PROFESSIONAL SCRUM MASTER (PSM II)

Quick Reference Guide

Pass Your Exam On Your First Try.

Author: Sid Bathia
BE, MS, MCSE, CCNA, PMP, PSM, PSD, PSU,SPS & PSPO

Version 32.0 © 2019 Sid Bathia. All rights reserved.

ISBN: 978-1-7326579-9-1
1/1/2019

Quick Reference Guide & Exam Questions
Professional Scrum Master II (PSM II)

Version 32.0 "© 2019 Sid Bathia. All rights reserved."

Contents

Introduction

Welcome! Kudos on taking the step towards preparing for the Professional Scrum Master II (Level 2). The Professional Scrum Master II (Level 2) exam is an advanced level assessment from Scrum.org aimed at demonstrating that that one understands the Scrum theory and also knows how to apply it in the real world.

The PSM II assessment is positioned between PSM I and PSM III in terms of difficulty and is an achievable certification for those that have attended a Professional Scrum Master course and/or have sufficient real-world experience.

The PSM II assessment is structured in a similar way to PSM I. It is comprised of 30 multiple choice questions. You have 90 minutes to complete the assessment and must score 85%+ to achieve the certification. The questions and answer options tend to be longer than PSM I and it takes more time to read and understand. As with all Scrum.org assessments, it is challenging and designed to test your real understanding of Scrum.

The Guide summarizes and highlights important information needed for PSM II exam. It also contains Questions and Answers which will help you prepare for the Professional Scrum Master II (PSM II) and / or Professional Scrum Product Owner II (Level 2) Exam. Information in this Guide references:

- The Scrum Guide. (Nov 2020)
- The Nexus Guide. (Jan 2021)
- The Kanban Guide. (Jan 2021)
- Professional Scrum Development Scrum Topics.
- Evidence Based Management Guide.
- Scrum Org Professional Scrum Master Learning Path.
- Scrum Org Professional Scrum Product Owner Learning Path.
- Scrum Org Professional Agile Learning Path.
- Scrum Forums, white papers, articles and training videos (Scrum.Org).
- Other Scrum sites and books.
- Practice Questions and Answers.
  - 160 Professional Scrum Master Basics Questions and Answers.
  - 130 Scaled Professional Scrum Questions and Answers.
  - 160 Professional Scrum Developer Questions and Answers.
  - 134 Kanban Questions and Answers.
  - 132 PAL-E and Professional Scrum Master (Level 2) Questions and Answers.
  - 80 Professional Scrum Master II (Level 2) Questions and Answers.

Exam Prep Steps

1. If you are very new to Scrum and have never been part of a Scrum team, then I would recommend you take a course. Attend a Scrum.org Professional Scrum Master I or Professional Scrum Product Owner I course.
2. **Read the Scrum Guide.**
3. Go through the **Scrum Guide Reference Table** mentioned in this book. Go through the questions and answers mentioned in the Book. These questions are compiled very carefully. Go through the answers and make sure you understand the concepts.

4. **Do the Professional Scrum Master Open assessment (https://www.scrum.org/open-assessments) until you score close to 100% 3 times in a row.**
5. **Read the Nexus Guide.**
6. Go through the Nexus **Guide Reference Table** mentioned in this book. Go through the questions and answers mentioned in the Book. These questions are compiled very carefully. Go through the answers and make sure you understand the concepts.
7. **Do the Nexus Open assessment (https://www.scrum.org/open-assessments) until you score close to 100% 3 times in a row.**
8. Go through the **Scrum Developer Reference Table** mention in this book. Go through the questions and answers mentioned in the Book. These questions are compiled very carefully. Go through the answers and make sure you understand the concepts.
9. **Do the Developer Open assessment (https://www.scrum.org/open-assessments) until you score close to 100% 3 times in a row.**
10. **Read the Kanban Guide.**
11. Go through the **Kanban Guide Reference Table** mention in this book. Go through the questions and answers mentioned in the Book. These questions are compiled very carefully. Go through the answers and make sure you understand the concepts.
12. **Do the Kanban Open assessment (https://www.scrum.org/open-assessments) until you score close to 100% 3 times in a row.**
13. Go through the Leadership Learning Path on Scrum.org.
14. Go through the PAL Reference Table.
15. **Read the Evidence Based Management Guide.**
16. Go through the Evidence Based Management **Reference Table** mention in this book. Go through the questions and answers mentioned in the Book. These questions are compiled very carefully. Go through the answers and make sure you understand the concepts.
17. **Do the Evidence Based Open assessment (https://www.scrum.org/open-assessments) until you score close to 100% 3 times in a row.**
18. Next best preparation for the Professional Scrum Master II (PSM II) is to attend a Scrum.org Professional Scrum Master course. This will teach you all the theory you need with real world examples to bring your learning to life. It is of course possible to take and pass PSM II without attending a course if you have sufficient knowledge and experience.
19. Read – "Scrum – A Pocket Guide" by Gunther Verheyen. (Highly recommended but optional)
20. Go through the PSM II Assessments at the end of this book. Make sure you understand the explanations / answers to the questions.

Book Recommendations

Good Books to Read:

1. Scrum - A Pocket Guide: By Gunther Verheyen
2. Agile Software Development with Scrum; By Ken Schwaber and Mike Beedle
3. Software in 30 Days: By Ken Schwaber, Jeff Sutherland

Exam Sequence

To Pass the PSM II exam, one must have knowledge about the contents which are tested in PSM I, PSPO I, PSD, PSK, PAL and SPS exams. You can choose to directly take the PSM II after the PSM I exam. However, make sure you cover all the topics tested in PSPO I, PSD, PSK, PAL and SPS exams. You can also choose to appear for the following exam sequence before you take PSM II. Please note that this is only a recommendation and not a must. This book contains the needed reference material to guide you through all the required topics for PSM II.

PSM-I > PSPO-I > PSD > SPS > PSM-II > PAL-I> PSK-I > PSPO-II > PSM-III>PSPO-III

Each certification in Scrum.org is part of one of the three possible difficulty tiers: beginner, intermediate and mastery. The basic recommendation here is to pass in all exams from **one level before going to the next** one, since inside a certain level the type of the questions is similar.

Tier 1 : Certifications that are part of the beginner tier are **PSM-I, PSPO-I and PSD.** They demand little (or none) practical experience and its theoretical content is significantly smaller than of the other assessments.

Tier II : The intermediate tier is the biggest one, with four different certifications. It is composed by the exams SPS, PSM-II, PAL-I and PSK-I and it presents a bigger challenge in terms of quantity of theoretical and practice content assessed. Also, this exam uses many study cases and real-world situations to test the practical knowledge of the candidate. It is common for the questions in this tier to have more than one correct answer, demanding that the candidate choose the best option accordingly with the situation at hand.

Tier III :

Finally, the advanced tier currently has two certifications: PSPO-II and PSM-III. Both have the biggest exam time (2 hours each) because of the disassortative questions they present in addition to the same complex multiple-choice questions that are present in the intermediate tier.

Trademark and References

This content is neither endorsed or affiliated with Scrum.org. This document uses content adapted from the Scrum Guide, Nexus Guide and other Scrum.org articles. All content related to the Guides is taken from scrumguides.org and is under the Attribution ShareAlike license of Creative Commons. Further information is accessible at http://creativecommons.org/licenses/by-sa/4.0/legalcode and also described in summary form at http://creativecommons.org/licenses/by-sa/4.0/. This document also uses content from the Scrum Glossary at https://www.scrum.org/resources/scrum-glossary. Professional Scrum™, Professional Scrum Master, PSM, PSM I, Scaled Professional Scrum, PSPO, PSPO I, etc. are trademarks and the protected brand of Scrum.org.

The statements made and opinions expressed herein belong exclusively to the creator of this course and are not shared by or represent the viewpoint of Scrum .org or Scrum Alliance. This training does not constitute an endorsement of any product, service or point of view. Scrum .org and Scrum Alliance makes no representations, warranties or assurances of any kind, express or implied, as to the completeness, accuracy, reliability, suitability, availability or currency of the content contained in this presentation or any material related to this presentation. In no event shall Scrum .org or Scrum Alliance, its agents, officers, employees, licensees or affiliates be liable for any damages whatsoever (including, without limitation, damages for loss of profits, business information, loss of information) arising out of the information or statements contained in the training. Any reliance you place on such content is strictly at your own risk.

PSM II Focus Areas

The PSM II Exam questions can be broken down into the following Focus Areas.

Focus Area	Summary of Results By Section	
	The questions in this test were organized by section. This table details a summary of scores by section.	
	Section/Subject Area	Percentage Scored
Understanding and Applying the Scrum Framework: Empiricism, Scrum Values, Roles, Events, Artifacts, Done.	Coaching and Facilitation (PSM II) - The Scrum Master enables the Scrum Team. Understanding the Scrum Master's role in working with people, and fostering teamwork and collaboration.	80.0%
	Cross-Functional, Self-Organizing Teams (PSM II) - A Scrum Development Team autonomously makes all decisions for the work to do that it has forecast for a Sprint. Self-organization fosters collaboration and increases commitment, feeling of ownership and creativity.	100.0%
Developing People and Teams: Self-Organizing Teams, Facilitation, Leadership Styles, Coaching and Mentoring.	Done and Undone (PSM II) - A core purpose of Scrum is the creation of releasable, "Done" Increments of software by the end of every Sprint. The definition of "Done" provides transparency. "Done" Increments enable empiricism and agility.	100.0%
	Maximizing Value (PSM II) - The Product Owner is responsible for maximizing the value of the product and the work of the Development Team. There are different aspects to value; from having a definition for it to measuring it, and ways to optimize value.	100.0%
Managing Products with Agility: Product Backlog Management, Stakeholders & Customers.	Product Backlog Management (PSM II) - The Product Backlog is the single source of work that emerges for the product. Product Backlog management includes creating, clarifying and maintaining the Product Backlog in order to plan releases, report and capitalize on unforeseen business opportunities.	66.7%
	Scaling Fundamentals (PSM II) - Scaling Scrum effectively requires a firm understanding of the Scrum Framework and how it is founded on empirical theory. This includes an understanding of the Scrum principles and values, and a focus on technical excellence.	100.0%
Developing and Delivering Products Professionally: Managing Technical Risk.	Scrum Framework (PSM II) - Rules and roles of Scrum per the Scrum Guide.	100.0%
Evolving the Agile Organization: Organizational Design & Culture.	Scrum Theory and Principles (PSM II) - Understanding of Scrum theory, how it is founded on empirical theory, and the principles and values of Scrum.	100.0%

Thank You

Thank You to Scrum.Org for giving us the opportunity to grow with Scrum.

Reviews

My goal is to continue offering a good reference guide and your review could greatly help me in doing so. Your review would mean the world to me. Please do leave one when you find the time.

CHAPTER 1: SCRUM BASICS

This chapter is designed to help you **earn / Revise / take a second Look at PSM I**. You should be very confident with PSM I while preparing for PSM II exam. The Level I certification exam is based on the Official Scrum Guide and helps to pass PSM II certification exam.

1. If you are very new to Scrum and have never been part of a Scrum team, then I would recommend you take a course. Attend a Scrum.org Professional Scrum Master I or Professional Scrum Product Owner I course.
2. **Read the Scrum Guide.**
3. Go through the **Scrum Guide Reference Table (Chapter 1)** mentioned in this book. Go through the questions and answers mentioned in the Book. These questions are compiled very carefully. Go through the answers and make sure you understand the concepts.
4. **Do the Professional Scrum Master Open assessment (https://www.scrum.org/open-assessments) until you score close to 100% 3 times in a row.**

Scrum Guide Reference Table

Time-Box, Effort of Size	Important

Scrum Definition	Scrum is a **lightweight** framework that helps people, teams and organizations **generate value** by creating **adaptive solutions** for **complex** problems. Scrum requires a Scrum Master to foster / maintain an environment where: 1. A Product Owner **orders the work** for a complex problem into a Product Backlog. 2. The Scrum Team **turns a selection of the work into an Increment (of value)** during a Sprint. 3. The Scrum Team and stakeholders **inspect the results** and adjust for the next Sprint. 4. Steps 1 through 3 are repeated for all sprints.
	The Scrum framework is **purposefully incomplete**. It only defines the parts required to implement Scrum theory.
	Scrum **wraps around existing practices** or removes the practices which are unnecessary. Scrum brings transparency to the effectiveness (or ineffectiveness) of the current management, environment, and work techniques, **so that improvements can be made.**
	The Scrum framework consists of 1) Scrum Teams 2) Roles / Accountabilities 3) Artifacts 4) Rules Each component within the framework **serves a specific purpose and is essential** to Scrum's success and usage. The rules of Scrum bind together the accountabilities, events, and artifacts, governing the relationships and interactions between them.
	Scrum recommends **using all the Scrum components** and rules (not just the ones which suit the project). While implementing only parts of Scrum is possible, the result is not Scrum. Scrum exists only in its entirety and functions well as a container for other techniques, methodologies, and practices. **Example 1**: A Team cannot decide that Sprint Retrospective Meeting would not be implemented since it is not needed. **Example 2:** Developers cannot choose to skip the Daily Scrum Meetings because they might be busy with writing code or developing the Product.
	Scrum proves especially effective in an iterative and incremental knowledge transfers.

	Scrum is founded on: 1) **Empirical process control theory**, or Empiricism. **Empiricism** asserts that knowledge comes from **experience** and **making decisions based on what is known.** 2) **Lean Thinking**: Lean thinking reduces waste and focuses on the essentials.
	Scrum is: 1) **Not a process, technique, or definitive method.** 2) **A framework** within which can employ various processes and techniques. 3) Employs an **iterative, incremental approach** to optimize predictability and to **control risk.** 4) Lightweight. 5) Simple to understand.

Scrum Values	Scrum Values **give direction to the work done in Scrum**, along with the work ethics the Scrum team should have.
1. **C**ommitment 2. **C**ourage 3. **F**ocus 4. **O**penness 5. **R**espect **Memorize: CCFOR** **Lack of Trust impacts all the above Values.**	**Commitment**: The Scrum Team members should personally commit to achieving the Scrum Goals. Commitment is about **dedication and applies to the actions, the effort, not the final result.** The Scrum Teams should: • Commit to quality, commit to collaborate. • Commit to learn, commit to do the best they can, every day again. • Commit to the Sprint Goal, commit to be professional. • Commit to self-organize, commit to excellence. • Commit to the agile principles, commit to create working software. • Commit to look for improvements, commit to the Definition of Done. • Commit to the Scrum framework, commit to focus on Value. • Commit to finish work, commit to inspect & adapt. • Commit to transparency.
	Courage: The Scrum Team members should have courage to do the right thing and work on tough problems. Note: • Courage in admitting requirements will never be perfect and that no plan can capture reality and complexity. • The Scrum Team members should have courage to consider change as a source of inspiration and innovation. • The Scrum Team members should have courage to not deliver undone software. • The Scrum Team members should have courage in sharing all possible information (transparency) that might help the team and the organization. • The Scrum Team members should have courage in admitting that nobody is perfect. The Scrum Team members should have courage to change direction. The Scrum Team members should have courage to share risks and benefits. • The Scrum Team members should have courage to promote Scrum and empiricism to deal with complexity. • The Scrum Team members should have courage to let go of the feint certainties of the past. The Scrum Team members should show courage to support the Scrum Values.
	Focus: Everyone in the Scrum Team **should focus on the work of the Sprint and the goals of the Scrum Team**. An iterative-incremental approach like Scrum and the time-boxing of Scrum allow the Scrum team to focus. • The Team should focus on what's most important now without being bothered by considerations of what might stand a chance to become important. • The Team should focus on what they know now. • The Team should focus on what's most nearby in time as the future is highly uncertain and the team should learn from the present to gain experience for future work. • The team should focus on the Sprint work to get things done.

Openness (No Hiding): The Scrum Team and its stakeholders should agree to be open about all the work and the challenges with performing the work. The empiricism of Scrum requires transparency and openness. The Scrum Team would always want to inspect reality in order to make sensible adaptations.

- The Scrum Team should be open about our work, progress, learnings and problems.
- The Scrum Team should also be open, flexible and adopt to different people working styles acknowledging people to be people, and not resources, robots or pieces of machinery.
- The Scrum Team should be open to collaborate across disciplines and skills.
- The Scrum Team should be open to collaborate with stakeholders.
- The Scrum Team should be open in sharing feedback and learning from one another.
- The Scrum Team should be open for change as the organization and the world it operates in, changes unpredictably, unexpectedly and constantly.

Respect: Scrum Team members respect each other to be capable, independent people.
- The Scrum Team should show respect for people, their experience and their personal background.
- The Scrum Team should respect diversity (it makes one stronger).
- The Scrum Team should respect different opinions (The Scrum Team might learn from it).
- The Scrum Team should how respect sponsors by not building unrequired features.
- The Scrum Team should show respect by not wasting money on things that are not valuable or might never being implemented or used.
- The Scrum Team should show respect for users by fixing their problems. The Scrum Team should respect the Scrum framework. The Scrum Team should respect our wider environment by not behaving as an isolated island in the world. The Scrum Team should respect each other's skills, expertise and insights.
- The Scrum Team should respect the accountabilities of the Scrum roles.

Reference: Scrum Guide and There's value in the Scrum Values – Gunter Verheyen
https://guntherverheyen.com/2013/05/03/theres-value-in-the-scrum-values/

Three Pillars of Scrum	Transparency
  1. Transparency 2. Inspection 3. Adaptation Memorize: TIA 	Transparency implies that all aspects of the process **must be visible.** Visibility or transparency should exist between: 1) The Scrum team members performing the work. 2) The Scrum team members and stakeholders responsible for receiving the work / outcome.
	Transparency means sharing a common standard and a common language.
	Important decisions are made based on the state of the Sprint backlog, Product backlog and the Product Increment. Thus, these three artifacts should be extremely transparent.
	Artifacts having **low transparency can lead to decisions that diminish value and increase risk.**
	Transparency enables inspection. Inspection without transparency is misleading and wasteful.
	Example: Scrum Team members (within the same scrum Team) performing the work and inspecting the resulting increment must **share a Common Definition of "Done".**
	Inspection
	Scrum users must frequently inspect scrum artifacts and progress made toward a Sprint Goal, to detect undesirable variances. Inspection **should not impact the work being done.**
	Inspections are most beneficial when diligently performed by skilled inspectors.
	Inspection enables adaptation. Inspection without adaptation is considered pointless. Scrum events are designed to provoke change.
	Adaptation
	If an inspector determined that one or more aspects of a process deviated outside acceptable limits, and that the resulting product was unacceptable, the process or the material being processed must **be adjusted as soon as possible or immediately.**
	A Scrum Team is expected to adapt the moment it learns anything new through inspection.
	In case of variances from the unexpected, an adjustment must be made **as soon as possible** to minimize deviation.
	Scrum prescribes **five** mandatory events **for Inspection and Adaptation:** 1. Sprint Planning 2. Daily Scrum 3. Sprint Review 4. Sprint Retrospective 5. The Sprint (Container of the above four events). The **event that contains the four formal events** is called the Sprint.

Scrum Team Accountabilities: 1. Scrum Master 2. Product Owner 3. Developers Scrum Team = Developers + Scrum Master + Product Owner. 	A Scrum Team is a cohesive unit of professionals focused on one objective at a time, **the Product Goal.**
	The Scrum Team consists of the following **accountabilities (previously known as roles)**: 1) One Product Owner. 2) Developers. 3) One Scrum Master.
	The **entire Scrum Team** is: 1) **Responsible** for **all product-related activities** from stakeholder collaboration, verification, maintenance, operation, experimentation, research, development, documentation and anything else that might be required. 2) **Accountable** for creating **a valuable, useful Increment** every Sprint.
	A Scrum Team **does not consist** of Project Managers or Functional Managers.
	The Scrum Team is small enough to remain nimble and large enough to complete significant work within a Sprint, **typically 10 or fewer people**. Remember 10 is just a Guideline. A Scrum Team can be 11 people if needed but it should stay small enough to stay nimble.
	Scrum Teams are **Cross-functional teams** that **have all competencies needed** to accomplish the work without depending on others outside the team.
	Scrum Teams are cross-functional teams having all the skills (as a team) needed to create a Product Increment.
	Scrum Teams are **Self-managing** which means they internally decide who does what, when, and how.
	Self-managing teams: 1) Manage their own work. 2) Decide how to achieve goals. 3) Grow as a team. 4) Continuously improve. 5) Manage stakeholders. 6) Help other teams and co-workers to grow, improve and thrive. 7) Constantly collaborate with other teams, pinpoint improvements and learn fast, making them more motivated and productive.
	Scrum Teams are structured and empowered by the organization **to manage their own work.**
	Scrum engages groups of people **who collectively have all the skills and expertise** to do the work. The Scrum teams can share or acquire such skills as needed.
	Sub-team formations (or hierarchies) in the Scrum Team **is not allowed**. Sub-Teams such as testing teams or an operation teams are not allowed to be formed in the Scrum Team.

	Titles are **not assigned** to the developers within the Scrum Team members, regardless of the type of work they perform.
	All the test cases (and documentation) are written and executed by members of the Scrum Team.
	The duty of the Scrum Team is to be transparent. **Users seeking for information** about the work done / completed by the Scrum Team **are responsible for getting it**. People interested in such information can: 1. Investigate the artifacts (Product Backlog, Sprint Backlog) created by the Scrum Team. 2. Visit the next Sprint Review meeting if needed. **No one in the Scrum Team is responsible for creating status reports.**
	Scrum Teams deliver products iteratively and incrementally.
	Scrum Team collectively decides on the Scrum Length.
	Scrum Team **delivers a "Done" increment every Sprint** to ensure a valuable version of a working product is always available. However, **it is up to the Product Owner to "Release" it.**
	Different Teams working on the same Product: • Must have the Same Product Backlog. • Must have the Same Product Owner. • Must have the Same Product Goal. • Must have different Sprint Backlogs. (one for each team) • Must have a shared Definition of Done. • Can have **different Sprint Lengths**. • Can have **different Scrum Masters**.

Product Owner (Sole person responsible for the Product Backlog) 	The Product Owner is **accountable for managing the Product Backlog. He / she is also accountable for maximizing the value of the Product and the work the Developers do.**
	The Product Owner is accountable for: 1) **Creating the Product Goal.** 2) **Explicitly communicating the Product Goal.**
	The Product Owner is responsible **for creating and clearly expressing Product Backlog items.**
	The Product Owner is also accountable for ensuring that the **Product Backlog is transparent, visible and understood.**
	The Product Owner is **accountable** for **prioritizing / ordering** the items in the Product Backlog to best achieve the Product goal and missions.
	The Product Owner is responsible **for optimizing / maximizing the value of the work the Developers performs.**
	The Product Owner is responsible for ensuring that the **Product Backlog is visible, transparent, and clear** to all.
	A Product should always have only one Product Owner no matter the size of the Product or Backlog.
	A Product Owner may represent **the desires of stakeholders** using the Product Backlog. This typically requires Product Owners active interaction with them.
	For the Product Owner to succeed, the entire organization must respect / provide autonomy to his or her decisions.
	No one can force (not even the CEO) the Developers to work on a different set of requirements, then what is agreed by the Product Owner.
	Only the **Product Owner has the authority to cancel the Sprint**, although he or she may do so under an influence, based on feedback received from the stakeholders, the Developers, or the Scrum Master.
	The Product Owner **tracks total work remaining at least once every Sprint Review.**
	The Product Owner prioritizes the Product Backlog items as deemed appropriate to him.
	The decisions made by the Product Owner are visible in: 1) The content of the Product Backlog. 2) The ordering of the Product Backlog. 3) The inspectable Increment at the Sprint Review.

Product Owner	The Product Owner is accountable for maximizing the value of the product resulting from the work of the Scrum Team. How this is done may vary widely across organizations, Scrum Teams, and individuals. Product Owner should focus on: → **Key Stakeholder Involvement** In order to maximize Product value, the Product Owner should identify the key stakeholders for the product and involve them as necessary throughout the development effort. → **Product Marketplace** The Product Owner should be expertly aware of the marketplace for the product. They should constantly be gathering and re-gathering information regarding the marketplace, so that the product value is maximized. → **Product Release Decisions** The Product Owner is the one and only person who can decide whether to release the latest Increment of the Product. For Product value to be captured, a release of the product must occur.
	The Product Owner: 1. The Product Owner is one person, not a committee. 2. Communicates regularly with the Stakeholders. 3. Creates new items in the Product Backlog. 4. Revises the priority of Product Backlog items 5. Work with the **Developers on Product Backlog refinement**. 6. Answers questions about the Product Backlog items and makes sure that everyone **has the right understanding** of Product Backlog items. 7. Checks the completed items with the Developers to ensure they are Done based on the "Definition of Done". 8. Collaborate with stakeholders, user communities, and subject matter experts.
	The Product owner is not only accountable for development and release of a product, but also **the cost of maintaining and operating the product**. If a person 'owns' the product, he/she is expected to be responsible for the complete lifecycle of a product.

Developers **(Sole Owners of the Sprint Backlog)**	Developers are professionals in the Scrum team who work towards delivering a useful and valuable Increment of "Done" product, at the end of each Sprint.
	The entire Scrum Team is accountable for creating a valuable, useful Increment every Sprint. (Not just the developers)
	Developers within the Scrum Team are **self-organizing**. The Scrum Master, Product Owner and Developers work together to turn Product Backlog into Increments of valuable functionality.
	Sub-team formations (or hierarchies) within the Scrum Team **is not allowed**. Sub-Teams where Developers might be categorized as testing teams or an operation teams are not allowed to be formed in the Scrum Team.
	Titles are **not assigned** to the developers within the Scrum Team members, regardless of the type of work they perform.
	Developers or people doing the work are **responsible for all estimates in the Product Backlog**. Product Owner can only influence.
	Scrum **does not prohibit** the Product Owner & Scrum Master to do Development work.
	Developers within the Scrum Team range between be between 3 to 8 Members. Changing developers typically reduces cohesion, performance and productivity in the short term.
	Developers are accountable for: 1. **Creating and managing** the Sprint Backlog (plan for the Sprint). 2. Creating and prioritizing tasks within the Sprint Backlog. 3. Instilling quality by adhering to a Definition of Done. 4. Running Daily Scrums. 5. Adapting **their plan each day toward the Sprint Goal.** 6. Holding each other accountable as professionals. 7. Measuring the Sprint performance.
	Different Teams working on the same Product: • Must have the Same Product Backlog. • Must have the Same Product Owner. • Must have the Same Product Goal. • Must have different Sprint Backlogs. (one for each team) • Must have a shared Definition of Done. • Can have **different Sprint Lengths.** • Can have **different Scrum Masters.**
	At least one functionality **is recommended** to be delivered every sprint by the Developers. (Not Mandatory)

Scrum Master	The Scrum Master is accountable for **establishing, promoting and supporting** Scrum.
	The Scrum Master helps within the team and throughout the entire organization to understand Scrum theory and practice.
	The Scrum Master is accountable for the **Scrum Team's effectiveness**.
	The Scrum Master facilitates Inspection and Adaption opportunities as requested or as needed.
	The Scrum Master **serves the Scrum Team** by: 1) **Coaching** the team members self-management and cross-functionality. 2) Helping the Scrum Team **focus** on creating high-value Increments that meet the Definition of Done. 3) **Removing impediments** to the Scrum Team's progress. 4) Ensuring that all **Scrum events take place** and are positive, productive, and kept within the timebox.
	The Scrum Master **serves the Product Owner** by: 1) Helping the Product Owner **find techniques** for effective **Product Goal definition** and Product Backlog management. 2) Helping the Scrum Team understand the need for clear and concise Product Backlog items. 3) Helping **establish empirical product planning** for a complex environment 4) **Facilitating** stakeholder collaboration as requested or needed.
	The Scrum Master serves the organization by: 1) **Leading, training, and coaching the organization** in its Scrum adoption. 2) **Planning and advising Scrum implementations** within the organization. 3) Helping employees and stakeholders **understand and enact an empirical approach** for complex work. 4) **Removing barriers** between stakeholders and Scrum Teams.
	Scrum **Masters are true leaders** who serve the Scrum Team and the larger organization.
	The Scrum Master helps those outside the Scrum Team understand which of their interactions with the Scrum Team are helpful and which aren't.
	The Scrum Master helps finding techniques for effective management of the Product Backlog.
	The Scrum Master ensures that the Scrum Team is meeting as needed and teaches the Scrum Team to keep the meetings within the time-box.

Sprints	
  	The **heart of Scrum is a Sprint where ideas are turned into value.**
	Each Sprint may be considered a short project.
	Sprint a time-box of **one month or less** during which a "Done", useable, and valuable Product Increment is created.
	All the work **necessary to achieve the Product Goal**, including Sprint Planning, Daily Scrums, Sprint Review, and Sprint Retrospective, **happen within Sprints**.
	Each Sprint has: 1) A goal of what is to be built. (Sprint Goal) 2) A design and flexible plan that will guide building the Product. 3) Work which is done. 4) Resultant Product Increments.
	Different Scrum Teams working on the same product can have different Sprint length. The duration of a **Sprint is fixed and should not be shortened or lengthened once the Sprint has started.**
	A Sprint event is held at the same place and time.
	At least **one functionality** should be implemented in a Sprint. (including the first Sprint). This is a recommendation and not **mandatory.**
	During the Sprint: 1) The Product Backlog is refined as needed. 2) Deliverables or Sprint items are worked on. 3) **No changes are made that would endanger the Sprint Goal.** 4) Quality does not decrease. 5) Scope may be clarified and re-negotiated between the Product Owner and Developers.
	The purpose of each Sprint (including the first Sprint) is to deliver Increments of **valuable functionality** that adhere to the Scrum Team's current Definition of "Done."
	Sprints enable **predictability** by ensuring **inspection and adaptation of progress** toward a **Product Goal** at least every calendar month.
	A new Sprint **starts immediately after the conclusion of the previous Sprint.** There is no gap or work done between Sprints.
	When a **Sprint's horizon is too long:** 1) The Sprint Goal may become invalid. 2) Complexity may rise. 3) Risk may increase. **Shorter Sprints can be employed to** generate: 1) More learning cycles. 2) Limit risk of **cost** to a smaller time frame. 3) Limit risk of **effort** to a smaller time frame.

	Various practices exist to forecast progress, like burndowns, burn-ups, or cumulative flows. While proven useful, these do not replace the importance of empiricism. In complex environments, what will happen is unknown. Only what has already happened may be used for forward-looking decision making.
	Only the **Product Owner** can cancel the Sprint.
	A Sprint should be cancelled in case the **Sprint Goal becomes obsolete.** (even if the Sprint Time Box is not over).
	When a Sprint is cancelled: 1) All completed and "Done" Product Backlog items are reviewed. 2) If part of the work is valuable, the Product Owner typically accepts it. 3) All incomplete Product Backlog Items are re-estimated and put back on the Product Backlog.

Daily Scrum	The purpose of the Daily Scrum is to:
	1) Inspect progress toward the Sprint Goal. **2) Adapt the Sprint Backlog as necessary**, adjusting the upcoming planned work.
	The Daily Scrum is a 15-minute time-boxed event for the Developers. The Daily Scrum is held every day of the Sprint at the same place and same time.
	Every day in the Daily Scrum, the Developers understands how they intends to work together (as a self-Managing team) to accomplish the Sprint Goal. Developers also work towards creating the anticipated Increment by the end of the Sprint.
	Only the people doing the work (described in the Sprint Backlog) need to inspect and adapt at the Daily Scrum. **If the Product Owner or Scrum Master are actively working on items in the Sprint Backlog, they participate as Developers** and will need to be at the Daily Scrum. Otherwise, the Scrum Master simply must make sure the Developers knows how to conduct a Daily Scrum and does so.
Mandatory : Yes	Developers uses the Daily Scrum to track and inspect how its progressing towards completing the work in the Sprint Backlog.
	The structure and agenda of the meeting is set by the Developers and can be conducted in different ways, if it focuses on progress toward the Sprint Goal.
	Developers can select whatever **structure and techniques they want** as long as: 1) Daily Scrum focuses on progress toward the Sprint Goal 2) They produce an actionable plan for the next day of work. This creates focus and improves self-management.
	The Scrum Master ensures that the Developers have the Daily scrum meeting but **does not have to be present in the meeting.**
	If people outside the Scrum Team are present in the Daily Scum, the Scrum Master ensures that they do not **disrupt the meeting.**
	Product Owner and Scrum **Master are not required in the Daily scrum**. However, Developers members must be present.
	Daily Scrums: 1) Improve Communications. 2) Identify impediments for removal. 3) Improve Team members knowledge. 4) Promote quick decision-making. 5) Consequently, eliminate the need for other meetings.
	The Daily Scrum is not the only time Developers can adjust their plan. They often meet throughout the day for more detailed discussions about adapting or re-planning the rest of the Sprint's work.

Sprint Planning (Scrum Team Effort) Mandatory :Yes	The work to be performed in the Sprint **is planned** in a meeting / event called the Sprint Planning.
	Sprint Planning **initiates the Sprint** by laying out the work to be performed for the Sprint. This resulting plan is created by the **collaborative work of the entire Scrum Team.**
	The Product Owner ensures **that attendees are prepared to discuss the most important Product Backlog items and how they map to the Product Goal.**
	Technical Domain Experts and other people (invited **by the Scrum Team**) may attend Sprint Planning to give advice.
	Sprint Planning addresses the following topics: **Topic One: Why is this Sprint valuable?** The **Product Owner** proposes how the product could increase its value and utility in the current Sprint. The **whole Scrum Team then collaborates to define a Sprint Goal** that communicates why the Sprint is valuable to stakeholders. The **Sprint Goal must be finalized prior to the end of Sprint Planning.** **Topic Two: What can be Done this Sprint?** Through discussion with the Product Owner, the **Developers select items from the Product Backlog to include in the current Sprint.** The selected items get moved to the Sprint Backlog. **The Scrum Team** may refine these items during this process, which increases understanding and confidence. Selecting how much can be completed within a Sprint may be challenging. However, the more the Developers will be more confident about how much work they can do in the sprint / sprint forecasts based on knowing more about: 1) Developers past performance. 2) Developers upcoming capacity. 3) Definition of Done. **Topic Three: How will the chosen work get done?** For each selected Product Backlog item: 1) **The Developers plan the work necessary to create an Increment that meets the Definition of Done.** 2) This is **often done by decomposing Product Backlog items into smaller work items of one day or less.** 3) The decomposing of Product backlog items into smaller work items is at the sole discretion of the **Developers.** No one else tells them how to turn Product Backlog items into Increments of value.
	The Inputs to Sprint Planning are: 1) Prioritized Product Backlog along with the Definition of Done. 2) Developers past performance. 3) Developers upcoming capacity. 4) Projected capacity of the Developers. (based on their past performance)
	The **objective of the Sprint & Sprint Goal is decided in the Sprint Planning meeting.**

	The number of items selected **from the Product Backlog for the Sprint is solely up to the Developers**. Based on the discussions with the product owner, the Developers can best assess what can be accomplished over the upcoming Sprint.
	The Sprint Planning **is a maximum of 8 Hours** per Monthly Sprint. For shorter Sprints, the event is usually shorter.
	Work for the entire sprint is planned by the entire Scrum team and the Developers decompose the selected items by the end of this meeting. (Often in units of one day or less)
	During Sprint Planning, the Sprint Backlog should be groomed, defined and decomposed enough **so the developers can create its best forecast of what it can do and start the first several days of the Sprint.**
	Sprint Planning answers the following questions: 1) **Why is this Sprint valuable?** 2) **What can be delivered** in the Increment resulting from the upcoming Sprint? 3) **How will the work** (needed to deliver the Increment) be achieved?
	By the end of the Sprint Planning, **the Developers should be able to:** 1) **Explain to the Product Owner and Scrum Master,** how it intends to work as a self-organizing team to accomplish the Sprint Goal 2) Clearly Vision the anticipated **Increment.**

Sprint Review	
Sprint Review Mandatory :Yes 	A meeting / event called the Sprint Review is typically held at the end of the Sprint to: 1) Inspect the Increment. 2) Adapt the Product Backlog.
	The **purpose** of the Sprint Review is to inspect the outcome of the Sprint and determine future adaptations.
	The Sprint Review is a working session and the Scrum Team **should avoid limiting it to a presentation.**
	The Sprint Review is the second to last event of the Sprint.
	During the Sprint Review, **the Scrum Team and Key Stakeholders** (people outside the Scrum Team) **collaborate** to discuss and review: 1) What was **achieved / accomplished** in the current Sprint? 2) What has **changed** in their environment? Based on this information, attendees collaborate on what to do next. The Product Backlog may also be adjusted to meet **new opportunities.**
	Multiple Increments **may be created within a Sprint. The sum of the Increments is presented at the Sprint Review** thus supporting empiricism.
	In the Sprint Review, the **Next things that could be done to optimize Product value, are also reviewed**.
	The result of a Sprint Review is a revised Product Backlog that defines the probable Product Backlog items for the next Sprint. (which also get discussed in the Next **Sprint Planning Meeting**)
	The Sprint Review meeting is at most a **four-hour meeting** for one-month Sprints. (or shorter)
	The Scrum Masters ensures that the Sprint Review meeting takes place.
	The **Scrum Team explains what Product Backlog items have been "Done"** and what has not been "Done" in the Sprint Review Meeting.
	The **Scrum Team** discusses what went well during the Sprint, what problems it ran into, and how those problems were solved, in the Sprint Review Meeting.
	The **Scrum Team demonstrates the work that it has "Done"** and answers questions about the Increment in the Sprint Review Meeting.
	The Key Stakeholders are **allowed to participate only in the Sprint Review meeting**. However, any member of the Scrum Team can interact with them any time.
	The Sprint Review **should never be considered a gate to releasing value.**
	The Sprint Review will review the Increment in the context of both the **Sprint Goal and the Product Goal**. This encourages Sprint Reviews to put some context around their findings and ask questions about how much progress has been made toward the Product **Goal**. These findings will be very useful in Sprint Planning as they can help create focus and form decisions about the next Sprint.

Sprint Retrospective Mandatory :Yes 	The Sprint Retrospective is an opportunity for the Scrum Team to inspect itself **and create an improvement plan** which can be enacted.
	The purpose of the Sprint Retrospective is to plan ways to **increase quality and effectiveness**
	The Sprint Retrospective occurs after the Sprint Review and prior to the next Sprint Planning.

	In the Sprint Retrospective:
	1) The Scrum team inspects how the last Sprint went with regards to individuals, interactions, processes, tools, and their Definition of Done.
	2) The Scrum Team discusses:
	   o What went well during the Sprint.
	   o The problems they encountered.
	   o How those problems were (or were not) solved.
	3) The Scrum team identifies and orders the major items that went well along with the potential improvements.

	The most impactful improvements are addressed as soon as possible. They may even be added to the Sprint Backlog for the next Sprint.
	After the Retrospective discussion **all the improvement items discussed are placed in the Product Backlog.**
	The most impactful improvements **may** even be added to the Sprint Backlog for the next Sprint. (Not Mandatory)
	The Sprint Retrospective is at most a three-hour meeting for one-month Sprints or shorter.
	The Scrum Master and Product Owner **participate as a peer team member** in the meeting.

Scrum Artifacts and Commitments	The three Scrum Artifacts are: 1) Product Backlog. 2) Sprint Backlog. 3) Product Increment.
	Scrum's artifacts represent work or value.
	Scrum's artifacts are designed to maximize transparency of key

	Each artifact contains a commitment. **Commitments** ensure that:
	   1) They **provide information** that **enhances transparency.**
	   2) They **provide focus** against which **progress can be measured.**
	   3) They exist to **reinforce empiricism** and the **Scrum values** for the Scrum Team and their stakeholders.

	Artifacts that have low transparency can lead to decisions that diminish value and increase risk. Transparency enables inspection. Inspection without transparency is misleading and wasteful.

	Remember:
	  • The commitment for the Product Backlog, is the Product Goal.
	  • The commitment for the Sprint Backlog, is the Sprint Goal.
	  • The commitment for the Increment is the Definition of Done.

	Are commitments mandatory? Yes, if a team is using Scrum, they must provide a commitment for each artifact.
	Who creates the commitments? They are part of the existing artifacts and as such whoever is accountable for that artifact is accountable for that commitment. Product Goal is created by the Product Owner working with the Scrum Team. The Sprint Goal is created by the Scrum Team. And, the Definition of Done is created by the Scrum Team.

Remember:

Artifact	Commitment	Creator / Owner
Product Backlog	Product Goal	Product Owner
Sprint Backlog	Sprint Goal	Scrum Team
Product Increment	Definition of Done	Scrum Team

Product Backlog (Owner : Product Owner)	The Product Backlog lists all features, functions, requirements, enhancements, and fixes that constitute the changes to be made to a Product.
	The Product Backlog is **an emergent**, **ordered list** of what is needed to improve the product.
	The Product Backlog is **the single source of work** undertaken by the Scrum Team. All the work which the Scrum Team does needs to be originated from the Product Backlog.
	A Product Backlog is never complete & is always evolving. It is a living artifact.
(Ongoing Process)	A Product cannot exist without a Product Backlog. A single Product can have only **one Product Backlog**.
	Product Backlog Refinement
	Product Backlog Refinement is the act of adding detail, estimates, order and other attributes to items in the Product Backlog. Refinement ensures that members of the Scrum team understands items in the Product Backlog to the level needed.
Memorize : DOEV / DOVE	Product Backlog items that can be "Done" **by the Scrum Team** within one Sprint are deemed "**Ready**" for selection.
	Product Backlog refinement is the act of **breaking down and further defining Product Backlog items into smaller more precise items.**
	Developers should participate in the Product Refinement as soon as possible.
	Refinement includes analyzing, designing and decomposing the Product Backlog items. Programming and testing do not happen during refinement.
	The Scrum Team **decides how and when refinement is done.**
	Product Owner and the Developers collaborate and refine the Product Backlog items together.
	Developers typically gives input on **Technical dependencies during** refining a Product Backlog item.
	During refinement, Developers understand and clarifies requirements. This could result to expanding the Product backlog item, if needed.

(!)	**Product Backlog Management**
	The Product Owner is also accountable for effective Product Backlog management, which includes: 1) Developing and explicitly communicating the Product Goal. 2) **Creating and Clearly expressing** Product Backlog items. 3) **Ordering** the items in the Product Backlog to best achieve goals and missions. 4) Ensuring that the Product Backlog is **visible, transparent,** and clear to all. The Product **Owner can delegate above to others however remains accountable for it.**
	Product Backlog items Order
(!)	The earliest version of the Product Backlog only lays out the initially known and best-understood requirements. The Product Backlog **evolves as the product and the environment in which it will be used evolves.**
	Average number of items in the Product Backlog are usually larger than items in a single Sprint Backlog. This is how it works: [A] Items with different sizes are added to the Product Backlog. [B] Items are sorted based on their business value. [C] Large items on the top of the Product Backlog are broken down into smaller ones. These are more detailed than the ones at the bottom. That's why the items on the top are smaller than those on the bottom. Remember that size is not a basis for ordering the Product Backlog items.
	Higher ordered Product Backlog items are usually clearer and **more detailed than lower ordered ones, as they would be worked on first.**
	Once the Refinement is complete, the detailed Product backlog items are moved to the Sprint backlog.
	Product Backlog items can be updated at any time by the Product Owner or at the Product Owner's discretion.

	Estimates
	Developers **are responsible for all estimates**. The Product Owner may influence the Developers by helping them understand the requirements, dependencies and trade-offs.
	Accountability of the Product Owner
	The Product Owner is responsible for the Product Backlog, including its content, availability, and ordering.
	The Product Owner tracks **the total work remaining at least every Sprint Review.**
	The **Product Owner decides the order of the Product backlog based on the complexity, risk, dependency and size of each** Product backlog item. However, it is up to the Product Owner to prioritize as needed to achieve the product's goals and to optimize the value received.
Product Goal	**Product Backlog Commitment: Product Goal**
	Product Goals are steppingstones towards the Product Vision. Scrum Teams and stakeholders can "see" how they connect.
	Product Goal provides context to the Product Backlog. It can be thought of as the 'why' the scrum is doing all of the work.
	The commitment for the Product Backlog is the **Product Goal.**
	The Product Goal describes a **future state of the product** which can serve as a target for the Scrum Team to plan against.
	The works items in the Product Backlog emerge to define "what" will fulfill the Product Goal.
	The Product Goal is the long-term objective for the Scrum Team.
	There can be **one "Active / Current" Product Goal for the Product Backlog at any one time.**
	The Scrum Team **must** fulfill (or abandon) one Product Goal / Objective before taking on the next.

Note:

1) Product Goals are like milestones on the Product roadmap. At any point in time, the next Product Goal is a single point to focus on for the Scrum teams. Product Goals are what the Scrum teams should work towards. For instance, if you put all your current work-in-progress on a Kanban board or look at all the items in a Sprint Backlog, they need to be all towards the next Product Goal. Getting teams to focus on the Product Goals keeps them focused on the product. This creates shared purpose.

2) A Product Backlog can have Product Backlog items which could tie to more than one Product Goals.

3) There can be only one "active / current" Product Goal at a time. This is the one Product Goal; the entire Scrum team focuses on.

4) During Sprint Planning, while considering Product Backlog items for a Sprint, the team should select the items which belong to that one "active" Product Goal.

5) During Sprint Review, the progress made towards the "active" Product Goal should be discussed.

6) If multiple teams are working, they should all work on the same "active" Product Goal.

7) During refinement, new Product Backlog items which tie to a different Product Goal could evolve. They should be placed in the Product Backlog.

8) As the Scrum Guide states, the Scrum team must fulfill (or abandon) one objective before taking on the next.

Who makes the Product Goal?
The **Product Owner is accountable for the development and communication of the Product Goal**; however, they would work with the Scrum Team and stakeholders to make sure that it is clear and easy to understand.

What happens when the current Product Goal is achieved?
A Scrum team can only have one Product Goal, so when the current Product Goal is achieved a new one would be created.

What happens when the goal changes?
Context of the situation or the environment the team is working in will influence what happens next.

1) Some teams will cancel the Sprint (which is the decision of the Product Owner) and go back to the stakeholders and present their findings

2) If there is a significant change in context and the current Product Goal has not been achieved, some Scrum Team would replace the Product Goal with a more fitting one.

What happens when the Product is no longer relevant?
If the Product is no longer relevant in the market (remember floppy disks, video cassettes, etc.), then the existence of the organization would end.

If this change to the Product Goal happens in a Sprint it remains in the authority of the Product Owner to cancel the Sprint if the goal of Sprint no longer aligns with the updated Product Goal.

The Product Goal should be:
1) Tangible and measurable (which provides real guidance on what's most potentially valuable).
2) Clear and concise.
3) Achievable.
4) Made transparent in the Product Backlog in the same way that the Sprint Goal is made transparent in the Sprint Backlog.
5) They communicate intent and not solution.

Product Goal example: There are many ways to capture product goals. Let's take an example from Melissa Perri Product Goals Canvas which clearly distinguishes the Product Vision from the measurable Product Goal (target condition).

Product Strategy Canvas

PRODUX labs

VISION
This is the lofty, futuristic goal for where your company or division is heading. Think long term.

In [10 years / time frame] [Uber / Company, division] will be [the cheaper alternative to owning a car or taking public transportation / Vision statement]

CHALLENGE
The first big goal to tackle on your way to the vision. Think in terms of user journeys, ideal states, objectives and KPIs that relate to the product lifecycle.

In order to reach our vision, we need to [reduce the wait time in key cities to less than 5 minutes / measureable objective] by [January 30, 2018 / time frame].

TARGET CONDITION
This is a smaller, measurable objective that teams can start exploring today.

In order to reach our Challenge, we first need to

[have at least one driver for every 50 people in each of those city by January 30, 2017. / measureable objective]

CURRENT STATE
What's the status today as it relates to the target condition?

After measuring, we know our current state is

[on average one driver for every 300 people in those cities. / measurements of current state]

Sprint Backlog (Sole Owner : Developers)	The Sprint Backlog is created during the beginning of the Sprint. The Sprint Backlog captures all the work which the **developers identify as necessary**, to meet the Sprint Goal.
	The Sprint Backlog is a plan by and for the Developers.
	The Sprint Backlog is made up of: 1) The Sprint Goal. 2) The Product Backlog items selected for the Sprint. 3) **The actionable plan for delivering them are together as an increment** and realizing the Sprint Goal.
	The Sprint Backlog is **created during the Sprint Planning**. The Sprint Backlog includes: 1) Items selected from the Product Backlog. 2) Tasks created by decomposing the selected Product Backlog items (during refinement).
	The Sprint Backlog is highly visible, real-time picture of the work that the Developers plan to accomplish during the Sprint in order to achieve the Sprint Goal.
	The Sprint Backlog is updated throughout the Sprint as more is learned. Developers keep adding tasks during the Sprint, so, the **Sprint Backlog keeps getting updated**. The Sprint Backlog is the Developers plan for the current Sprint. This plan is not detailed upfront.
	If the Developers cannot deliver some of the items from the Sprint Backlog, the items can be moved **back to the Product Backlog**. The incomplete items do not go to the next Sprint automatically.
	If the work turns out to be different than they expected, developers collaborate with the Product Owner to negotiate the scope of the Sprint Backlog within the Sprint **without affecting the Sprint Goal.**
	Each task in the Sprint backlog could be assigned to one developer or a pair of developers, **but the ownership is still shared across all the Developers in the Scrum Team.**
	Only the Developers can change the Sprint Backlog during a Sprint.
	Developers modifies the Sprint Backlog **throughout the Sprint**, and the Sprint Backlog emerges during the Sprint.
	Developers should not take any work into a Sprint if there are some unresolved external dependencies associated with that work.
	All Sprint Backlog Items **are "owned" by all the Developers in the Scrum Team**, even though each one may be implemented by an individual Developer.

Spring Goal	Sprint Backlog Commitment: Sprint Goal
   	The Sprint Goal is an **objective set for the Sprint** that can be met through the implementation of the Sprint Backlog items selected in a Sprint. It provides guidance to the Scrum Team on why it is building the Increment.
	During **Sprint Planning, the whole Scrum Team collaborates** to define a Sprint Goal that communicates why the Sprint is valuable to stakeholders.
	The Sprint Goal is the single objective for the Sprint.
	The Sprint Goal is fixed and if changed would result into cancellation of the Sprint.
	A Sprint **should be cancelled in case the Sprint Goal becomes obsolete**. (even if the Sprint Time Box is not over). Only the Product Owner can cancel the Sprint. When a Sprint is cancelled, all completed and "Done" Product Backlog items are reviewed. If part of the work is valuable, the Product Owner typically accepts it. All incomplete Product Backlog Items are re-estimated and put back on the Product Backlog.
	The Sprint Goal must be finalized prior to the end of Sprint Planning then added to the Sprint Backlog.
	Three important purposes of Sprint Goals: 1. The goal gives guidance during the Sprint on the objective that the Scrum Team wants to achieve in the Sprint, as well as why that is important. 2. They help the Scrum Team focus on what (kind of) work is important, and what is not. 3. Promote collaboration by giving Scrum Teams one clear purpose to work on, instead of separate initiatives.
	Sprint Goal Example 1: This Sprint exists to set up our deployment infrastructure to deploy a secure, working login page. Sprint Goal Example 2: This Sprint exists to build the interface for entering hours.
	Advantages of a Sprint Goal: 1. The Sprint Goal gives sense to the tasks and motivates the Team. People tend to be more enthusiastic and enjoy their work when they understand what it's for and how they contribute to the common cause. 2. The Sprint Goal unites the Scrum Team. 3. The Sprint Goal helps in managing risks. Each Sprint can be considered a project with a fixed budget and date. The Sprint Goal indicates the risk that the Scrum Team mitigates during the current Sprint. The risk can be associated with functionality, technologies, human factors, the external environment, etc. 4. The Sprint Goal helps with focus, making decisions & manage stakeholders' expectations.

Missing Sprint Goals	Without a clear and shared objective for the Sprint:
	1) A wide variety of items will be pulled from the Product Backlog during Sprint Planning.
	2) Unexpected problems, uncertainties and issues are likely to arise that require more time. With time being a purposefully scarce resource in a Sprint, and without a clear and shared objective, the Scrum Team would not have guidance on how to decide where to invest time and what to let go
	3) It will be hard to know when a Sprint is successful.
	4) There will be no obvious incentive to collaborate.
	5) Members will complete 'all their work' at different moments during the Sprint.
	6) It will be hard to know who to invite for the Sprint Review
	7) the Daily Scrum takes the form of a status update where members announce what they've been working on and what they plan to work on.
	8) Without there being a shared objective, known both to the team and its stakeholders, the Sprint Backlog is likely what Developers implicitly (or explicitly) commit to instead.
	9) People are likely to complain that Scrum Events take a lot of time and feel ineffective.
	Remember:
	A) The Sprint Goal should not be too big.
	B) The Sprint Goal should not be too vague.
	C) The team should pay attention to the Sprint Goal during the Sprint.
	D) The Sprint Goal should be meaningful.
	Myth: Having A Sprint Goal Is Optional In Scrum - Christiaan Verwijs https://www.scrum.org/resources/blog/myth-having-sprint-goal-optional-scrum
	Getting to Done: Creating Good Sprint Goals - Stephanie Ockerman https://www.scrum.org/resources/blog/getting-done-creating-good-sprint-goals

Product Increment (!)	Scrum requires the team **to create (at minimum) a valuable, useful Increment every Sprint.** Scrum's empiricism encourages the creation of multiple valuable increments during the Sprint to enable fast inspect and adapt feedback loops.
	An Increment is the sum of all the Product Backlog items completed during the Sprint plus the value of the increments of all previous Sprints.
	An Increment is a **concrete steppingstone** toward the **Product Goal.**
	Each Increment is additive to all prior Increments and thoroughly verified, ensuring that all Increments work together.
	In order to provide value, the Increment must be usable.
	An Increment may be delivered to stakeholders prior to the end of the Sprint.
Definition of Done (!)	**Increment Commitment: Definition of Done.**
	The Definition of Done is a formal description of **the state of the Increment when it meets the quality measures required for the product.**
	The moment a Product Backlog item **meets the Definition of Done, an Increment is born.**
	The Definition of Done creates transparency by providing everyone a **shared understanding of what work was completed** as part of the Increment.
	If a Product Backlog item **does not meet the Definition of Done:** 1) It cannot be released. 2) It cannot be even presented at the Sprint Review.
	If a Product Backlog item **does not meet the Definition of Done**, it returns to the Product Backlog for future consideration.
	All members of a **Scrum Team** must have a shared understanding of what it means for work to be complete, to ensure transparency.
	Definition of done should include: 1) Conventions, standards and guidelines of the Organization which need to be followed at the minimum should be a part of the definition of one. 2) Any compliance or regulatory requirements
	If "Done" for an increment is **not** a convention of the organization, the entire **Scrum Team must define a Definition of "Done"** appropriate for the product.

The entire **Scrum Team must define a Definition of "Done"**:

1) **Developers** have the knowledge and skills to do the work to create useable Increments, so they should bring this expertise into the Definition of Done.
2) **Product Owners** often have inputs related to quality from the business perspective.
3) **Scrum Masters** helps facilitate improvements to a Definition of Done as part of their accountability for the Scrum Team's effectiveness. A Scrum Master can help create greater transparency for the Scrum Team to identify where quality needs to improve.

The entire Scrum Team would need to work together to change the definition of "Done". If more than one Scrum teams use the same definition of "Done", then those Scrum teams should be involved in changing the Definition of Done as well.

The Developers are required to **conform to the Definition of Done.**

The Scrum Team plans ways to increase product quality **by adapting and improving the Definition of "Done" as appropriate.** So, Definition of Done changes with time.

A good time to change the **Definition of Done is at the Retrospective right before the next Sprint. However, this is not mandatory.**

A Good Definition of Done provides:
- Guidance on the specific patterns to be implemented in code.
- Communicates about the Quality Standard needed.

Each team might be working on a different part of the product (e.g. desktop application, mobile application, web application), or simply have different styles of work. If there are multiple Scrum Teams working together on a product, they must mutually define and comply with a **shared Definition of Done.**

A Few Good Criteria to include in the Definition of Done are:

- Unit tests passed.
- Code reviewed Completed.
- Acceptance criteria met / Acceptance test passed.
- Functional tests passed
- Non-Functional requirements met.
- Integrated into a clean build
- Automated regression tests pass
- Feature level functional tests passed
- Meets compliance requirements

Things that do not Exist	Scrum does not acknowledge: 1) Hardening Phases. 2) Sprint 0. 3) Technical Sprints that consists only of tasks which help reduce the technical debt and do not add any functionality to the Product.
Burn-down Charts 	Burn-down chart shows the evolution of remaining effort against time.
	A burn down chart is a graphical representation of work left to do versus time. That is, it is a run chart of outstanding work.
	X-Axis on the Burn-down chart shows he project/iteration timeline Y-Axis on the Burn-down chart the work that needs to be completed for the project. The Lines on the Graph show the **Actual Task Remaining Vs the Ideal Task Remaining.**
Additional Meetings	Scrum allows additional meetings if they facilitate achieving the Sprint and Product Goal.
Cone of Uncertainty	The Cone of Uncertainty describes the evolution of the amount of uncertainty during a project.
Opportunities to Adapt and Inspect	Remember, **including the Sprint itself** (which is a container for all other events), **each event** (Daily Scrum, Sprint Review, Sprint Retrospective and Daily Scrum) in Scrum is a formal opportunity to inspect and adapt something. These events are specifically designed to enable critical transparency and inspection.
Time-boxed events	Time-boxed events are events that have a maximum duration.

Product Release	The Product Increment should be usable and valuable at the end of every Sprint, but it **does not have to be released** to the client or published.
Role of Management	The Management supports the Product Owner with insights and information which helps with developing a high value product. The Management also supports the Scrum Master to cause organizational changes that foster empiricism, self-organization, bottom-up intelligence, and intelligent release of software. The Management has no active role in the actual product development through Scrum. However, Management external to the Scrum team is incredibly important in setting the vision and strategy to guide the overall direction of the organization.
Value of the Product	The Value of the product increases with Increased **Customer Satisfaction, Reduced Long Term Operational Cost and Time to market.**
Non-Functional Requirements	Non-functional requirements describe qualities of the system being developed. E.g. the system should be secure, extensible and have acceptable performance. The way to meet such requirements is: 1) Have them as a part of the Definition of Done and check the applicable Increment against these criteria. 2) Add them as the Acceptance Criteria to the applicable Product Backlog item. 3) Include them as Product Backlog item itself.
Scrum Team Velocity	Velocity is a measure of the amount of work a Team can tackle during a single Sprint and is the key metric in Scrum. Velocity is calculated at the end of the Sprint by totaling the Points for all fully completed User Stories.
Benefits of Self - Organization	The preferred leadership style in Scrum is "servant leadership", which emphasizes achieving results by focusing on the needs of the Scrum Team. Some of the benefits of Self-organization are: • Team buy-in and shared ownership • Motivation, which leads to an enhanced performance level of the team • Innovative and **Creative environment** conducive to growth • Increased Self Accountability, & Commitment to achieving the goals of the Scrum Team.

Technical Debt	Technical debt (also known as design debt or code debt) is a concept in software development that reflects **the implied cost of rework caused by choosing an easy solution "now" instead of using a better approach that would take longer**. Like any other debt, a large accumulation of Technical Debt (bad code) can impact future maintainability of the product.
	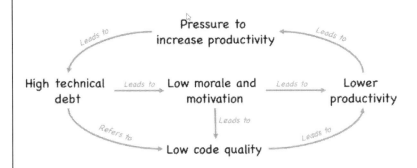
	The downsides of Technical Debt are as follows: 1. It **misleads** the Product Owners, Scrum Masters and Developers about **the "Current state" of the System**. For example, if Product Backlog item A is assumed to be completed in a day, it might take three days for it to complete, because of unseen bad code or Technical Debt. 2. The **Product becomes more unstable**, as more functionality is added over bad code (or existing technical debt). It is far more likely to impact components which crosscut a range of features. Moreover, if the necessary refactoring is significant it could impact the entire product, and it could affect features in uneven ways. Technical Debt is a **result of a bad technical decision** taken in order to save time or effort.
	Technical debt causes a greater percentage of the product's budget to be spent on maintenance of the product.
	The velocity at which new functionality can be created is reduced when you have technical debt.

PSM and PSPO Questions & Answers

Please go through these questions and check the answers you go along. The Scrum Assessments **online** (**https://www.scrum.org/open-assessments**) are the best way to judge where you stand. The Questions and Answers below will only make sure you understand the concepts and help you help you prepare for the PSM I and PSPO I. Go through the answers regardless of you answering the questions right or wrong. Don't try to time yourself. Rather focus on understanding the answers and thus the concepts.

1) A company in France has a heavy management layer. (Many Mangers, Project Managers etc.). The company just hired four Project Managers, a CEO and a CTO. This company should not implement Scrum as the management team really does not contribute to Scrum and implementing such methodology would not help the company. A. True B. False	**Correct answer: B** Remember, although Management does not actively involve itself in the Daily Scrum meetings, it does not mean they have no role at all. Management supports the Product Owner with insights and information needed to develop a high value product. They also Support the Scrum Master to cause organizational change that fosters empiricism, self-organization, bottom-up intelligence and intelligent release of software. Management external to the Scrum team is incredibly important in setting the vision and strategy to guide the overall direction of the organization.
2) Which activities does the accountability "functional manager" perform in Scrum? A. Lend their team members to the Scrum Team Leads as needed. B. Monitor and manage the Developers in the Scrum Team. C. Monitor everyone's productivity. D. Scrum has no such accountability as functional manager.	**Correct answer: D** A Scrum Team is a cohesive unit of professionals focused on one objective at a time, the Product Goal. The Scrum Team consists of the following accountabilities (previously known as roles): 1) One Product Owner. 2) Developers. 3) One Scrum Master. No Project Managers or Functional Managers exist within the Scrum Team.

3) A Sprint Backlog item has not been completed. It is now the last day of the Sprint (before the Sprint Retrospective and Sprint Review begins). Who is responsible if that Sprint Backlog item is not completed? (Choose the best answer) A. The Product Owner is responsible as he is responsible for the entire Product and Product Backlog. B. The entire Scrum Team is responsible even if one person is working on it. C. Only the Developers in the Scrum Team are accountable as they are the owners of the Sprint Backlog. D. The person assigned to the incomplete Sprint Backlog item is responsible. E. No one is responsible. The Sprint Backlog is just a forecast and if work is not completed, it gets moved back to the Product Backlog.	**Correct answer: E** The **entire Scrum Team** is: 1) **Responsible** for **all product-related activities** from stakeholder collaboration, **verification,** maintenance, operation, experimentation, research, development, documentation and anything else that might be required. 2) **Accountable** for creating **a valuable, useful Increment** every Sprint. The Sprint Backlog is a plan by and for the Developers. Remember the Sprint backlog is just a forecast of the work necessary for the Sprint Goal to be met. It is not a commitment. The people who undertake that work (which continues to emerge and evolve during the Sprint) are all Developers. However, If the Developers cannot deliver some of the items from the Sprint Backlog, the items get moved **back to the Product Backlog**. Since the Sprint Backlog is just a forecast and not a commitment, no one is responsible if the Product Backlog item is not completed.
4) The maximum length of the Sprint Review is: A. 4 hours regardless of the Sprint Length B. 4 hours for monthly sprint. For shorter Sprints it is usually shorter. C. 4 hours for biweekly sprints. D. As long as needed.	**Correct answer: B** A meeting / event called the Sprint Review is typically held at the end of the Sprint to: 1) Inspect the Increment. 2) Adapt the Product Backlog. The purpose of the Sprint Review is to inspect the outcome of the Sprint and determine future adaptations. The Sprint Review is at most a four-hour meeting for one-month Sprints. (Or shorter)

5) You must explain "Scrum" briefly to one of your potential clients. How would you best describe Scrum? (Choose three) A. Scrum is an old method that can be used to only develop software. (Only Applicable to Software Development) B. Scrum is a collection is of best practices for software and other industry development. C. Scrum is a framework within which complex products are developed. D. Scrum is a lightweight framework that helps people, teams and organizations generate value through adaptive solutions for complex problems. E. Various processes, techniques and methods can be employed within the framework.	**Correct answer: C, D, E** Scrum is a **lightweight** framework that helps people, teams and organizations **generate value** by creating **adaptive solutions** for **complex** problems. Scrum requires a Scrum Master to foster / maintain an environment where: 1. A Product Owner **orders the work** for a complex problem into a Product Backlog. 2. The Scrum Team **turns a selection of the work into an Increment (of value)** during a Sprint. 3. The Scrum Team and stakeholders **inspect the results** and adjust for the next Sprint. 4. Steps 1 through 3 are repeated for all sprints. Scrum is: 1) **Not a process, technique, or definitive method.** 2) **A framework** within which can employ various processes and techniques. 3) Employs an **iterative, incremental approach** to optimize predictability and to **control risk.** 4) Lightweight. 5) Simple to understand.
6) The maximum length of the Daily Sprint is: A. 15 Mins Timeboxed. B. 15 Mins or longer. C. 15 Mins for monthly sprint. For shorter Sprints it is usually shorter. D. As long as needed.	**Correct answer: A** The purpose of the Daily Scrum is to: 1) **Inspect progress toward the Sprint Goal** 2) **Adapt the Sprint Backlog as necessary,** adjusting the upcoming planned work. Every day in the Daily Scrum, the Developers understands how they intends to work together (as a self-Managing team) to accomplish the Sprint Goal. Developers also work towards creating the anticipated Increment by the end of the Sprint. The Daily Scrum is a 15-minute time-boxed event for the Developers in the Scrum Team. Time-boxed events are events that have a maximum duration. If the meeting agenda ends earlier, the meeting would be ended earlier than 15 mins.

7) The length of a Sprint Planning meeting is: A. 8 hours Period regardless of the Sprint Length B. 4.5 hours. C. 8 hours for biweekly sprint. For shorter Sprints it is usually shorter. D. 8 hours for monthly sprint. For shorter Sprints it is usually shorter. E. 4 hours for biweekly sprints.	**Correct answer: D** Sprint Planning initiates the Sprint by laying out the work to be performed for the Sprint. This resulting plan is created by the collaborative work of the entire Scrum Team. The Sprint Planning is time-boxed to a maximum of eight hours for a one-month Sprint.
8) The maximum length of a monthly Sprint Retrospective is: A. 3 hours. B. 4.5 hours. C. 8 hours for biweekly sprint. For shorter Sprints it is usually shorter. D. 8 hours for monthly sprint. For shorter Sprints it is usually shorter. E. 4 hours for biweekly sprints. F. As long as needed.	**Correct answer: A** The Sprint Retrospective is an opportunity for the Scrum Team to inspect itself and create an improvement plan which can be enacted. The purpose of the Sprint Retrospective is to plan ways to increase quality and effectiveness. The Sprint Retrospective occurs after the Sprint Review and prior to the next Sprint Planning. This is at most a three-hour meeting for one-month Sprints or shorter.
9) The three pillars of Scrum are: A. Watch, Learn and Develop. B. Planning, Develop, Test. C. Inspection, Transparency, Adaptation. D. Planning, Inspection, Adaptation.	**Correct answer: C** Scrum is founded on: 1) Empirical process control theory, or Empiricism. Empiricism asserts that knowledge comes from experience and making decisions based on what is known. 2) Lean Thinking: Lean thinking reduces waste and focuses on the essentials. Three pillars uphold every implementation of empirical process control: transparency, inspection, and adaptation.

10) When does a Sprint begin and end? A. The Sprint beginning and ending is decided by the Product Owner or Developer. It has no limitations. B. A Sprint begins right after the previous sprint ends & ends depending upon the length of the Sprint. C. A Sprint begins right after the previous sprint ends & ends based on when the work gets over. D. A Sprint begins and ends based on what the Scrum Master decides with the Lead Developer.	**Correct answer: B** A Sprint begins right after the previous sprint ends & ends depending upon the length of the Sprint. The duration of a Sprint is fixed and cannot be shortened or lengthened. A new Sprint starts immediately after the conclusion of the previous Sprint. There is no gap or work done between Sprints.
11) The Product Owner always releases the Product to the client's end of every Sprint. This would make sense as the Scrum Team also works towards creating a complete product / increment by the end of each Sprint. A) True B) False	**Correct answer: B** The product increment should be **usable and valuable** at the end of every Sprint, but it does not have to be "released" by the Product Owner.
12) The length of a Sprint could be: A. Weekly. B. Biweekly. C. Monthly. D. Short enough to keep the risk acceptable to the Product Owner. E. All the Above.	**Correct answer: E** Sprints are limited to one calendar month or shorter. The length of a Sprint thus could be Weekly, Biweekly or Monthly. Sprint should be short enough to keep the risk acceptable to the Product Owner.

13) The length of a Sprint could be: A. Quarterly for huge products. B. No more than one month. C. Short enough to not let the Sprint Goal may become invalid, allow complexity or increase risk. D. Short enough to generate more learning cycles and limit risk of cost and effort to a smaller time frame.	Correct answer: B, C, D Sprints enable predictability by ensuring inspection and adaptation of progress toward a Product Goal at least every calendar month. When a Sprint's horizon is too long the Sprint Goal may become invalid, complexity may rise, and risk may increase. Shorter Sprints can be employed to generate more learning cycles and limit risk of cost and effort to a smaller time frame. Each Sprint may be considered a short project. Sprints are limited to one calendar month or shorter. The length of a Sprint thus could be Weekly, Biweekly or Monthly. Sprint should be short enough to keep the risk acceptable to the Product Owner.
14) A company has recently added a new Scrum Team. The Scrum Team often has difficulties focusing on creating high-value Increments that meet the Definition of Done. Who is responsible for working with the Scrum team to correct this? A. Product Owner. B. Developers. C. Scrum Master. D. Scrum Lead.	Correct answer: C The Scrum Master is accountable for the Scrum Team's effectiveness. The Scrum Master helps those outside the Scrum Team understand which of their interactions with the Scrum Team are helpful and which aren't. The Scrum Master helps change interactions to maximize the value created by the Scrum Team. The Scrum Guide Says the following: The Scrum Master **serves the Scrum Team** by: 1) **Coaching** the team members self-management and cross-functionality. 2) Helping the Scrum Team **focus** on creating high-value Increments that meet the Definition of Done. 3) **Removing impediments** to the Scrum Team's progress. 4) Ensuring that all **Scrum events take place** and are positive, productive, and kept within the timebox.

15) The Sprint Retrospective occurs: A. After the Sprint Review and prior to the next Sprint Planning. B. Before the Sprint Review and after the Sprint Planning. C. After the Daily Scrum and before the next Sprint Review. D. Is optional, flexible and can be scheduled based on the Scrum teams need.	**Correct answer: A** The purpose of the Sprint Retrospective is to plan ways to increase quality and effectiveness. The Scrum Team inspects how the last Sprint went with regards to individuals, interactions, processes, tools, and their Definition of Done. Inspected elements often vary with the domain of work. Assumptions that led them astray are identified and their origins explored. The Sprint Planning occurs after the Sprint Review and prior to the next Sprint Planning.
16) Members of a Scrum Team (Developers) are facing two difficulties in general. The first difficulty is that they do not get the required server (hardware) from the external vendors on time. The second difficulty is they often have issues getting access to the cloud server from Jack. Jack is a member of an external cloud team. Who is responsible for removing impediments that hinder the progress of the Scrum Team? A. Product Owner. B. Developers. C. Scrum Master. D. Scrum Lead.	**Correct answer: C** The Scrum Master is accountable for the Scrum Team's effectiveness. The Scrum Master helps those outside the Scrum Team understand which of their interactions with the Scrum Team are helpful and which aren't. The Scrum Master helps change interactions to maximize the value created by the Scrum Team. The Scrum Guide states the following: The Scrum Master **serves the Scrum Team** by: 1) **Coaching** the team members self-management and cross-functionality. 2) Helping the Scrum Team **focus** on creating high-value Increments that meet the Definition of Done. 3) **Removing impediments** to the Scrum Team's progress. 4) Ensuring that all **Scrum events take place** and are positive, productive, and kept within the timebox.

17) A development company often shares resources (Developers) across Scrum Teams. These Developers are often busy and try to avoid attending meetings (including the Daily Scrum meetings). Who can most likely skip attending the Daily Scrum Meeting, if needed? (Choose one best answer) A. Developers. B. The Scrum Team. C. Developers and Scrum Master. D. The Scrum Master and Product Owner. (assuming they do not work on the Sprint Backlog items)	**Correct answer: D** The Daily Scrum is a 15-minute event **for the Developers** of the Scrum Team. Since it is a meeting is for the Developers, it is expected that the needed Developers would attend the Daily Scrum. The Scrum Master ensures that Developers in the Scrum Team have the Daily scrum meeting however does not have to be present himself in the meeting. If people outside the Scrum Team are present in the Daily Scum, the Scrum Master ensures that they do not disrupt the meeting. If the Product Owner or Scrum Master are actively working on items in the Sprint Backlog, they participate as Developers.
18) Which of the below accountabilities can be assigned to members of a Scrum Team? A. Project Manager, Scrum Lead, Development Lead and Developers. B. Project Manager, Scrum Lead and Developer. C. Product Owner, Scrum Lead and Developers. D. None of the above	**Correct answer: D** The Scrum Team consists only of the following accountabilities: • Product Owner. • Developer. • Scrum Master.
19) Developers in the Scrum Team keep changing the Daily Scrum meeting place and time based on the availability of conference rooms. The Team is: A. Doing the right thing as daily scrum has to be held every day. B. Increasing complexity by increasing inconsistency. C. Decreasing complexity by increasing inconsistency.	**Correct answer: B** The Daily Scrum is a 15-minute time-boxed event for the Developers. The Daily Scrum is held every day of the Sprint at the same place and same time to maintain consistency. Remember, it's not just the Daily Scrum Meeting. All Scrum events should be held at the same time and place to reduce complexity.

20) What is the recommended size for a Scrum Team including the Product Owner and Scrum Master? A. Minimal 7. B. Less or equal to 10. C. 12. D. 3 to 9.	**Correct answer: B** The Scrum Team is small enough to remain nimble and large enough to complete significant work within a Sprint, typically 10 or fewer people. Remember 10 is just a Guideline. A Scrum Team can be 11 people if needed but it should stay small enough to stay nimble.
21) An organization has recently started practicing Scrum. The Sprint Planning meetings have been taking a long time because the Scrum team members and stakeholders do not have the knowledge about the content or priority of the Product backlog items being considered. Whose responsibility is it prepare the Sprint Planning attendees to help with better discussions? **A.** Product Owner. **B.** Developers. **C.** Scrum Master. **D.** The Scrum Team.	**Correct answer: A** The Product Owner should ensure that attendees are prepared to discuss the most important Product Backlog items and how they map to the Product Goal.
22) A software development company is making a software for an Airport Terminal. 7 Scrum Teams are working together on this huge software. For such a complicated software each team should: (Select two best answers) A. Maintain one Product Backlog and coordinate with only one Product Owner. B. Maintain a shared "Definition of Done". C. Maintain one Scrum Master. D. Maintain a separate Product Backlog and Product Owner based on specific functions. E. Maintain a separate Scrum Master to manage the added complications.	**Correct answer: A, B** Multiple Scrum Teams often work together on the same product. One Product Backlog should be used to describe the upcoming work on the product (managed by one Product Owner). Each team might be working on a different part of the product (e.g. desktop application, mobile application, web application), or simply have different styles of work. If there are multiple Scrum Teams working together on a product, they must mutually define and comply with a shared **Definition of Done.**

23) A finance company is developing a product / software. Functions within the product are complex and some of them take longer than a Sprint to develop. Regardless, the Scrum Team must deliver an increment of "Releasable" software every Sprint. A. False B. True	**Correct answer: A** The term "potentially releasable" no longer used to describe the Increment. The Scrum Team should work on and deliver a product increment which usable and valuable at the end of every Sprint.
24) For each Sprint, a Sprint Review should be conducted just to display and show the stake holders what was achieved. Once the demo is done and client feedback is received, the Sprint Review is considered complete. A. False B. True	**Correct answer: A** The purpose of the Sprint Review is to inspect the outcome of the Sprint and determine future adaptations. The Scrum Team presents the results of their work to key stakeholders and progress toward the Product Goal is discussed. During the event, the Scrum Team and stakeholders review what was accomplished in the Sprint and what has changed in their environment. Based on this information, attendees collaborate on what to do next. The Sprint Review is a working session and the Scrum Team should avoid limiting it to just a presentation.
25) Sprint Review includes discussion on what should be selected in the upcoming Sprint. A. False B. True	**Correct answer: B** During the Sprint Review, the Scrum Team and stakeholders collaborate about what was done in the Sprint. Based on that and changes made to the Product Backlog during the Sprint, attendees collaborate on the next things that could be done to optimize value.

26) Which of the following statements are true about the Sprint Retrospective?
 	
A. The Scrum team inspects how the last Sprint went with regards to individuals, interactions, processes, tools, and their Definition of Done.
 	
B. The Scrum Team discusses, what went well during the Sprint, the problems they encountered and How those problems were (or were not) solved.
 	
C. The Scrum team identifies and orders the major items that went well along with the potential improvements.
 	
D. The Scrum Master and Product Owner do not participate in the Sprint retrospectives.
	Correct answer: A, B, C
	
	In the Sprint Retrospective:
	1) The Scrum team inspects how the last Sprint went with regards to individuals, interactions, processes, tools, and their Definition of Done.
	2) The Scrum Team discusses:
	   o What went well during the Sprint.
	   o The problems they encountered.
	   o How those problems were (or were not) solved.
	
	The Scrum team identifies and orders the major items that went well along with the potential improvements.

27) Can the key stakeholders participate in the Sprint Reviews meetings? **A.** No **B.** Yes	**Correct answer: B** During the Sprint Review, **the Scrum Team and Key Stakeholders** (people outside the Scrum Team) **collaborate** to discuss and review: 1) What was **achieved / accomplished** in the current Sprint? 2) What has **changed** in their environment?
28) Technical experts can attend the Sprint Planning Meetings. **A.** False **B.** True	**Correct answer: B** Technical Domain Experts or people outside the Scrum Team (if invited by the Scrum Team) may attend Sprint Planning to give advice.

29) Which of the following statements are true about Sprint Goals? (Choose all that apply) **A.** The Sprint Goal is an objective set for the Sprint that can be met through the implementation of the Sprint Backlog items selected in a Sprint. It provides guidance to the Scrum Team on why it is building the Increment. **B.** During Sprint Planning, the whole Scrum Team collaborates to define a Sprint Goal that communicates why the Sprint is valuable to stakeholders. **C.** The Sprint Goal is the single objective for the Sprint. **D.** The Sprint Goal is fixed and if changed would result into cancellation of the Sprint.	**Correct answer: A, B, C, D** The Sprint Goal is an objective set for the Sprint that can be met through the implementation of the Sprint Backlog items selected in a Sprint. It provides guidance to the Scrum Team on why it is building the Increment. During Sprint Planning, the whole Scrum Team collaborates to define a Sprint Goal that communicates why the Sprint is valuable to stakeholders. The Sprint Goal is the single objective for the Sprint. The Sprint Goal is fixed and if changed would result into cancellation of the Sprint. A Sprint should be cancelled in case the Sprint Goal becomes obsolete. (even if the Sprint Time Box is not over). Only the Product Owner can cancel the Sprint. When a Sprint is cancelled, all completed and "Done" Product Backlog items are reviewed. If part of the work is potentially valuable, the Product Owner typically accepts it. All incomplete Product Backlog Items are re-estimated and put back on the Product Backlog.
30) Can people outside the Scrum Team participate regularly and actively in the ongoing Daily Scrums calls? **A.** False **B.** True	**Correct answer: A** People outside the Scrum Team can attend the Daily Scrums; however, they cannot participate (participate actively). They are involvement is controlled and guided by the Scrum Master. Remember that the developers might need help from other business or technical users. The Team might invite others on the call to have a few questions answered. Only the Developers actively participates in the Daily Scrum Calls. If the question was can people outside the Scrum Team attend (as opposed to participate) a Daily Scrum call? The answer would have been true, they could attend if invited.

31) During Sprint Planning, who selects items from the Product Backlog to the Sprint Backlog? A. Product Owner. B. Developers. C. Scrum Master. D. Scrum Lead.	**Correct answer: B** During Sprint Planning, through discussion with the Product Owner, the Developers select items from the Product Backlog to include in the current Sprint. The selected items get moved to the Sprint Backlog. The Scrum Team may refine these items during this process, which increases understanding and confidence.
32) When is the Sprint Goal created? A. Sprint Review B. Daily Sprint. C. Sprint Retrospective. D. Sprint Planning.	**Correct answer: D** During Sprint Planning, the whole Scrum Team collaborates to define a Sprint Goal that communicates why the Sprint is valuable to stakeholders.
33) People outside the Scrum Team can attend a Daily Scrum call. A. False B. True	**Correct answer: B** People outside the Scrum Team can attend the Daily Scrums; however, they cannot participate (participate actively). They are involvement is controlled and guided by the Scrum Master. Remember that the developers might need help from other business or technical users. The Team might invite others on the call to have a few questions answered. People outside the Scrum team can attend this meeting however they cannot actively participate. Only the Developers can actively participate in the ongoing Daily Scrum Calls.

34) A Sprint Review is in process. The clients invited to the review realize that the Developers are not very clear about the requirements captured in form of Product Backlog items. Who is responsible for clarifying the requirements to the Developers? A. The Scrum Team. B. The Product Owner. C. The Scrum Master. D. The Scrum Master and Product Owner.	**Correct answer: B** The Product Owner keeps communicating with the stakeholders, creates new items in the Product Backlog, revises the order of items and answers questions to makes sure that everyone has the right understanding of items. The Product Owner is also accountable for effective Product Backlog management, which includes: • Developing and explicitly communicating the Product Goal. • Creating and **clearly communicating Product Backlog items.** • Ordering Product Backlog items; and, • Ensuring that the Product Backlog is transparent, visible and **understood**.
35) At the Sprint Review, only the Developers should explain which Product Backlog items have been completed and what has not been "Done" to the key stakeholders as they have been working on these items. **A.** False **B.** True	**Correct answer: A** The purpose of the Sprint Review is to inspect the outcome of the Sprint and determine future adaptations. The entire **Scrum Team** presents the results of their work to key stakeholders and progress toward the Product Goal is discussed. During the Sprint Review, **the Scrum Team and Key Stakeholders** (people outside the Scrum Team) **collaborate** to discuss and review: 1) What was **achieved / accomplished** in the current Sprint? 2) What has **changed** in their environment?
36) At the Sprint Review, the entire Scrum Team collaborates (with the stakeholders) on what to do next. Thus, the Sprint Review provides valuable input to subsequent Sprint Planning. **A.** False **B.** True	**Correct answer: B** During the Sprint Review, the Scrum Team and Key Stakeholders (people outside the Scrum Team) collaborate about what was done in the Sprint. In the Sprint Review the next things that could be done to optimize value is also reviewed. The result of the Sprint Review is a revised Product Backlog that defines the probable Product Backlog items for the next Sprint.

37) A Scrum Team decides they need to create a UI mockup to better understand the existing product capabilities. Can they proceed without anyone's permission? **A.** Yes **B.** No	**Correct answer: A** Yes, the Scrum team are responsible to manage their own work, the way they want it. Scrum Teams are **Self-managing** which means they internally decide who does what, when, and how. Self-managing teams: 1) Manage their own work. 2) Decide how to achieve goals. 3) Grow as a team. 4) Continuously improve. 5) Manage stakeholders. 6) Help other teams and co-workers to grow, improve and thrive. 7) Constantly collaborate with other teams, pinpoint improvements and learn fast, making them more motivated and productive
38) The Definition of "Done" is created by: **A.** Product Owner. **B.** Developers. **C.** Scrum Master. **D.** The Scrum Team.	**Correct answer: D** The entire **Scrum Team must define a Definition of "Done"**: 1) **Developers** have the knowledge and skills to do the work to create useable Increments, so they should bring this expertise into the Definition of Done. 2) **Product Owners** often have inputs related to quality from the business perspective. 3) **Scrum Masters** helps facilitate improvements to a Definition of Done as part of their accountability for the Scrum Team's effectiveness. A Scrum Master can help create greater transparency for the Scrum Team to identify where quality needs to improve.

39) A Scrum Team is just formed, and they are about to begin work. There is no Sprint 0 and the Product backlog items haven't even started. While the Product Owner works on getting the Product backlog started, what is enough to start a first Sprint? A. A first Sprint requires no more than a Product Owner, Developers, and enough ideas. B. A complete Product Backlog. C. A groomed Sprint Backlog. D. A requirement documents.	**Correct answer: A** A first Sprint requires no more than a Product Owner, Developers, and enough ideas to potentially complete a full Sprint. Remember Scrum is founded on empiricism and lean thinking. Empiricism asserts that knowledge comes from experience and making decisions based on what is observed. Lean thinking reduces waste and focuses on the essentials. Both Empiricism and Lean encourage starting the work rather than having prolonged discussions about it.
40) In a large firm, some of the external stakeholders do not have visibility about the progress made by the Scrum team. They are a bit concerned. What's the best way to inform people about the progress made by the Scrum Team? A. Share the Product Backlog and ask them to visit the next Sprint Review. B. Share a status report. C. Share a roadblock document. D. All of the above.	**Correct answer: A** The duty of the Scrum Team is to be transparent. Those who need information are responsible for getting it. So, people concerned about the progress can investigate the artifacts of the Scrum Team (Product Backlog, Sprint Backlog and Product increment) and visit the next Sprint Review, if needed.

41) The Product Owner can have the Developers work on clearly expressing Product Backlog items. A. True B. False	**Correct answer: A** The Product Owner is also accountable for effective Product Backlog management, which includes: 1) Developing and explicitly communicating the Product Goal. 2) **Creating and Clearly expressing** Product Backlog items. 3) **Ordering** the items in the Product Backlog to best achieve goals and missions. 4) Ensuring that the Product Backlog is **visible, transparent,** and clear to all. The Product **Owner can delegate above to others however remains accountable for it.**
42) The Product Owner can make the developers work on communicating the Product Goal and ordering the items in the Product Backlog to best achieve goals and missions. A. True B. False	**Correct answer: A** The Product Owner is also accountable for effective Product Backlog management, which includes: 1) Developing and explicitly communicating the Product Goal. 2) **Creating and Clearly expressing** Product Backlog items. 3) **Ordering** the items in the Product Backlog to best achieve goals and missions. 4) Ensuring that the Product Backlog is **visible, transparent,** and clear to all. The Product **Owner can delegate above to others however remains accountable for it.**

43) What items might a Scrum Product Owner focus on to ensure his product delivers value? **A.** Key Stake Holder Involvement. **B.** Product Market Place. **C.** Product Release Decisions. **D.** Each Developers work hours and resultant velocity. **E.** All of the Above.	**Correct answer: A, B, C** The Product Owner is accountable for maximizing the value of the product resulting from the work of the Scrum Team. How this is done may vary widely across organizations, Scrum Teams, and individuals. Product Owner should focus on: → **Key Stakeholder Involvement.** In order to maximize value, the Product Owner should identify the key stakeholders for the product and involve them as necessary throughout the development effort. → **Product Marketplace.** The Product Owner should be expertly aware of the marketplace for the product. They should constantly be gathering and re-gathering information and data regarding the marketplace, so that the product value is maximized. → **Product Release Decisions** The Product Owner is the one and only person who can decide whether to release the latest increment of the Product. For value to be captured, a release of the product must occur.
44) There are 60 items selected in a Sprint. With 6 Developers each developer must at least select one or more Sprint Backlog items (ideally 10 for equal work distribution). A. True B. False	**Correct answer: B** The Sprint Backlog is created during the beginning of the Sprint. The Sprint Backlog captures all the work which the developers identify as necessary, to meet the Sprint Goal. The Sprint Backlog is a plan by and for the Developers. The Sprint Backlog is made up of: 1) The Sprint Goal. 2) The Product Backlog items selected for the Sprint. 3) The actionable plan for delivering them are together as an increment and realizing the Sprint Goal. Each task in the Sprint backlog could be assigned to one developer or a pair of developers, but the ownership is still shared across all the Developers in the Scrum Team. Developers can assign or distribute the work as needed. (Self-managing)

45) In an old company, there are a set of developers who have been working for 16 to 18 years. These developers do not share information about the product and keep the important coding documentation to themselves. Which Scrum values are impacted? (Choose all that apply)

A. Commitment.
B. Courage.
C. Focus.
D. Strength.
E. Openness.

Correct answer: A, B, C, E

Scrum Values give direction to the Scrum Team with regard to their work, actions, and behavior. They also help define the work ethics the Scrum team should have. The Scrum Team members learn and explore the values as they work with the Scrum events and artifacts. Different Scrum Values are:

1. **Commitment**: The Scrum Team members personally commit to achieving the Scrum Goals and to supporting each other.
2. **Courage:** The Scrum Team members have courage to do the right thing and work on tough problems.
3. **Focus**: Everyone focuses on the work of the Sprint and the best possible progress made toward the goals of the Scrum Team.
4. **Openness** (No Hiding): The Scrum Team and its stakeholders agree to be open about all the work and the challenges with performing the work.
5. **Respect**: Scrum Team members respect each other to be capable, independent people. Scrum Team members are respected by the people with whom they work.

All Scrum Values are all impacted by lack of trust or transparency. Strength is not a value.

46) Scrum Team A and Scrum Team B are working on the same Product. Team A has decided that their Sprint Length is going to be 4 weeks long. Team B has decided that their Sprint length is going to be 2 weeks long. Team A and Team B can: (Choose all that apply) A. Have different Sprint Lengths. B. Have different Scrum Masters. C. Have different Product Owners. D. Have different Product Backlogs.	**Correct answer: A, B** Different Teams working on the same Product can: • Have **different Sprint Lengths**. • Have different Scrum Masters. • Have only one Product Owner. • Have a shared Definition of Done.
47) No one has the authority to replace an item in the Sprint Backlog. Only Developers within the Scrum Team have the rights to do so once they talk to the Product Owner. A. True B. False	**Correct answer: A** Only the Developers in a Scrum Team can change their Sprint Backlog during a Sprint. The Product Owner might help or influence the team to help select and plan items for a Sprint Backlog however the Developers within the Scrum Team have the final authority and control over the sprint backlog as it's the "developers work queue".
48) The number of items selected from the Product Backlog for the Sprint is solely up to the Developers. Based on the discussions with the product owner, the Developers can best assess what can be accomplished over the upcoming Sprint. A. True B. False	**Correct answer: A** The number of items selected from the Product Backlog for the Sprint is solely up to the Developers. Based on the discussions with the product owner, the Developers can best assess what can be accomplished over the upcoming Sprint. Selecting how much can be completed within a Sprint may be challenging. However, the more the Developers know about their past performance, their upcoming capacity, and their Definition of Done, the more confident they will be in their Sprint forecasts

49) The Product Owner has all the authority to add and manage items in the Product Backlog. A. True B. False	**Correct answer: A** The Product Owner is responsible for managing the Product Backlog maximizing the value of the Product. He can add remove items as needed from the Product Backlog. The Product Owner is accountable for effective Product Backlog management, which includes: 1) Developing and explicitly communicating the Product Goal. 2) **Creating and Clearly expressing** Product Backlog items. 3) **Ordering** the items in the Product Backlog to best achieve goals and missions. 4) **Optimizing the value** of the work for the Developers to performs. 5) Ensuring that the Product Backlog is **visible, transparent,** and clear to all.
50) During the 10th sprint, a client realizes that a critical functionality is missing. Which meetings did they probably miss where they could have provided feedback about the missing functionality or the change, the product needed? A. Sprint Review. B. Daily Sprint. C. Sprint Retrospective. D. Management Meeting.	**Correct answer: A** Sprint Review is a meeting where Members external to the Scrum Team can actively participate to give feedback.
51) Who creates the commitments for the Scrum artifacts? A. Product Goal is created by the Product Owner working with the Scrum Team. The Sprint Goal is created by the Scrum Team. And, the Definition of Done is created by the Scrum Team. B. Commitments are created by organization managers.	**Correct answer: A** Artifact commitments are part of the existing artifacts and as such whoever is accountable for that artifact is accountable for that commitment. Product Goal is created by the Product Owner working with the Scrum Team. The Sprint Goal is created by the Scrum Team. And, the Definition of Done is created by the Scrum Team.

52) On asking a Developer about details as to how the product development was going, the Developer referred the person to the Product Backlog (and the Sprint Backlog). He also invited the person to the next Sprint Review. Did the Developer do the right thing? A. True B. False	**Correct answer: A** A duty of the Scrum Team is to be transparent. Those who need information are responsible for getting it. So, the managers can investigate the artifacts of the Scrum Team (Product Backlog, Sprint Backlog) and visit the next Sprint Review if needed.
53) During a Sprint Retrospective, what is the Scrum Master responsible for? A. Taking Notes Meeting Minutes. B. Scrum Master and Product Owners should not attend the Sprint Retrospective. C. Only reserving the rooms. D. The Scrum Master participates as a peer team member in the Retrospective. E. The Scrum Master is not allowed in the Sprint Retrospective.	**Correct answer: D** The Scrum Master and Product Owner participates as a peer team member in the Sprint Retrospective. Everyone in the Scrum Team inspects how the last Sprint went with regards to individuals, interactions, processes, tools, and their Definition of Done. Inspected elements often vary with the domain of work. Assumptions that led them astray are identified and their origins explored. The Scrum Team discusses what went well during the Sprint, what problems it encountered, and how those problems were (or were not) solved. Everyone in the Scrum Team identifies the most helpful changes to improve its effectiveness.

54) The client is concerned with the Product. The Product seems to have all the functionalities asked for however it seems to crash / stop quite often. Performance testing of the Products is a concern. What should one do next? A. Create special test documentation for the client explaining the issues. B. Ask the client to do acceptance testing before accepting the Product. C. Adapt a new Definition of Done which includes improved performance testing as soon as possible. D. Adapt a new Definition of Done which includes improved Performance testing during Sprint Retrospective, as Definition of Done can only be changed during Sprint Retrospective.	**Correct answer: C** During each Sprint Retrospective, the Scrum Team plans ways to increase product quality by improving work processes or adapting an improved definition of "Done", if appropriate and not in conflict with product or organizational standards. Typically, it is advised to wait for the Sprint retrospective to improve the terms of quality in the Definition of "Done" for the product, however it's not mandatory and can be changed right away.
55) A Definition of "Done" can only be changed by the Product Owner. A. True B. False	**Correct answer: B** The entire Scrum Team would need to get together to change the definition of "Done". If more than one Scrum teams use the definition of "Done", then both the Scrum teams (or at least the appropriate representatives) should be involved in changing the Definition of Done.

56) After a Retrospective meeting, John sends out the meeting minutes with the few high priority action items identified by the team, which will improve its effectiveness. What would the team do next? (Choose all that apply) A. Add all the items into the Product Backlog. B. The most impactful improvements must be addressed as soon as possible. C. The most impactful improvements may even be added to the Sprint Backlog for the next Sprint. **D.** The most impactful improvements should be sent to the process improvement team for further review. E. At least one impactful improvement must be added to the Sprint Backlog for the next Sprint.	**Correct answer: A, B, C** The Scrum Team inspects how the last Sprint went with regards to individuals, interactions, processes, tools, and their Definition of Done. Inspected elements often vary with the domain of work. Assumptions that led them astray are identified and their origins explored. The Scrum Team discusses what went well during the Sprint, what problems it encountered, and how those problems were (or were not) solved. The Scrum Team identifies the most helpful changes to improve its effectiveness. The most impactful improvements are addressed as soon as possible. They may even be added to the Sprint Backlog for the next Sprint. "At least one impactful improvement must be added to the Sprint Backlog for the next Sprint." - This is no longer mandator based on the latest Scrum Guide.
57) Who has the authority to cancel a Sprint? A. The Sponsor. B. The Scrum Master. C. Developers. D. The Product Owner.	**Correct answer: D** Only the Product Owner can cancel a Sprint. As seen below in the Scrum Guide "A Sprint could be cancelled if the Sprint Goal becomes obsolete. Only the Product Owner has the authority to cancel the Sprint."
58) What is the Sprint Backlog? A. Set of Product Backlog items selected for the current Sprint plus the plan for delivering them. B. Set of Product Backlog items selected for the current Sprint. **C.** Set of Product Backlog items selected for the current Sprint plus a set of internal tasks. **D.** A subset of the Product Backlog.	**Correct answer: A** The Sprint Backlog is the set of Product Backlog items selected for the Sprint, plus a plan for delivering the product Increment and realizing the Sprint Goal. The Sprint Backlog is created during the beginning of the Sprint. The Sprint Backlog captures all the work which the developers identify as necessary, to meet the Sprint Goal. The Sprint Backlog is a plan by and for the Developers. The Sprint Backlog is made up of: 1) The Sprint Goal. 2) The Product Backlog items selected for the Sprint. 3) The actionable plan for delivering them are together as an increment and realizing the Sprint Goal. The Sprint Backlog is created during the Sprint Planning. The Sprint Backlog includes:

		1) Items selected from the Product Backlog. 2) Tasks created by decomposing the selected Product Backlog items (during refinement).
59)	A Product Owner is looking at a Product Backlog. How would he / she see the Product backlog items typically ordered in the Product Backlog? (Choose all that Apply.) A. Higher Ordered Product Backlog items are usually clear, detailed and on the top in the Product Backlog. B. Less detailed items at the bottom of the Product Backlog. C. First in Top up i.e. the recently added items are seen at the top in the Product Backlog. D. The less described items are seen at the top in the Product Backlog. E. The Product Backlog items are ordered based on the Numerical number assigned to them.	**Correct answer: A, B** Average number of items in the Product Backlog are usually more than items in the Sprint Backlog. This is how it works: [A] Items with different sizes are added to the Product Backlog. [B] Items are sorted based on their business value. [C] Large items on the top of the Product Backlog are broken down into smaller ones (during refinement). These are more detailed than the ones at the bottom. That's why the items on the top are smaller than those on the bottom. Remember that size is not a basis for ordering the Product Backlog items.
60)	During one of the Sprints, the Scrum Master decides to help the Developers by executing (working on and completing) a few items in the Sprint Backlog. Can the Scrum Master do that? A. Yes B. No	**Correct answer: A** Yes. The Scrum Master can be a Developer however it's not recommended as it may impact the responsibilities the Scrum Master is supposed to accomplish.

61) What provides guidance to the Developer on why they are building the Increment? (Choose two) A. The Company Guidelines. B. The Sprint Backlog. C. The Scrum Master. D. The Sprint Goal. E. The Product Goal.	**Correct answer: D, E** The Sprint Goal is an objective set for the Sprint that can be met through the implementation of Product Backlog. It provides guidance to the Developers on why it is building the Increment. Three important purposes of Sprint Goals: 1. The goal gives guidance during the Sprint on the objective that the Scrum Team wants to achieve in the Sprint, as well as why that is important; 2. They help the Scrum Team focus on what (kind of) work is important, and what is not. 3. Promote collaboration by giving Scrum Teams one clear purpose to work on, instead of separate initiatives. Product Goal provides context to the Product Backlog. It can be thought of as the 'why' the scrum is doing all of the work. The commitment for the Product Backlog is the Product Goal.
62) A Developer needs to make changes to the Product Backlog. Which of the following statements are true? A. He is not allowed to make the changes, only the Product Owner can. B. He can make changes if the Product Owner has granted permission. C. He can make changes, but it's not recommended. D. He can make changes without any permissions.	**Correct answer: B** The Product Owner is responsible for the Product Backlog. The Product Owner can delegate the following changes to the Product Backlog: 1) Developing and explicitly communicating the Product Goal. 2) **Creating and Clearly expressing** Product Backlog items. 3) **Ordering** the items in the Product Backlog to best achieve goals and missions. 4) **Optimizing the value** of the work for the Developers to performs. 5) Ensuring that the Product Backlog is **visible, transparent,** and clear to all.

63) Developers are prohibited to add new work into the Sprint Backlog after the Sprint Planning is completed. A. False **B.** True	**Correct answer: A** Developers modifies the Sprint Backlog throughout the Sprint, and the Sprint Backlog emerges during the Sprint. This emergence occurs as the Scrum Team works through the plan and learns more about the work needed to achieve the Sprint Goal. As new work is recognized, the Developers adds it to the Sprint Backlog.
64) Who is responsible for tracking the total work remaining in the Sprint Backlog to project the likelihood of achieving the Sprint Goal? A. The Scrum Master. B. Development Lead. C. Developers **D.** The Product Owner.	**Correct answer: C** The Sprint Goal is the single objective for the Sprint. Although the Sprint Goal is a commitment by the Developers, it provides flexibility in terms of the exact work needed to achieve it. The Sprint Goal also creates coherence and focus, encouraging the Scrum Team to work together rather than on separate initiatives. The Sprint Goal is created during the Sprint Planning event and then added to the Sprint Backlog. As the Developers work during the Sprint, they keep the Sprint Goal in mind. If the work turns out to be different than they expected, **they collaborate with the Product Owner to negotiate the scope of the Sprint Backlog within the sprint without affecting the Sprint Goal.**
65) A Product can have only one Product Goal throughout its life. A. True B. False	**Correct answer: B** A Scrum team can only have one "active" Product Goal, so when the current Product Goal is achieved a new one would be created. This is the one Product Goal; the entire Scrum team focuses on.

66) Which are the inputs to the Sprint Planning? A. Prioritized Product Backlog items and Definition of Done. B. Developers past performance and upcoming capacity. C. Amount of Technical backlog remaining. D. Sprint Goal and updated Sprint Backlog with refined Product Backlog items.	**Correct answer: A, B** During Sprint Planning, the Product Owner ensures that attendees are prepared to discuss the most important Product Backlog items and how they map to the Product Goal. Through discussion with the Product Owner, the Developers select items from the Product Backlog to include in the current Sprint. The selected items get moved to the Sprint Backlog. The Scrum Team may refine these items during this process, which increases understanding and confidence. Selecting how much can be completed within a Sprint may be challenging. However, the more the Developers will be more confident about how much work they can do in the sprint / sprint forecasts based on knowing more about: 1) Developers past performance. 2) Developers upcoming capacity. 3) Definition of Done. Thus, the Inputs to Sprint Planning are: 1) Prioritized Product Backlog along with the Definition of Done. 2) Developers past performance. 3) Developers upcoming capacity. 4) Projected capacity of the Developers. (based on their past performance) The outputs of Sprint Planning are a Sprint Goal and an updated Sprint Backlog with refined Product Backlog items.
67) Scrum recommends using only those Scrum components and rules which suit most for the given project. A. True B. False	**Correct answer: B** Each component within the Scrum framework serves a specific purpose and is essential to Scrum's success and usage. Just the way one can't skip creating a Product or Sprint Backlog, similarly, one can't skip scheduling a meeting.

68) Scrum is founded on: (Choose two) A. Common sense. B. Agile methods. C. Waterfall method. D. Old Methodologies Combined. E. Empiricism. F. Lean Thinking.	**Correct answer: E, F** Scrum is founded on empirical process control theory, or empiricism. Empiricism asserts that knowledge comes from experience and making decisions based on what is known. Scrum is founded on: 1) Empirical process control theory, or Empiricism. Empiricism asserts that knowledge comes from experience and making decisions based on what is known. 2) Lean Thinking: Lean thinking reduces waste and focuses on the essentials.
69) Who is responsible for all the estimates in the Product Backlog? A. The Scrum Master. B. The Product Owner. C. The Product Owner and Developers. D. Developers. **E.** The Product Owner and the Scrum Master.	**Correct answer: D** Developers in the Scrum Team are responsible for all estimates in the Product Backlog. The Product Owner may influence the Developers by helping it understand and select trade-offs, but the people who will perform the work make the final estimate.
70) Which of the following are the Scrum Artifacts? Select all applicable items. A. Increment. B. Sprint Backlog. C. Product Backlog. D. The Sprint Goal. E. Project Reports.	**Correct answer: A, B, C** Scrum Artifacts are: • Product Backlog. • Sprint Backlog. • Increments.
71) Every day in the Daily Scrum meeting, the Developers understands how they intends to work together (as a self-organizing team) to accomplish the Sprint Goal. A. True B. False	**Correct answer: A** Every day in the Daily Scrum meeting, the Developers understands how they intends to work together (as a self-Managing team) to accomplish the Sprint Goal. Developers also work towards creating the anticipated Increment along with the rest of the team by the end of the Sprint.

72) A company has been practicing Scrum for years. Midway through the Sprint, the company has withdrawn all Scrum funding as the company has decided to sunset the Product. The Sprint Goals are now obsolete. The Product owner has decided to cancel the sprint. What happens typically when a Sprint is cancelled? (Choose all that apply). **A.** The completed and "Done" Product Backlog items are reviewed. **B.** If part of the work is potentially valuable, the Product Owner typically accepts it. **C.** All incomplete Product Backlog Items are re-estimated and put back on the Product Backlog. **D.** All the complete and incomplete work is discarded as it does not matter anymore.	**Correct answer: A, B, C** When a Sprint is cancelled, any completed and "Done" Product Backlog items are reviewed. If part of the work is potentially valuable, the Product Owner typically accepts it. All incomplete Product Backlog Items are re-estimated and put back on the Product Backlog. The work done on them depreciates quickly and must be frequently re-estimated.
73) Check all the opportunities to inspect and adapt. **A.** The Sprint Review. **B.** The Daily Scrum. **C.** The Sprint Planning. **D.** The Sprint Retrospective. **E.** The Sprint.	Correct answer: A, B, C, D, E Scrum combines four formal events for inspection and adaptation within a containing event, the Sprint. To help with inspection, Scrum provides cadence in the form of its five events. Scrum prescribes **five** mandatory events **for Inspection and Adaptation:** 1. Sprint Planning 2. Daily Scrum 3. Sprint Review 4. Sprint Retrospective 5. The Sprint (Container of the above four events). The **event that contains the four formal events** is called the Sprint.

74) A Scrum Team is composed of the following accountabilities: **A.** Scrum Master **B.** Project Manager **C.** Scrum Lead **D.** Development Lead **E.** Developers **F.** Product Lead **G.** Product Owner **H.** Architects	**Correct answer: A, E, G** The Scrum Team is composed of the Scrum Master, Developers and Product Owner. As seen below in the Scrum Guide
75) What questions does the Sprint Planning answer? Select three. **A.** What can be delivered in the Increment using the upcoming Sprint? **B.** How will the work needed to deliver the Increment be achieved? **C.** What new technologies could be used to speed up the Scrum Team velocity? **D.** What is the size of the Technical Debt and how it could be removed? **E.** Why is the work selected in the Sprint important? **F.** Who will be responsible for each item in the Sprint Backlog?	**Correct answer: A, B, E** **Sprint Planning addresses the following topics:** **Topic One: Why is this Sprint valuable?** The **Product Owner** proposes how the product could increase its value and utility in the current Sprint. The **whole Scrum Team then collaborates to define a Sprint Goal** that communicates why the Sprint is valuable to stakeholders. The **Sprint Goal must be finalized prior to the end of Sprint Planning.** **Topic Two: What can be Done this Sprint?** Through discussion with the Product Owner, the **Developers select items from the Product Backlog to include in the current Sprint.** The selected items get moved to the Sprint Backlog. **The Scrum Team** may refine these items during this process, which increases understanding and confidence. Selecting how much can be completed within a Sprint may be challenging. However, the more the Developers will be more confident about how much work they can do in the sprint / sprint forecasts based on knowing more about: 1) Developers past performance. 2) Developers upcoming capacity. 3) Definition of Done. **Topic Three: How will the chosen work get done?** For each selected Product Backlog item: 1) **The Developers plan the work necessary to create an Increment that meets the Definition of Done.**

	2) This is **often done by decomposing Product Backlog items into smaller work items of one day or less.** 3) The decomposing of Product backlog items into smaller work items is at the sole discretion of the **Developers.** No one else tells them how to turn Product Backlog items into Increments of value.
76) During a Sprint, the quality of the items delivered can be decreased if needed. Quality can always be compensated for, in the next sprint. **A.** True **B.** False	**Correct answer: B** During the Sprint: • No changes are made that would endanger the Sprint Goal. • Quality goals do not decrease. • Scope may be clarified and re-negotiated between the Product Owner and Developers as more is learned.
77) A Good Scrum team would always have all the items in the Product Backlog complete. **A.** True **B.** False	**Correct answer: B** A Product Backlog is never complete. The earliest development of it only lays out the initially known and best-understood requirements. The Product Backlog evolves as the product and the environment in which it will be used evolves. The Product Backlog is dynamic; it constantly changes to identify what the product needs to be appropriate, competitive, and useful. As long as a product exists, its Product Backlog also exists.
78) The purpose of the Sprint Review is to inspect the outcome of the Sprint. Scrum Teams demo the Sprints work which is already complete. No Adaption activities are done in Sprint Review. **A.** True **B.** False	**Correct answer: B** A meeting / event called the Sprint Review is typically held at the end of the Sprint to: 1) Inspect the Increment. 2) Adapt the Product Backlog. The purpose of the Sprint Review is to inspect the outcome of the Sprint and determine future adaptations. The Sprint Review is a working session and the Scrum Team should avoid limiting it to a presentation.

79) Which of the following statements about the Sprint Length are true? (Choose all that apply) **A.** Different Scrum Teams working on the same product can have different Sprint lengths. The duration of a Sprint is fixed and should not be shortened or lengthened once the Sprint has started. **B.** When a Sprint's length is too long, the Sprint Goal may become invalid. Complexity may rise and Risk may increase. **C.** Shorter Sprints can be employed to generate more learning cycles based on the quick feedback loops from the stakeholders. **D.** Shorter Sprints limit risk of cost to a smaller time frame Limit risk of effort to a smaller time frame.	**Correct answer: A, B, C, D** Different Scrum Teams working on the same product can have different Sprint length. The duration of a Sprint is fixed and should not be shortened or lengthened once the Sprint has started. When a Sprint's horizon is too long, the Sprint Goal may become invalid. Complexity may rise and Risk may increase. Shorter Sprints can be employed to generate more learning cycles based on the quick feedback loops from the stakeholders. Shorter Sprints limit risk of cost to a smaller time frame Limit risk of effort to a smaller time frame.

80) Which of the following statements are true about the Daily Scum? (Choose all that apply)
A. The purpose of the Daily Scrum is to inspect progress toward the Sprint Goal and adapt the Sprint Backlog as necessary, adjusting the upcoming planned work.
B. The Daily Scrum is a 15-minute event for the Developers of the Scrum Team.
C. To reduce complexity, it is held at the same time and place every working day of the Sprint.
D. If the Product Owner or Scrum Master are actively working on items in the Sprint Backlog, they participate as Developers.
	Correct answer: A, B, C, D
	
	The purpose of the Daily Scrum is:
	   1) To inspect progress made by the developers toward the Sprint Goal
	   2) Adapt the Sprint Backlog as necessary, adjusting the upcoming planned work.
	
	The Daily Scrum is a 15-minute event for the Developers of the Scrum Team. To reduce complexity, it is held at the same time and place every working day of the Sprint.
	If the Product Owner or Scrum Master are actively working on items in the Sprint Backlog, they participate as Developers

81) Who ensures that the Sprint Review meeting takes place? **A.** The Stake Holders. **B.** Developers. **C.** The Product Owner **D.** The Scrum Master.	**Correct answer: D** Scrum Master ensures that the meeting takes place but does not have to be present in the meeting. The Scrum Master serves the Scrum Team in several ways, including: • Coaching the team members in self-management and cross-functionality. • Helping the Scrum Team focus on creating high-value Increments that meet the Definition of Done. • Causing the removal of impediments to the Scrum Team's progress. • Ensuring that **all Scrum events take place and are positive, productive, and kept within the timebox.**
82) Who demonstrates the work the team has "Done" and answers questions about the Increment in the Sprint Review Meeting? **A.** Product Owner **B.** Scrum Master **C.** QA Team **D.** The Scrum Team **E.** Developers	**Correct answer: D** The purpose of the Sprint Review is to inspect the outcome of the Sprint and determine future adaptations. The Scrum Team presents the results of their work to key stakeholders and progress toward the Product Goal is discussed.
83) The Developers use the Daily Scrum to inspect progress toward the Sprint Goal. They also use the Daily Scrum to inspect how progress is trending toward completing the remaining work in the Sprint Backlog. **A.** True **B.** False	**Correct answer: A** Developers in the Scrum Team uses the Daily Scrum to inspect progress toward the Sprint Goal and to inspect how progress is trending toward completing the remaining work in the Sprint Backlog.

84) Who decides on the structure and agenda of the Daily Scrum meeting? A. Product Owner B. Scrum Master C. QA Team D. Developers	**Correct Answer: D** The purpose of the Daily Scrum is to inspect progress toward the Sprint Goal and adapt the Sprint Backlog as necessary, adjusting the upcoming planned work. The Developers can select whatever structure and techniques they want, as long as their Daily Scrum focuses on progress toward the Sprint Goal and produces an actionable plan for the next day of work. This creates focus and improves self-management.
85) Once a Sprint begins, its duration is fixed and its recommended that its length should not be shortened or lengthened. A. True B. False	**Correct answer: A** The Scrum framework does not require the same Sprint length or aligned Sprints for all teams. So, the start date can be different. However, the Sprint length should not be shortened or lengthened.
86) The result of the Sprint Review is: A. All Product Backlog Items closed and completed in the Sprint Backlog. B. Reviewed Product Backlog Items and incomplete items moved to the top of the Product Backlog. C. A revised Product Backlog that defines the probable Product Backlog items for the next Sprint. D. Reviewed Product Backlog Items and incomplete items moved to the top of the next Sprint Backlog.	**Correct answer: C** The purpose of the Sprint Review is to inspect the outcome of the Sprint and determine future adaptations. The Scrum Team presents the results of their work to key stakeholders and progress toward the Product Goal is discussed. During the event, the Scrum Team and stakeholders review what was accomplished in the Sprint and what has changed in their environment. Based on this information, attendees collaborate on what to do next. Sprint Review is a meeting in which the stakeholders see what was done. They also collectively decide on what needs to be done in the next sprint. Everything which needs to be done flows through the Product backlog. Thus, the result of the Sprint Review is a revised Product Backlog that defines the probable Product Backlog items for the next Sprint. Remember not all the incomplete items get moved to the top of the Product Backlog or the next Sprint Backlog. While this might be common, the next sprint priorities might change, and the incomplete items might be considered at a later point in time.

87) Product Backlog refinement is: **A.** A daily mandatory event. **B.** An occasional Scrum event. **C.** Carried out once per Sprint, during the beginning of the Sprint. **D.** An ongoing process in which the Product Owner and the Developers collaborate to add details, estimates and order to the Product Backlog items.	**Correct Answer: D** Product Backlog refinement is an ongoing process which is the act of adding detail, estimates, and order to items in the Product Backlog. The Scrum Team decides how and when refinement is done.
88) The Daily Scrum is the only time the Developers can meet to adjust their plan to deliver the Sprints work. **A.** True **B.** False	**Correct Answer: B** The Daily Scrum is not the only time Developers can adjust their plan. They often meet throughout the day for more detailed discussions about adapting or re-planning the rest of the Sprint's work.
89) A Product Backlog is never complete **A.** True - If a product exists, its Product Backlog also exists. **B.** False - A Complete Product Backlog should be created before starting the first Sprint.	**Correct Answer: A** A Product Backlog is never complete. As long as a product exists, its Product Backlog also exists.
90) The Scrum Master must always facilitate the Daily Scrum. **A.** False **B.** True	**Correct Answer: A** The Scrum Master does not have to be present in the Daily Scrum meetings. Developers own this meeting and runs it.

91) A company has two products. Which of the following is an acceptable way of forming Scrum teams? Choose all that apply. **A.** There should be a Product Owner for each product. He / She can be shared across Products. **B.** There should at least be one Scrum Master for each product. He / She can be shared across Products. **C.** There should be a different Scum Master for each team. **D.** There should be one Product Owner supported by a Junior Product Owner. **E.** There should be a Chief Product Owner and one Product Owner for each product. **F.** There should be a single Definition of Done across Products.	**Correct Answer: A, B** One Product should at least have one Product Owner. However, the same Product Owner can work across Products. (Not recommended). There "should" be at least one Scrum master for every product and in fact for every Scrum Team. One cannot have a Scrum Team without a Scrum Master (and a Product Owner). Its ok if the same Scum Master is shared across Scrum Teams and Products. (Not recommended). Be careful. Definition of Done should be shared across teams working on the same Product, not across Products.
92) Which of the following is the single source of requirements for all changes to the product? **A.** The Increment **B.** The Sprint Retrospective **C.** The Product Backlog **D.** The Sprint Backlog **E.** The Product's vision	**Correct Answer: C** The Product Backlog is an ordered list of everything that is known to be needed in the product. It is the single source of requirements for any changes to be made to the product. The Product Owner is responsible for the Product Backlog, including its content, availability, and ordering.
93) Which of the following statements about Sprints are true? (Choose all that apply) **A.** All the work necessary to achieve the Product Goal, including Sprint Planning, Daily Scrums, Sprint Review, and Sprint Retrospective, happen within Sprints. Nothing happens outside the Sprint. **B.** Sprints enable predictability by ensuring inspection and adaptation of progress toward a Product Goal at least every calendar month. **C.** The heart of Scrum is a Sprint where ideas are turned into value. **D.** Sprint a time-box of two weeks or less during which a "Done", useable, and potentially releasable Product Increment is created.	**Correct Answer: A, B, C** All the work necessary to achieve the Product Goal, including Sprint Planning, Daily Scrums, Sprint Review, and Sprint Retrospective, happen within Sprints. Sprints enable predictability by ensuring inspection and adaptation of progress toward a Product Goal at least every calendar month. The heart of Scrum is a Sprint where ideas are turned into value. Sprint a time-box of one month or less during which a "Done", useable, and potentially releasable Product Increment is created.

94) Which Scrum event is an opportunity for the Scrum Team to inspect itself and create a plan for improvements? **A.** Sprint Planning **B.** Sprint Retrospective **C.** Daily Scrum **D.** Sprint Review	**Correct Answer: B** The purpose of the Sprint Retrospective is to plan ways to increase quality and effectiveness. The Scrum Team discusses what went well during the Sprint, what problems it encountered, and how those problems were (or were not) solved. The Scrum Team identifies the most helpful changes to improve its effectiveness. The most impactful improvements are addressed as soon as possible. They may even be added to the Sprint Backlog for the next Sprint. The purpose of the Sprint Retrospective is to: • Inspect how the last Sprint went with regards to people, relationships, process, tools and Definition of Done. • Identify and order the major items that went well and potential improvements. • Create a plan for implementing improvements to the way the Scrum Team does its work.
95) A Team is organizing Scrum. What is a "must have" factor for the Scrum Team? Choose all that Apply. **A.** The Scrum Team should have years of experience. **B.** The Scrum Team should be very knowledgeable about the Domain. **C.** The Scrum Team should have good communication. **D.** The Scrum Team should be self-Managing. **E.** The Scrum Team should look for ways to continuously Improve. **F.** The Scrum Team should constantly collaborate with other teams, pinpoint improvements and learn fast, making them more motivated and productive.	**Correct Answer: C, D, E, F** Remember. Scrum Teams are cross-functional teams having all the skills (as a team) needed to create a Product Increment. Scrum Teams are Self-managing which means they internally decide who does what, when, and how. Self-managing teams: 1) Manage their own work. 2) Decide how to achieve goals. 3) Grow as a team. 4) Continuously improve. 5) Manage stakeholders. 6) Help other teams and co-workers to grow, improve and thrive. 7) Constantly collaborate with other teams, pinpoint improvements and learn fast, making them more motivated and productive.

96) A New Scrum Team is busy documenting all the client requirements in a requirement document. They are working as quickly as they can. They want to finish this before the Sprint starts. The Scrum Team: (Choose all that apply) A. Should be documenting all the requirements. The Sprint can start only once all the requirements are documented. B. Would not need a Product backlog as all the requirements are present in the requirement documents. C. Should be maintaining the Product Backlog by adding all the requirements as they are recognized. D. Should focus more on the requirements which are going to be developed first up.	**Correct Answer: C,D** Documenting all the requirements at the same time is not preferred or advised. Instead the Product Owner should focus more on the items which are going to be picked up in the sprint. He / she may continue to elaborate on the rest of the items as he / she find the time.
97) Where are the requirements stored? A. Product Backlog. B. Secured Database. C. On a Server. D. Depends upon the Product Owner.	**Correct Answer: A** In Scrum, the source of all requirements and changes is the Product Backlog.
98) The Developers failed to complete all the items they had selected for a Sprint. The Product Owner should: A. Fire the Developers. B. Ask the Developers to work overtime and complete those items. C. Push the Sprint End date to accommodate the remaining work. D. Move the remaining items back to the Product Backlog. E. Move the remaining items to the next Sprint Backlog.	**Correct Answer: D** In the real world, almost every sprint will have at least one or two sprint backlog items which won't be completed. In such situations, the Developers will work with the Product Owner to move it back to the Product Backlog. These items might (and not necessarily) be moved to the Next Sprint Backlog from the Product Backlog, if they are needed for the next sprints goal.

99) The Sprint Goal needs to be corrected. Who should be present? **A.** Product Owner Only. **B.** Product Owner and Developers. **C.** Entire Scrum Team. **D.** CEO of the Company.	**Correct Answer: C** Remember the Sprint Goal is crafted by the whole Scrum Team, just not the Product Owner. If it needs to be changed, the entire team (or the appropriate representatives) should be present.
100) Which of the following statements about Scrum are true? (Choose all that apply). **A.** Scrum is a lightweight framework that helps people, teams and organizations generate value by creating adaptive solutions for complex problems. **B.** The Scrum framework is purposefully incomplete and only defines the parts required to implement Scrum theory. **C.** Scrum wraps around existing practices or renders them unnecessary. **D.** Scrum brings transparency to the effectiveness (or ineffectiveness) of the current management, environment, and work techniques, so that improvements can be made.	**Correct Answer: A, B, C, D** Scrum is a lightweight framework that helps people, teams and organizations generate value by creating adaptive solutions for complex problems. The Scrum framework is purposefully incomplete and only defines the parts required to implement Scrum theory. Scrum wraps around existing practices or renders them unnecessary. Scrum brings transparency to the effectiveness (or ineffectiveness) of the current management, environment, and work techniques, so that improvements can be made.
101) What questions does the Sprint review answer? (Choose two) **A.** What was achieved / accomplished in the current Sprint? **B.** What has changed in their environment? **C.** Why was the work taken / importance of the work? **D.** Who finished the work in the sprint?	**Correct Answer: A, B** The purpose of the Sprint Review is to inspect the outcome of the Sprint and determine future adaptations. The entire Scrum Team presents the results of their work to key stakeholders and progress toward the Product Goal is discussed. During the Sprint Review, the Scrum Team and Key Stakeholders (people outside the Scrum Team) collaborate to discuss and review: 1) What was achieved / accomplished in the current Sprint? 2) What has changed in their environment?

102) Scrum requires a Scrum Master to foster / maintain an environment where: (Choose all the Apply) A. A Product Owner orders the work for a complex problem into a Product Backlog. B. Stakeholders order the work in the Product Backlog. C. Developers (and only developers) turn the selection of the work into an Increment (of value) during a Sprint. D. The Scrum Team turns a selection of the work into an Increment (of value) during a Sprint. E. The Scrum Team and stakeholders inspect the results and adjust for the next Sprint.	**Correct Answer: A, D, E** Scrum requires a Scrum Master to foster / maintain an environment where: 1. A Product Owner **orders the work** for a complex problem into a Product Backlog. 2. The Scrum Team **turns a selection of the work into an Increment (of value)** during a Sprint. 3. The Scrum Team and stakeholders **inspect the results** and adjust for the next Sprint.
103) The Scrum framework is **purposefully incomplete**. It only defines the parts required to implement Scrum theory. A. True B. False	**Correct Answer: A** The Scrum framework is **purposefully incomplete**. It only defines the parts required to implement Scrum theory.
104) Which of the following statements about Scrum are true? (Choose all that apply) A. Scrum is not a process, technique, or definitive method. B. Scrum is a framework within which can employ various processes and techniques. C. Scrum employs an iterative, incremental approach to optimize predictability and to control risk. D. Scrum is lightweight and simple to understand.	**Correct Answer: A, B, C, D** Scrum is: A. **Not a process, technique, or definitive method**. B. **A framework** within which can employ various processes and techniques. C. Employs an **iterative, incremental approach** to optimize predictability and to **control risk**. D. Lightweight. E. Simple to understand. F. Difficult to master.
105) Which of the following is true about Artifact commitments? A. The commitment for the Product Backlog, is the Product Goal. B. The commitment for the Sprint Backlog, is the Definition of Done. C. The commitment for the Increment is the Product Goal and the Sprint Goal. D. All of the above.	**Correct Answer: A** Remember: • For the Product Backlog, the commitment is the Product Goal. • For the Sprint Backlog, the commitment is the Sprint Goal. • For the Increment, the commitment is the Definition of Done.

106) Important decisions are made based on the state of the Sprint backlog, Product backlog and the Product Increment. Thus, these three artifacts should be extremely transparent. Artifacts having low transparency can lead to: **A.** Decisions that increase product value and decrease risk. **B.** Decisions that diminish product value and increase risk.	**Correct Answer: B** Important decisions are made based on the state of the Sprint backlog, Product backlog and the Product Increment. Thus, these three artifacts should be extremely transparent. Artifacts having low transparency can lead to decisions that diminish value and increase risk.
107) Who is responsible for all product-related activities from stakeholder collaboration, verification, maintenance, operation, experimentation, research, development, documentation and anything else that might be required? A. Product Owner. B. Developers. C. Scrum Master. D. Scrum Team.	**Correct Answer: D** The **entire Scrum Team** is: 1) **Responsible** for **all product-related activities** from stakeholder collaboration, verification, maintenance, operation, experimentation, research, development, documentation and anything else that might be required. 2) **Accountable** for creating **a valuable, useful Increment** every Sprint.
108) In Scrum, each artifact contains a commitment. Commitments ensure that: A. They provide information that enhances transparency. B. They provide focus against which progress can be measured. C. They exist to reinforce empiricism and the Scrum values for the Scrum Team and their stakeholders. D. All of the above.	**Correct Answer: D** Each artifact contains a commitment. Commitment ensure that: 1) It provides information that enhances transparency. 2) It provides focus against which progress can be measured. 3) They exist to reinforce empiricism and the Scrum values for the Scrum Team and their stakeholders.

109) Who is accountable for creating a valuable, useful Increment every Sprint? A. Product Owner. B. Developers. C. Scrum Master. D. Scrum Team.	**Correct Answer: D** The **entire Scrum Team** is: 1) **Responsible** for **all product-related activities** from stakeholder collaboration, verification, maintenance, operation, experimentation, research, development, documentation and anything else that might be required. 2) **Accountable** for creating **a valuable, useful Increment** every Sprint.
110) Which of the following statements about a Scrum Team are true? A. Sub-team formations (or hierarchies) in the Scrum Team is not allowed. B. Titles are not assigned to the developers within the Scrum Team members, regardless of the type of work they perform. C. Scrum Team collectively decides on the Scrum length. D. Scrum Team delivers a "Done" product every Sprint to ensure a potentially useful version of a working product is always available. However, it is up to the Product Owner to "Release" it.	**Correct Answer: A, B, C, D** Sub-team formations (or hierarchies) in the Scrum Team **is not allowed**. Sub-Teams such as testing teams or an operation teams are not allowed to be formed in the Scrum Team. Titles are **not assigned** to the developers within the Scrum Team members, regardless of the type of work they perform. Scrum Team collectively decides on the Scrum Length. Scrum Team **delivers a "Done" product every Sprint** to ensure a potentially useful version of a working product is always available. However, **it is up to the Product Owner to "Release" it.**
111) Which of the following is true about multiple Scrum teams working on the same Product? (Choose all that apply). A. Scrum teams would have the same Product Backlog. B. Scrum teams would have the same Product Owner. C. Scrum teams would have different Sprint Backlogs. (one for each team) D. Scrum teams would have a shared Definition of Done.	**Correct Answer: A, B, C, D** Different Teams working on the same Product: • Must have the Same Product Backlog. • Must have the Same Product Owner. • Must have the Same Product Goal. • Must have different Sprint Backlogs. (one for each team) • Must have a shared Definition of Done. • Can have **different Sprint Lengths.** • Can have **different Scrum Masters.**

112) Which of the following statements are true about a Product Owner? A. The Product Owner is accountable for maximizing the value of the Product and the work the Developers do. B. The Product Owner is accountable for creating the Product Goal. C. The Product Owner is accountable for creating the Sprint Goal. D. The Product Owner is accountable explicitly communicating the Product Goal.	**Correct Answer: A, B, D** The Product Owner is **accountable for managing the Product Backlog. He / she is also accountable for maximizing the value of the Product and the work the Developers do** The Product Owner is accountable for: 1) **Creating the Product Goal.** 2) **Explicitly communicating the Product Goal.** The entire Scrum team is responsible for creating the Sprint Goal.
113) The Product Owner is also accountable for effective Product Backlog management, which includes: (Choose all that apply) A. Developing and explicitly communicating the Product Goal. B. Creating and Clearly expressing Product Backlog items. C. Ordering the items in the Product Backlog to best achieve goals and missions. D. Ordering the items in the Sprint Backlog to best achieve Sprint goals. E. Ensuring that the Product Backlog is visible, transparent, and clear to all. F. Ensuring that the Product Backlog is always complete.	**Correct Answer: A, B, C, E** The Product Owner is also accountable for effective Product Backlog management, which includes: 1) Developing and explicitly communicating the Product Goal. 2) **Creating and Clearly expressing** Product Backlog items. 3) **Ordering** the items in the Product Backlog to best achieve goals and missions. 4) **Optimizing the value** of the work for the Developers to performs. 5) Ensuring that the Product Backlog is **visible, transparent,** and clear to all.

114) Which of the following activities can be delegated to others by the Product Owner? A. Developing and explicitly communicating the Product Goal. B. Creating and Clearly expressing Product Backlog items. C. Ordering the items in the Product Backlog to best achieve goals and missions. D. Optimizing the value of the work for the Developers to performs. E. Ensuring that the Product Backlog is visible, transparent, and clear to all.	**Correct Answer: A, B, C, E** The Product Owner is also accountable for effective Product Backlog management, which includes: 1) Developing and explicitly communicating the Product Goal. 2) **Creating and Clearly expressing** Product Backlog items. 3) **Ordering** the items in the Product Backlog to best achieve goals and missions 4) Ensuring that the Product Backlog is **visible, transparent,** and clear to all. The Product Owner can delegate above to others however remains accountable for it. Optimizing the value of the product is the Product Owners responsibility and should not delegated.
115) For larger and complicated products, the Product Owner accountability can be represented by a committee. A. True B. False	**Correct Answer: B** The Product Owner is one person, not a committee.
116) Who is accountable for the Scrum Teams effectiveness? A. Product Owner. B. Developers. C. Scrum Master. D. Scrum Lead.	**Correct answer: C** The Scrum Master is accountable for the Scrum Team's effectiveness.

117) A new Scrum team is formed in an organization. Almost all the team members have experience in the waterfall methodology and have very little idea about how scum works. A new scrum master has been hired. He should: (Choose all that apply) A. Coach the team members self-management. B. Help the Scrum Team focus on creating high-value Increments. C. Help the Scrum Team by removing impediments to the Scrum Team's progress. D. Help the Scrum Team by ensuring that all Scrum events take place and are positive, productive, and kept within the timebox.	**Correct Answer: A, B, C, D** The Scrum Master **serves the Scrum Team** by: 1) **Coaching** the team members self-management and cross-functionality. 2) Helping the Scrum Team **focus** on creating high-value Increments that meet the Definition of Done. 3) **Removing impediments** to the Scrum Team's progress. 4) Ensuring that all **Scrum events take place** and are positive, productive, and kept within the timebox.
118) A Product has 16 active clients. The product is evolving and every month lots of enhancements request flow in from the stakeholders. The Product owner is struggling to manage the Product backlog. He also needs help with the stakeholder's meetings as they are not very product focused, often resulting to a lot of derailed discussions. Who should help the Product Owner and how? (Choose all that apply) A. The Scrum master should help the Product Owner find techniques for effective Product Backlog management. B. The Scrum Master should help the Product Owner by facilitating stakeholder collaboration as requested or needed. C. Managers in the organization should help the Product Owner find techniques for effective Product Backlog management. D. The Product Owners boss should step in and help the product Owner by facilitating stakeholder collaboration as requested or needed.	**Correct answer: A, B** The Scrum Master **serves the Product Owner** by: 1) Helping the Product Owner **find techniques** for effective **Product Goal definition** and Product Backlog management. 2) Helping the Scrum Team understand the need for clear and concise Product Backlog items. 3) Helping **establish empirical product planning** for a complex environment 4) **Facilitating** stakeholder collaboration as requested or needed.

119) A Scrum team is not so good at maintaining detailed Product backlog items. Who should help the Scrum Team understand the need for clear and concise Product Backlog items? A. Product Owner. B. Developers. C. Scrum Master. D. Scrum Lead.	**Correct answer: C** The Scrum Master **serves the Product Owner** by: 1) Helping the Product Owner **find techniques** for effective **Product Goal definition** and Product Backlog management. 2) Helping the Scrum Team understand the need for clear and concise Product Backlog items. 3) Helping **establish empirical product planning** for a complex environment 4) **Facilitating** stakeholder collaboration as requested or needed.
120) Who should help with the Planning of Scrum implementations within the organization? A. The Product Owner. B. Scrum Team. C. Developers. D. Scrum Master.	**Correct answer: D** The Scrum Master serves the organization by: 1) **Leading, training, and coaching the organization** in its Scrum adoption. 2) **Planning and advising Scrum implementations** within the organization. 3) Helping employees and stakeholders **understand and enact an empirical approach** for complex work. 4) **Removing barriers** between stakeholders and Scrum Teams.

121) Who makes the Product Goal and is responsible for communicating it across the stakeholders? A. The Product Owner is accountable for the development of the Product Goal. The communication of the Product Goal is done by the Scrum Master. B. The Product Owner is accountable for the development and communication of the Product Goal; however, they would work with the Scrum Team and stakeholders to make sure that it is clear and easy to understand. C. The Scrum Team is accountable for the development and communication of the Product Goal. D. The management team is accountable for the development of the Product Goal. The communication of the Product Goal is done by the Scrum Master.	**Correct answer: B** The Product Owner is accountable for the development and communication of the Product Goal; however, they would work with the Scrum Team and stakeholders to make sure that it is clear and easy to understand.
122) Which of the following statements are true about a definition of done? (Choose all that apply) A. The Definition of Done is a formal description of the state of the Increment when it meets the quality measures required for the product. B. The moment a Product Backlog item meets the Definition of Done, an Increment is born. C. The Definition of Done creates transparency by providing everyone a shared understanding of what work was completed as part of the Increment. D. All members of a Scrum Team must have a shared understanding of what it means for work to be complete, to ensure transparency.	**Correct answer: A, B, C, D** The Definition of Done is a formal description of the state of the Increment when it meets the quality measures required for the product. The moment a Product Backlog item meets the Definition of Done, an Increment is born. The Definition of Done creates transparency by providing everyone a shared understanding of what work was completed as part of the Increment. If a Product Backlog item does not meet the Definition of Done, it returns to the Product Backlog for future consideration. All members of a Scrum Team must have a shared understanding of what it means for work to be complete, to ensure transparency.

| 123) There should be only one "active / current" Product Goal at a time. This is the one Product Goal; the entire Scrum team focuses on.

A. True
B. False | **Correct answer: A**

1) Product Goals are like milestones on the Product roadmap. At any point in time, the next Product Goal is a single point to focus on for the Scrum teams. Product Goals are what the Scrum teams should work towards. For instance, if you put all your current work-in-progress on a Kanban board or look at all the items in a Sprint Backlog, they need to be all towards the next Product Goal. Getting teams to focus on the Product Goals keeps them focused on the product. This creates shared purpose.
2) A Product Backlog can have Product Backlog items which could tie to more than one Product Goals.
3) There can be only one "active / current" Product Goal at a time. This is the one Product Goal; the entire Scrum team focuses on.
4) During Sprint Planning, while considering Product Backlog items for a Sprint, the team should select the items which belong to that one "active" Product Goal.
5) During Sprint Review, the progress made towards the "active" Product Goal should be discussed.
6) If multiple teams are working, they should all work on the same "active" Product Goal.
7) During refinement, new Product Backlog items which tie to a different Product Goal could evolve. They should be placed in the Product Backlog.
8) As the Scrum Guide states, the Scrum team must fulfill (or abandon) one objective before taking on the next. |

124) Which of the following statements about a Product increment are true? (Choose all that apply). A. An Increment is the sum of all the Product Backlog items completed during the Sprint plus the value of the increments of all previous Sprints. B. An Increment is a concrete steppingstone toward the Product Goal. C. Each Increment is additive to all prior Increments and thoroughly verified, ensuring that all Increments work together. D. In order to provide value, the Increment must be usable. E. An Increment may be delivered to stakeholders prior to the end of the Sprint.	**Correct answer: A, B, C, D, E** An Increment is the sum of all the Product Backlog items completed during the Sprint plus the value of the increments of all previous Sprints. An Increment is a concrete steppingstone toward the Product Goal. Each Increment is additive to all prior Increments and thoroughly verified, ensuring that all Increments work together. In order to provide value, the Increment must be usable. An Increment may be delivered to stakeholders prior to the end of the Sprint.
125) Developers within a Scrum Team, have remote team members who typically spends time before the Daily Scrum to go through Architectural designs, code designs, code reviews, high priorities bugs, concerns etc. How should the Scrum Master handle this situation? A. Ask the Developers to discuss the same in the Daily meetings. Meetings outside the Scrum Events are not allowed. They are a waste of time. B. Allow the Developers to self-manage and decide for themselves. C. Inform the Management about such meetings. Try and reduce such meetings as much as possible so the developers can get more time to develop. D. Get involved and start facilitating such meetings.	**Correct Answer: B** As a self-organized team, the scrum team (including the Developers) will decide for themselves how to best manage communication between team members. The Daily Scrum is not the only time Developers can adjust their plan. They often meet throughout the day for more detailed discussions about adapting or re-planning the rest of the Sprint's work. The Scrum Master will only act if requested or if he/she observes that there is a potential problem.

126) You are the Scrum Master who has just joined a Scrum Team in an organization. One of the developers notify you that they will need full-time help of a technical specialist in the upcoming two Sprints. This specialist Is not a part of the Scrum Team. What concerns should the Scrum Master take into consideration? A. The Team velocity will increase as the specialist will be added to the Team for the next two Sprints. B. The Team velocity will decrease as the specialist will be doing some work in the next two Sprints. External resources velocity is not considered in the Team velocity. C. The Team is not cross-functional enough to do the work themselves. A Scrum Team should be self-supporting. D. All of the above.	**Correct Answer: C** Scrum Teams should be Cross-functional teams that they should all the competencies needed to accomplish the work without depending on others outside the team. Scrum Teams should have all the skills necessary to create value each Sprint. Scrum Teams should also be self-managing, meaning they internally decide who does what, when, and how.
127) Developers within the Scrum Team are requesting to extend the Sprint an extra 5 days in order to complete the Product Backlog items in the Sprint Backlog. They are worried that management team members will be upset if they are not able to finish all of the items before the end of the Sprint. As a Product Owner, what should you do? A. Remind the Developers, that once they have selected Product Backlog items in the Sprint Backlog and they must complete it. B. Ask the Developers to work over the weekend to complete the work. C. Do not extend the Sprint. Work with the stakeholders and explain the reasons for the delay. Transparency and Openness are important in an empirical Process. D. Its ok to extend the Sprint. Developers have the freedom to work and deliver as needed.	**Correct Answer: C** Time-boxes helps everyone focus on the same problem at the same time and encourages the people who are closest to the problem to create the best possible result in the time allotted, give the current context. The Sprint Backlog is a forecast of functionality that will be developed during the Sprint if completed would achieve the Sprint Goal. It is not a commitment. If the Developers determines it has too much or too little work, it may renegotiate the selected Product Backlog items with the Product Owner in order to produce a valuable Increment and achieve the Sprint Goal.

128) Your team committed to delivering 20 story points this iteration, but it looks like they will only complete 8. You should: A. Extend the iteration. B. Add more resources to the team. C. Complete 8 points and put 12 back in the Product backlog. D. Complete 8 points and put 12 back in next Sprint backlog.	**Correct answer: C** Since iterations are timeboxed, the duration won't be changed. You also wouldn't change the iteration plan or expand the team. Instead, work that isn't completed within the iteration is returned to the Product backlog. Therefore, the choice of completing 8 points and returning 12 points to the backlog is the correct option. Remember it's not always necessary that the incomplete work would be picked up in the next Sprint, so that option is invalid.
129) Developers in the Scrum Team failed to complete a few of the items they had selected for a Sprint. The Product Owner should: (Select two) A. Fire the Developers responsible. B. Ask the Team to work overtime and complete those items. C. Push the Sprint End date. D. Move the incomplete and remaining items back to the Product Backlog. E. Only consider the completed part and create product backlog items for the incomplete part. F. Not consider the incomplete Product backlog item as a part of the increment.	**Correct Answer: D, F** In the real world, almost every sprint will have at least one or two sprint backlog items which won't be completed. In such situations, Developers will work with the Product Owner to move it back to the Product Backlog. These items would typically (and not always) be moved to the Next Sprint Backlog from the Product Backlog, through the Product Backlog.

130) You are a Scrum Team Lead and are going to start working with the team to build a new Product. The Scrum Teams are not created yet and it is your responsibilities to create the agile teams that will be working on this new product. Prior to this job, you have years of experience leading the HR (Human resources) department and are very well acquainted with the interview process, salary negotiations etc. which are standard practices in a Traditional Waterfall organization. How would you decide which member will belong to which team?

A. You should distribute team members into group according to individual velocities.

B. You should allocate the team members into functional teams where each team focuses on a specific area of expertise.

C. Allocate the team members into groups based on the features they are going to develops.

D. You should work with the Product Owner, bring the involved members together, discuss the vision and goals for the product, let the group self-organize and divide itself into teams.

Correct Answer: D

This question tries to confuse the reader by mentioning the Scrum Leaders past experience which has nothing to do with how the team should be selected in Scrum.

Providing the proper guidelines will help promote self-organization, creativity, and problem solving. The decisions on who and how to work together in order to deliver Valuable increments is best decided by the Scrum team and team members involved with doing the work.

131) The Product Owner (and Developers) talk to the stakeholders only during the Sprint Reviews or customer interviews. A. True B. False	**Correct answer: B** The Product Owner keeps communicating with the stakeholders, creates new items in the Product Backlog, revises the order of items, answers questions, makes sure that everyone has the right understanding of items, and checks the completed items with the Developers to ensure they are Done based on the Definition of Done. The Product Owner is responsible for clearly expressing Product Backlog items to the Developers and making trade-offs. The Product Owner would thus know the requirements (business needs) of the Product Backlog items. The Product Owner is responsible for ordering the items in the Product Backlog to best achieve goals and missions. Product Owner is continuously in touch with the stakeholders. Similarly, the Scrum team Developers can talk to the stakeholders as required.
132) New Scrum Teams have been created to build one product. Jack and John are Developers on the Scrum team. They are concerned that their work is not going to remain aligned with Charles who is now in the other Scrum Team. What advice should you give to Jack and John? A. Ask Jack and John to collect the Sprint tasks from the teams at the end of their Sprint Planning and merge that into a consolidated plan. B. Tell Jack and John that it is their responsibility to work with Charles to create an integrated Increment. They can choose a form of communication which suites them the best. C. Visit Charles each day to inspect that his work is aligned. **D.** Ask the Product Owner to lead the developers in a way which would avoid overlap during a Sprint.	Correct answer: B It is the responsibility of the Developers to work with the other Scrum Teams members as needed to make sure that their Sprint work is aligned to create an integrated Increment.

133) A company has recently added a new Scrum Team. Developers in the Scrum Team are not clear about the functional requirements. Who is responsible for clarifying the Developers questions about the functional requirements? A. Product Owner. B. Developers themselves. C. Scrum Master. D. Scrum Lead.	**Correct answer: A** The Product Owner is responsible for clearly expressing Product Backlog items to the Developers and making trade-offs. The Product Owner would thus know the requirements (business needs) of the Product backlog items. The Product Owner is responsible for ordering the items in the Product Backlog to best achieve goals and missions.
134) Who is responsible for optimizing the value of the Product (and is also known as the Value optimizer)? A. Scrum Master. B. Developers themselves. C. Product Owner. D. Scrum Team.	**Correct answer: C** A great Product Owner has a focus on functionality and the non-functional aspects of the product. Hours or even story points are less important. The goal of the Product Owner is to maximize value for the customer. It's the functionality that has value; therefore, this is the main focus for the Product Owner. A great Product Owner has in depth (non-)functional product knowledge and understands the technical composition. For large products it might be difficult to understand all the details and scaling the Product Owner role might be an option. However, the Product Owner should always know the larger pieces of the puzzle and hereby make conscious, solid decisions.

135) Two Scrum teams are working together on the same product. During Sprint Planning, they are getting ready to create their own individual Sprint Backlogs. Which of the following statement is true? A. The Product Owner will decide on which Product Backlog items will go in the Sprint Backlogs as he is responsible for the delivery of the Product. B. The Scrum Master will decide on which Product Backlog items will go in each teams Sprint Backlogs. He should take the Sprint velocity into considerations. C. Developers within the Scrum Team will decide on which Product Backlog items will go in each teams Sprint Backlog. This has to be in agreement with the Product Owner. D. Team with the highest velocity will decide on which Product Backlog items will go in their Backlog first.	**Correct answer: C** Multiple Scrum Teams can work on the same product. Developers in each team would typically maintain their own Sprint Backlog and pull work from the Product Backlog during Sprint Planning. This has to be in agreement with the Product Owner.
136) Mark Jones is the CFO of a company. He realizes that he needs a different type of report created and his need is urgent. He walks to the Developers and does ask them to add this need to their current Sprint. What should the Developers do? A. Developers in the Scrum Team should add the item to the current Sprint. If this result into more work than what they can handle, then the Scrum Master should add additional team members. B. Developers should add the item to the current Sprint and drop an item of equal size. C. Developers should add the item to the next Sprint. D. Developers should inform the Product Owner so he/she can work with the CEO.	**Correct answer: D** The current items selected for a Sprint have been selected as most valuable with the Product Owner. These items serve the Sprint's goal. No changes should be made that endanger the Sprint Goal. No one external to the Scrum Team can force changes on the Developers (Sprint Backlog) and the Product Owner (Product Backlog). All changes which need to be made to the Product show flow through the Product Backlog and the Product Owner.

137) A Project Manager working with your Scrum Team has raised concerns about the progress made and the money spent, by the Scrum Team. What are the two best responses? (choose the best two answers) A. Scrum doesn't have Project Managers so disregard their concerns. B. Have a discussion with the Project Manager; share the current impediments and forecast for the Sprint. C. Promote transparency by sharing the Product Backlog and ensuring the Project Manager has access. D. Share the last stakeholder briefing document prepared by the Product Owner. E. Show the Earned Value Analysis (EVA) report.	**Correct answer: B, C** The Product Owner and / or the Scrum Master should promote transparency by sharing the Product Backlog and ensuring all the stakeholders have the needed access to it. The Scrum Master and the Product Owner should always be open to discussing the impediments and forecast with the concerned parties.
138) Non-functional requirements can be incorporated in the product by: (Choose all that apply) A. Having them as a part of the Definition of Done and checking the applicable Increment against these criterias. B. Adding them as the Acceptance Criteria to the applicable Product Backlog item. C. Including them as Product Backlog item itself. D. Sharing Non-Functional Requirement documents with the developers.	**Correct answer: A, B, C** Non-functional requirements describe the quality of the system being developed. E.g. the system should be secure, extensible and have acceptable performance. The way to meet such requirements is: 1) Have them as a part of the Definition of Done and check the applicable Increment against these criteria. 2) Add them as the Acceptance Criteria to the applicable Product Backlog item. 3) Including them as Product Backlog item itself.
139) Three Scrum Teams are working on the same Product. It is recommended that the teams must merge their code before the Sprint ends. A. True. B. False.	**Correct answer: A** A single Increment is needed at the end of the Sprint. Regardless of the number of teams, the teams should merge their code to have one single valuable Increment by the End of the Sprint. The Product owner and stakeholders would not be able to inspect the increment accurately if the code is not merged.

140) What happens during Product Backlog Refinement? (Choose two) A. Planning of which Product Backlog items will be selected and their completion dates. B. Analysis and decomposing of the Product Backlog items. C. Designing of the Product Backlog items. D. Testing of the Product Backlog items. E. Programming of the Product Backlog items.	**Correct Answer: B, C** Planning of which Product Backlog items will be selected, and their completion dates happens during Sprint Planning. Product Backlog refinement is the act of breaking down and further defining Product Backlog items into smaller more precise items. During Sprint planning, decomposing, designing (flow charts, logic Diagrams etc.) of the Sprint Backlog items are done. Through discussion with the Product Owner, the Developers select items from the Product Backlog to include in the current Sprint. The Scrum Team may refine these items during this process, which increases understanding and confidence.
141) What is the most effective way to order the Product Backlog? A) Order the Product Backlog based only on the complexity of the Product Backlog item. B) Order the Product Backlog based only on the risk and size of the Product Backlog item. C) Order the Product Backlog based on Client needs. D) Order the Product Backlog based on what the Product Owner decides. The Product Owner will take different factors into consideration.	**Correct Answer: D** The **Product Owner decides the order of the Product Backlog based on the complexity, risk, dependency and size of each** Product Backlog item.
142) Which two things **do not** occur in the first Sprint? A) Detailing all the Product Backlog items present in the Product Backlog. B) Creating a useful and valuable software. C) Defining the complete architecture. D) Developing something of value to customer.	**Correct Answer: A, C** A Product Backlog is never complete and is always evolving. It is a living artifact. It does not get finalized in any of the Sprints. The System's architecture is decided throughout the project, as understanding emerges and the Scrum Team learns more about the project.

143)	John is Developer and wants to remove a few items from the Sprint Backlog. He thinks they are now unnecessary and are not required to meet anymore to meet the Sprint Goal. John can: A) Remove the items with the Scrum Masters Permission. B) Remove the items. The Product Owner should agree with him. C) Cannot remove the items as the Sprint Backlog is being worked on. D) Cannot remove the items as the Sprint Backlog is a commitment of the work which needs to be delivered made by the Developers.	**Correct answer: B** A Sprint Backlog is a forecast of the work which would be accomplished in the Sprint. A Sprint backlog is expected to change as the Sprint progresses. It is not a commitment. As new work is realized, developers work with the Product Owner to adds items to the Sprint Backlog. As work is performed or completed, the estimated remaining work is updated. When elements of the plan are deemed unnecessary, they are removed.
144)	Jack is a Developer in a Scrum Team and is asked to prepare the Sprint Backlog. Jack can only add the functional Items which are required to meet the Sprint Goal in the Sprint Backlog. A) True B) False	**Correct answer: B** The Sprint Backlog is a collection of work items planned for the Sprint. This work would need to be identified and made visible to all as it would need to be completed to meet the Sprint Goal. This would include the functional and nonfunctional work needed. The Scrum Glossary gives the following definition for Product Backlog: "The Product Backlog is an emergent, ordered list of what is needed to improve the product. It is the single source of work undertaken by the Scrum Team." So, Scrum is not specific about exactly what a Product Backlog Item is or how it should be expressed. It is just about the work which needs to be done. A Product Backlog can contain knowledge acquisition tasks, prototyping, technical chores etc. A Product Backlog should typically contain items that the Product Owner cares about, in the sense that they add clear business value and can be ordered by him or her. If there are some "Developer Stories", i.e. removing technical debt, they can be introduced by the Developers (if the Product Owner agrees) into the Product Backlog from where they would be moved to the Sprint Backlog.

145)	Product Backlog items that completed or be "Done" by the Developers within one Sprint are deemed "Ready" for selection in Sprint Planning. A) True. B) False.	Correct answer: A Product Backlog items that can be "Done" by the Scrum Team within one Sprint are deemed "Ready" for selection in Sprint Planning. They usually acquire this degree of transparency after refining activities. Product Backlog refinement is the act of breaking down and further defining Product Backlog items into smaller more precise items. This is an ongoing activity to add details, such as a description, order, and size. Attributes often vary with the domain of work.
146)	A HR (human resource) personal is looking to hire a new Scrum Team member. A few important skills that the HR personal should be looking for are: (Choose all that apply) A) The Team members must have domain knowledge. B) The team members must have java or development skills. C) The Team members must show respect towards others. D) They should be able to best finish the work assigned to them.	**Correct answer: C, D** The Scrum guide states, "Scrum Team members respect each other to be capable, independent people, and are respected as such by the people with whom they work." The guide also states, "Their primary focus is on the work of the Sprint to make the best possible progress toward these goals." Technical skills and domain knowledge are nice to haves, however not mandatory.
147)	If an inspector determines that one or more aspects of a process deviate outside acceptable limits, and that the resulting product will be unacceptable, the process or the material being processed must be: A) Adjusted as soon as possible or immediately. B) Adjusted in the next Sprint. C) Adjusted after the next Sprint retrospective. D) Adjusted after discussing it with the management.	Correct answer: A During each Sprint Retrospective, the Scrum Team inspects how the last Sprint went with regards to individuals, interactions, processes, tools, and their Definition of Done. Thus, it would be best to wait for the Sprint retrospective and improve the terms of quality in the Definition of "Done" for the product. This is however recommended. For situations where the increment is going to be impacted to a level where the product would be unacceptable, the changes to the process / material / DOD / product should be made right away. The Guide clearly states "The Scrum Team identifies the most helpful changes to improve its effectiveness. The most impactful improvements are addressed as soon as possible."

148)	One of the Pillars of the Empirical Process demands significant aspects to be defined by a minimum common standard, so observers share a common understanding of what is being inspected. This Pillar is: A) Inspection. B) Adoption. C) Transparency.	**Correct answer: C** The emergent process and work must be visible to those performing the work as well as those receiving the work. With Scrum, important decisions are based on the perceived state of its three formal artifacts. Artifacts that have low transparency can lead to decisions that diminish value and increase risk. Transparency enables inspection. Inspection without transparency is misleading and wasteful. Significant aspects of the process must be visible to those responsible for the outcome. Transparency requires those aspects be defined by a common standard, so observers share a common understanding of what is being seen.
149)	A Company is forming a new Scrum Team. The Scrum Team members insist on forming sub-teams based on domains such as testing, architecture and operations. Is this allowed? A) True. B) False.	**Correct answer: B** Scrum does not recognize sub-teams regardless of domains that need to be addressed like testing, architecture, operations or business analysis.
150)	Developers in the Scrum Team have the capability to self-organizes to undertake the work from the Product Backlog (and move it to the Sprint Backlog). The process of moving the Product Backlog items from the Product Backlog to the Sprint Backlog is done during Sprint Planning and could be repeated as needed throughout the Sprint. A) True. B) False.	**Correct answer: A** Developers in the Scrum Team self-organizes and self-manage to undertake the work in the Sprint Backlog, during Sprint Planning and as needed throughout the Sprint. They coordinate with the Product Owner as needed.

151) The purpose of the Sprint Retrospective is to: (Choose all that apply) A) Check how the last Sprint went with regards to people, relationships, process, and tools. B) Identify and order the major items that went well and potential improvements. C) Create a plan for implementing improvements to the way the Scrum Team does its work. D) Plan on the next Sprint Backlog items.	**Correct answer: A, B, C** The purpose of the Sprint Retrospective is to: • Inspect how the last Sprint went with regards to people, relationships, process, and tools; • Identify and order the major items that went well and potential improvements; and, • Create a plan for implementing improvements to the way the Scrum Team does its work. Planning of the Sprint Backlog items does not happen in the Sprint Retrospective meeting.
152) The Sprint Goal and Definition of Done is crafted by: A) Product Owner. B) Scrum Master. C) Scrum Team. D) Developers within the Scrum Team.	**Correct answer: C** During Sprint Planning the entire Scrum Team crafts the Sprint Goal. The Definition of Done for an increment is part of the standards of the organization, all Scrum Teams must follow it as a minimum. If it is not an organizational standard, the entire Scrum Team must create a Definition of Done appropriate for the product.
153) All Sprint Goals should align with the Product Goal. A) True B) False	**Correct answer: A** The Sprint Goal is the single objective for the Sprint. Every increment created under the guidance of the Sprint Goal is a concrete steppingstone toward the Product Goal. Thus, all the Sprint Goals should be all aligned.

154)	Developers in a Scrum team are running short of time and will not be able to complete a few items which are the Sprint Backlog. They have decided to push off / postpone the testing for a few Product Backlog items and create new product backlog items (worth 0 points) just for testing these items in the next Sprint. Scrum allows this. A) True B) False	**Correct answer: B** During the Sprint: • No changes are made that would endanger the Sprint Goal. • Quality should not decrease. • Scope may be clarified and re-negotiated between the Product Owner and Developers as more is learned. The Product Backlog items should not be postpone the testing as it would compromise on the quality.
155)	Does the productivity increase right away when two Scrum Teams are merged? A) Yes. B) No.	**Correct answer: B** In the Short term, the productivity will decrease because the new teams will spend time to get up to speed with the Product. The old team will spend a lot of time communicating and training the new team.
156)	Scrum Team consists of professionals who: A) Do the work of delivering a valuable increment and always achieve their commitments. B) Do the work of delivering a valuable Increment of "Done" product at the end of each Sprint. C) Do the work of delivering a potentially releasable Increment of "Done" product at the end of each Release. D) Are skilled in coding and testing.	**Correct answer: B** The Scrum Team consists of professionals who do the work of delivering a valuable Increment of "Done" product at the end of each Sprint.

157)	John is a new Product Owner and he invites a few stakeholders to the Product Backlog Refinement sessions. The Stakeholders instruct John on the what the priorities of the Product Backlog items should be. The stakeholders at this point more about the functional requirements of these items. Should John only prioritize the Product Backlog items based on the received stakeholder feedback? A) Yes. B) No.	**Correct answer: B** The Product Owners do not usually do this. A Product Owner must be the arbiter of Product Value and how it is represented to the team. Many times key stakeholders do not know exactly what they want and how it can be achieved. This is a job for the Product Owner to understand their needs, decide how they can be fulfilled with the maximum value. Probably, in rare cases a key stakeholder can be invited as a domain expert to a product refinement session. In this case, even if they know about the details of the Product backlog item, how it adds value to the Product and its priority should be decided by the Product Owner taking everything (technical challenges, market needs, dependencies) into consideration. The Product Owner should have the final word.
158)	What is the Scrum Team responsible for? (Choose all that apply) A) Resolving internal team conflicts. B) Creating the Increment. C) Organizing the work required to meet the Sprint Goal. D) Working within the boundaries of their functional job descriptions and nicely handing off work from analyst to developer to tester to integration.	**Correct answer: A, B, C** The Scrum Team members are self-managing and self-organizing. No one (not even the Scrum Master) tells the Scrum Team knows how to turn Product Backlog into Increments of valuable functionality. The value which the Scrum Team brings to the table can be measured based on the Increment they deliver. Option D is the only incorrect answer here as the Scrum team needs to resolve any internal conflicts and work across their functional titles.
159)	A Scrum Team should plan at least one improvement from the previous Sprint Retrospective in the upcoming Sprint Backlog. This is mandatory. A) True B) False	**Correct answer: B** The Scrum Guide no longer states this as a rule. There may be times when a Scrum Team decides not to plan any actionable improvements in a Sprint. The intention behind this change is to no longer prescribe this practice, and instead, let the Scrum Team decide. However, remember that inspection without adaptation is pointless.

160) Technical debt (also known as design debt or code debt) is a concept in software development that reflects the implied cost of rework caused by choosing an easy solution now instead of using a better approach that would take longer. Which of the following statement is true about technical debt?

A. The amount of technical debt is representation of the quality of the code and development practices.
B. Only the developers need to be concerned with tech debt
C. Technical debt can be handled after delivery during the maintenance period
D. Tech debt is a threat to the long-term viability of a product.

Correct Answer: D

Like any other debt, a large accumulation of Technical Debt (bad code) can impact future maintainability of the product. The downsides of Technical Debt are as follows:

1. It **misleads** the Product Owners, Scrum Masters and even the developers with their assumptions about the **"Current state" of the System**. For example, if Product Backlog item A is assumed to be completed in a day, it might take three days for it to complete, because of unseen bad code or Technical Debt.

2. The **Product becomes more unstable**, as more functionality is added over bad code (or existing technical debt). Example: Let's assume that the team decided to delay some important refactoring to facilitate an early release. Technical debt starts to accrue at that point, and it may not map cleanly to specific items on the Product Backlog. It is far more likely to impact components which crosscut a range of features. Moreover, if the necessary refactoring is significant it could impact the entire product, and it could affect features in uneven ways.

CHAPTER 2: Scaled Scrum / Nexus

This chapter is designed to help you take a learn / revise / take a **second Look at the Nexus Framework and concepts necessary to apply scrum in scaled projects.** This exam also introduces many important themes, including the synchronization of the work between several teams, which appears in virtually all certifications from now on.

1. **Read the Nexus Guide.**
2. Go through the Nexus **Guide Reference Table** mentioned in this book. Go through the questions and answers mentioned in the Book. These questions are compiled very carefully. Go through the answers and make sure you understand the concepts.
3. **Do the Nexus Open assessment (https://www.scrum.org/open-assessments) until you score close to 100% 3 times in a row.**

Nexus Guide Reference Table

Nexus Definition and Theory ⚠	Nexus is the **exoskeleton of Scrum**. Nexus is **based on the Scrum framework** and uses an iterative and incremental approach to scaling software and product development. Nexus **minimally extends the Scrum framework only where absolutely necessary** to enable multiple teams to work from a single Product Backlog to build an Integrated Increment that meets a goal.
	Nexus is a **process framework** for **Multiple Scrum Teams** working together to create an Integrated Increment.
	Nexus is a framework **that bind and weaves together** the work of the Scrum Teams. Nexus consist of Accountabilities, Events and Artifacts.
	A Nexus is a group of **approximately three to nine Scrum** Teams that work together to deliver a single product (working on a **single Product Backlog).** This allows building an Integrated Increment that meets a goal.
	At its heart, **Nexus seeks to preserve and enhance Scrum's foundational bottom-up intelligence and empiricism.** It enables a group of Scrum Teams to deliver more value than can be achieved by a single team.
	The goal of Nexus is to scale the value that a group of Scrum Teams, working on a single product is able to deliver. It does this by reducing the complexity that those teams encounter as they collaborate to deliver **an integrated, valuable, useful product Increment at least once every Sprint.**
	Nexus is consistent with Scrum. The difference is that more attention is **paid to dependencies** and interoperation between Scrum Teams.
	Nexus builds upon Scrum by enhancing the foundational elements of Scrum in ways that help solve the **dependency and collaboration challenges of cross-team work.**
	Nexus delivers a valuable, useful Integrated Increment at least once every Sprint.
	All Scrum Teams use the same, single Product Backlog. These Scrum Team's however maintain their own individual Sprint Backlog.

Nexus Challenges & Dependencies	The Nexus Framework helps teams solve common scaling challenges like: 1. Reducing cross-team dependencies 2. Preserving team self-management and transparency 3. Ensuring accountability. **Dependencies is one of the most important concerns** when multiple Scrum Teams work together. Nexus helps to make transparent dependencies. These dependencies are often caused by mismatches related to: 1. Product structure: **The degree to which different concerns are independently separated** in the product will greatly affect the complexity of creating an integrated product release. The scope of the requirements may overlap if not separated as needed. The order in which these requirements are implemented may also affect each other. While **ordering** the Product Backlog and selecting the Product Backlog items in the Sprint Backlog, one should make sure that such dependencies are accommodated. 2. Communication structure: **The way that people communicate within and between teams affects their ability to get work done**; delays in communication and feedback reduce the flow of work.
	Nexus provides opportunities to change the process, product structure, and communication structure to reduce or remove these dependencies.
	Scaling the value that is delivered does not always require adding more people. Increasing the number of people and the size of a product increases complexity and dependencies, the need for collaboration, and the number of communication pathways involved in making decisions. Scaling-down, reducing the number of people who work on something, can be an important practice in delivering more value.

Nexus Process Flow

- 1) Refine the Product Backlog
- 2) Nexus Sprint Planning
- 3) Development Work
- 4) Nexus Daily Scrum
- 5) Nexus Sprint Review
- 6) Nexus Retrospective

Step 1: Refine the Product Backlog / Cross- Team Refinement.
- The Product Backlog is decomposed to **identify, remove or minimize dependencies**.
- Product Backlog items are refined into **thinly sliced pieces of functionality**.
- The **Scrum team** likely to do the work **should be identified**.
- Where needed, each Scrum Team will continue their own refinement in order for the Product Backlog items to be ready for selection in a Nexus Sprint Planning event. An adequately refined Product Backlog will minimize the emergence of new dependencies during Nexus Sprint Planning.

Step 2: Nexus Sprint Planning
- Appropriate Representatives from each Scrum Team meet to review the refined Product Backlog.
- The Representatives select Product Backlog items for each team.
- Each Scrum Team then plans its own Sprint. They interact with other teams as appropriate.

Step 3: Development work
- All teams frequently integrate their work into a common environment that can be tested to ensure that the integration is done.

Step 4: Nexus Daily Scrum
- Represented Developers from each Scrum Team meet daily in the Nexus Daily Scrum to **identify if any integration issues exist**. If integration issues are identified, this information is transferred back to each Scrum Team's Daily Scrum.
- Scrum Teams use their Daily Scrum making sure to address the integration issues raised during the Nexus Daily Scrum.

Step 5: Nexus Sprint Review
- The Nexus Sprint Review is conducted to provide feedback on the Integrated Increment that a Nexus has built over the Sprint.
- All individual Scrum Teams meet with stakeholders to review the Integrated Increment.
- Adjustments may be made to the Product Backlog based on the feedback provided by the Stakeholders.

Step 6: Nexus Sprint Retrospective
- In the Nexus Sprint Retrospective, appropriate representatives from each Scrum Team meet to identify shared challenges.
- Each Scrum Team holds individual Sprint Retrospectives.
- Appropriate representatives from each team meet again to discuss any actions needed based on shared challenges to provide bottom-up intelligence.

Nexus Integration Team	A Nexus consists of Scrum Teams that work together toward a Product Goal. The Scrum framework defines three specific sets of accountabilities within a Scrum Team: the Developers, the Product Owner, and the Scrum Master. These accountabilities are prescribed in the Scrum Guide. In Nexus, an additional accountability is introduced, the Nexus Integration Team.
	The Nexus Integration team provides the focus **that makes possible the accountability of multiple Scrum Teams to come together to create valuable, useful Increments, as prescribed in Scrum.**
	The Nexus Integration Team provides a focal point of integration for the Nexus. Integration includes addressing **technical and non-technical cross-functional team constraints that may impede a Nexus' ability to deliver a constantly Integrated Increment.**
	The Nexus Integration Team should use bottom-up intelligence from within the Nexus to achieve resolution.
	The Nexus Integration Team **owns responsibility for the:** • **Integration issues.** • **Delivering a valuable integrated done Increment at least once every Sprint.** • **Coaching and guiding the Scrum Teams** to acquire, implement, and learn practices and tools that improve their ability to produce a valuable, useful Increment. **Remember an integrated increment represents the current sum of all integrated work completed across all the teams.**
	The Nexus Integration Team is a Scrum Team that consists of: • The Product Owner. • A Scrum Master. • Nexus Integration Team Members.
	Composition of the Nexus Integration Team may change over time to reflect the current needs.
	Common activities the Nexus Integration Team might perform include • Coaching. • Consulting. • Highlighting awareness of dependencies and cross-team issues.

Nexus Integration Team – Team Members	The Nexus Integration Team consists of professionals who are skilled in the use of tools, Various Practices and the field of Systems Engineering. The Nexus Integration Team often consists of Scrum Team members who help the Scrum Teams to adopt tools and practices that contribute to the Scrum Teams' ability to deliver a valuable and useful Integrated Increment that frequently meets the Definition of Done.
	Nexus Integration Team Members ensure that: 1) The Scrum Teams within the Nexus **understand and implement the practices and tools** needed to detect dependencies. 2) The Scrum Teams **frequently integrate all artifacts** to the definition of "Done."
	Nexus Integration Team: • **Does not do the Integration work themselves**. They guide the Scrum Teams to do it. • **Does not coordinate the day to day work between the Scrum Teams**. It is the Scrum Teams responsibility to work with the other Teams to create an integrated Increment.
	Nexus Integration Team Members Raises Transparency by **coaching and guiding the Scrum Teams to acquire, implement, and learn the Nexus practices and needed tools**.
	The Nexus Integration Team will take ownership of integration issues. However, they **may not necessarily do the work required to resolve these when they occur**. They may work with 1 or more Scrum Teams to help them resolve issues around integration. At other times they may deliver tools and technology to help make integration run more smoothly.
	The Nexus Integration Team coaches the individual Scrum Teams on the necessary **development, infrastructural, or architectural standards** required by the organization to ensure the development of quality Integrated Increments.
	If the primary responsibility of the Nexus Team Member is satisfied, **Nexus Integration Team Members may also work as Developers** in one or more Scrum Teams.
	Membership in the Nexus Integration Team takes precedence over individual Scrum Team membership. As long as their Nexus Integration Team responsibility is satisfied, they can work as team members of their respective Scrum Teams. This preference helps ensure that the work to resolve issues affecting multiple teams has priority.
	It is the **responsibility of the Scrum Team Members** to work with the other teams to make sure that their Sprint work is aligned to create an integrated Increment.

Nexus Integration Team – Product Owner	A Nexus has a **single Product Owner who manages a single Product Backlog from which the Scrum Teams work.**
	The **Product Owner is a member of the Nexus Integration Team.**
	In Scrum or Scrum with Nexus, **there will be only one Product Backlog and a Single Product Owner (for a single Product).**
	Scrum Teams working on the same product will integrate their work in the same Nexus and thereby provide value to the same Product Owner.
	The Product Owner is **responsible for maximizing the value** of the product and the integrated work performed by the Scrum Teams (in a Nexus framework).
Nexus Integration Team – Scrum Master	The Scrum Master is a member of the Nexus Integration Team.
	The Scrum Master in the Nexus Integration Team has the **overall responsibility** for ensuring the Nexus framework is understood and enacted.
	The **Scrum Master ensures that the Nexus Integration Team** is meeting daily during the Nexus Daily Scrum Meetings. He / She will also ensure that all the Nexus Meetings are conducted. (Nexus Refinements, Nexus Retrospectives, Nexus Retrospectives etc.).
	The **Nexus Scrum Master may also be a Scrum Master in one or more of the Scrum Teams**.
Nexus Events	Events are appended to, placed around, or replace regular Scrum events to augment them. As modified, they serve both the overall effort of all Scrum Teams in the Nexus, and each individual team.
	Nexus adds to or extends the events defined by Scrum.
	The duration of Nexus events is guided by the length of the corresponding events in the Scrum Guide. They are timeboxed in addition to their corresponding Scrum events.
	At scale, it may not be practical for all members of the Nexus to participate to share information or to come to an agreement. Nexus events are attended by whichever members of the Nexus are needed to achieve the intended outcome of the event most effectively.

Nexus Cross-Team Refinement (Nexus Event)	**Product Backlog Refinement** is the act of: 1. Understanding and **decomposing** the Product Backlog items. 2. Adding detail to the Product Backlog items. 3. Estimating & Ordering the Product Backlog items.
	Refinement of the Product Backlog serves two purposes. 1) Refinement helps the Scrum Teams **forecast which team may deliver** which Product Backlog items. 2) Refinement **identifies dependencies** across those teams. The **frequency, duration, and attendance** of Cross-Team Refinement varies to optimize these two purposes.
	In Scrum, **Product Backlog refinement is an ongoing activity for a single team**; however, it is not a mandatory event. Due to the added complexity of many teams working together on a single product, **Refinement is an official and required event in the Nexus Framework.** Teams in a Nexus need to be involved in a shared Refinement event, because Refinement is **focused on decomposing** Product Backlog Items enough so that the teams can understand which work, they could deliver and in what sequence over upcoming Sprints.
	Product Backlog items pass through different levels of decomposition from very **large and vague requests to actionable work that a single Scrum Team could deliver inside a Sprint.** Refinement of Product Backlog Items by the Nexus continues until the Product Backlog Items **are sufficiently independent (actionable work) to be worked on by a single Scrum Team** without excessive conflict.
	The number, frequency, duration and attendance of Refinement is based on the **dependencies and uncertainty** inherent in the Product Backlog.
	Where needed, **each Scrum Team will continue their own refinement in order for the Product Backlog items to be ready for selection in a Nexus Sprint Planning event.** An adequately refined Product Backlog will minimize the emergence of new dependencies during Nexus Sprint Planning.

	The advantages Product Backlog Refinement are:
	<ul><li>Allows **Scrum Teams to identify, reduces or eliminates** cross-team dependencies between Product Backlog items as early as possible and seeks to reduce them so individual Scrum Teams can work more independently during Sprints.</li><li>Helps assigns Teams to the Product Backlog items.</li><li>Helps to make big batches of complex work manageable by breaking large pieces of functionality into smaller more manageable units.</li><li>Allows Scrum team members to explore and understand upcoming Product Backlog items, in advance of the Sprint.</li><li>Facilitates the input of multiple Scrum teams into the exploration, detailing and estimating of each Product Backlog Item. This helps ensure a greater understanding of the work.</li><li>Allows external Subject Matter Experts to get involved and offers assistance in planning and design ahead of implementation.</li><li>Allows the Scrum Teams to guide the Product Owner in the efficient ordering of the Product Backlog.</li></ul>

Nexus Sprint Planning (Nexus Event)	Nexus Sprint Planning is conducted **to coordinate the activities of all Scrum Teams** for a **single Sprint.** **Note:** The following should be done **prior to the Nexus Sprint Planning:** 1) The Product Backlog should be adequately refined. Having a Product **Backlog refined to "Ready"** is likely to be an **essential prerequisite to allow planning to proceed effectively.** 2) The Dependencies within the Product Backlog items should be identified and removed or minimized.
	During Nexus Sprint Planning: 1) **Appropriate Representatives (& not all Team Members)** from each Scrum Team meet to review the refined Product Backlog. Each Scrum Team further validates and adjusts the ordering of the Backlog items (created during Refinement events). The ordering will help reduce dependencies between Scrum Teams in the Nexus during the Sprint. 2) **The Team will be working a single Nexus Sprint Backlog t**hat represents the work of the Nexus toward the Nexus Sprint **Goal. The Nexus Sprint Goal will be formulated in Nexus Sprint Planning**. It will describe the purpose that will be achieved by the Nexus during the Sprint. 3) Product Backlog Items will be then be selected by an appropriate Scrum Team **(in their individual Sprint Backlogs)** that has the skills required to deliver them with no (or minimal) dependencies on other Scrum Teams. The Scrum Team should have all the cross functional skills required to translate the Product Backlog Item into an integrated Increment by the end of the Sprint. 4) Each Scrum Team then plans its own Sprint (**Individual Teams Sprint Planning event**), **Sprint Goal which will align to the Nexus Sprint Goal**. They interact with other teams to share newly found dependencies or update the existing dependencies.
	In the Nexus Sprint Planning, the Product Owner: 1) Discusses the Nexus Sprint Goal. 2) Provides Domain knowledge. 3) Guides backlog item selection. 4) Provides backlog item Priorities and related decisions.
	New dependencies can be identified during Sprint Planning. As **new dependencies** emerge during **Nexus Sprint Planning:** 1) The dependencies should be made transparent on the Nexus Sprint Backlog. 2) The sequence of work across teams may also be adjusted. Note: An **adequately refined Product Backlog** which is refined extensively will minimize the emergence of new dependencies during Nexus Sprint Planning.
	Nexus Sprint Planning time box would be 8 hours for a 1-month Sprint (not mandated). However, in Nexus, Inspection and adaption may lead to this being adjusted over time as required.

	The result of Nexus Sprint Planning is: • A **Nexus Sprint Goal** that aligns with the Product Goal and describes the purpose that will be achieved by the Nexus during the Sprint. • A **Sprint Goal for each Scrum** Team that aligns with the Nexus Sprint Goal. • A **single Nexus Sprint Backlog** that represents the work of the Nexus toward the Nexus Sprint Goal and makes cross-team dependencies transparent. • **A Sprint Backlog for each Scrum Team**, which makes transparent the work they will do in support of the Nexus Sprint Goal.
	Nexus Sprint Planning is complete when **each Scrum Team has finished their individual Sprint Planning events.**

Nexus Daily Scrum (Nexus Event) 	The Nexus Daily Scrum is the scaled version of the Daily Scrum event from the Scrum framework.
	The Nexus Daily Scrum is an event which: 1) **Inspects the current state of the Integrated Increment against the Nexus Sprint Goal.** 2) Is an **opportunity to Identifies** Integration issues and make them Transparent. 3) Identifies newly discovered cross-team dependencies. 4) Identifies cross-team impacts.
	Each Scrum Team's Daily Scrum complements the Nexus Daily Scrum by creating plans for the day, **focused primarily on addressing the integration issues raised during the Nexus Daily Scrum.**
	Appropriate **represented Developers from individual Scrum Teams attend the Nexus Daily Scrum.** **All Developers from all the Scrum Teams are not required** to attend the Nexus Daily Scrum. However, they are required to attend their Internal Daily Scrum Call.
	At least **every Nexus Daily Scrum**, the **Nexus Sprint Backlog should be inspected (adjusted** if needed) to reflect the current understanding of the work of the Scrum Teams within the Nexus. Remember: The **Nexus Daily Scrum is not the only time Scrum Teams in the Nexus are allowed to adjust their plan / Sprint backlogs.** Cross-team communication can occur throughout the day for more detailed discussions about adapting or re-planning the rest of the Sprint's work.
	Appropriate Representatives (Developers) from each Scrum Team meet daily to identify if any integration issues exist. If **integration issues are identified, this information is transferred back to each Scrum Team's Daily Scrum.**
	During the Nexus Daily Scrum, attendees should focus on each team's impact on the Integrated Increment and discuss: 1) Was the previous day's work successfully integrated? If not, why not? 2) What new dependencies or impacts have been identified? 3) What information needs to be shared across teams in the Nexus?
	The Nexus framework does suggest that the duration of Nexus events be guided by the length of the corresponding events in the Scrum framework. So, for the Nexus Daily Scrum the target for the time box would be 15 minutes. However, Inspection and adaption may lead to this being adjusted over time as required.

Nexus Sprint Review (Nexus Event)	The Objective of the Nexus Sprint Review is: 1. To review the completed integrated Increment 2. Generate feedback based on new learnings and viewpoints.
	The Nexus Sprint Review is **held at the end of the Sprint** to **provide feedback on the done Integrated Increment** that the Nexus has built over the Sprint and **determine future adaptations**.
	During Nexus Sprint Review, the Nexus presents the results of their work to key stakeholders and **progress toward the Product Goal is discussed.**
	A Nexus Sprint Review **replaces individual Scrum Team Sprint Reviews**, because the entire Integrated Increment is the focus for capturing feedback from stakeholders.
	The Nexus Sprint Review is conducted **so feedback can be provided by all the stakeholders** on the Integrated Increment that has been built over the Sprint. It **may not be possible to show all completed work done by each team** in detail. Techniques may be necessary to maximize stakeholder feedback.
	Representatives of each of the Scrum Teams attend the Nexus Sprint Review. The Scrum teams within themselves, decide the most appropriate people to attend. This may change over **time and vary from one Nexus Sprint Review to another.**
	Adjustments may be made to the **Product Backlog based on the feedback provided** by the Stakeholders. The **result of the Nexus Sprint Review** is a **revised Product Backlog.**
	Time box for the Nexus Sprint Review is recommended to be 3 hours for a 1-month Sprint. (not mandated). However, Inspection and adaption may lead to this being adjusted over time as required.

Nexus Sprint Retrospective (Nexus Event)	The purpose of the Nexus Sprint Retrospective is **to plan ways to increase quality and effectiveness across the whole Nexus.**
	The Nexus Sprint Retrospective is a formal opportunity to inspect and adapt itself. The Nexus Sprint Retrospective **enables the team to create a plan for improvements** which would be enacted during the next Sprint to ensure continuous improvement.
	The Nexus Sprint **Retrospective occurs after the Nexus Sprint Review** and prior to the next **Nexus Sprint Planning.**
	The **Nexus Sprint Retrospective concludes the Sprint.**
	The Nexus Sprint **Retrospective** inspects how the last Sprint went with regards to individuals, teams, interactions, processes, tools, and its Definition of Done.
	The Scrum Teams' Sprint Retrospectives complement the Nexus Sprint Retrospective by using **bottom-up intelligence** to focus on issues that affect the Nexus as a whole. The Retrospective typically consists of three parts: **Part 1: Nexus Retrospective:** Appropriate representatives from each scrum team meet to **Identify issues** that have impacted **more than a single Scrum team**. The purpose is to make shared issues transparent to all Scrum Teams. **Part 2: Individual Scrum Team Sprint Retrospectives:** Each Scrum Team **holds their own Sprint Retrospective** as described in the Scrum framework. They can **use issues raised from the Nexus Retrospective** as input to their team discussions. The individual Scrum Teams should form actions to address these issues during their individual Scrum Team Sprint Retrospectives. **Part 3:** Synchronize: Third part is an **opportunity for appropriate representatives from the Scrum Teams to meet again and agree on how to visualize and track the identified actions.** The Nexus Retrospective is considered **complete only when all the Individual Retrospectives are complete.** **Note :** These 3 parts were removed in the Jan 2021 Version of the Scrum Guide. However the use of the word "bottom up intelligence" aligns with the same 3 part process.

	Every Retrospective should address the following subjects: 1. Was any planned work left undone? Did the Nexus generate technical debt? 2. Were all artifacts, particularly code, frequently (as often as every day) successfully integrated? 3. Was the software successfully built, tested, and deployed often enough to prevent the overwhelming accumulation of unresolved dependencies? For the questions above, address if necessary: 1. Why did this happen? 2. How can technical debt be undone? 3. How can the recurrence be prevented?
	Nexus scales the value that a group of Scrum Teams, working on a single Product. Nexus reduces the complexity that those teams encounter as they collaborate to **deliver an integrated, valuable, useful product Increment at least once every Sprint.**

Nexus Artifacts & Commitments	Artifacts represent work or value, and are designed to maximize transparency, as described in the Scrum Guide.
	The Nexus Integration Team works with the Scrum Teams within a Nexus to ensure that transparency is achieved across all artifacts and that the state of the Integrated Increment is widely understood.
	In the Nexus Framework, there are three backlogs which are used: 1. Product Backlog 2. Nexus Sprint Backlog 3. Scrum Team's Individual Sprint Backlog

Remember:

Artifact	Commitment	Creator / Owner
Product Backlog	Product Goal	Product Owner
Nexus Sprint Backlog	Nexus Sprint Goal – Finalized during Nexus Sprint Planning.	Nexus Integration Team
Sprint Backlog	Sprint Goal – Finalized during Individual Scrum Teams Sprint Planning.	Scrum Team
Product Increment	Definition of Done	Scrum Team

Remember:

- A **Sprint Goal** created by Individual teams **should always align to the Nexus Sprint Goal.**
- A **Nexus Sprint Goal** created by the Nexus Integration teams should always align to the **Product Goal.**
- The purpose of the **Nexus Daily Scrum** is to identify any integration issues and inspect progress toward **the Nexus Sprint Goal.**
- The purpose of **the Individual Team's Daily Scrum** is to Inspect progress toward the **Individual Teams Sprint Goal.**
- During Sprint Review, the Nexus presents the results of their work to key stakeholders and **progress toward the Product Goal** is discussed.
- The Integrated Increment represents the current sum of all integrated work completed by a **Nexus toward the Product Goal.**

Product Backlog Nexus Perspective	The Product Backlog lists all features, functions, requirements, enhancements, and fixes that constitute the changes to be made to a Product.
	The Product Owner is responsible for the Product Backlog, including its content, availability, and ordering.
	A Product Backlog is never complete & is always evolving. It is a living artifact.
	A Product cannot exist without a Product Backlog. A single Product can have only **one Product Backlog.**
	Only One Product Backlog and Only One Product Owner can exist for a Product. This is true in Regular Scrum framework or in Nexus. Multiple Scrum Teams work on the Same Product Backlog.
	At scale, the Product Backlog must be understood at a level where dependencies can be detected and minimized.
	Different Scrum Teams working on the same Product (in Nexus) can: • Have different Sprint Lengths. • Have different Scrum Masters. • Have only one Product Owner. • Have only one Product Backlog. • Have a shared Definition of Done.
	A Product Backlog must be understood at a level where dependencies can be detected and minimized in advance of the actual implementation work to deliver the items in a Sprint.
	Product Backlog items are often broken down to a level / **granularity called "thinly sliced" functionality.**
	During Refinement, Product Backlog items **are deemed as "Ready" before the Nexus Sprint Planning meeting. The Scrum Teams can select and work on these items with no or minimal dependencies** on other Scrum Teams.
	The **commitment** for the **Product Backlog is the Product Goal**. The Product Goal, which describes the future state of the product and serves as a long-term goal of the Nexus.

Nexus Sprint Backlog. (Different from **Individual Sprint Backlog** and **Product Backlog**)	The Nexus Sprint Backlog will be created **during Nexus Sprint Planning**.
	A Nexus Sprint Backlog is the composite of : • The Nexus Sprint Goal • The Product Backlog items from the Sprint Backlogs of the individual Scrum
	The Nexus Sprint Backlog is used to highlight dependencies and the flow of work during the Sprint.
	The Nexus Sprint Backlog contains the Product Backlog Items being worked on by all of the teams plus the subset of work that identifies dependencies between teams. It also includes the work done by the individuals teams to ensure that the work is delivered and fully integrated.
	• The Nexus Sprint Backlog provides a **single view** of all the Product Backlog items **in a Sprint.** • The Nexus Sprint Backlog is an **aggregation of each team's individual Sprint Backlog.** • The Nexus Sprint Backlog is the composite of Product Backlog items from the Sprint Backlogs of the all individual Scrum Teams.
	• As the Product Backlog items are refined and made ready, **indicators of which Scrum team will do the work inside a Sprint are made transparent in the Nexus Sprint Backlog.** • The Nexus Sprint Backlog makes all the **Scrum Team's (not just the Integration Team) work transparent by exposing the dependencies.**
	The Nexus Sprint Backlog is used to **highlight dependencies and the flow of work during the Sprint.** It focuses on the coordination between teams to ensure the **Nexus Sprint Goal is achieved.**
	The Nexus Sprint Backlog is **throughout the Sprint as more is learned** , often as part of the Nexus Daily Scrum.
	The primary owner is the **Nexus Integration Team**. Note: 1) If anyone on any of the Scrum teams identifies new work that would extend across two or more teams in the Nexus, they would be able to add it to **the Nexus Sprint Backlog** through the team's representative on the Nexus Integration Team. 2) The members of the Nexus Integration Team "are often members of the individual Scrum Teams in the Nexus" and that their membership in the Nexus Integration Team "takes **precedence over individual Scrum Team membership**". That would mean that the members of the Nexus Integration Team are responsible for and accountable for ensuring that the **cross-team work items added to the Nexus Sprint Backlog are complete.** A **Nexus Sprint Backlog** exists to assist with transparency during the Sprint.

Nexus Sprint Goal	The commitment for the Nexus Sprint Backlog is the Nexus Sprint Goal. The Nexus Sprint
	The Nexus Sprint Goal is a single objective for the Nexus.
	The Nexus Sprint Goal is discussed and **finalized during Nexus Sprint Planning**. The Nexus Sprint Goal is then communicated to the rest of the Individual Scrum Teams to reflect the shared purpose of Nexus.
	Individual Scrum Team Sprint Goals are set during Individual Scrum Team Sprint Planning sessions. (not during the Nexus Sprint Planning).
	The Nexus Sprint Goal describes the purpose that will be achieved by all the Scrum Teams during the Sprint.
	Nexus Sprint Goal = Sum of **Sprint Goals** Across all the Team {In a SPRINT} + the **Work done** by all the Teams {In a SPRINT}
	The Nexus Sprint Goal creates coherence and focus for the Nexus for the Sprint by encouraging the Scrum Teams to work together rather than on separate initiatives.
	The Nexus should demonstrate the valuable and useful functionality that is done to achieve the Nexus Sprint Goal at the Nexus Sprint Review in order to receive stakeholder feedback.
	• A Sprint Goal created by Individual teams should always align to the Nexus Sprint Goal. • A Nexus Sprint Goal created by the Nexus Integration teams should always align with the Product Goal.

Integrated Increment	The **Integrated Increment represents the current sum of all integrated work completed by a Nexus, toward the Product Goal.** The Integrated Increment must be usable and **valuable each sprint** which means it must meet the definition of "Done". The Integrated Increment is inspected at the Nexus Sprint Review.
⚠	Individual Team **increments should be integrated every Sprint**. If increments are not integrated every Sprint then : • **The state of the product becomes unclear** (due to undiscovered problems that could arise during integration and complete product increment tests) • The **Product Owner would not know whether the increment he/she was presented is potential shippable** • It would not be transparent to the organization what the next reasonable steps would be.
	The Integrated Increment is inspected at the Nexus Sprint Review, but may be delivered to stakeholders before the end of the Sprint.
	The commitment for the Integrated Increment is the Definition of Done.
Nexus Definition of Done	The commitment for the Integrated Increment is the Definition of Done, which defines **the state of the integrated work when it meets the quality** and measures required for the product.
	The Increment is done only when **integrated, valuable, and usable.**
	When Multiple Scrum teams working on 1 product, there would be a shared understanding of what **Definition of "Done"** means. This can be called the Nexus Definition of Done.
⚠	When multiple teams are working on the same product, **there can be more than one Definition of "Done" for all of them.** Each team might be working on a different part of the product (e.g. desktop application, mobile application, web application), or simply have different styles of work. If there are multiple Scrum Teams working together on a product, they must mutually define and comply **with a shared Definition of Done. They can add their own specific criteria on top of this Definition of "Done" Criteria.**
	When different teams are working on the same product, they must observe a common Definition of Done which qualifies for the integrated increment. The **Definition of Done observed by an individual team** should reinforce and not contradict any shared Definition for a product increment. For example, a team may incorporate a shared DoD as a subset of their own.
⚠	**Scrum Teams Definition of "Done" = Nexus Definition of "Done" + Optional Scrum Team Specific Definition of "Done" Criteria.**

⚠	Individual Scrum Teams may choose to **apply a more stringent definition** of "Done" within their own teams but cannot apply less rigorous criteria than agreed for the Increment.
	The Increment is "Done" only when: 1. All team increments are integrated. 2. Integrated increment is usable. 3. Integrated increment is potentially releasable by the Product Owner.
	The **best time to change the Definition of "Done" is during the Sprint retrospective where** the team discusses how to increase product quality. However, this is not mandatory.
	1. During the **Nexus Sprint Retrospective**, the **Definition of "Done"** is revised If needed. 2. These changes are then communicated to the Individual teams to be incorporated. 3. Once Adapted by the Team, they are then implemented in each Sprint. Note: **The Individuals Teams must incorporate the Definition of "Done" to their own Definition of "Done".**
	The **Nexus Integration Team is responsible for a Definition of "Done"** that can be applied to the Integrated Increment developed each Sprint. That doesn't mean that the Nexus integration team members are the only ones who define the Definition of Done. The Nexus Integration Team make sure there is a DOD which works across all the teams. Everyone in the Nexus needs to contribute to creating a usable increment that meets certain standards.
	All Scrum Teams within the Nexus must define and adhere to this Definition of Done
	Each Sprint, all Scrum Teams have a "Done" Increment which integrates with the other "Done" Increments.
	Decisions made based on the state of artifacts are only as effective as the level of artifact transparency. Incomplete or partial information will lead to incorrect or flawed decisions. The impact of those decisions can be magnified at the scale of Nexus.

Nexus Sprint Length	All Scrum Teams in a nexus **do not have to have same sprint length**.
	All Scrum Teams in a nexus **can have different Sprint Start and End Dates,**
	Each team in a Nexus **must respect and observe the Nexus Sprint** (e.g. a 4 week cadence), but there's nothing to stop a team from having shorter Sprints which align to it (e.g. a 2 week cadence).
	Factors Impacting the Sprint Length: • Risk of **being disconnected from the Stakeholders** • **Level of uncertainty over the technology** used and velocity • **Market Competition & Time to release.**
Transparency	Just like its building block, Scrum, Nexus is based on transparency. **The Nexus Integration Team works with the Scrum Teams within a Nexus and the organization to ensure that transparency is apparent across all artifacts and that the integrated state of the Integrated Increment is widely understood.** Decisions made based on the state of Nexus artifacts are only as effective as the level of artifact transparency. Incomplete or partial information will lead to incorrect or flawed decisions. The impact of those decisions can be magnified at the scale of Nexus. Software must be developed so that dependencies are detected and resolved before technical debt becomes unacceptable to the Nexus. A lack of complete transparency will make it impossible to guide a Nexus effectively to minimize risk and maximize value.
Things that do not exist (for your exam).	Scrum does not acknowledge: 1) Hardening Phases. 2) Sprint 0. 3) Technical Sprints that consists only of tasks which help reduce the technical debt and do not add any functionality to the Product. 4) Stabilization Period. 5) The phrase or word "Scrum of Scrums" 6) First Part, Second Part of Sprint Planning. It means Sprint Planning. Only First, Second & Third Part of Nexus Sprint Retrospective exist. 7) Nexus Phases (Development Phase, integration Phase etc.)

Application Architecture	Developers in the Scrum Teams (or selective Experts) should design and build a platform / a foundation (**of Non-Functional requirements and High Value Functions) which would be used by as a Shared Architecture.** Each set of Scrum Team would work on this (to begin with) and work with each other to enhance it with time.
	Developers in the Scrum Team are **responsible for creating the architecture. T**he architectural and technical design discussions start as early as sprint planning and continue throughout the sprint as the design is being implemented (i.e. coding/construction).
	Defects, non-functional testing (such as performance, reliability, usability testing) also uncover design issues or problems which result in design discussions and may result in changes to the underlying application architecture or specific components or designs.
	The Applications overall architecture **is not designed upfront**, as the actual implementation of it emerges. The emergence of the Architecture is based on guidelines and agreed principles.
	The System's architecture is decided throughout the project, as **understanding emerges, and the Developers learns more about the project.**
	Developers should **have a set of Guiding Architecture Principles** that they understand and follows when writing code.
	There is no assigned Role (e.g. a software architect) whose job it is to makes sure a consistent architecture is developed. Developers makes sure that the architecture evolves based on the needs.
	Developers plans some time each Sprint to discuss the architecture needed for the features planned in that Sprint.

Version 32.0 "© 2019 Sid Bathia. All rights reserved."

Technical Debt	Technical debt (also known as design debt or code debt) is a concept in software development that reflects the implied cost of rework caused by choosing an easy solution now instead of using a better approach that would take longer. Like any other debt, a large accumulation of Technical Debt (bad code) can impact future maintainability of the product. The downsides of Technical Debt are as follows:
	1. It **misleads** the Product Owners, Scrum Masters and even the developers with their assumptions about **the "Current state" of the System**. For example, if Product Backlog item A is assumed to be completed in a day, it might take three days for it to complete, because of unseen bad code or Technical Debt.
	2. The **Product becomes more unstable**, as more functionality is added over bad code (or existing technical debt). Example: Let's assume that the team decided to delay some important refactoring to facilitate an early release. Technical debt starts to accrue at that point, and it may not map cleanly to specific items on the Product Backlog. It is far more likely to impact components which cross-cut a range of features. Moreover, if the necessary refactoring is significant it could impact the entire product, and it could affect features in uneven ways.
	Technical debt causes a greater percentage of the product's budget to be spent on maintenance of the product.
	The velocity at which new functionality can be created is reduced when you have technical debt.

Benefits of Self - Organization	The preferred leadership style in Scrum is "servant leadership", which emphasizes achieving results by focusing on the needs of the Scrum Team. Some of the benefits of Self-organization are: • Team buy-in and shared ownership • Motivation, which leads to an enhanced performance level of the team • Innovative and **Creative environment** conducive to growth • Increased Self Accountability, & Commitment to achieving the goals of the Scrum Team.
Feature Teams Vs Component Teams	A feature team is a long-lived, cross-functional, cross-component team that completes many end-to-end customer features. A component team is a team whose primary area of concern is restricted to a specific component.

Component team	Feature team
Can be implemented in a Scrum Framework	Can be implemented in a Scrum Framework
More Communication Overhead	Less Communication Overhead
Optimized for delivering the maximum number of lines of code	Optimized for delivering the maximum customer value
Focus on increased individual productivity by implementing 'easy' lower-value features	Focus on high-value features and system productivity (value throughput)
Dependencies between teams leads to additional planning	Minimizes dependencies between teams to increase flexibility
Focus on single specialization	Focus on multiple specializations
individual/team code ownership	Shared product code ownership
Clear individual responsibilities	Shared team responsibilities

Cross – Team Refinement Board	Cross Team Refinement Board
	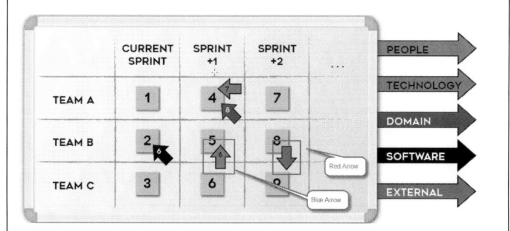 1. The Team Refinement Board visualization helps the teams within the Nexus identify the 'critical path' of work throughout the upcoming Sprints. 2. The Team Refinement Board provides the basis for conversations about ways to remove or minimize the impact of these dependencies. 3. In the Cross – Team Refinement Board, more arrows associated to a Product Backlog item indicate high risk due to the number of dependent items impacted. 4. The Red downward facing vertical dependency arrow is external and represents "In Sprint" dependency. A team is relying on an item delivered by an external group in the same Sprint to build a subsequent item. This is an extremely high-risk item. 5. The blue arrow shows dependency across teams within a single Sprint is vertical. One team will build an item in a Sprint that is needed by an item that will be delivered in the same Sprint by a different team. This dependency gives little room for delay or unexpected complexity. This is a high-risk relationship.

Nexus Summary Table	The Table below helps highlight the difference between the Scrum Framework and the Nexus Framework. Read the Table Once you are done reading the entire Reference Guide.	

	Scrum Team Specific	**Nexus- Across Scrum Teams**
Product Backlog	Only One Product Backlog can exist for a Product. Multiple Scrum Teams work on the Same Product Backlog, **on the Same Product Goal.**	
Sprint Backlog	Sprint Backlog ~	Nexus Sprint Backlog~
Refinement	Due to the added complexity of many teams working together on a single product, Refinement is an official and required event in the Nexus Framework. (unlike in Scrum Framework).	
Daily Scrum	Daily Scrum~	Nexus Daily Scrum~
Sprint Planning	Sprint Planning~	Nexus Sprint Planning~
Sprint Review	A Nexus Sprint Review replaces individual Scrum Team Sprint Reviews, because the entire Integrated Increment is the focus for capturing feedback from stakeholders.	
Sprint Retrospective	Sprint Retrospective~	Nexus Sprint Retrospective~
Product Owner	Only One Product Owner exist for a Product. Thus, the same Product Owner would participate in the Nexus Sprint Planning sessions and Team Specific Sprint Planning sessions, as needed.	
Scrum Master	Scrum Master	Scrum Master
Team Members	Developers	Nexus Integration Team Members*
Increment	Increment	Integrated Increment
Sprint Goal	Scrum Team Sprint Goal #	Nexus Sprint Goal #

Note:
1) (~) The Following are not the same. Refer to the Reference Table above to find more details:
    2.1 **Sprint Backlog and Nexus Sprint Backlog are different backlogs.**
    2.2 **Daily Scrum and Nexus Daily Scrum are different Meetings.**
    2.3 **Sprint Planning and Nexus Sprint Planning are different Meetings.**
    2.4 **Sprint Retrospective and Nexus Sprint Retrospective are different Meetings.**

2) Scrum Master and the Nexus Integration Scrum Master could be the same.
3) Nexus Integration Team Members may also work as Developers in one or more Scrum Teams.

Nexus Event Attendance

Roles / Events	Nexus Refinement	Nexus Sprint Planning	Nexus Daily Sprints	Nexus Sprint Review	Nexus Sprint Retrospective
Product Owner	Yes	Mandatory. (Actively Participates)	Optional.	Mandatory. (Actively Participates)	Mandatory . The Product Owner will be unable to attend each Scrum Teams Retrospective (part 2). This may be an instance where they will need to have specialist assistance to represent them at the individual Scrum Teams level.
Developers from Scrum Team			The Nexus Daily Scrum is attended by represented developers from each Scrum Team. Developers in the Scrum Team will self-organize to decide who is the right person to attend this event. As with all things in Scrum, inspection and adaption may lead to the attendees to this event changing over time.		Mandatory.
Scrum Master	As requested or required to facilitate this event.	Mandatory. (Actively Participates)	Optional.	Mandatory. (Actively Participates)	Mandatory.
Stake Holders		NA	NA	Stakeholders should also be present to assist in the inspection/adaption of this session.	Not Required.
Others		Technical and Domain Consultants may be invited by Scrum Team.	NA	-	-
Representatives of Each Scrum Team	It is likely that Teams are now operating at scale. It will not be practical to have all Scrum Team members from every team present during this event. Therefore, the Scrum Teams will Self-manage to decide who is the right person or people to attend this event.		NA		The first and third parts of the Nexus Sprint Retrospective should be attended by appropriate representatives from each Scrum Team.
All Scrum Team Members		Based on the Guide, "All members of the Scrum Teams should participate to minimize communication issues.". In reality it can be tough to coordinate this large number of people, so each Scrum Teams should nominate a smaller number of appropriate people to represent the team when planning discussions are carried out at the Nexus level. Once individual Scrum Teams take their Product Backlog Items for Sprint Planning at the team level, all Scrum Team members of each team should take part as they would using Scrum.	NA	Based on the Scrum Guide, "All individual Scrum Teams meet with stakeholders to review the Integrated Increment" However, it may not be possible or sensible for ALL members of ALL teams to attend. So appropriate representatives of each team must attend.	In part 2 of the Nexus Sprint Retrospective, all members of each Scrum Team should take part.

Nexus Guide Questions and Answers

Please go through these questions and check the answers as you go along. The Nexus Assessments **online (https://www.scrum.org/open-assessments)** are the best way to assess your knowledge. The Questions and Answers below will ensure you understand the concepts and help you help you prepare for the SPS exam. Go through the answers regardless of whether you answered the questions correctly or not. Don't try to time yourself. Focus on understanding the answers and the concepts. As you go through these questions, make your own notes to the Quick reference tables.

Question 1	Correct answer: B
Eight Scrum Teams in an organization are working together on a single Product. These eight Teams are using Nexus. There are many concerns these teams have with respect to integrations. One of the most important concerns which could directly impact the work of the Team Members is: A. Transparency. B. Dependency. C. Testing. D. Requirements.	**Dependencies is one of the most important concerns** when multiple Scrum Teams work together. The Nexus Framework helps teams solve common scaling challenges like: 1. Reducing cross-team dependencies 2. Preserving team self-management and transparency 3. Ensuring accountability.
Question 2 Nexus is a framework that binds together the work done by approximately: A. Three to Nine Scrum Teams. B. Four to Five Scrum Teams. C. Not more than 4 Scrum Teams. D. Not more than 8 Scrum Teams.	Correct answer: A Nexus is a framework which consist of roles, events, artifacts, and rules that bind together the work of approximately **three to nine Scrum Teams** working on a **single Product Backlog** to build an Integrated Increment that meets a goal. Remember it says **approximately** three to nine teams.

Question 3	**Correct answer: A, B**

Many dependencies exist when multiple teams collaborate to create a complete and "Done" Increment. These dependencies are typically related to: (Choose 2 best answers)
 	
   A. Product Structure.
   B. Communication Structure.
   C. Software Architecture.
   D. Accountabilities.
	The Nexus Framework helps teams solve common scaling challenges like:
	1. Reducing cross-team dependencies
	2. Preserving team self-management and transparency
	3. Ensuring accountability.
	
	Dependencies is one of the most important concerns when multiple Scrum Teams work together. Nexus helps to make transparent dependencies. These dependencies are often caused by mismatches related to:
	
	Product structure: The degree to which different concerns are independently separated in the product will greatly affect the complexity of creating an integrated product release. The scope of the requirements may overlap if not separated as needed. The order in which these requirements are implemented may also affect each other. While ordering the Product Backlog and selecting the Product Backlog items in the Sprint Backlog, one should make sure that such dependencies are accommodated.
	
	2. Communication structure: The way that people communicate within and between teams affects their ability to get work done; delays in communication and feedback reduce the flow of work.

Question 4
 	
A Team has four lead resources who have years of experience and lots of specific product knowledge. This team is getting split into multiple teams. Instead of keeping these seven resources in one team, these resources with specific knowledge should be distributed across the Scrum Teams to ensure that all the teams have the knowledge they need to do their work.
   A. True
   B. False
	Correct answer: A
	
	Team Member's knowledge should be distributed across the Scrum Teams to ensure that the teams have the knowledge they need to do their work. This would minimize interruptions between Scrum Teams during a Sprint.

Question 5	Correct answer: A

John is a Product Owner. During Backlog refinement he realized that the scope of the requirements overlaps, and the order in which they are implemented also affect each other. What should John do?
 	
  A. While ordering the Product Backlog and selecting the Product Backlog items in the Sprint Backlog, John should make sure that such dependencies are accommodated.
  B. Items which are dependent on each other should be merged into one Product Backlog item.
  C. Developers should manage the dependencies all by themselves.
	The scope of the requirements may overlap, and the order in which they are implemented may also affect each other. While ordering the Product Backlog and selecting the Product Backlog items in the Sprint Backlog, one should make sure that such dependencies are accommodated to avoid / reduce dependencies.

Question 6	Correct answer: B

Scrum Team A consist of eight Developers. All eight Team Members are required to attend the Nexus Daily Scrum Call.
 	
  A. True
  B. False
	The Nexus Daily Scrum is the scaled version of the Daily Scrum event from the Scrum framework. The Nexus Daily Scrum is an event which:
	
	1) Inspects the current state of the Integrated Increment against the Nexus Sprint Goal.
	
	2) Is an opportunity to Identifies Integration issues and make them Transparent
	
	3) Identifies newly discovered cross-team dependencies
	
	4) Identifies cross-team impacts.
	
	Appropriate represented Developers from individual Scrum Teams attend the Nexus Daily Scrum. All Developers from all the Scrum Teams are not required to attend the Nexus Daily Scrum. However, they are required to attend their Internal Daily Scrum Call.

Question 7	**Correct answer: A**
Scrum Team A consist of seven Developers. All these developers are not required to attend the Nexus Daily Sprint however they are required to attend their own Internal Daily Scrum calls A. True B. False	The Nexus Daily Scrum is the scaled version of the Daily Scrum event from the Scrum framework. The Nexus Daily Scrum is an event which: 1) Inspects the current state of the Integrated Increment against the Nexus Sprint Goal. 2) Is an opportunity to Identifies Integration issues and make them Transparent 3) Identifies newly discovered cross-team dependencies 4) Identifies cross-team impacts. Appropriate represented Developers from individual Scrum Teams attend the Nexus Daily Scrum. All Developers from all the Scrum Teams are not required to attend the Nexus Daily Scrum. However, they are required to attend their Internal Daily Scrum Call.
Question 8	**Correct answer: A**
Nexus Sprint Retrospective consist of three parts. During the first part of the Nexus Sprint Retrospective: A. The Team identifies the issues that have impacted more than a single Scrum Team. B. The Team identifies the issues that have impacted a single Scrum Teams work. C. The Team identify the dependencies. D. The Team talk about how to improve their internal Scrum Processes.	The purpose of the Nexus Sprint Retrospective is to plan ways to increase quality and effectiveness across the whole Nexus. The Nexus inspects how the last Sprint went with regards to individuals, teams, interactions, processes, tools, and its Definition of Done. In addition to individual team improvements, the Scrum Teams' Sprint Retrospectives complement the Nexus Sprint Retrospective by using bottom-up intelligence to focus on issues that affect the Nexus as a whole. The Nexus Retrospective consists of three parts: Part 1: **Nexus Retrospective: Representatives from all the Scrum teams meet to Identify issues** that have impacted **more than a single Scrum team**. The purpose is to make shared issues transparent to all Scrum Teams. Part 2: **Individual Scrum Team Sprint Retrospectives:** Each Scrum Team **holds their**

	own Sprint Retrospective as described in the Scrum framework. They can **use issues raised from the Nexus Retrospective** as input to their team discussions. The individual Scrum Teams should form actions to address these issues during their individual Scrum Team Sprint Retrospectives. Part 3: Synchronize: Third part is an **opportunity for appropriate representatives from the Scrum Teams to meet again and agree on how to visualize and track the identified actions**.
Question 9 Which part of the Nexus Sprint Retrospective is an opportunity for **appropriate representatives from the Scrum Teams to meet again and agree on how to visualize and track the identified actions**? A. First Part. B. Second Part. C. Fourth Part. D. Third Part.	**Correct answer: D** The Retrospective consists of three parts: Part 1: **Nexus Retrospective: Representatives from all the Scrum teams meet to Identify issues** that have impacted **more than a single Scrum team**. The purpose is to make shared issues transparent to all Scrum Teams. Part 2: **Individual Scrum Team Sprint Retrospectives:** Each Scrum Team **holds their own Sprint Retrospective** as described in the Scrum framework. They can **use issues raised from the Nexus Retrospective** as input to their team discussions. The individual Scrum Teams should form actions to address these issues during their individual Scrum Team Sprint Retrospectives. Part 3: Synchronize: Third part is an **opportunity for appropriate representatives from the Scrum Teams to meet again and agree on how to visualize and track the identified actions**.

Question 10 In the Second Part of the Nexus Sprint Retrospective: A. Each Scrum Team holds their own Sprint Retrospective as described in the Scrum framework. They can use issues raised from the Nexus Retrospective as input to their team discussions. B. The Team identifies the issues that have impacted more than a single Scrum Team. C. The Team identifies the issues that have impacted a single Scrum Teams work. D. The Team identify the dependencies.	**Correct answer: A** The Retrospective consists of three parts: Part 1: **Nexus Retrospective: Representatives from all the Scrum teams meet to Identify issues** that have impacted **more than a single Scrum team**. The purpose is to make shared issues transparent to all Scrum Teams. Part 2: **Individual Scrum Team Sprint Retrospectives:** Each Scrum Team **holds their own Sprint Retrospective** as described in the Scrum framework. They can **use issues raised from the Nexus Retrospective** as input to their team discussions. The individual Scrum Teams should form actions to address these issues during their individual Scrum Team Sprint Retrospectives. Part 3: Synchronize: Third part is an **opportunity for appropriate representatives from the Scrum Teams to meet again and agree on how to visualize and track the identified actions**.
Question 11 James is a Product Owner and he wants to add more Value to the Product. He decides to add more resources to the Scrum Team. Will this increase the value of the Product? A. True B. False	**Correct answer: B** Product Owner should focus on: → **Key Stakeholder Involvement** **In order to maximize Product value**, the Product Owner should identify the key stakeholders for the product and involve them as necessary throughout the development effort. → **Product Marketplace** The Product Owner should be **expertly aware of the marketplace for the product**. They should constantly be gathering and re-gathering information regarding the marketplace, so that the **product value is maximized**. → **Product Release Decisions** The Product Owner is the one and only person who can decide whether to release the latest Increment of the Product. **For Product value to be captured, a release of the product must occur.**

	Note: Product Value does not increase by simply adding more resources to the Scrum Team.
Question 12 Team A and Team B are Scrum Teams. Team C Is the Nexus Integration Team. Who is responsible for doing the actual integration Work? 　A. Team A since it has the highest velocity. 　B. Team A and Team B 　C. Team C 　D. Team A, B and Team C.	**Correct answer: B** Nexus Integration Team Members ensure that: 1) The Scrum Teams within the Nexus understand and implement the practices and tools needed to detect dependencies. 2) The Scrum Teams frequently integrate all artifacts to the definition of "Done." Nexus Integration Team does not do the Integration work. They guide the Scrum Teams to do it.
Question 13 The Nexus Sprint Backlog **provides a single view of all the Product Backlog items selected across all the teams (working on the same Product) in a Sprint.** 　A. True 　B. False	**Correct answer: A** In the Nexus Framework, there are three backlogs which are used: 　1. Product Backlog 　2. Nexus Sprint Backlog 　3. Scrum Team's Individual Sprint Backlog The Nexus Sprint Backlog provides a single view of all the Product Backlog items in a Sprint. The Nexus Sprint Backlog is a compilation of each team's individual Sprint Backlog. The Nexus Sprint Backlog is the composite of Product Backlog items from the Sprint Backlogs of the all individual Scrum Teams. As the Product Backlog items are refined and made ready, indicators of which Scrum team will do the work inside a Sprint are made transparent in the Nexus Sprint Backlog. The Nexus Sprint Backlog makes all the Scrum Team's (not just the Integration Team) work transparent by exposing the dependencies. The Nexus Sprint Backlog is used to highlight dependencies and the flow of work during the Sprint. It focuses on the coordination between teams to ensure the Nexus Sprint Goal is achieved. The Nexus Sprint Backlog is updated daily, often as part of the Nexus Daily Scrum.

Question 14	Correct answer: D
The advantages of Nexus Sprint Backlog are: A. It exposes the dependencies between teams. B. It provides a single view of all the Product Backlog items in a Sprint. C. It helps focus on the coordination between teams to ensure the Nexus Sprint Goal is achieved. D. All of the Above.	The Nexus Sprint Backlog provides a single view of all the Product Backlog items **in a Sprint**. As the Product Backlog items are refined and made ready, indicators of which Scrum team will do the work inside a Sprint are made transparent in the Nexus Sprint Backlog. The Nexus Sprint Backlog **makes the work of all Scrum Team's transparent (& not just the Integration Team) by exposing the dependencies.** The Nexus Sprint Backlog is used to highlight dependencies and the flow of work during the Sprint. **It focuses on the coordination between teams to ensure the Nexus Sprint Goal is achieved.**
Question 15	Correct answer: D
What factors should be considered when establishing the Sprint length? A. Risk of being disconnected from the stakeholders B. Level of uncertainty over the technology used and velocity C. Market competition D. All of the above.	Few factors which need to be consider for the sprint length are: **Risk Appetite and Market viability** One of the factors to be considered is the risk appetite of the business as well as the market viability. In scenarios where competition is stiff, the business might not have an appetite to take a risk and would like to deliver products frequently. The sprint duration is accordingly planned and with low risk appetite, the team might plan for a shorter duration. **Uncertainty** When there is uncertainty with respect to the change, technology stack and velocity, it is better to go for shorter duration so that the team would get opportunities to get more frequent feedbacks from the stakeholders as well as will get more opportunities to inspect and adapt accordingly.

Question 16	Correct answer: B
The system's architecture is finalized right in the beginning of the project. A. True B. False	The System's architecture is decided throughout the project, as **understanding emerges and the Developers learn more about the project.**
Question 17 New Scrum Teams have been created to build one product. Jack and John who are Developers are concerned that their work is not going to remain aligned with Charles who is in the other Scrum Team. What advice should you give to Jack and John? A. Ask Jack and John to collect the Sprint tasks from the teams at the end of their Sprint Planning and merge that into a consolidated plan. B. Tell Jack and John that it is their responsibility to work with Charles to create an integrated Increment. They should coordinate as needed. C. Visit Charles each day to inspect that his work is aligned. D. Ask the Product Owner to lead the developers in a way which would avoid overlap during a Sprint.	Correct answer: B It is the **responsibility of the Developers** to work with the other teams to make sure that their Sprint work is aligned to create an integrated Increment.
Question 18 Developers within the Scrum Team are responsible for creating the architecture. A. True B. False	Correct answer: A **Developers within the Scrum Team are responsible for creating the architecture.** The architectural and technical design discussions start as early as sprint planning and continues throughout the sprint as the design is being implemented (i.e. coding/construction).

Question 19	Correct answer: B

An applications overall architecture is designed upfront during Sprint 0.
  A. True
  B. False
	The applications overall architecture is not designed upfront, as the actual implementation of it emerges. The emergence of the Architecture is based on guidelines and agreed principles. The System's architecture is decided throughout the project, as understanding emerges and the Developers learns more about the project.

Question 20
 	
Before starting development of a new product, an overall architecture and design is needed. Which approach is the most effective?
 	
  A. Have select developers create a base design and architecture. Have them also create design models which the rest of the developers can use.
  B. Developers (or selective Experts) should design and build a platform / a foundation (of Non-Functional requirements and High Value Functions) which would be used by as a shared architecture.
  C. Form a team of Architects who would consult the Developers as needed.
	Correct answer: B
	Developers (or selective Experts) should design and build a platform / a foundation (**of Non-Functional requirements and High Value Functions**) which would be used by as a Shared Architecture. Each set of Scrum Team would work on this (to begin with) and work with each other to enhance it with time. Developers within the Scrum Team are responsible for creating the architecture. The architectural and technical design discussions start as early as sprint planning and continue throughout the sprint as the design is being implemented (i.e. coding/construction). Remember a Non-functional foundation (with no designs) and just some high value function is all that is needed in the beginning. Scrum Developers will work on it together as requirements get translated to Product Backlog items and the Product starts to build.

Question 21
 	
Who is responsible for a definition of "Done" that can be applied to the Integrated Increment (developed each Sprint)?
 	
  A. Scrum Master.
  B. Individual Scrum Teams.
  C. Product Owner.
  D. The Nexus Integration Team.
	Correct answer: D
	
	The Nexus Integration Team is responsible for a definition of "Done" that can be applied to the Integrated Increment developed each Sprint. The Nexus Integration Team is responsible. That doesn't mean they are the only ones who define the Definition of Done. The Nexus Integration Team make sure there is a DOD which works across all the teams. Everyone in the Nexus needs to contribute to creating a usable increment that meets certain standards.

Question 22

Individual Scrum Teams may choose to apply a less stringent criteria definition of done (than agreed for the Increment during Nexus Retrospective) within their own teams.

    A. True
    B. False

Correct answer: B

The Nexus Integration Team is responsible for a Definition of "Done" that can be applied to the Integrated Increment developed each Sprint. That doesn't mean that the Nexus integration team members are the only ones who define the Definition of Done. The Nexus Integration Team make sure there is a DOD which works across all the teams. Everyone in the Nexus needs to contribute to creating a usable increment that meets certain standards.

Each Sprint, all Scrum Teams have a "Done" Increment which integrates with the other "Done" Increments.

When different teams are working on the same product, they must observe a common Definition of Done which qualifies for the integrated increment. The Definition of Done observed by an individual team should reinforce and not contradict any shared Definition for a product increment. For example, a team may incorporate a shared DoD as a subset of their own.

Scrum Teams Definition of "Done" = Nexus Definition of "Done" + Optional Scrum Team Specific Definition of "Done" Criteria.

Individual Scrum Teams can choose to apply a more stringent definition of "Done" within their own teams but cannot apply less rigorous criteria than agreed (in nexus) for the Increment.

Question 23
 	
In the Nexus Daily Scrum, if integration issues are identified:
 	
  A. The information is transferred back to each Scrum Team's Daily Scrum, so they can resolve it.
  B. The issue identified by the Nexus Daily Scrum Team is resolved right away.
	Correct answer: A
	
	Selected Developers from each Scrum Team would meet daily to identify if any integration issues exist. If integration issues are identified, this information is transferred back to each Scrum Team's Daily Scrum.

Question 24
 	
The Nexus Daily Scrum is an event which: (Choose all that apply)
 	
  1) Inspects the current state of the integrated increment against the Nexus Sprint Goal.
  2) Is an opportunity to Identifies Integration issues and make them Transparent
  3) Identifies newly discovered cross-team dependencies
  4) Identifies cross-team impacts.
	Correct answer: A,B,C,D
	
	The Nexus Daily Scrum is the scaled version of the Daily Scrum event from the Scrum framework. The Nexus Daily Scrum is an event which:
	
	1) Inspects the current state of the integrated increment against the Nexus Sprint Goal.
	
	2) Is an opportunity to Identifies Integration issues and make them Transparent
	
	3) Identifies newly discovered cross-team dependencies
	
	4) Identifies cross-team impacts.

Question 25
 	
Who is responsible for the Integrated Increment developed each Sprint in Nexus?
 	
  A. Scrum Master.
  B. Individual Scrum Team.
  C. Product Owner.
  D. The Nexus Integration Team.
	Correct answer: D
	
	The Nexus Integration Team is responsible for the Integration issues and Integrated Increment developed each Sprint.

Question 26	**Correct answer: C**
Seven Scrum Teams (in Nexus) are planning to work on one Product. How should these teams coordinate work (on daily basis) with the other teams? A. The Nexus Team Integration team should coordinate the work between teams. B. Create a Project Plan (for each team) of all the "To-do's" once the Sprint Planning is over. Merge the Plan for all the Teams. C. It is the Scrum Teams responsibility to work with the other Teams to create an integrated Increment. D. Ask the Scrum Master to work with each team lead developer on sequencing the Product Backlog that would avoid overlaps during a Sprint.	Remember there are no Team Leads in Scrum or in Nexus. Also, Nexus Team Integration team is not responsible for coordinating the work between the Scrum Teams. The Scrum Teams are responsible themselves. One cannot completely avoid overlaps by simply sequencing the Product Backlogs. The Scrum Team Members must make sure that they take the responsibility to coordinate with other team members to decrease or reduce dependency.
Question 27 A Technical Debt (Select 2): A. Misleads the Product Owners, Scrum Masters and even the developers with their assumptions about the "Current state" of the System. B. Makes the Product more stable. C. Makes the Product more unstable. D. Enhances the Transparency.	**Correct answers: A, C** Technical debt (also known as design debt or code debt) is a concept in software development that reflects the implied cost of rework caused by choosing an easy solution "now" instead of using a better approach that would take longer. Like any other debt, a large accumulation of Technical Debt (bad code) can impact future maintainability of the product. **A Technical debt reduces Transparency.** It **misleads** the Product Owners, Scrum Masters and even the developers with their assumptions about **the "Current state" of the System**. For example, if Product Backlog item A is assumed to be completed in a day, it might take three days for it to complete, because of unseen bad code or Technical Debt. The **Product becomes more unstable**, as more functionality / features added over bad code (or existing technical debt). For example, suppose that the team decided to delay some important refactoring to facilitate an early release. Technical debt starts to accrue at that point, and it may not map cleanly to specific

	items on the Product Backlog. It is far more likely to impact components which cross-cut a range of features. Moreover, if the necessary refactoring is significant it could impact the entire product, and it could affect features in uneven ways.

Question 28
 	
When are the **dependencies between the Product Backlog items discovered or identified in Nexus**? Select all that Apply
 	
  A. Nexus Sprint Retrospective.
  B. Nexus Refinement.
  C. Nexus Sprint Planning.
  D. All of the above.
	Correct answers: B, C
	
	Refinement of the Product Backlog at scale serves a dual purpose.
	  • It helps the Scrum Teams forecast which team will deliver which Product Backlog items
	  • it **identifies dependencies** across those teams.
	
	Ideally, the Product Backlog should be adequately refined with **dependencies identified and removed or minimized prior to Nexus Sprint Planning. However** New dependencies may emerge during Nexus Sprint Planning.
	
	Note: **Sprint Planning is another opportunity to identify and eliminate or reduce dependencies** between Product Backlog Items, so Scrum Teams can plan and work on them independently.

Question 29	Correct answers: A, B
A company has two products. Which of the following is an acceptable way of forming Scrum teams? Choose all that apply. A. There must be a single Product Owner for each product. B. There can be a single Product Owner across two products however a Single Product cannot have more than one Product Owner. C. There should be one Product Owner supported by a Junior Product Owner. D. There should be a Chief Product Owner and one Product Owner for each product.	**Only One Product Backlog and Only One Product Owner can exist for** a Product (Regular Scrum framework or in Nexus). Multiple Scrum Teams work on the Same Product Backlog. Thus, the same Product Owner would participate in the Nexus Sprint Planning sessions and Team Specific Sprint Planning sessions, as needed. Different Scrum Teams working on the same Product (in Nexus) can: • Have different Sprint Lengths. • Have different Scrum Masters. • Have only one Product Owner. • Have only one Product Backlog. A Product owner can act as Product Owner for more than one Products however this is not recommended. Remember: A) For a given Product, there should be only one Product Owner. E.g. Charles and John both cannot be Product Owners for the same Product (Product XYZ) in an Organization. One Product can only have one Product Owner. B) The same person can be a Product Owner for more than one Products. This might not be recommended, however is still allowed in Scrum. For e.g Charles can be a Product Owner for Product A and Product B, at the same time. Thus Both A and B are true.

Question 30

A company has 20 products and 5 Product Owners. Which of the following is an acceptable way of forming Scrum teams? Choose all that apply.

- A. There must be a single Product Owner for each product.
- B. 5 Product Owners are assigned 4 Products each. The Product Owner may delegate work to others.
- C. There should be one Product Owner supported by a Junior Product Owner.
- D. There should be a Chief Product Owner and one Product Owner for each product.
- E. Each Product can have more than one Product owner.

Correct answers: A, B

Only One Product Backlog and Only One Product Owner can exist for a Product (Regular Scrum framework or in Nexus).

The Same Product Owner may work as a Product Owner for multiple Products. (Not Recommended)

The Product **Owner can delegate the following capabilities** to Developers:
1. Clearly expressing Product Backlog items;
2. Ordering the items in the Product Backlog to best achieve goals and missions

Note:

A) If there are 20 Products, each Product should have a single assigned Product Owner. This does not mean that we have 20 different individuals working on these 20 Products. It means that no two people can act as a Product Owner on a single product.

B) 5 Product Owners can be assigned 4 products each.
Example:
- Charles can be a Product Owner for Products 1,2,3, 4
- James can be a Product Owner for Products 5 ,6,7, 8
- John can be a Product Owner for Products 9,10,11,12
- Mathew can be a Product Owner for Products 13,14,15,16
- Roger can be a Product Owner for Products 17,18,19,20

Question 31	**Correct answers: B, D**
There are 6 Scrum Teams in a company. These 6 Teams are working on the same Product. Which of the below is true? **(Choose two)** A. Each Team should have its own Product Backlog. B. Each Team should have its own Sprint Backlog. C. Each Team should have its own Product Owner. D. All the Scrum Teams will have the Same Product Owner.	Regardless of the Number of Scrum Teams working on a Product, a Product would have only One Product Owner and only One Product Backlog. The teams would pull the Backlog items from the Product Backlog or from the Nexus Sprint Backlog to their own individual Sprint Backlogs.
Question 32 The Product Owner decides on the number of Product Backlog items which should be assigned to a Teams Sprint Backlog. A. True B. False	**Correct answers: B** The Sprint Backlog is created during the beginning of the Sprint. Developers within the Scrum Team work with the Product Owner to pull in the work, into their individual Sprint Backlogs. The Sprint Backlog captures all the work which the Developers identifies as necessary, to meet the Sprint Goal. Developers keep adding tasks during the Sprint, so, the Sprint Backlog keeps getting updated. The Sprint Backlog is the plan for the Developers for the current Sprint. This plan is not detailed upfront. Only the **Developers can change its Sprint Backlog during a Sprint**. The Product Owner has to agree to the changes to make sure they don't impact the Sprint Goal.
Question 33 50 Product Backlog items exist in a current Nexus Sprint Backlog. The Product Owner should assign 10 items to the 5 Scrum Teams so balance of work is maintained. A. True B. False	**Correct answers: B** The Product Owner does not assign work to individual Scrum Teams or Sprint Backlogs. Developers in the Scrum Team work with the Product Owner to pull the items during Nexus Sprint Planning. It is not necessary that equal items be assigned to the Scrum Teams.

Question 34	Correct answers: B
The Scrum Team with the highest velocity can choose items from the Nexus Product Backlog over teams with a lower velocity. A. True B. False	Velocity is a measure of the amount of work a Team can tackle during a single Sprint and is the key metric in Scrum. Velocity is calculated at the end of the Sprint by totaling the Points for all fully completed User Stories. Team velocity has nothing to do when it comes to prioritizing and choosing items in a teams Sprint backlog. The Sprint Backlog is created during the beginning of the Sprint. Developers within the Scrum Team work with the Product Owner to pull in the work, into their individual Sprint Backlogs. The Sprint Backlog captures all the work which the Developers identifies as necessary, to meet the Sprint Goal.
Question 35	Correct answers: B
Team A and Team B are working on the same product. They must have the same sprint start date. A. True B. False	Nexus doesn't require that team Sprints within the Nexus start or stop at the same time. It is certainly strongly implied, as doing so makes integration between teams much easier, but there's nothing in the framework that stops you from having a two-week iteration for one team, and a four-week iteration for another, or having one team end its Sprints on Wednesdays while another team ends theirs on Fridays.

Question 36	Correct answers: B
3 Scrum Teams are added to a Product which already has 2 Scrum Teams working on it. The Productivity of the existing Scrum Teams will immediately increase as 3 Scrum Teams are added. A. True B. False	In a short term the productivity will decrease because the new teams will spend time to get up to speed with the Product. The old team will spend a lot of time communicating with the new teams. Adding more Members to a Team or adding more teams would **lead to immediate decrease in Productivity as communication and coordination time between the Scrum Teams increase.**
Question 37	Correct answers: A
The Purpose of the Nexus Integration Team Members is to: A) Increase **Transparency across teams working on the same Product.** B) Work and resolve the integration issues identified across teams.	Nexus Integration Team Members Raises Transparency by **coaching and guiding the Scrum Teams to acquire, implement, and learn the nexus practices and needed tools.**
Question 38	Correct answers: A
Team A, Team B, Team C and Team D are working on the same Product in Nexus. Their work / increment should be integrated every Sprint. A. True B. False	If increments are not integrated every Sprint then, - The state of the product becomes unclear (due to undiscovered problems that could arise during integration and complete product increment tests). - The Product Owner would not know whether the increment he/she was presented is potential shippable. - It would not be transparent to the organization what the next reasonable steps would be.

Question 39	Correct answers: D
Team A and Team B are working on the same product. They must have: A. Same Product Backlog. B. Same Nexus Sprint Backlog. C. Different Individual Sprint Backlogs. D. All of the above.	Regardless of the Number of Scrum Teams working on a Product, a Product would have only One Product Owner and only One Product Backlog. The Teams would **They must have:** A. Same Product Backlog. B. Same Nexus Sprint Backlog. C. Different Individual Sprint Backlogs.
Question 40 Integration could happen multiple times during the sprint as and when required. A. True B. False	**Correct answers: A** Integration could happen multiple times during the sprint as and when required. For e.g. Multiple teams working on the same product could integrate twice a day for End to End Testing. Continuous integration is a software development practice where developers regularly merge their code changes into a central repository, after which automated builds and tests are run. Continuous Integration is a software development practice where members of a Scrum team integrate and verify their work frequently, often multiple times each day to detect integration errors as quickly as possible. In the past, developers on a team worked in isolation for an extended period of time, only merging their changes to the master branch once their work was completed. This made merging code changes difficult and time-consuming. It also resulted in bugs accumulating for a long time without correction. These factors made it harder to deliver updates to customers quickly. The purpose of Continuous Integration is to avoid last minute integration surprises and find code issues right away.

	Integration could happen multiple times during the sprint as and when required. For e.g. Multiple teams working on the same product could integrate twice a day for End to End Testing.

Question 41
 	
A good time to change the Nexus Definition of Done is at the Nexus Retrospective. It is however not mandatory to change it during the Nexus Sprint Retrospective.
 	
   A. True
   B. False
	Correct answers: A
	
	The best time to change the Definition of Done is during the Sprint Retrospective where the team discusses how to increase product quality. It is however not mandatory to change it during the Nexus Sprint Retrospective. If needed it can be changed as soon as possible. (as long as all Scrum Team members work towards the change).

Question 42
 	
Seven Scrum Teams are working on a complicated financial software. These 7 Teams don't integrate their individual increments before the Sprint Review. Each Team simply shows the increment they have worked on to the clients. The Clients feedback has reduced to a point that most of them don't give any feedback at all. What are the impacts, if this continues?
 	
   A. This will be a missed opportunity to adapt and inspect as the Scrum team is are not getting much feedback from the clients.
   B. The product would be considered as unstable as the increments are not integrated.
   C. Technical debt will increase as the team might rush to integrate their work in the end.
   D. All of the above.
	Correct answers: D
	
	In Nexus, a Product Backlog item can be considered "Done" when the planned functionality has been successfully added to the product and integrated into the final Increment.
	
	All Scrum Teams are responsible for developing and integrating their work into an Increment, however the Nexus Integration Team owns the accountability.
	
	Nexus Sprint Reviews replace Individual Sprint Reviews with the expectation that the stakeholders would get a chance to give feedback for the Integrated increment. If there is no feedback, this would be a considered a missed opportunity to adapt. The Value of the Product would be compromised as it depends on client's feedback.
	
	As Teams starts delaying the integration, more chances of bugs and tech debt rises. The delay might lead to reduced testing, unknown last-minute issues etc.
	
	Thus, all of the answers are true.

Question 43	Correct answers: B
Two Teams working on the same product, need to have the exact same definition of done. A. True B. False	When Multiple Scrum teams working on 1 product, there would be a shared understanding of what Definition of "Done" means. This can be called the Nexus Definition of Done. When multiple teams are working on the same product, there can be more than one Definition of "Done" for all of them. Each team might be working on a different part of the product (e.g. desktop application, mobile application, web application), or simply have different styles of work. If there are multiple Scrum Teams working together on a product, they must mutually define and comply with a shared Definition of Done. They can add their own specific criteria on top of this Definition of "Done" Criteria. When different teams are working on the same product, they must observe a common Definition of Done which qualifies for the integrated increment. The Definition of Done observed by an individual team should reinforce and not contradict any shared Definition for a product increment. For example, a team may incorporate a shared DoD as a subset of their own. Scrum Teams Definition of "Done" = Nexus Definition of "Done" + Optional Scrum Team Specific Definition of "Done" Criteria. Individual Scrum Teams may choose to apply a more stringent definition of "Done" within their own teams but cannot apply less rigorous criteria than agreed for the Increment.

Question 44	**Correct answers: B**
What happens when the Definition of "Done" changes? (Select one Best Answer) A. The changed definition of Done should be communicated to all the clients. B. The Nexus Integration Team will discuss the Definition of "Done" during the Nexus Sprint Retrospective and let the individual Scrum Teams adapt to it. The changed Definition of Done might not be implemented right away. C. Based on the new definition of done, Individual Scrum teams include all the changes in the current Sprint or next Sprint.	When Multiple Scrum teams working on 1 product, there would be a shared understanding of what Definition of "Done" means. This can be called the Nexus Definition of Done. 1. During the **Nexus Sprint Retrospective**, the **Definition of "Done"** can be revised If needed. 2. These changes would be then communicated to the Individual teams to be incorporated. 3. Once Adapted by the Individual Scrum Team, they would implemented / applied to the Product Backlog items in each Sprint. Note: **The Individuals Teams must incorporate the changed Nexus Definition of "Done" criteria to their own Definition of "Done".** The Nexus Definition of "Done" **cannot be implemented by Scrum Teams without the individual teams adapting to it.**
Question 45 Advantages of a Self – Organizing Team are: A. Team Buy-in B. Shared Ownership C. Motivation D. Innovation E. Creativity F. Self-Accountability G. Commitment H. All of the Above.	**Correct answers: H** Some of the benefits of Self-organizing team are: • Team buy-in and shared ownership • Motivation, which leads to an enhanced performance level of the team • Innovative and **Creative environment** conducive to growth • **Increased Self Accountability & Commitment** to achieving the goals of the Scrum Team.

Question 46	Correct answers: A, C
Representatives of Scrum Team A and Scrum Team B are participating in Sprint Planning. Each Team has 8 Development Members. These Teams have quite a few dependencies (resource and work selected) on each other in Sprint 1. Which techniques will help with reducing these dependencies? (Select 2) A. Reassign the Team Members from Scrum Team A to Scrum Team B (and Vice versa) to decrease the cross-team dependencies. B. Extend the Length of Sprint 1, to allow more time for Scrum Team A and Scrum Team B. C. Order the Nexus Sprint Backlog appropriately so backlog items are picked up in the correct sequence. D. Merge the Teams.	Remember the following with respect to dependencies: The scope of the requirements may overlap, and the order in which they are implemented may also affect each other. While ordering the Product Backlog and selecting the Product Backlog items in the Sprint Backlog, one should make sure that such dependencies are accommodated. Team Member's knowledge should be distributed across the Scrum Teams to ensure that the teams have the knowledge they need to do their work. This would minimize interruptions between Scrum Teams during a Sprint. Extending the Sprint Length is not an option under any situations. Merging the Team is not possible as well as the team should remain small enough to be flexible.
Question 47 Who reports to the Nexus Integration Team? A. Product Owner. B. All Individual Scrum Teams. C. Scrum Master. D. All of the above. E. None of the above.	**Correct answers: E** Under the Scrum and Nexus Frameworks, No one "reports" to the Nexus Integrations Team. Developers and Scrum Masters working in an Individual Scrum Teams can be a part of the Nexus Integration Team, however they do not report to anyone.
Question 48 The Role of the Nexus Integration Team is: (Choose all that apply) A. Raise Transparency by coaching and guiding the Scrum Teams to acquire, implement, and learn the nexus practices and needed tools. B. Take ownership of integration issues. C. Work with 1 or more Scrum Teams to help them resolve issues around integration.	**Correct answers: A, B, C, D, E** Nexus Integration Team: • Does not do the Integration work themselves. They guide the Scrum Teams to do it. • Does not coordinate the day to day work between the Scrum Teams. It is the Scrum Teams responsibility to work with the other Teams to create an integrated Increment.

D. Deliver tools and technology to help make integration run more smoothly. E. Coach the individual Scrum Teams on the necessary development, infrastructural, or architectural standards required by the organization to ensure the development of quality Integrated Increments. F. Develop and merge the code if needed, to integrate the increments.	Nexus Integration Team Members Raises Transparency by coaching and guiding the Scrum Teams to acquire, implement, and learn the nexus practices and needed tools. The Nexus Integration Team will take ownership of integration issues. However, they may not necessarily do the work required to resolve these when they occur. They may work with 1 or more Scrum Teams to help them resolve issues around integration. At other times they may deliver tools and technology to help make integration run more smoothly. Additionally, the Nexus Integration Team coaches the individual Scrum Teams on the necessary development, infrastructural, or architectural standards required by the organization to ensure the development of quality Integrated Increments.

Question 49
 	
The Nexus Sprint Goal is discussed and finalized during Nexus Sprint Retrospective.
 	
   A. True
   B. False
	Correct answers: B
	
	The Nexus Sprint Goal is discussed and finalized during Nexus Sprint Planning.

Question 50
 	
Team A and Team C are busy building their individual Increments. The Nexus Integration team steps in and offers to merge their existing code, so deadlines can be met. The Nexus Integration Team should do so, if needed.
 	
   A. True
   B. False
	Correct answers: B
	
	Nexus Integration Team:
	• **Does not do the Integration work themselves.** They guide the Scrum Teams to do it.
	• Does not coordinate the day to day work between the Scrum Teams. It is the Scrum Teams responsibility to work with the other Teams to create an integrated Increment.

Question 51.	Correct answers: A
There are 8 Scrum Teams working together. Recently during the Sprint Review, they displayed their own individual increments. The teams did not show the integrated increment as it doesn't exist yet. Which one of the below is a strong possibility? A. The Nexus Integration Team does not Exist. B. The Product Owner does not exist. C. The Scrum Master does not exist. D. Scrum allows non-integrated increments as long as they are valuable to the clients.	Scrum promotes a single integrated increment end of each sprint. The Nexus Integration Team **owns responsibility for the:** <ul><li>**Integration issues.**</li><li>**Integrated Increment.**</li></ul> If the integrated increment is missing, then probably the team responsible for it is nonexistent. (or the team did not meet its definition of done)

Question 52	Correct answers: D
Which of the following is true about the Cross-Team Refinement Board? 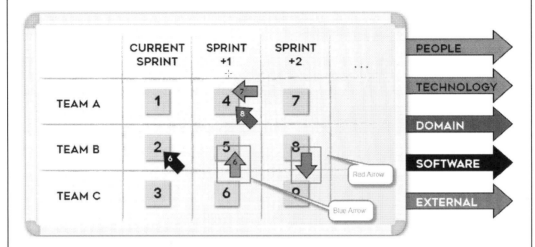 A. More arrows indicate point a work items indicates high risk due to the number of dependent items impacted. B. This visualization helps the teams within the Nexus identify the 'critical path' of work throughout the upcoming Sprints. C. This visualization provides the basis for conversations about ways to remove or minimize the impact of these dependencies. D. All of the above.	In the Cross – Team Refinement Board, more arrows associated to a Product Backlog item indicate high risk due to the number of dependent items impacted. The Team Refinement Board visualization helps the teams within the Nexus identify the 'critical path' of work throughout the upcoming Sprints. The Team Refinement Board provides the basis for conversations about ways to remove or minimize the impact of these dependencies.

Question 53

The Team Refinement Board visualization helps the teams within the Nexus identify the 'critical path' of work throughout the upcoming Sprints. The Team Refinement Board provides the basis for conversations about ways to remove or minimize the impact of these dependencies.
Which is the riskiest item in the Cross-Team Refinement Board drawn below?
(8→9 Red Arrow = External Dependency), (6→5 Blue Arrow = People Dependency.)

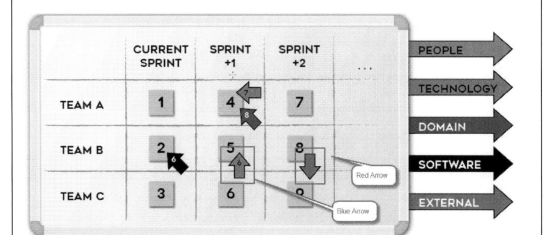

A. Product Backlog item 4.
B. Backlog item 2.
C. Backlog item 7.
D. Backlog item 9.

Correct answers: D

The Red Downward facing vertical (dependency arrow) is external and represents "In Sprint" dependency. A team is relying on an item delivered by an external group in the same Sprint in order to build a subsequent item. This is an extremely high-risk item.

Question 54. Which is the highest Relationship Risk item in the Cross-Team Refinement Board drawn below? **(8→9 Red Arrow = External Dependency), (6→5 Blue Arrow = People Dependency.)** 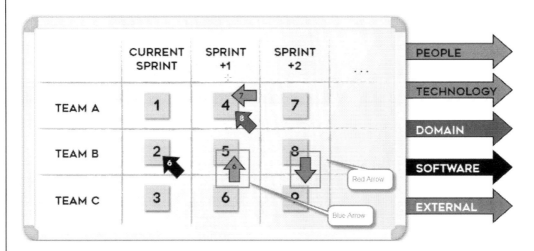 A. Product Backlog item 4. B. Backlog item 2. C. Backlog item 5. D. Backlog item 9.	**Correct answers: C** The blue vertical arrow shows dependency across teams within a single Sprint. One team will build an item in a Sprint that is needed by an item that will be delivered in the same Sprint by a different team. This dependency gives little room for delay or unexpected complexity. This is a high-risk relationship.
Question 55 Team A is a component-based Team. Team B is feature based Team. Both the teams can use the Scrum Framework. A. True B. False	**Correct answers: A** Scrum supports component based and feature based Teams.

Question 56. Team A is a component-based Team. Team B is feature based Team. Both the Teams can use the Scrum Framework. Team A would have less communication overhead as compared to Team B. A. True B. False	**Correct answers: B** Remember the following comparison table.

Component team	Feature team
Can be implemented in a Scrum Framework	Can be implemented in a Scrum Framework
More Communication Overhead	Less Communication Overhead
Optimized for delivering the maximum number of lines of code	Optimized for delivering the maximum customer value

Question 57. Who coaches the individual Scrum Teams on the necessary **development, infrastructural, or architectural standards** required by the organization? A. Product Owner. B. All Individual Scrum Team Leads. C. Scrum Master. D. The Nexus Integration Team.	**Correct answers: D** The Nexus Integration Team coaches the individual Scrum Teams on the necessary **development, infrastructural, or architectural standards** required by the organization to ensure the development of quality Integrated Increments.
Question 58. **Nexus Integration Team Members may also work as Developers** in one or more Scrum Teams. A. True B. False	**Correct answers: A** If the primary responsibility of the Nexus Team Member is satisfied, **Nexus Integration Team Members may also work as Developers** in one or more Scrum Teams.
Question 59 The Product Owner in the Nexus Integration Team has the **overall responsibility** for ensuring the Nexus framework is understood and enacted. A. True B. False	**Correct answers: B** The Scrum Master in the Nexus Integration Team has the **overall responsibility** for ensuring the Nexus framework is understood and enacted.

Question 60.	Correct answers: A
The Nexus Scrum Master / Scrum Master in the Nexus Team: A. May also be a Scrum Master in one or more of the Scrum Teams. B. Cannot be a Scrum Master in one or more of the Scrum Teams.	The **Nexus Scrum Master may also be a Scrum Master in one or more of the Scrum Teams.**
Question 61 In a Nexus Sprint Review, the Stakeholders are not satisfied because the Integrated increment was not shown. Individuals showed all their individual Increments. Which of the following options is / are true? A. The Stakeholders were not satisfied because the Nexus Goal was not met. B. The Stakeholders were not satisfied because the right team of attendees might not be involved. C. Showing an integrated increment is needed during Nexus Sprint Review, for the Nexus Sprint Goal to be met. D. None of the above.	**Correct answers: A, C** The Nexus Sprint Goal is an objective set for the Sprints across Teams. The Nexus Sprint Goal is discussed and finalized during Nexus Sprint Planning. The Nexus Sprint Goal is then communicated to the rest of the Individual Scrum Teams to reflect the shared purpose of Nexus. Individual Scrum Team Sprint Goals are set during Individual Scrum Team Sprint Planning sessions. (not during the Nexus Sprint Planning). The Nexus Sprint Goal describes the purpose that will be achieved by all the Scrum Teams during the Sprint. Remember Nexus Sprint Goal = Sum of Sprint Goals Across all the Team {In a SPRINT} + the Work done by all the Teams {In a SPRINT}. Only the integrated increment will show if Nexus Sprint Goal is met. Thus, it is a must that an Integrated Increment is shown in the Nexus Sprint Reviews.

Question 62	Correct answers: B
How does the Nexus Daily Scrum relate to the Daily Scrum in each Scrum Team? A. These events are completely separate. Members at the Nexus Daily Scrum only cross-team members identify and resolve the issues. B. Work that is identified during the Nexus Daily Scrum is then taken back to individual Scrum Teams for planning inside their Daily Scrum events. C. Nexus Daily Scrum is the Scrum of Daily Scrums. D. All the above.	The Nexus Daily Scrum is the scaled version of the Daily Scrum event from the Scrum framework. The Nexus Daily Scrum is an event which: 1) Inspects the current state of the Integrated Increment against the Nexus Sprint Goal. 2) Is an opportunity to Identifies Integration issues and make them Transparent 3) Identifies newly discovered cross-team dependencies 4) Identifies cross-team impacts. Appropriate represented Developers from individual Scrum Teams attend the Nexus Daily Scrum. All Developers from all the Scrum Teams are not required to attend the Nexus Daily Scrum. However, they are required to attend their Internal Daily Scrum Call. At least **every Nexus Daily Scrum**, the **Nexus Sprint Backlog should be inspected (adjusted** if needed) to reflect the current understanding of the work of the Scrum Teams within the Nexus. Appropriate Representatives (Developers) from each Scrum Team meet daily to identify if any integration issues exist. If integration issues are identified, this **information is transferred back to each Scrum Team's Daily Scrum.** Scrum Teams use their Daily Scrum making sure to address the integration issues raised during the Nexus Daily Scrum

Question 63	Correct answers: B, C, D
The Nexus Integration Team consists of professionals who: A. Are not allowed to work as Developers in Scrum Teams. B. Coach the individual Scrum Teams on the necessary development, infrastructural, or architectural standards required by the organization to ensure the development of quality Integrated Increments. C. Ensure the Scrum Teams within the Nexus understand and implement the practices and tools needed to detect dependencies, and frequently integrate all artifacts. D. Are skilled in the use of tools, various practices, and the general field of systems engineering.	The Nexus Integration Team consists of professionals who are skilled in the use of tools, various practices, and the general field of systems engineering. Nexus Integration Team Members ensure the Scrum Teams within the Nexus understand and implement the practices and tools needed to detect dependencies, and frequently integrate all artifacts. Nexus Integration Team Members are responsible for coaching and guiding the Scrum Teams in a Nexus to acquire, implement, and learn these practices and tools. Additionally, the Nexus Integration Team coaches the individual Scrum Teams on the necessary development, infrastructural, or architectural standards required by the organization to ensure the development of quality Integrated Increments.

Question 64	Correct answers: A, B, D, F, G
What are the best ways to improve productivity of all Scrum teams? Choose Five. A. Reduce cross functional dependencies as much as possible. B. Appropriately distribute domain knowledge between the Scrum Teams. C. Add a Nexus expert into each Scrum Team. D. Preserve Teams self-management and transparency. E. Organize a training on the Nexus framework for all developers. F. Sequence the Product Backlog items to reduce dependencies during Refinement. G. Ensure Accountability	The Nexus Framework helps teams solve common scaling challenges like: 1. Reducing cross-team dependencies 2. Preserving team self-management and transparency 3. Ensuring accountability. Dependencies is one of the most important concerns when multiple Scrum Teams work together. Nexus helps to make transparent dependencies. These dependencies are often caused by mismatches related to: 1. Product structure: The degree to which different concerns are independently separated in the product will greatly affect the complexity of creating an integrated product release. The scope of the requirements may overlap if not separated as needed. The order in which these requirements are implemented may also affect each other. While ordering the Product Backlog and selecting the Product Backlog items in the Sprint Backlog, one should make sure that such dependencies are accommodated. 2. Communication structure: The way that people communicate within and between teams affects their ability to get work done; delays in communication and feedback reduce the flow of work.
Question 65 **How does Nexus relate to Scrum?** A. Nexus and Scrum are two different frameworks addressing complex adaptive problems in different ways. B. Nexus is just a part of the Scrum framework. C. Nexus is an "Unit of development" and hardly relates to Scrum. D. Nexus uses Scrum as its building block.	Correct answers: D Nexus is a framework for developing and sustaining scaled product and software development initiatives. It uses Scrum as its building block.

Question 66	Correct answers: B, C
Are there any prerequisites before starting the Nexus Sprint Planning? (Choose all that apply) A. No, there are no any additional requirements above the standard Scrum requirements for this case. B. The Product Backlog should be adequately refined. The Product Backlog refined to "Ready" is an essential prerequisite to allow planning to proceed effectively. C. The Dependencies within the Product Backlog items should be identified and removed or minimized. D. All Team members should meet in the same room during Nexus Sprint Planning.	Nexus Sprint Planning is conducted to coordinate the activities of all Scrum Teams for a single Sprint. Note: The following should be done prior to the Nexus Sprint Planning: 1) The Product Backlog should be adequately refined. Having a Product Backlog refined to "Ready" is likely to be an essential prerequisite to allow planning to proceed effectively. 2) The Dependencies within the Product Backlog items should be identified and removed or minimized. During Nexus Sprint Planning: 1) Appropriate Representatives (& not all Team Members) from each Scrum Team meet to review the refined Product Backlog. Each Scrum Team validates and adjusts the ordering of the Backlog items (created during Refinement events). The ordering will help reduce dependencies between Scrum Teams in the Nexus during the Sprint. 2) Product Backlog Items will be then be selected by an appropriate Scrum Team that has the skills required to deliver them with no (or minimal) dependencies on other Scrum Teams. The Scrum Team should have all the cross functional skills required to translate the Product Backlog Item into an integrated Increment by the end of the Sprint. 3) The Nexus Sprint Goal will be formulated in Nexus Sprint Planning. It will describe the purpose that will be achieved by the Nexus during the Sprint. 4) Each Scrum Team then plans its own Sprint. They interact with other teams to share newly found dependencies or update the existing dependencies.

Question 67	**Correct answers: A, B**
When is the Nexus Sprint Planning considered complete? (Choose two) A. After the Nexus Sprint Planning, when all individual Scrum Teams finish their individual Sprint Planning events, the Nexus Sprint Planning is considered complete. B. After the Nexus Sprint Goal is formulated. C. When the Product Backlog is refined with all the dependencies identified and completely removed. D. When the Nexus Sprint Planning event or meeting is over.	Nexus Sprint Planning is complete when each Scrum Team has finished their individual Sprint Planning events. The Nexus Sprint Goal is formulated during Nexus Sprint Planning. The Nexus Sprint Goal is an objective set for the Sprint. It is the sum of all the work and Sprint Goals of the Scrum Teams within the Nexus. The Nexus should demonstrate the functionality that it has "Done" developed to achieve the Nexus Sprint Goal at the Nexus Sprint Review in order to receive stakeholder feedback.

Question 68	Correct answers: A, E
What are the main purposes of Product Backlog Refinement at scale? Select two. A. Forecasting which team will deliver which Product Backlog items. B. Completely documenting all the Product Backlog Items in the Product Backlog. C. Decomposing large Product Backlog items into stories which can be consumed by one Individual in one Sprint. D. Adding new items into the Product Backlog. E. Identifying dependencies across the teams.	Product Backlog Refinement is the act of: 1. Understand and Decomposing the Product Backlog items. 2. Adding detail to the Product Backlog items. 3. Estimating & Ordering the Product Backlog items. Refinement of the Product Backlog serves two purposes. 1) Refinement helps the Scrum Teams forecast which team will deliver which Product Backlog items. 2) Refinement identifies dependencies across those teams. In Scrum, Product Backlog refinement is an ongoing activity for a single team; however, it is not a mandatory event. Due to the added complexity of many teams working together on a single product, Refinement is an official and required event in the Nexus Framework. Teams in a Nexus need to be involved in a shared Refinement event, because Refinement is focused on decomposing Product Backlog Items enough so that the teams can understand which work they could deliver and in what sequence over upcoming Sprints.
Question 69 **What are the responsibilities of the Nexus Integration Team?** A. Ensure that the Product Backlog Items are visible, transparent, and clear to all. B. Maximize the value of the product and the work of the Developers. C. Do the work of delivering a potentially releasable Increment of "Done" product at the end of each Sprint. D. Coordinate, coach, and supervise the application of Nexus and the operation of Scrum so the best outcomes are derived.	Correct answers: D The Nexus Integration Team exists to coordinate, coach, and supervise the application of Nexus and the operation of Scrum so the best outcomes are derived. It is the responsibility of the Product Owner to: A. Ensure that the Product Backlog Items are visible, transparent, and clear to all. B. Maximize the value of the product and the work of the Developers in the Scrum Team.

Question 70	Correct answers: A,B
What is the purpose of the Nexus Sprint Backlog? A. To highlight dependencies and the flow of work during the Sprint. B. To makes all the Scrum Team's (not just the Integration Team) work transparent by exposing the dependencies. C. There is no such a thing as the Nexus Sprint Backlog. D. To manage the work owned by the Nexus Integration Team only. E. To manage the work which only appears because of dependency (where more than one team have to work on it).	The Nexus Sprint Backlog contains the Product Backlog Items being worked on by all of the teams plus the subset of work that identifies dependencies between teams. It also includes the work done by the individuals teams to ensure that the work is delivered and fully integrated. The Nexus Sprint Backlog provides a single view of all the Product Backlog items in a Sprint. The Nexus Sprint Backlog is a compilation of each team's individual Sprint Backlog. The Nexus Sprint Backlog is the composite of Product Backlog items from the Sprint Backlogs of the all individual Scrum Teams. As the Product Backlog items are refined and made ready, indicators of which Scrum team will do the work inside a Sprint are made transparent in the Nexus Sprint Backlog. The Nexus Sprint Backlog makes all the Scrum Team's (not just the Integration Team) work transparent by exposing the dependencies. The Nexus Sprint Backlog is used to highlight dependencies and the flow of work during the Sprint. It focuses on the coordination between teams to ensure the Nexus Sprint Goal is achieved.
Question 71	Correct answers: A
How many Sprint Review / Sprint Reviews should be conducted (or are mandatory) in a nexus environment? A. One Nexus Sprint Review replaces all individual Scrum Team Sprint Reviews. B. One Nexus Sprint Review and one Sprint Review for each Scrum Team. C. There is no such event as the Nexus Sprint Review, but only individual Scrum Team Sprint Reviews, one per team. D. Depends upon the Scrum Master.	A Nexus Sprint Review replaces individual Scrum Team Sprint Reviews, because the entire Integrated Increment is the focus for capturing feedback from stakeholders. It may not be possible to show all completed work done by each team in detail. Techniques may be necessary to maximize stakeholder feedback.

Question 72	**Correct answers: A, B, D**
What are the main questions asked in a Nexus Daily Scrum? Select three. A. What information needs to be shared across teams in the Nexus? B. What new dependencies have been identified? C. What are the results of previous day work for each Scrum Team? D. Was the previous day's work successfully integrated? If not, why not? E. What are the plans for the next day for each Scrum Team? F. What are the impediments of each Scrum Team?	During the Nexus Daily Scrum, attendees should focus on each team's impact on the Integrated Increment and discuss: 1. Was the previous day's work successfully integrated? If not, why not? 2. What new dependencies have been identified? 3. What information needs to be shared across teams in the Nexus?
Question 73	**Correct answers: B, C, D**
What are the purposes of the Nexus Sprint Planning? Select three. A. All Nexus Sprint Backlog items are groomed and estimated in detail. B. Cross team dependencies are detected. C. The Nexus Sprint Goal is formulated. D. The sequence of work across teams is adjusted.	Nexus Sprint Planning is conducted to coordinate the activities of all Scrum Teams for a single Sprint. Note: The following should be done prior to the Nexus Sprint Planning: 1) The Product Backlog should be adequately refined. Having a Product Backlog refined to "Ready" is likely to be an essential prerequisite to allow planning to proceed effectively. 2) The Dependencies within the Product Backlog items should be identified and removed or minimized. During Nexus Sprint Planning: 1) Appropriate Representatives (& not all Team Members) from each Scrum Team meet to review the refined Product Backlog. Each Scrum Team validates and adjusts the ordering of the Backlog items (created during Refinement events). The ordering will help reduce dependencies between Scrum Teams in the Nexus during the Sprint. 2) Product Backlog Items will be then be selected by an appropriate Scrum Team that has the skills required to deliver them with no (or minimal) dependencies on other

	Scrum Teams. The Scrum Team should have all the cross functional skills required to translate the Product Backlog Item into an integrated Increment by the end of the Sprint.
	3) The Nexus Sprint Goal will be formulated in Nexus Sprint Planning. It will describe the purpose that will be achieved by the Nexus during the Sprint.
	4) Each Scrum Team then plans its own Sprint. They interact with other teams to share newly found dependencies or update the existing dependencies.
	The outcomes of a Nexus Sprint Planning meeting are:
	1) A set of Sprint Goals that align with the overarching Nexus Sprint Goal 2) Each Scrum Team's Individual Sprint Backlog. 3) Adjustments to the Nexus Sprint Backlog.
Question 74 **What are the subjects discussed in a Nexus Sprint Retrospective? (Choose all that apply)** A. Was the software successfully built, tested, and deployed often enough? B. Did the Nexus generate technical debt? C. Were all artifacts frequently and successfully integrated? **D.** Was any work left undone?	**Correct answers: A, B, C, D** The Nexus Sprint Retrospective is a formal opportunity to inspect and adapt itself. The Nexus Sprint Retrospective enables the team to create a plan for improvements which would be enacted during the next Sprint to ensure continuous improvement. The Nexus Sprint Retrospective occurs after the Nexus Sprint Review and prior to the next Nexus Sprint Planning. Because they are common scaling dysfunctions, every Retrospective should address the following subjects: • Was any work left undone? Did the Nexus generate technical debt? • Were all artifacts, particularly code, frequently (as often as every day) successfully integrated? • Was the software successfully built, tested, and deployed often enough to prevent the overwhelming accumulation of unresolved dependencies?

Question 75	**Correct answers: C**
Who is responsible for maximizing the value of the product including the integrated work performed by the Scrum Teams (in a Nexus framework)?	The Product Owner is responsible for maximizing the value of the product and the integrated work performed by the Scrum Teams (in a Nexus framework).
A. The Nexus Integration Team. B. Individual Scrum Team. C. Product Owner. D. Scrum Master.	
Question 76	**Correct answers: A**
Who has the overall responsibility for ensuring the Nexus framework is understood and enacted? Select 1 answer. A. The Scrum Master in the Nexus Integration Team. B. The Product Owner. C. The Nexus Specialist Scrum Master. D. Developers in the Nexus Teams.	The Scrum Master is a member of the Nexus Integration Team. A Nexus Integration Team has one Scrum Master. The Scrum Master in the Nexus Integration Team has the overall responsibility for ensuring the Nexus framework is understood and enacted. The Nexus Integration Team is responsible for coaching and guiding the Scrum Teams to acquire, implement, and learn practices and tools that improve their ability to produce a valuable, useful Increment.
Question 77	**Correct answers: B**
All Teams must demo their individual work in the Nexus Sprint Review. A. True B. False	The Objectives of the Nexus Sprint Review are: 1. To review the completed integrated Increment 2. Generate feedback based on new learnings and viewpoints. The Nexus Sprint Review is held at the end of the Sprint. A Nexus Sprint Review replaces individual Scrum Team Sprint Reviews, because the entire Integrated Increment is the focus for capturing feedback from stakeholders. The Nexus Sprint Review is conducted so feedback can be provided by all the stakeholders on the Integrated Increment that has been built over the Sprint. It may not be possible to show all completed work done by each team in detail. Techniques may be necessary to maximize stakeholder feedback.

	Representatives of each of the Scrum Teams attend the Nexus Sprint Review. The Scrum teams within themselves, decide the most appropriate people to attend. This may change over time and vary from one Nexus Sprint Review to another.
	Adjustments may be made to the Product Backlog based on the feedback provided by the Stakeholders. The result of the Nexus Sprint Review is a revised Product Backlog. It may not be possible to show all completed work done by each team in detail.

Question 78
 	
What is the time box for the Nexus Sprint Planning Event?
 	
Select 1 answer.
 	
  A. 8 hours.
  B. 4 hours.
  C. The time box will be guided by the corresponding event in the Scrum Framework. It may be 8 hours for a 1-month Sprint. Inspection and Adaptation will guide the time box for this event.
  D. The time box will be guided by the corresponding event in the Scrum Framework. it must be 8 hours for a 1-month Sprint.
	Correct answers: C
	
	Nexus Sprint Planning time box would be 8 hours for a 1-month Sprint (not mandated). However, in Nexus, Inspection and adaption may lead to this being adjusted over time as required.

Question 79
 	
The members of the Nexus Integration Team should not change (should remain in the same team) over time.
 	
True or False.
 	
  A. True.
  B. False.
	Correct answers: B
	
	The Nexus Integration Team consists of professionals who are skilled in the use of:
	
	1. Tools
	2. Various Practices
	3. The field of Systems Engineering.
	
	Nexus Integration Team Members ensure that:
	1) The Scrum Teams within the Nexus understand and implement the practices and tools needed to detect dependencies.
	2) The Scrum Teams frequently integrate all artifacts to the definition of "Done."

Nexus Integration Team:
• Does not do the Integration work themselves. They guide the Scrum Teams to do it.

• Does not coordinate the day to day work between the Scrum Teams. It is the Scrum Teams responsibility to work with the other Teams to create an integrated Increment.

Nexus Integration Team Members raises Transparency by coaching and guiding the Scrum Teams to acquire, implement, and learn the Nexus practices and needed tools. The Nexus Integration Team will take ownership of integration issues. However, they may not necessarily do the work required to resolve these when they occur. They may work with 1 or more Scrum Teams to help them resolve issues around integration. At other times they may deliver tools and technology to help make integration run more smoothly.

The Nexus Integration Team coaches the individual Scrum Teams on the necessary development, infrastructural, or architectural standards required by the organization to ensure the development of quality Integrated Increments. If the primary responsibility of the Nexus Team Member is satisfied, Nexus Integration Team Members may also work as Developers in one or more Scrum Teams. It is the responsibility of the Scrum Team Members to work with the other teams to make sure that their Sprint work is aligned to create an integrated Increment.

Like any other Team, Nexus Integration Team can also change over time, based on the phase and needs and expertise needed on the Project.

Question 80	Correct answers: A,D,E
The Nexus framework consist of the following accountability / role: Select all that apply. A. Nexus Integration Team. B. Nexus Specialist Scrum Master. C. Nexus Specialist Product Owner. D. Product Owner. E. Scrum Master	The Nexus Integration Team is a new role in Nexus that consists of: • The Product Owner. • A Scrum Master. • Nexus Integration Team Members.
Question 81	**Correct answers: C, D**
Which of the following are mandated by the Nexus framework? Select all that apply. A. Individual Team Sprint Reviews. B. Technical Reviews. C. Nexus Sprint Planning. D. Product Backlog Refinement.	The Following Event are mandatory in Nexus: • Refinement. • Nexus Daily Scrum. • Nexus Sprint Planning. • Nexus Sprint Review. • Nexus Sprint Retrospective.
Question 82	**Correct answers: A**
Nexus Sprint Planning is not complete till the Nexus Sprint Goal and Individual Team's Sprint Goals are complete. A. True B. False	The Nexus Sprint Goal is an objective set for the Sprints across Teams. The Nexus Sprint Goal is discussed and finalized during Nexus Sprint Planning. The Nexus Sprint Goal is then communicated to the rest of the Individual Scrum Teams to reflect the shared purpose of Nexus. Individual Scrum Team Sprint Goals are set during Individual Scrum Team Sprint Planning sessions. (not during the Nexus Sprint Planning). The Nexus Sprint Goal describes the purpose that will be achieved by all the Scrum Teams during the Sprint. Nexus Sprint Goal = Sum of Sprint Goals Across all the Team {In a SPRINT} + the Work done by all the Teams {In a SPRINT}

Question 83	**Correct answers: C**

The time box for the Nexus Daily Scrum is:
Select 1 answer.
    A. 15 minutes for part 1 and 15 minutes for part 2.
    B. 15 minutes.
    C. Guided by the length of the Daily Scrum event from the Scrum framework.
    D. 30 minutes.
	The Nexus Daily Scrum is the scaled version of the Daily Scrum event from the Scrum framework. The Nexus Daily Scrum is an event which:
	
	1) Inspects the current state of the Integrated Increment against the Nexus Sprint Goal.
	2) Is an opportunity to Identifies Integration issues and make them Transparent
	3) Identifies newly discovered cross-team dependencies
	4) Identifies cross-team impacts.
	Appropriate represented Developers from individual Scrum Teams attend the Nexus Daily Scrum. All Developers from all the Scrum Teams are not required to attend the Nexus Daily Scrum. However, they are required to attend their Internal Daily Scrum Call.
	
	At least **every Nexus Daily Scrum**, the **Nexus Sprint Backlog should be inspected (adjusted** if needed) to reflect the current understanding of the work of the Scrum Teams within the Nexus.
	
	The Nexus framework does suggest that the duration of Nexus events be guided by the length of the corresponding events in the Scrum framework. So for the Nexus Daily Scrum the target for the time box would be 15 minutes. However, Inspection and adaption may lead to this being adjusted over time as required.

Question 84	Correct answers: A
The Nexus Sprint Goal once decided is communicated to the rest of the Individual Scrum Teams to reflect the shared purpose of Nexus. All Individuals Sprint goals tie up to / are aligned to / are subsets of the overall Nexus Sprint Goal. A. True B. False	The Nexus Sprint Goal is an objective set for the Sprints across Teams. The Nexus Sprint Goal is discussed and finalized during Nexus Sprint Planning. The Nexus Sprint Goal is then communicated to the rest of the Individual Scrum Teams to reflect the shared purpose of Nexus. Individual Scrum Team Sprint Goals are set during Individual Scrum Team Sprint Planning sessions. (not during the Nexus Sprint Planning). The Nexus Sprint Goal describes the purpose that will be achieved by all the Scrum Teams during the Sprint. Nexus Sprint Goal = Sum of Sprint Goals Across all the Team {In a SPRINT} + the Work done by all the Teams {In a SPRINT}
Question 85 Which of the following are likely to be vital to a successful Nexus Sprint Planning? Select all that apply. A. A Product Backlog refined to "ready" with dependencies reduced/eliminated. B. Effective facilitation of the event by a Scrum Master. C. The presence and active participation of the Product Owner. D. Product Backlog Items with an indication of which team may work on them in the Sprint, by the end of the Sprint Planning.	**Correct answers: A,B,C,D** Be careful in how you read the question. **During Nexus Sprint Planning:** 1) **Appropriate Representatives (& not all Team Members)** from each Scrum Team meet to review the refined Product Backlog. Each Scrum Team validates and adjusts the ordering of the Backlog items (created during Refinement events). The ordering will help reduce dependencies between Scrum Teams in the Nexus during the Sprint. 2) Product Backlog Items will be then be selected by an appropriate Scrum Team that has the skills required to deliver them with no (or minimal) dependencies on other Scrum Teams. The Scrum Team should have all the cross functional skills required to translate the Product Backlog Item into an integrated Increment by the end of the Sprint. 3) The Nexus Sprint Goal will be formulated in Nexus Sprint Planning. It will describe the purpose that will be achieved by the Nexus during the Sprint. 4) Each Scrum Team then plans its own Sprint. They interact with other teams to share newly found dependencies or update the existing dependencies. The following should be done **prior to the Nexus Sprint Planning:**

	1) The Product Backlog should be adequately refined. Having a Product **Backlog refined to "Ready"** with dependencies reduced/eliminated and an indication of which Scrum Team will deliver each Product Backlog Item is likely to be an **essential prerequisite to allow planning to proceed effectively.** 2) The Dependencies within the Product Backlog items should be identified and removed or minimized. Also, the question is not asking what should be done prior to the Nexus Sprint Planning. Effective Facilitation and Presence of the Product Owner will also help lead to a successful Nexus Sprint Planning.

Question 86
 	
How many parts are there to a Nexus Sprint Retrospective?
Select 1 answer.
 	
   A. 1.
   B. 2.
   C. 3.
   D. 4.
	Correct answers: C
	
	The Retrospective consists of three parts:
	
	Part 1: **Nexus Retrospective: Identify issues** that have impacted **more than a single Scrum team**. The purpose is to make shared issues transparent to all Scrum Teams.
	
	Part 2: **Individual Scrum Team Sprint Retrospectives:** Each Scrum Team **holds their own Sprint Retrospective** as described in the Scrum framework. They can **use issues raised from the Nexus Retrospective** as input to their team discussions. The individual Scrum Teams should form actions to address these issues during their individual Scrum Team Sprint Retrospectives.
	
	Part 3: Synchronize: Third part is an **opportunity for appropriate representatives from the Scrum Teams to meet again and agree on how to visualize and track the identified actions**.

Question 87 The time box for Nexus Product Backlog Refinement event should be: Select 1 answer. A. Not mandated. Inspection and adaptation will lead to the Nexus defining its own time box for this event. B. 10% of the Scrum Team's capacity during the Sprint.	**Correct answers: A** The Nexus Product Backlog is suggested to be Timeboxed (not mandated) up to 10% of the capacity of a Scrum Team during a Sprint. However, Inspection and adaption may lead to this being adjusted over time as required.
Question 88 What happens during the Product Backlog Refinement event? Select all that apply. A. The Scrum Teams work together to reduce large batches of work to smaller more manageable units. B. The Scrum Teams explore and understand the Product Backlog Items. C. The Scrum Teams order the Product Backlog Items. D. The Scrum Teams estimate the Product Backlog Items.	**Correct answers: A,B,C,D** Product Backlog Refinement is the act of adding detail, estimates, and order to items in the Product Backlog. Refinement of the Product Backlog serves two purposes. 1) Refinement helps the Scrum Teams forecast which team will deliver which Product Backlog items. 2) Refinement identifies dependencies across those teams.
Question 89 Objectives of the Nexus Daily Scrum include: Select 2 answers. A. Identify cross team dependencies. B. Make the newly discovered integration issues transparent. C. Review progress made with the Product Owner. D. Seek to solve issues challenging an individual Scrum Team.	**Correct answers: A,B** The Nexus Daily Scrum is an event which: 1) Inspects the current state of the integrated increment against the Nexus Sprint Goal. 2) Is an **opportunity to Identify** Integration issues and make them Transparent 3) Identifies newly discovered cross-team dependencies 4) Identifies cross-team impacts.

Question 90
 	
Nexus is the **exoskeleton of Scrum**.
 	
True or False.
 	
    A. True.
    B. False.
	Correct answers: A
	
	Nexus is **based on the Scrum framework** and uses an iterative and incremental approach to scaling software and product development. Nexus **augments (adds to) Scrum** minimally with one new role and some expanded events and artifacts. **It preserves Scrum.**

Question 91
 	
The Nexus Integration Team is responsible for:
 	
Select 1 answer.
 	
    A. Verifying the work done by the Scrum Teams.
    B. Fixing the integration issues found during a Sprint.
    C. Ensuring that an integrated Increment is produced at least every Sprint.
    D. Carrying out integration work where individual Scrum Teams have less capacity to consume it.
	Correct answers: C
	
	The Nexus Integration Team **owns responsibility for the:**
	  • **Integration issues.**
	  • **Integrated Increment which needs to be produced every Sprint.**
	
	Nexus scales the value that a group of Scrum Teams, working on a single Product. Nexus reduces the complexity that those teams encounter as they collaborate to deliver an integrated, valuable, useful product **Increment at least once every Sprint.**

Question 92
 	
Select the statement that is correct about Scaled Professional Scrum and the Product Backlog:
 	
Select 1 answer.
    A. There will be a single Product Backlogs. All Scrum Team will work from this Product Backlog.
    B. There can be multiple Product Backlogs for a Product. Each Scrum Team will work from a Product Backlog that contains the PBI's they need to deliver.
	Correct answers: A
	
	Different Scrum Teams working on the same Product (in Nexus) can:
	  • Have different Sprint Lengths.
	  • Have different Scrum Masters.
	  • Have only one Product Owner.
	  • Have only one Product Backlog.

Question 93	Correct answers: D
The Nexus Sprint Retrospective replaces the need for individual Scrum team Sprint Retrospectives.	The Retrospective consists of three parts:

Question 93

The Nexus Sprint Retrospective replaces the need for individual Scrum team Sprint Retrospectives.

Select 1 answer.

- A. True. A single Nexus level Retrospective is all that is needed in a Nexus environment.
- B. True. Scrum Team level Sprint Retrospectives are optional in a Nexus environment.
- C. False. Individual teams may combine and conduct a shared Sprint Retrospective.
- D. False. Individual Scrum Team Sprint Retrospectives still happen as part of the Nexus Sprint Retrospective.

Correct answers: D

The Retrospective consists of three parts:
Part 1: Nexus Retrospective: Appropriate representatives from each scrum team meet to Identify issues that have impacted more than a single Scrum team. The purpose is to make shared issues transparent to all Scrum Teams.

Part 2: Individual Scrum Team Sprint Retrospectives: Each Scrum Team holds their own Sprint Retrospective as described in the Scrum framework. They can use issues raised from the Nexus Retrospective as input to their team discussions. The individual Scrum Teams should form actions to address these issues during their individual Scrum Team Sprint Retrospectives.

Part 3: Synchronize: Third part is an opportunity for appropriate representatives from the Scrum Teams to meet again and agree on how to visualize and track the identified actions.
The Nexus Retrospective is considered complete only when all the Individual Retrospectives are complete.

Only the Sprint Review for Individual Team is replaced by Nexus Sprint Review. In Part 2 of Nexus Scrum Team Sprint Retrospectives, each Scrum Team holds their own Sprint Retrospective as described in the Scrum framework. They can use issues raised from the Nexus Retrospective (Part 1) as input to their team discussions. The individual Scrum Teams should form actions to address these issues during their individual Scrum Team Sprint Retrospectives.

Even though the Scrum Guide does not prescribe the Retrospective "Parts (Part 1, 2 and 3), the general idea of how a nexus retrospective is conducted and the process remains the same.

Question 94	Correct Answer: B
The Nexus Sprint Backlog provides a **single view** of all the Product Backlog items. A. True B. False	Read the Question Carefully. The Product backlog provides a Single View of all the Product Backlog items. However, the Nexus Sprint Backlog provides a **single view** of all the Product Backlog items **in a Sprint, across all teams.**
Question 95	**Correct Answer: A**
The Nexus Sprint Backlog is a compilation of each team's individual Sprint Backlog, for a given Sprint. A. True B. False	Remember the following: • The Nexus Sprint Backlog provides a **single view** of all the Product Backlog items **in a Sprint.** • The Nexus Sprint Backlog is a **compilation of each team's individual Sprint Backlog.** • The Nexus Sprint Backlog is the composite of Product Backlog items from the Sprint Backlogs of the all individual Scrum Teams.
Question 96	**Correct Answer: B**
The Nexus Sprint Backlog makes the work of only the Nexus Integration Teams transparent by exposing the dependencies. A. True **B. False**	The Nexus Sprint Backlog will be created during Nexus Sprint Planning. This will be a combination of the Sprint Backlogs created by individual Scrum Teams and will additionally highlight cross team dependencies. The Nexus Sprint Backlog contains the Product Backlog Items being worked on by all of the teams plus the subset of work that identifies dependencies between teams. It also includes the work done by the individuals teams to ensure that the work is delivered and fully integrated. As the Product Backlog items are refined and made ready, indicators of which Scrum team will do the work inside a Sprint are made transparent in the Nexus Sprint Backlog. The Nexus Sprint Backlog makes all the Scrum Team's (not just the Integration Team) work transparent by exposing the dependencies.

Question 97 The Nexus Sprint Backlog is updated: A. Daily, often as part of the Nexus Daily Scrum. B. Whenever the Nexus Integration Team meets. C. At Least once, in the Nexus Retrospective. D. At Least once in the Sprint.	**Correct Answer: A** The Nexus Sprint Backlog is **updated Daily**, often as part of the Nexus Daily Scrum.
Question 98 During Refinement, Product Backlog items **are deemed as _____ before the Nexus Sprint Planning meeting.** A. Hardened. B. Independent. C. Ready. D. Groomed.	**Correct Answer: C** During Refinement, Product Backlog items **are deemed as "Ready "before the Nexus Sprint Planning meeting. The Scrum Teams can select and work on these items with no or minimal dependencies** on other Scrum Teams.
Question 99 When do the appropriate Representatives from each Team meet to **identify dependencies?** (Choose all that Apply) A. Nexus Daily Scrum. B. Nexus Refinement. C. Nexus Sprint Planning. D. Nexus Retrospective.	**Correct Answer: A, B, C** Refinement of the Product Backlog serves two purposes. 1) Refinement helps the Scrum Teams forecast which team will deliver which Product Backlog items. 2) Refinement identifies dependencies across those teams. New dependencies can be identified during Sprint Planning as well. As new dependencies emerge during Nexus Sprint Planning: 1) The dependencies should be made transparent on the Nexus Sprint Backlog. 2) The sequence of work across teams may also be adjusted. Remember during Nexus Daily Scrum, appropriate Developer Representatives from each Scrum Team meet daily to identify if any integration issues and not dependencies. If integration issues are identified, this information is transferred back to each Scrum Team's Daily Scrum.

Question 100	Correct Answer: C
Who ensures that the Nexus Integration Team is meeting daily during the Nexus Daily Scrum Meetings and the Nexus Sprint Retrospectives are conducted as well? A. The Product Owner. B. The Nexus Integration Team. C. The Scrum Master in the Nexus Integration Team. D. The Company HR.	The Scrum Master ensures that the Nexus Integration Team is meeting daily during the Nexus Daily Scrum Meetings. He / She will also ensure that all the Nexus Meetings are conducted. (Nexus Refinements, Nexus Retrospectives, Nexus Retrospectives etc).
Question 101	**Correct Answer: A,B**
The objectives of the Nexus Sprint Review are: A. To review the completed integrated Increment. B. Generate feedback based on new learnings and viewpoints. C. Show all the work done by each team to the stakeholders. D. Only Display all the integrated work.	A Nexus Sprint Review replaces individual Scrum Team Sprint Reviews, because the entire Integrated Increment is the focus for capturing feedback from stakeholders. The Nexus Sprint Review is conducted so feedback can be provided by all the stakeholders on the Integrated Increment that has been built over the Sprint. It may not be possible to show all completed work done by each team in detail. Techniques may be necessary to maximize stakeholder feedback. A Nexus Sprint Review helps: 1. To review the completed integrated Increment. 2. Generate feedback based on new learnings and viewpoints." Remember not all the work completed by all the teams would be displayed or demoed in the Sprint Review Sessions.

Question 102	**Correct answers: A**
The Scrum Master ensures that the Developers are meeting daily during the Daily Scrum Meeting. A. True B. False	The Scrum Master ensures that the Developers in the Scrum Team are meeting and teaches the Scrum Team to keep the meetings within the time-box.
Question 103	**Correct answers: B**
Teams should integrate their Increments into the common environment at the very end of a Nexus. True or false? A. True B. False	All teams frequently integrate their work into a common environment that can be tested to ensure that the integration is done.
Question 104	**Correct answers: B**
How many Sprint Backlogs are used in Nexus framework? Select the most applicable answer. A. It depends on the number of Scrum Teams. Usually two-three Scrum Teams share the same Sprint Backlog. B. Each Scrum Team has its own Sprint Backlog. All the items from these backlogs compose the single Nexus Sprint Backlog. C. Single Sprint Backlog.	There is a single Nexus Sprint Backlog. It is the composite of Product Backlog items from the Sprint Backlogs of the individual Scrum Teams. All Scrum Teams maintain their individual Sprint Backlogs.
Question 105	**Correct answers: A**
The Nexus Integration Team **owns responsibility for an Integrated Increment to be produced every Sprint.** A. True B. False	The Nexus Integration Team **owns responsibility for:** • **Integration issues.** • **Integrated Increment every Sprint.**

Question 106	Correct answers: B
Each Scrum Team delivers an increment that gets integrated into one final increment during the stabilization prior to the release. A. True B. False	Scrum Teams should merge their increments at least once during the Sprint. They can do this as many times needed in a Sprint. There is no such "Stabilization Period "defined in a Sprint.

Question 107	Correct answers: C
Which meeting provides a Bottom-up intelligence to improve how teams should work together in Nexus? A. Individual Sprint Sessions. B. Refinement. C. Nexus Sprint Retrospective. D. Nexus Sprint Planning.	The Nexus Sprint Retrospective is a formal opportunity to inspect and adapt itself. Appropriate representatives from across the Scrum Teams meet. The Sprint Retrospective: • Inspects how the last Sprint went with regards to people, relationships, process, and tools. • Identifies the potential improvements.

Question 108	Correct answers: A
Three Scrums Teams are working together. All three teams understand the work which needs to be completed very well. The work needs to be completed quickly. During Sprint Planning the teams realize that they have a large number of dependencies on each other's work. What should the teams do reduce these dependencies? Choose all that Apply. A. Merge the three Scrum Teams. B. Increase Refinement time to increase the clarity on what work needs to be completed. C. Increase / have additional quarterly meetings to nail down all the dependencies. D. All of the Above.	Cautiously, the answer is A. Option B: Increase the refinement time to clarify on what needs to be completed, does not seem to be a bad option, however the team has no issues understanding the work which needs to be completed. They have issues working with the dependencies. So, this option is the wrong answer. Option C is not a bad answer either, however a quarterly meeting is a long gap for biweekly and monthly Sprints and would not help much. The only option left is Option A.

Question 109

A financial Product is very sensitive to code changes. A small change may have huge impacts on the results. Specialized individuals outside the Nexus Teams are called to make such kind of changes. There have been issues in the past dealing with such kind of dependencies. What should one do to minimize such situations or dependencies?

A. Make sure that the outside experts are available during Sprint Planning and have a quick way to communicate with them, physically or virtually.

B. Make sure that the representatives in the Nexus integration assign the work to the Scrum Team so they can schedule and align such dependencies.

C. All of the above.

D. None of the above.

Correct answers: C

Nexus Sprint Planning is conducted **to coordinate the activities of all Scrum Teams** for a **single Sprint. Note:** The following should be done **prior to the Nexus Sprint Planning:**

1) The Product Backlog should be adequately refined. Having a Product **Backlog refined to "Ready"** is likely to be an **essential prerequisite to allow planning to proceed effectively.**

2) The Dependencies within the Product Backlog items should be identified and removed or minimized.

During Nexus Sprint Planning:

1) **Appropriate Representatives (& not all Team Members)** from each Scrum Team meet to review the refined Product Backlog. Each Scrum Team further validates and adjusts the ordering of the Backlog items (created during Refinement events). The ordering will help reduce dependencies between Scrum Teams in the Nexus during the Sprint.

2) **The Team will be working a single Nexus Sprint Backlog** that represents the work of the Nexus toward the Nexus Sprint **Goal. The Nexus Sprint Goal will be formulated in Nexus Sprint Planning**. It will describe the purpose that will be achieved by the Nexus during the Sprint.

3) Product Backlog Items will be then be selected by an appropriate Scrum Team **(in their individual Sprint Backlogs)** that has the skills required to deliver them with no (or minimal) dependencies on other Scrum Teams. The Scrum Team should have all the cross functional skills required to translate the Product Backlog Item into an integrated Increment by the end of the Sprint.

4) Each Scrum Team then plans its own Sprint (**Individual Teams Sprint Planning event**), **Sprint Goal which will align to the Nexus Sprint Goal**. They interact with other teams to share newly found dependencies or update the existing dependencies.

Question 110
 	
What impacts the number, frequency, duration and attendance of Nexus Refinement meetings, the most?
 	
   A. Number of items in the Product Backlog.
   B. Clarity of items in the Product Backlog.
   C. Dependencies and uncertainty inherent in the Product Backlog.
   D. How well large items in the Product Backlog are decomposed into smaller ones.
	Correct answers: C
	
	In Scrum, Product Backlog refinement is an ongoing activity for a single team; however, it is not a mandatory event. Due to the added complexity of many teams working together on a single product, Refinement is an official and required event in the Nexus Framework.
	
	Teams in a Nexus need to be involved in a shared Refinement event, because Refinement is focused on decomposing Product Backlog Items enough so that the teams can understand which work they could deliver and in what sequence over upcoming Sprints.
	
	Refinement of Product Backlog Items by the Nexus continues until the Product Backlog Items are sufficiently independent (actionable work) to be worked on by a single Scrum Team without excessive conflict.
	
	The number, frequency, duration and attendance of Refinement is based on the dependencies and uncertainty inherent in the Product Backlog.

Question 111
 	
When is the Scrum Team who may be responsible for implementing a piece of functionality, usually identified?
 	
   A. During Product Backlog Refinement.
   B. At the Nexus Retrospective meeting.
   C. At the Nexus Daily Scrum meeting.
   D. At the Nexus Sprint Planning meeting.
	Correct answers: A
	
	In the process of Product Backlog Refinement items are refined into thinly sliced pieces of functionality and the team likely to do the work is usually identified. Refinement of the Product Backlog at scale serves a dual purpose. It helps the Scrum Teams forecast which team will deliver which Product Backlog items, and it identifies dependencies across those teams.

Question 112
Which factors Impact the Sprint Length?
(Choose all that Apply)
 	
   A. Risk of being disconnected from the Stakeholders
   B. Level of uncertainty over the technology used and velocity
   C. Market Competition & Time to release.
   D. Product Owners Vision of a Release.
   E. Total Cost of the Product.
	Correct answers: A,B,C
	
	Factors Impacting the Sprint Length:
	  • Risk of **being disconnected from the Stakeholders**
	  • **Level of uncertainty over the technology** used and velocity
	  • **Market Competition & Time to release.**

Question 113	**Correct answers: A**

Product Backlog Refinement is a mandatory part of the Nexus framework?
 	
True or False.
 	
   A.   True.
   B.   False.
	In Scrum, Product Backlog refinement is an ongoing activity for a single team; however, it is not a mandatory event. Due to the added complexity of many teams working together on a single product, **Refinement is an official and required event in the Nexus Framework.** Teams in a Nexus need to be involved in a shared Refinement event, because Refinement is focused on decomposing Product Backlog Items enough so that the teams can understand which work they could deliver and in what sequence over upcoming Sprints.

Question 114
 	
The Nexus Sprint Backlog will be created during:
 	
   A.   Nexus Sprint Planning.
   B.   Nexus Daily Sprints.
   C.   Daily Sprints.
   D.   Sprint Retrospectives.
	Correct answers: A
	
	The Nexus Sprint Backlog will be created during Nexus Sprint Planning. This will be a combination of the Sprint Backlogs created by individual Scrum Teams and will additionally highlight cross team dependencies.

Question 115	Correct answers: A.B,C,D
Which of the following statements are true about a Nexus Sprint Backlog? (Choose all that apply) A. The Nexus Sprint Backlog will be created during Nexus Sprint Planning. B. The Nexus Sprint Backlog contains the Product Backlog Items being worked on by all of the teams plus the subset of work that identifies dependencies between teams. It also includes the work done by the individual teams to ensure that the work is delivered and fully integrated. C. The primary owner of the Nexus Sprint Backlog is the Nexus Integration Team. D. The members of the Nexus Integration Team are responsible for and accountable for ensuring that the cross-team work items added to the Nexus Sprint Backlog are complete.	The Nexus Sprint Backlog will be created during Nexus Sprint Planning. This will be a combination of the Sprint Backlogs created by individual Scrum Teams and will additionally highlight cross team dependencies. The Nexus Sprint Backlog contains the Product Backlog Items being worked on by all of the teams plus the subset of work that identifies dependencies between teams. It also includes the work done by the individual teams to ensure that the work is delivered and fully integrated. The primary owner is the Nexus Integration Team. If any one on any of the Scrum teams identifies new work that would extend across two or more teams in the Nexus, they would be able to add it to the Nexus Sprint Backlog through the team's representative on the Nexus Integration Team. The members of the Nexus Integration Team "are often members of the individual Scrum Teams in the Nexus" and that their membership in the Nexus Integration Team "takes precedence over individual Scrum Team membership". That would mean that the members of the Nexus Integration Team are responsible for and accountable for ensuring that the cross-team work items added to the Nexus Sprint Backlog are complete.

Question 116	Correct answers: A.B,C,D,E
Which of the following are true statements about the Nexus Sprint Goal? A. The Nexus Sprint Goal is an objective set for the Sprints across Teams. B. The Nexus Sprint Goal is discussed and finalized during Nexus Sprint Planning. The Nexus Sprint Goal is then communicated to the rest of the Individual Scrum Teams to reflect the shared purpose of Nexus. C. Individual Scrum Team Sprint Goals are set during Individual Scrum Team Sprint Planning sessions. (not during the Nexus Sprint Planning). D. The Nexus Sprint Goal describes the purpose that will be achieved by all the Scrum Teams during the Sprint. E. Nexus Sprint Goal = Sum of Sprint Goals Across all the Team {In a SPRINT} + the Work done by all the Teams {In a SPRINT}	The Nexus Sprint Goal is an objective set for the Sprints across Teams. The Nexus Sprint Goal is discussed and finalized during Nexus Sprint Planning. The Nexus Sprint Goal is then communicated to the rest of the Individual Scrum Teams to reflect the shared purpose of Nexus. Individual Scrum Team Sprint Goals are set during Individual Scrum Team Sprint Planning sessions. (not during the Nexus Sprint Planning). The Nexus Sprint Goal describes the purpose that will be achieved by all the Scrum Teams during the Sprint. Nexus Sprint Goal = Sum of Sprint Goals Across all the Team {In a SPRINT} + the Work done by all the Teams {In a SPRINT}
Question 117 Which of the following statements are true? A. Nexus Integration Team Members ensure that the Scrum Teams within the Nexus understand and implement the practices and tools needed to detect dependencies. B. Nexus Integration Team Members ensure that the Scrum Teams frequently integrate all artifacts to the definition of "Done." C. Nexus Integration Team does do all the Integration work themselves. D. Nexus Integration coordinates the day to day work between the Scrum Teams.	Correct answers: A,B Nexus Integration Team Members ensure that the Scrum Teams within the Nexus understand and implement the practices and tools needed to detect dependencies. Nexus Integration Team Members ensure that the Scrum Teams frequently integrate all artifacts to the definition of "Done." Nexus Integration Team does not do the Integration work themselves. They guide the Scrum Teams to do it. Nexus Integration Team does not coordinate the day to day work between the Scrum Teams. It is the Scrum Teams responsibility to work with the other Teams to create an integrated Increment.

Question 118	Correct answers: A, C, D
Which of the following statements are true? A. Nexus Integration Team Members Raises Transparency by coaching and guiding the Scrum Teams to acquire, implement, and learn the Nexus practices and needed tools. B. The Nexus Integration Team will take ownership of the integration issues. They typically resolve the issues themselves. C. The Nexus Integration Team coaches the individual Scrum Teams on the necessary development, infrastructural, or architectural standards required by the organization to ensure the development of quality Integrated Increments. D. If the primary responsibility of the Nexus Team Member is satisfied, Nexus Integration Team Members may also work as Developers in one or more Scrum Teams.	Nexus Integration Team Members Raises Transparency by coaching and guiding the Scrum Teams to acquire, implement, and learn the Nexus practices and needed tools. The Nexus Integration Team will take ownership of integration issues. However, they may not necessarily do the work required to resolve these when they occur. They may work with 1 or more Scrum Teams to help them resolve issues around integration. At other times they may deliver tools and technology to help make integration run more smoothly. The Nexus Integration Team coaches the individual Scrum Teams on the necessary development, infrastructural, or architectural standards required by the organization to ensure the development of quality Integrated Increments. If the primary responsibility of the Nexus Team Member is satisfied, Nexus Integration Team Members may also work as Developers in one or more Scrum Teams. It is the responsibility of the Scrum Team Members to work with the other teams to make sure that their Sprint work is aligned to create an integrated Increment.
Question 119 The Nexus Scrum Master may also be a Scrum Master in one or more of the Scrum Teams. A. True B. False	Correct answers: A The **Nexus Scrum Master may also be a Scrum Master in one or more of the Scrum Teams**.

Question 120	**Correct answers: A,B,C,D**
Individual Team increments should be integrated every Sprint. What would happen If increments are not integrated every Sprint? (Choose all that apply) A. The state of the product becomes unclear (due to undiscovered problems that could arise during integration and complete product increment tests) B. The Product Owner would not know whether the increment he/she was presented is potential shippable. C. It would lead to incorrect or flawed decisions. D. It would lead to last minute integration issues and consume lots of time to integrate huge pieces of code which is not integrated frequently.	Individual Team increments should be integrated every Sprint. If increments are not integrated every Sprint then, · The state of the product becomes unclear (due to undiscovered problems that could arise during integration and complete product increment tests) · The Product Owner would not know whether the increment he/she was presented is potential shippable It would not be transparent to the organization what the next reasonable steps would be.
Question 121 Nexus is a framework that binds together the work done by approximately: (Select 2 best answers) A. Three to Nine Scrum Teams. B. Two to Ten Scrum Teams. C. Not more than 4 Scrum Teams. D. Not more than 8 Scrum Teams.	**Correct answer: A,B** Nexus is a framework which consist of roles, events, artifacts, and rules that bind together the work of approximately **three to nine Scrum Teams** working on a **single Product Backlog** to build an Integrated Increment that meets a goal. Remember it says **approximately** three to nine teams. Its only an approximation and recommendation.
Question 122 The Nexus Integration Team only deals with technical cross-functional team constraints that may impede a Nexus' ability to deliver a constantly Integrated Increment. Non-Technical cross-functional issues are managed only by the Product Owner. A. True B. False	**Correct Answer: B** The Nexus Integration Team provides a focal point of integration for the Nexus. Integration includes addressing technical and non-technical cross-functional team constraints that may impede a Nexus' ability to deliver a constantly Integrated Increment.

Question 123
 	
Implementing Nexus will automatically fix the process, product structure, and communication structure to reduce or remove the dependencies which exist between the teams.
 	
   A. True
   B. False
	Correct answer: B
	
	Nexus provides opportunities to change the process, product structure, and communication structure to reduce or remove these dependencies.

Question 124
 	
Scaling the value of the product (that is delivered) can be achieved by:
 	
   A. Increasing the number of people working on the Product.
   B. Reducing the number of people working on the Product.
	Correct answer: B
	
	Scaling the value that is delivered does not always require adding more people. Increasing the number of people and the size of a product increases complexity and dependencies, the need for collaboration, and the number of communication pathways involved in making decisions. Scaling-down, reducing the number of people who work on something, can be an important practice in delivering more value.
	.

Question 125
 	
Who provides a focal point of integration for the Nexus?
 	
   A. The Product Owner.
   B. The Nexus Integration Team.
   C. The Scrum Master in the Nexus Integration Team.
   D. The Company HR.
	Correct Answer: B
	
	The Nexus Integration Team provides a focal point of integration for the Nexus. Integration includes addressing technical and non-technical cross-functional team constraints that may impede a Nexus' ability to deliver a constantly Integrated Increment.

Question 126
 	
What kind of intelligence does the Nexus Integration Team should use from within the Nexus to achieve resolutions?
   A. Bottom Up – The Nexus Integration Team Talks to all the Teams (or representatives) during the Nexus Meetings and makes decisions based on the collected information.
   B. Top – Down – The Nexus Integration Team makes decisions during the Nexus Meetings and propagates the information to all the Scrum Teams.
	Correct Answer: A
	
	The Nexus Integration Team should use bottom-up intelligence from within the Nexus to achieve resolution.

Question 127	Correct Answer: A
Which of the following Statement is True? **A.** Membership in the Nexus Integration Team takes precedence over individual Scrum Team membership. As long as their Nexus Integration Team responsibility is satisfied, they can work as team members of their respective Scrum Teams. **B.** Membership in individual Scrum Team takes precedence over Nexus Integration Team membership. As long as Scrum Team members are able to finish their work, they can help integrate the product by working in the Nexus Integration Scrum Team. **C.** Individual Scrum Team members cannot work in Nexus Integration Teams. **D.** Team Members should be able to balance the work on their plate by self-organizing and self-managing. Precedence of one work over another is not required in Scrum.	Membership in the Nexus Integration Team takes precedence over individual Scrum Team membership. As long as their Nexus Integration Team responsibility is satisfied, they can work as team members of their respective Scrum Teams. This preference helps ensure that the work to resolve issues affecting multiple teams has priority.
Question 128	**Correct Answer: A,B,C,D**
Which of the following are results of the Nexus Sprint Planning discussion and meetings? (Choose all that apply) **A.** A Nexus Sprint Goal that aligns with the Product Goal. **B.** A Sprint Goal for each Scrum Team that aligns with the Nexus Sprint Goal. **C.** A single Nexus Sprint Backlog. **D.** A Sprint Backlog for each Scrum Team.	The result of Nexus Sprint Planning is: • A Nexus Sprint Goal that aligns with the Product Goal and describes the purpose that will be achieved by the Nexus during the Sprint. • A Sprint Goal for each Scrum Team that aligns with the Nexus Sprint Goal. • A single Nexus Sprint Backlog that represents the work of the Nexus toward the Nexus Sprint Goal and makes cross-team dependencies transparent. • A Sprint Backlog for each Scrum Team, which makes transparent the work they will do in support of the Nexus Sprint Goal.

Question 129	Correct Answer: A
Each Scrum Team's Daily Scrum complements the Nexus Daily Scrum by : A. Creating plans for the day, focused primarily on addressing the integration issues raised during the Nexus Daily Scrum. B. Creating their own version of a stringent Nexus Sprint Goal.	Each Scrum Team's Daily Scrum complements the Nexus Daily Scrum by creating plans for the day, focused primarily on addressing the integration issues raised during the Nexus Daily Scrum.
Question 130 At least every Nexus Daily Scrum, the Nexus Sprint Backlog should be inspected (and adjusted if needed) to reflect the current understanding of the work of the Scrum Teams within the Nexus. A. True B. False	**Correct Answer: A** At least **every Nexus Daily Scrum**, the **Nexus Sprint Backlog should be inspected (adjusted** if needed) to reflect the current understanding of the work of the Scrum Teams within the Nexus. Remember: The Nexus Daily Scrum is not the only time Scrum Teams in the Nexus are allowed to adjust their plan. Cross-team communication can occur throughout the day for more detailed discussions about adapting or re-planning the rest of the Sprint's work.

Question 131	Correct Answer: B, C, D, E
Which of the following statements are true? A. The Nexus Sprint Review is held in the beginning of the Sprint to provide feedback on the done Integrated Increment that the Nexus has built over the Sprint and determine future adaptations. B. A Nexus Sprint Review replaces individual Scrum Team Sprint Reviews. C. During Nexus Sprint Review event, the Nexus team presents the results of their work to key stakeholders. D. During Nexus Sprint Review event, progress toward the Product Goal is discussed. E. During Nexus Sprint Review Event, the Product Backlog may be adjusted to reflect these discussions.	The Nexus Sprint Review is held at the end of the Sprint to provide feedback on the done Integrated Increment that the Nexus has built over the Sprint and determine future adaptations. Since the entire Integrated Increment is the focus for capturing feedback from stakeholders, a Nexus Sprint Review replaces individual Scrum Team Sprint Reviews. During the event, the Nexus presents the results of their work to key stakeholders and progress toward the Product Goal is discussed, although it may not be possible to show all completed work in detail. Based on this information, attendees collaborate on what the Nexus should do to address the feedback. The Product Backlog may be adjusted to reflect these discussions.
Question 132	Correct Answer: E
Which Event in Nexus allows to plan ways to increase process quality and effectiveness across the whole Nexus? A. Nexus Sprint Planning. B. Nexus Daily Sprints. C. Daily Sprints. D. Sprint Retrospectives. E. Nexus Sprint Retrospective.	The purpose of the Nexus Sprint Retrospective is to plan ways to increase quality and effectiveness across the whole Nexus. The Nexus inspects how the last Sprint went with regards to individuals, teams, interactions, processes, tools, and its Definition of Done. In addition to individual team improvements, the Scrum Teams' Sprint Retrospectives complement the Nexus Sprint Retrospective by using bottom-up intelligence to focus on issues that affect the Nexus as a whole.

CHAPTER 3: Scrum Developer Basics

This chapter is designed to help you take a learn / revise / take a second look at a broader set of Development concepts. Its contents explains concepts like Continuous Integration and Test Automation

1. Go through the **Scrum Developer Reference Table** mention in this book. Go through the questions and answers mentioned in the Book. These questions are compiled very carefully. Go through the answers and make sure you understand the concepts.
2. **Do the Developer Open assessment (https://www.scrum.org/open-assessments) until you score close to 100% 3 times in a row.**

Scrum Developer (PSD) Reference Table

Important

Testing	Software testing is an **investigation conducted** to provide stakeholders with information about the **quality of the software product or service under test.**
	Test techniques include the process of executing programs or applications **with the intent of finding software bugs (errors or other defects) and verifying that the software products are fit for use.**
	Software testing involves the execution of a software component or system component to evaluate one or more properties of interest. In general, these properties indicate the extent to which the component or system under test: 1. Meets the requirements that guided its design and development. 2. Responds correctly to all kinds of inputs. 3. Performs its functions within an acceptable time. 4. Is sufficiently usable. 5. Can be installed and run in its intended environments, and 6. Achieves the general result its stakeholders desire.
Unit Testing	**Unit Test: A Unit test** is a way of testing a unit (**the smallest piece of code**) that can be logically isolated in a system.
	Unit testing, also known as component testing, is a level of software testing where individual units / components of a software are tested. The purpose is to validate that each unit of the software performs as designed.
	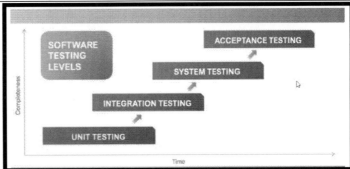
	In most programming languages, a **"Unit" is a function, a subroutine, a method or property.**
	A Unit test can be automated.
	Unit Test is a test that **Isolates and Verifies** Individual units of source code.

Quick Reference Guide & Exam Questions
Professional Scrum Master II (PSM II)

	Characteristics of a unit test are: A. Unit test **executes fast.** B. Code in each Unit test is **as small as possible**. Unit test help maintaining **readability** of the code. C. Each Unit test is **independent** of other unit tests. D. Each Unit test makes assertions about only **one logical concept.**
Regression Testing ⓘ	**Regression Test**: Whenever developers change or modify their software, a small tweak can have unexpected consequences. **Regression testing is testing existing software applications to make sure that a code change or addition hasn't broken any existing functionality.**
	The **purpose of Regression Test is to catch bugs that may have been accidentally introduced** into a new build or release candidate. **Its purpose is to ensure that previously eradicated bugs continue to stay dead.**
	During Regression Test, by re-running testing scenarios that were originally scripted when known problems were first fixed, one can make sure that any new changes to an application **haven't resulted in a regression or caused components that formerly worked to fail.**
	As software is updated or changed, emergence of new faults and/or re-emergence of old faults is quite common. Sometimes re-emergence occurs because a fix gets lost through poor revision control practices (or simple human error in revision control). Therefore, it is considered good coding practice, to record a test that exposes the bug and re-run that test regularly after subsequent changes to the program. Thus regression test suites tend to grow with each found defect, test automation is frequently involved.
	A Regression test can be automated.
Functional Testing	**Functional Test** is a form of testing that deals with **how applications functions**.
	Functional testing is traditionally implemented by a team of testers, **independent of the developers.**
	Functional testing is a type of black-box testing that bases its test cases on the specifications of the software component under test. Functions are tested by feeding them input and examining the output, and internal program structure is rarely considered (unlike white-box).
	Functional tests **can be automated.**
Integration Testing ⓘ	**Integration Test**: Integration testing, also known as Integration and Testing (I&T), is a type of testing in which **program units are combined and tested as groups. Testing is done in multiple ways.**
	Integration testing is performed **on the modules that are unit tested first** and then integration testing defines whether the combination of the modules give the desired output or not.
	Integration test is a **test of multiple units of functionality.**
	Integration test **can be automated.**

Exploratory Testing	**Exploratory Test**: Exploratory testing is all about discovery, investigation, and learning. **It emphasizes on personal freedom and responsibility** of the individual tester. It is defined as a type of testing **where Test cases are not created in advance**, but **testers check system on the fly.** They may note down ideas about what to test before test execution. The focus of exploratory testing is more on testing as a "thinking" activity.
	Exploratory test cannot be automated.
Smoke Testing	**Smoke Testing:** Smoke testing, also known as **"Build Verification Testing",** is a type of software testing **that comprises of a non-exhaustive set of tests** that aim at ensuring that the most important functions work.
	The result of Smoke testing is **used to decide if a build is stable enough to proceed with further testing.**
Black Box Testing	**Black Box Testing:** Black Box testing (also known **as Behavioral Testing)** is a software testing method in which the **internal structure/design/implementation of the item being tested is not known to the tester.**
	Black Box Testing, either functional or non-functional, is a testing **which has no reference to the internal structure of the component or system.**
	Black Box Testing Example: A tester, without knowledge of the internal structures of a website, would tests the web pages by using a browser; providing inputs (clicks, keystrokes) and verifying the outputs against the expected outcome.
White Box Testing	**White Box Testing**: White Box testing, also known as Clear Box Testing, Open Box Testing, Glass Box Testing, Transparent Box Testing, Code-Based Testing or Structural Testing.
	White Box Testing is a software testing method in which **the internal structure/design/implementation of the item being tested is known to the tester.**
Performance Testing ⓘ	Performance Testing is defined as a type of software testing to ensure software applications will perform well under their expected workload. Features and Functionality supported by a software system is not the only concern. A software application's performance like its response time, reliability, resource usage and scalability do matter. The goal of Performance Testing is not to find bugs but to eliminate performance bottlenecks. The focus of Performance Testing is checking a software program's • Speed - Determines whether the application responds quickly • Scalability - Determines maximum user load the software application can handle. • Stability - Determines if the application is stable under varying loads
	In Scrum performance **testing at the beginning of the development process and continue with it along with the whole evolution of the application.**

Code Coverage	Code Coverage is a measure which describes the degree to which the source code of the program has been tested.
	Code Coverage is a form of **white box testing** which shows the areas of the program **exercised by a set of test cases.**
	Measuring Code Coverage can help increase software quality **by identifying untested parts of codes in a product / application.**
	Code Coverage **is NOT a** metric of code quality.
	Code Coverage shows the **ratio between the tested and untested code.**
	Code Coverage **does not tell you anything** about the quality of the tests being run.
	Some Advantages of Code Coverage are: • It offers a **Quantitative Measurement**. • It defines the degree to which the source code has been tested.
	Some shortcomings of Code Coverage as a measurement are: • Code Coverage **does not ensure that the most important or highest risk areas of the code are being exercised by tests.** • Code Coverage does not necessarily **provide functional coverage.** • Code Coverage could create incentives to write tests that simply increase code coverage, **rather than tests that find bugs without increasing coverage.**
	Note: 1) There are always parts of code that are hard to test (e.g. I/O, multi-threaded and network code) and the benefits of testing them might not always worth the costs. 2) Writing unit tests for every new feature or change (preferably before writing production code, by practicing Test Driven Development) helps achieve Code Coverage automatically.

Types of Code Coverage - Statement Coverage	**Statement Coverage:** Statement Coverage is a white box test design technique which involves execution of all the statements (executable) in the source code, at least once. In any software, the source code is made up of a wide variety of elements like operators, functions, loops, exceptional handlers, etc. The goal of Statement Coverage is to cover all the possible path's, line, and statement in the code. $$Statement\ Coverage = \frac{Number\ of\ executed\ statements}{Total\ number\ of\ statements}\ x\ 100$$ What is covered by Statement Coverage Code Coverage? • Unused Statements • Dead Code • Unused Branches
Types of Code Coverage - Decision Coverage	**Decision Coverage:** Decision Coverage is a white box test design technique which reports the true or false outcomes of all the Boolean expressions, present in a code. $$Decision\ Coverage = \frac{Number\ of\ Decision\ Outcomes\ Excercised}{Total\ Number\ of\ Decision\ Outcomes}$$
Types of Code Coverage - Branch Coverage	**Branch Coverage:** In Branch Coverage, every **possible outcome** from a code module is tested. For example, if the outcomes are Pay a Car Claim VS Deny a Car Claim, both Paying, and Denying a Car Claim are tested. By using Branch coverage method, one can also measure the fraction of independent code segments. It also helps you to find out which is sections of code don't have any branches. $$Branch\ Coverage = \frac{Number\ of\ Executed\ Branches}{Total\ Number\ of\ Branches}$$

Types of Code Coverage - Condition Coverage	**Condition Coverage** Conditional coverage or expression coverage will reveal how the variables or subexpressions **in the conditional statement are evaluated**. In this coverage expressions with **logical operands** are only considered. Example: An expression with a Boolean operation like AND, OR, XOR indicate the total number of possibilities. $$Condition\ Coverage = \frac{Number\ of\ Executed\ Operands}{Total\ Number\ of\ Operands}$$
	Note: Remembering different types of Code Coverage is not required for the PSD Exam.

Test Driven Development (TDD) **Test First Development** 	**Test First Development is** also known as Test Driven Development (TDD). Test Driven Development is a development style in which **one writes the unit tests before writing the code**.
	Test Driven Development is a Predictable, Incremental and Emergent Software development approach / technique which relies **on Automated Test.**
	"Test-Driven Development" **refers to a style of programming in which three activities are tightly interwoven: Writing Test, Coding and Refactoring.** Example: Test Driven Development for a feature / aspect of a program can be concisely described by the following: • Write a **"Single" Unit Test describing** an aspect of the program. • **Run the test, which should fail** because the program **lacks** that feature. • **Write "just enough" code** to make the test pass. • "Refactor" the code until it conforms to the **Simplicity Criteria.** • Repeat, "Accumulating" unit tests over time. 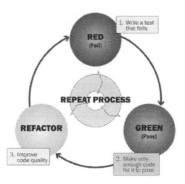
	A test written with Test-Driven Development **represents a technical requirement** that must be satisfied.
	Test-Driven Development is easier to implement in in applications designed to unit test.
	Benefits of Test-Driven Development: • It promotes good design and separation of concerns. • It improves quality and reduces bugs. • It leads to the construct of an automated test harness. • It speeds the **overall development process.** • IT reduces cost of maintenance over time.
	Note: Test Driven Development **does not test the existing test cases / software** before developing new functionality. It only tests the test cases written for the new functionality which needs to be developed.

Acceptance Test Driven Development (ATDD)	Acceptance Test Driven Development is a Test-First software development practice in which **acceptance criterias for new functionality are created before the implementation actually begins.** These acceptance tests are supported by examples and other necessary information.
	Acceptance Test Driven development is the **practice of expressing requirements as acceptance tests.**
	Acceptance Test Driven Development (ATDD) involves team members with different perspectives (customer, development, testing) collaborating to write acceptance criteria **in advance of implementing the corresponding functionality.**

ATDD can be broken down in four stages:

Discuss: In this stage of an ATDD cycle, the agile team along with the business stake holders gets into a discussion. The team develops a detailed understanding of the behavior of the system from the user point of view in the discussion. And on the basis of the understanding, the agile team creates acceptance tests that can be executed either automatically or programmatically.

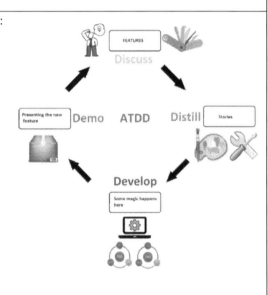

Distill: In this stage of an ATDD cycle, the agile tries to implements the acceptance tests in an automatic testing framework. In this stage the team ensures that the tests are not just remain specifications but can be actually executed in the project.

Develop: During this stage, the agile team follows a Test First Development TFD approach, i.e. they will first execute the tests, make sure what are making them fail and then proceed to write the code that will make the tests pass.

Demo: In this stage of ATDD cycle, the agile team provides a demo to the business stake holders. In the demo, they can also indicate the tests they have run and the vulnerabilities they have been identified through the tests.

Test case creation is moved to the beginning of the cycle thus reducing defects and bug fixing effort as project progresses.

	Advanced practices of test-driven development can lead to Acceptance Test-driven development (ATDD) where the criteria specified by the customer are **automated into acceptance tests. This** then drive the traditional unit test-driven development (UTDD) process.
Behavior Driven Development (BDD) (!)	Behavior Driven Development is a variation / extension of Test-Driven Development methodology, where the main **focus is on:** 1) **Behavioral specifications of the product or application (or its features).** 2) **User and System Interactions**
	When Behavior Driven Development is adapted in a project, the technical nitty-gritty **aspects of the requirements and implementation are outlined in a business-oriented language.**
	Behavior Driven Development uses Ubiquitous language that can be understood by the developers and stakeholders.
Specifications by Example (!)	Specification by example (SBE) is a **collaborative approach to defining requirements and business-oriented functional tests for software products, based on realistic examples instead of abstract statements.**
	Specification by Example is an agile software development practice based on Test Driven Development and Acceptance Test Driven Development.
	Specification by Example calls for using **realistic examples from past experience** instead of untested or abstract statements in the description of the desired functional behavior.

Differences between ATDD, TDD and BDD (!)

- Test Driven Development (TDD) is technical in nature and is written in the same language the feature is implemented in. If the feature is implemented in Java, JUnit test cases are written. Whereas Behavior Driven Development (BDD) & Acceptance Test Driven Development (ATDD) are written in simple English language
- The Test-Driven Development (TDD) approach focuses on the implementation of a feature. Behavior Driven Development (BDD) focuses on the behavior of the feature, and Acceptance Test Driven Development (ATDD) focuses on capturing the requirements (in form of acceptance criterias).
- To implement TDD, one needs to have technical knowledge. Whereas Behavior Driven Development (BDD) & Acceptance Test Driven Development (ATDD) do not require any technical knowledge. The beauty of Behavior Driven Development (BDD) / Acceptance Test Driven Development (ATDD) lies in the fact that both technical, as well as non-technical people, can participate in developing the feature.
- TDD, BDD and ATDD basically talk about the "test-First" approach, unlike the "test-last" approach used in traditional development methodologies.

Approaches / Comparison Parameters	ATDD	TDD	BDD
Users Involved and Scope	Communication mechanism between Business Users, Developers, Testers to ensure requirements are well documented.	Mechanism between Developers and Testers to create well written unit of code (module, class, function)	Communication mechanism between Product Owners, Developers and Testers to collaborate and understand the requirement.
Focus	Focus is on capturing requirements as an acceptance criterion which then drives the development. Customer gets involved in design phase.	"Test-Driven Development" refers to a style of programming in which three activities are tightly interwoven: Writing Test, Coding and Refactoring.	Focus is on behavioral aspect of system for Customer and Developer. The practice of writing tests before development still implies.
Input documentation	Acceptance Criteria + Examples (data and scenarios) = Acceptance Test	Requirement documentation will be base for development and testing.	Specification document (describing the expected behavior) in native language (Plain English)
Automation Required	Doesn't require automation but needed for regression purposes.	Yes. Must have.	Yes. Must have.
Story / Feature: Test Mapping	Each story should have acceptance test	Each functionality should have implementation of a unit test.	Each story should have implementation of a behavior test.
Tools in the market	Robot Framework, FitNesse FIT	Junit, TestNG, NUnit frameworks, Selenium tool (any open source tools)	MSpec, Specflow – used to define the behavior. Cucumber with Selenium / Serenity

Spike	A Spike is a story or task aimed at **answering a question or gathering information, rather than producing a shippable product.** In practice, the spikes which teams take on, are often **proof-of-concept** activities. By definition the work done for a spike **is not focused on the finished product.** A Spike may even be designed to be thrown away at the end.

	Two characteristics that spikes should have are:
	
	   A. **Clear objectives and outcomes**: Before implementing the Spike, the developer should be clear on the knowledge he / she is trying to gain and the problem(s) he / she is trying to address. It's easy for a team to stray off into something interesting and related, but not relevant.
	   B. **Timeboxed:** Spikes should be timeboxed, so one just works enough to get the value required.

	In Agile software development, the Architecture evolves to meet the needs of the Product Backlog Items (PBI's) forecasted in the given Sprint. It's lean. Developing business software does not necessarily **require all of the architecture defined upfront.** **Spikes are special type of stories that are used to drive out risk and uncertainty in a project.** A **Spike is a great way to mitigate risks early and promotes fluid iterations** later in the project. It allows the team an understanding of the upcoming Product Backlog items complexity.

	Spikes may be used for a number of reasons:
	   • The team may not have knowledge of a new domain, and **spikes may be used for basic research to familiarize the team with a new technology or domain.**
	   • The story may be too big to be estimated appropriately, and the team may use **a spike to analyze the implied behavior, so they can split the story into estimable pieces.**
	   • The story may contain significant technical risk, and the team may have to do some research or prototyping **to gain confidence** in a technological approach that will allow them to commit the user story to some future timebox.
	   • The story may contain significant functional risk. While the intent of the story may be understood, it's **may not be clear on how the system would need to interact with the user** to achieve the benefit implied, for which a spike might be used.

Technical Spike	Technical Spikes are used to research various technical approaches in a domain.
	Example of Technical Spikes: • Evaluation of potential performance or load impact due to a new user story. • Evaluation of specific implementation technologies that can be applied to a solution. • Team needs to develop more confidence by understanding the implications of a desired approach before committing the functionality to a timebox.
Functional Spike	Functional Spikes are used whenever there is **significant uncertainty as to how a user might interact with the system.** Functional spikes are often best evaluated through some level of prototyping, whether it be user interface mockups, wireframes, page flows, or whatever techniques is best suited to get feedback from the customer or stakeholders.
	Note: In the Exam, the difference between Technical and Functional Spike might not be asked.

Application Architecture	Developers in the Scrum Teams should design and build a platform / a foundation **of Non-Functional requirements and High Value Functions which would be used as a Shared Architecture.** Each set of Scrum Team would work on this shared Architecture and enhance it with time.
	Developers in the Scrum Team are **responsible for creating the architecture.**
	The architectural and technical design discussions start as early as sprint planning and **continue throughout the sprint**s as the design is implemented (i.e. coding/construction).
	Defects, Non-functional testing (such as performance, reliability, usability testing) and Design issues may result to underlying application architecture changes.
	The Applications overall architecture **is not designed upfront**. The emergence of the Architecture is based on guidelines and agreed principles.
	The System's architecture is decided throughout the project as the **understanding of the project increases.**
	Developers in the Scrum Team should **have a set of Guiding Architecture Principles** that every Developer understands and follows when writing code.
	There is **no assigned Role** (e.g. a software architect) whose job it is to makes sure a consistent architecture is developed. Developers in the **Scrum team makes sure that the architecture evolves** based on the needs.
	The Scrum Team **plans some time each Sprint** to discuss the architecture needed for the features planned in that Sprint.
	Cross – Cutting concerns (concerns across different layers / modules / classes) within the application should also be addressed. Example of some concerns are: • Performance & Scalability • Layering/partitioning Quality and validation • Reusability, Reliability, Availability, Serviceability, and Performance • Concurrency, Security • Maintenance, Error Handling • Logging • Caching and Transaction Management

Layered Application Architecture	**What Is Layered Architecture?** 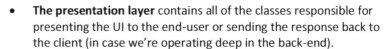 A Layered Architecture the organization of the project structure into four main categories: **presentation, application, domain, and infrastructure.** Each of the layers contains objects related to the particular concern it represents. • **The presentation layer** contains all of the classes responsible for presenting the UI to the end-user or sending the response back to the client (in case we're operating deep in the back-end). • **The application layer** contains all the logic that is required by the application to meet its functional requirements and, at the same time, is not a part of the domain rules. In most systems the application layer consisted of services orchestrating the domain objects to fulfill a use case scenario. • **The domain layer** represents the underlying domain, mostly consisting of domain entities and, in some cases, services. Business rules, like invariants and algorithms, should all stay in this layer. • **The infrastructure layer (also known as the persistence layer)** contains all the classes responsible for doing the technical stuff, like persisting the data in the database, like DAOs, repositories, or whatever else you're using.
	Layered Architecture has some benefits, including: • **Simplicity** – The concept is very easy to learn and visible in the project at first grasp. • **Maintainability** – Layering increases maintainability of a system by isolating functional responsibilities • Layering makes it easier to **reuse functions** • **Consistent across different projects** – the layers and the overall code organization is pretty much the same in every layered project. • **Guaranteed separation of concerns** – it is very easy to separate the concerns and the associated code organization with respect to the concern submitted. • **Browsability from a technical perspective** – when one wants to change something in some/all objects of a given kind, it's very easy to find and they're kept all together.

Extreme Programming (XP)	Extreme Programming (XP) is an agile software development framework with an **extreme focus on quality programming.**
	Extreme Programming takes the engineering practices to an extreme, **in order to create and release high quality code.**
	Extreme Programming (XP) is an agile software development framework that aims to produce higher quality software, and higher quality of life for the Scrum team. XP is the most specific of the agile frameworks regarding appropriate engineering practices for software development.
Extreme Programming Values	Extreme Programming (XP) is based on 5 values which are: 1. **Simplicity**: This value focuses on reducing complexity, extra features, and waste. XP teams keep the phrase "Find the simplest thing that could possibly work" in mind and build that solution first. The purpose of this is to avoid waste and do only absolutely necessary things such as keep the design of the system as simple as possible so that it is easier to maintain, support, and revise. 2.**Communication**: This value focuses on making sure all the team members know what is expected of them and what other people are working on. Software development is inherently a team sport that relies on communication to transfer knowledge from one team member to everyone else on the team. XP stresses the importance of the appropriate kind of communication – face to face discussion with the aid of a white board or other drawing mechanism. 3.**Feedback**: The team should get impressions of suitability early. Failing fast can be useful, especially if in doing so we get new information while the team still has time to improve the product. Through constant feedback about their previous efforts, teams can identify areas for improvement and revise their practices. Feedback also supports simple design. 4.**Courage**: It takes courage to allow our work to be entirely visible to others. Inpair programming making bold simplifications and changes to that code, back up by automated builds and unit tests, developers need to have the courage. One would need courage to stop doing something that doesn't work and try something else. One would also need courage to accept and act on feedback. 5.**Respect**: Respect is essential on XP projects, where people work together as a team and everyone is accountable for the success or failure of the project. Team members need to recognize that people work differently and respect those differences. Just like Scrum, Extreme Programming (XP) values Courage and Respect.

XP Roles	A typical XP team includes:
	The customer is the person who is responsible for writing user stories, setting priorities and formulating the product backlog. The XP Customer is expected to be actively engaged on the project and ideally becomes part of the team. The Customer role is responsible for making all of the business decisions regarding the project including:
	• What should the system do (What features are included and what do they accomplish)?
	• How do we know when the system is done (what are our acceptance criteria)?
	• How much do we have to spend (what is the available funding, what is the business case)?
	• What should we do next (in what order do we deliver these features)?
	The programmer is an ordinary developer, who writes the code and performs the entire amount of project tasks.
	The coach is the person who watches the team's work, controls it, and teaches its members to implement the most effective practices.
XP Practices	**The tracker** is the person whose main task is to monitor the progress of software development and to detect all problems in it. This is often one of the developers who spends part of their time each week filling this extra role. The main purpose of this role is to keep track of relevant metrics that the team feels necessary to track their progress and to identify areas for improvement. Key metrics that the team may track include velocity, reasons for changes to velocity, amount of overtime worked, and passing and failing tests. This is not a required role for the team, and is generally only established if your team determines a true need for keeping track of several metrics.
	Note: "Product Owner" and "Customer" are roughly equivalent roles, as are "Scrum Master" and "Coach."

1. Whole Team	**Practice 1**: Scrum and XP values whole team approach. Whole Team means: 1) All skills that are **required to turn the selected stories into avaluable software must be on the team.** 2) Anyone who is qualified to perform a role can undertake it. The roles are not reserved for people who specialize in one particular area.
2. Planning / Planning Games	This practice helps optimize the use of resources, since people who can perform multiple jobs are able to switch from one role to another as the demand arises. The practice also allows for more efficient sharing of information and helps eliminate the possibility that people in certain roles will be idle or overstretched at certain points in the project.
	Practice 2: Scrum is very focused on what happens in the Sprint. Scrum does not say anything about planning at a high level. XP has two primary planning activities or planning games—**Release planning and iteration / sprint planning.** During release planning: • Customer presents what is expected and the developers estimates the same at a high level. • The customer forecast the budget and plan for development. • The Scrum team forecast any skills they require.
3. Small Releases	**Practice 3**: Small Releases: Frequent, small releases to a test environment are encouraged in XP, both at the iteration level, to demonstrate progress and increase visibility to the customer, and at the release level, to rapidly deploy working software to the end users. Quality is maintained in these short delivery time frames by rigorous testing and through practices like continuous integration, in which suites of tests are run as frequently as possible.
4. Customers Test	**Practice 4**: The Customer describes one or more test criteria that will indicate that the software is working as intended. The team then builds automated tests to prove to the customer that the software has met those criteria. While Scrum does not require the customer to be on-site, Extreme Programming **recommends the customer on-site and continuously test with the team**. For Scrum Teams practicing Extreme Programming, during Sprint Review the Customer, Product Owner and Developers will review the product that is already in production.
5. Collective Code Ownership	**Practice 5**: In XP, any pair of developers can improve or amend any code. This means multiple people will work on all the code, which results in increased visibility and broader knowledge of the code base. This practice leads to a higher level of quality; with more people looking at the code, there is a greater chance defects will be discovered.

6. Code Standards	**Practice 6**: Code Standards: XP teams follow a consistent coding standard so that all the code looks as if it has been written by a single, knowledgeable programmer. The specifics of the standard each team uses are not important; what matters is that the team takes a consistent approach to writing the code
7. Sustainable Pace	**Practice 7**: XP recognizes that the highest level of productivity is achieved by a team operating at a sustainable pace. While periods of over time might be necessary, repeated long hours of work are unsustainable and counterproductive.
8. Metaphor	**Practice 8**: Metaphor: XP uses metaphors and similes to explain designs and create a shared technical vision. These descriptions establish comparisons that all the stakeholders can understand to help explain how the system should work. For example, "The billing module is like an accountant who makes sure transactions are entered into the appropriate accounts and balances are created." Even if the team cannot come up with an effective metaphor to describe something, they can use a common set of names for different elements to ensure everyone understands where and why changes should be applied.
9. Simple Design	**Practice 9**: Simple Design: By focusing on keeping the design simple but adequate, XP teams can develop code quickly and adapt it as necessary. The design is kept appropriate for what the project currently requires. It is then revisited iteratively and incrementally to ensure it remains appropriate.
	Practice 10: During Sprint Planning, Scrum Team who is practicing Extreme Programming will select the stories that can be **completed in a one- or two-week Sprint.**
10. Pair Programming 	Pair programming is an agile software development technique in which **two programmers work together at one workstation**. One of the developers (the driver) writes code while the other (the observer or navigator) reviews each line of code as it is typed in. The two programmers switch roles frequently. 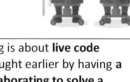 Scrum Team practicing Extreme Programming **will pair programmers throughout the Sprint.**
	Pair programming **is a micro feedback loop**. Pair programming is about **live code review**. Using Pair Programming, dirtiness in a code can be caught earlier by having **a live code review. Pair programming is about two people collaborating to solve a problem** together because two heads are better than one.
	Pair programming is an agile software development technique in which two programmers work together at one workstation. One, the driver, writes code while the other, the observer or navigator, reviews each line of code as it is typed in. The two programmers switch roles frequently. While reviewing, the observer also considers the "strategic" direction of the work, coming up with ideas for improvements and likely future problems to address. This is intended to free the driver to focus all of their attention on the "tactical" aspects of completing the current task, using the observer as a safety net and guide.

	Scrum Team practicing Extreme Programming will put pair programming in the definition of "Done".
	Pair programming configuration may be two developers working with one machine or a **programmer and a tester** working together.
	The Advantages of Pair Programming are: • Fewer Coding Mistakes and thus good Code Quality. • An effective way to share knowledge • Solve Problems Faster and Quicker • Train New People and Improve Interpersonal and Social Skills.
	Scrum Teams practicing Extreme Programming could have their **increment deployed to production daily.**
11. Ten Minute Build	**Practice 11 :** Ten Minute Build enables **automatically building the whole system and running all of the tests in ten minutes.** A build that takes longer than ten minutes will be used much less often, missing the opportunity for feedback.
	Ten Minute Build is another Extreme Programming practice that Scrum Teams find valuable. Extreme Programming requires the code to be integrated continuously and the build run for under ten minutes.
12. Continuous Integration 13. Test Driven Development 14. Refactoring	Ten Minute Build is non-negotiable rule from Extreme Programming. When the build runs more than ten minutes, developers get more reluctant to continuously integrate their code. When developers don't continuously integrate their code, they lose the opportunity to get feedback. Extreme Programming highly values feedback. Faster build means faster feedback.
	Practice 12: Continuous Integration, Test Driven Development and Refactoring are also principals adopted in XP and are explained below.
	Note: The PSD exam does not focus on Release Planning, Extreme Programming Roles or Extreme Programing Values.

XP Lifecycle	1. In XP, the team starts off by describing the desired results of the project by having customers define a set of stories.
	2. As these stories are being created, the team estimates the size of each story. This size estimate, along with relative benefit as estimated by the customer can provide an indication of relative value which the customer can use to determine priority of the stories.
	3. If the team identifies some stories that they are unable to estimate because they don't understand all of the technical considerations involved, they can introduce a spike to do some focused research on that particular story or a common aspect of multiple stories. Spikes are short, time-boxed time frames set aside for the purposes of doing research on a particular aspect of the project. Spikes can occur before regular iterations start or alongside ongoing iterations.
	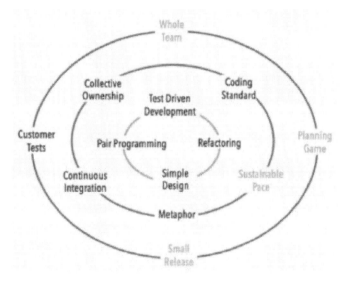
	4. Next, the entire team gets together to create a release plan that everyone feels is reasonable. This release plan is a first pass at what stories will be delivered in a particular quarter, or release. The stories delivered should be based on what value they provide and considerations about how various stories support each other.
	5. Then the team launches into a series of weekly cycles. At the beginning of each weekly cycle, the team (including the customer) gets together to decide which stories will be realized during that week. The team then breaks those stories into tasks to be completed within that week.
	6. At the end of the week, the team and customer review progress to date and the customer can decide whether the project should continue, or if sufficient value has been delivered.

Lean Product Development	Lean originated in the Toyota Production System that was developed to improve upon. Henry Ford's mass production system for building cars. Lean Thinking is a superset of agile and Kanban methods. Lean Product Development, Kanban, and agile methods (Scrum, XP) are all specialized instances of lean thinking.
	Eliminate waste: To maximize value, the team must minimize waste. Waste can take the form of partially done work, delays, handoffs, unnecessary features, etc.
	Empower the team: Rather than taking a micromanagement approach, the team should respect the team members' superior knowledge of the technical steps required on the project and let them make local decisions to be productive and successful.
	Deliver fast: Projects Return on investment (ROI) can be minimized by quickly producing valuable deliverables and iterating through designs. Teams find the best solution through the rapid evolution of options.
	Optimize the whole: Teams would need to go beyond the pieces of the project and look for how it aligns with the organization as whole. As part of optimizing the whole, team would focus on forming better intergroup relations.
	Build quality in: Lean development doesn't try to "test in" quality at the end; instead, teams build quality into the product and continually assure quality throughout the development process, using techniques like refactoring, continuous integration, and unit testing.
	Defer Decisions: Team balance early planning with making decisions and commitments as late as possible.
	Amplify learning: This concept involves facilitating communication early and often, getting feedback as soon as possible, and building on what teams learn

Seven Waste of Lean	Lean experts Mary and Tom Poppendieck, who have written extensively on the use of lean in software projects, have converted the seven traditional manufacturing wastes into seven comparable software development wastes, as shown below
	<table><tr><td>Waste</td><td>Description</td></tr><tr><td>Partially Done Work</td><td>Work started, but not complete.</td></tr><tr><td>Extra Processes</td><td>Extra work that does not add value</td></tr><tr><td>Extra Feature</td><td>Features that are not required, or are thought of as "nice-to-haves"</td></tr><tr><td>Task Switching</td><td>Multi-tasking between several different projects when there are context-switching penalties</td></tr><tr><td>Waiting</td><td>Delays waiting for reviews and approvals</td></tr><tr><td>Motion</td><td>The effort required to communicate or move information or deliverables from one group to another; if teams are not co-located, this effort may need to be greater</td></tr><tr><td>Defects</td><td>Defective documents or software that needs correction</td></tr></table>
Dynamic Systems Development Method (DSDM)	DSDM is an Agile method that focuses on the full project lifecycle. The Method brings more governance and discipline to this new iterative way of working. DSDM's success is due to the philosophy "that any project must be aligned to clearly defined strategic goals and focus upon early delivery of real benefits to the business." Supporting this philosophy with the eight principles allows teams to maintain focus and achieve project goals. The eight Principles of DSDM: 1. Focus on the business need 2. Deliver on time 3. Collaborate 4. Never compromise quality 5. Build incrementally from firm foundations 6. Develop iteratively 7. Communicate continuously and clearly 8. Demonstrate control

Crystal Methodology	The Crystal methodology is one of the most lightweight, adaptable approaches to software development. Crystal is actually comprised of a family of agile methodologies such as Crystal Clear, Crystal Yellow, Crystal Orange and others, whose unique characteristics are driven by several factors such **as team size, system criticality, and project priorities.** This Crystal family addresses the realization that each project may require a slightly tailored set of policies, practices, and processes in order to meet the project 's unique characteristics.
Moscow	MoSCoW prioritization, also known as the MoSCoW method or MoSCoW analysis, is a popular prioritization technique for managing requirements. The method is commonly used to help key stakeholders understand the significance of initiatives in a specific release. **MoSCoW Prioritization** **M** — Must have: Non-negotiable product needs that are mandatory for the team. **S** — Should have: Important initiatives that are not vital, but add significant value. **C** — Could have: Nice to have initiatives that will have a small impact if left out. **W** — Will not have: Initiatives that are not a priority for this specific time frame.

Modeling	"Agile Modeling" is a set of practices one can use in Agile teams for **effective modeling and documentation**. The types of agile models that can be created during agile modeling include Use case diagrams, Data models and » Screen designs. This method aligns with the Agile values and principles and still helps benefit from the power of modeling. The emphasis is on **models for conversation, not for handovers.**
	The **shared understanding of the system should be maintained somewhere as documentation to** share information which is not well communicated and retained by the code.
	Agile makes clear is the **value shift from documentation to conversation**, so writing heavy design documentation (which often duplicates information from the code) is not the right approach. Documentation that makes conversations effective is the approach which should be taken, and it should be the simplest possible set of models which works complementary to the code.
Static Analysis ①	Static analysis, also called static code analysis, **is a method of computer program debugging that is done by examining the code without executing the program.**
	Static Analysis provides an understanding of the code structure and can help to ensure that the code adheres to industry standards.
	Automated Static Analysis tools can scan the entire code base without executing the code.
	The principal advantage of static analysis is the fact that it can reveal errors that do not manifest themselves until a disaster occurs weeks, months or years after release.
	After static analysis has been done, dynamic analysis is often performed in an effort to uncover subtle defects or vulnerabilities.
	Benefits of Static Analysis are: 1. Static Code Analysis helps identify potential software quality issues during development phase before the software goes into production. 2. It detects the exact areas in code that needs re-factoring / simplification. 3. The analysis detects programming errors or flaws and shows them to you 4. Static Code Analysis improves communication in the Scrum team and helps training Developers to produce high-quality code.

Dynamic Analysis	Dynamic analysis involves the testing and evaluation of a program based on its execution. Static and dynamic analysis, considered together, are sometimes referred to as glass-box testing.
	Dynamic program analysis tools may require loading of special libraries or even recompilation of program code.
	Dynamic analysis is capable of exposing a subtle flaw or vulnerability too complicated for static analysis alone to reveal and can also be the more expedient method of testing.
	A dynamic test will only find defects in the part of the code that is actually executed.
Code Refactoring	Code Refactoring is an agile software development practice **in which code is adjusted (within the code base) without impacting the external, functional behavior of that code.**
	Code Refactoring is the **process of clarifying and simplifying the design of existing code**, without changing its behavior. Agile teams extend their code a lot from iteration to iteration with the help of code refactoring.
	There are two general benefits to the activity of refactoring: **Readability and Maintainability**. It is easier to fix bugs because the source code is easy to read, and the intent of its author is easy to grasp. Code Refactoring involves: • Reducing large monolithic routines into a set of individually concise, well-named, single-purpose methods. • Moving a method to a more appropriate class, or by removing misleading comments. **Extensibility**. It is easier to extend the capabilities of the application if the code uses recognizable design patterns.
	Refactoring does "not" include: • Rewriting the entire code • Fixing bugs • Improving observable aspects of software such as its interface

Simplicity Criteria	Simplicity Criteria is a set of criteria, in priority order, to judge whether some source code is "Simple". A source code is "Simple" if: • The code contains no duplication. • The code expresses separately, each distinct idea or responsibility. • The code is composed of minimum number of components (classes, methods, lines). • The code is verified by automated tests, and all such tests pass.
DRY (Don't Repeat Yourself) Code with Minimum Duplication. 	Don't Repeat Yourself (DRY) is a principle of software development which aims at reducing repetition of software patterns, replacing them with abstractions or data normalization. DRY reduces redundancy.
	The DRY principle states that "**Every piece of knowledge must have a single, unambiguous, authoritative representation within a system**". This principle has been formulated by Andy Hunt and Dave Thomas in their book The Pragmatic Programmer. DRY Benefits are: • It saves overall development time and effort • Code is easy to maintain • It reduces the chances of bugs
WET (Write Everything Twice) 	Violations of DRY are typically referred to as WET solutions. WET stands for "Write Everything Twice". It is difficult to manage changes when the same code is written in more than one place. Example: WET solutions are common **in multi-tiered architectures.** Example, adding a "comment" field on a form in a web application. The text string "comment" might be repeated in the label, the HTML tag, in a read function name, a private variable, database DDL, queries, and so on. A DRY approach eliminates redundancy by using frameworks that reduces or eliminate all duplicate code, performing the same task, leaving the extensibility of adding new knowledge variables in one place.

SOLID	SOLID principles are a set of principles which help software developers to achieve scalability by avoiding code breaks every time a change is made.

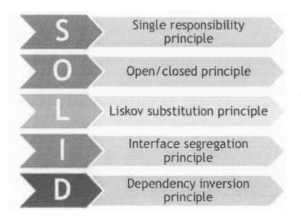

SOLID principles are a set of principles which help software developers to achieve scalability by avoiding code breaks every time a change is made.

S.O.L.I.D. stands for:

S – Single-Responsibility Principle - This principle states that an object/class should only have one responsibility and that it should be completely encapsulated by the class.

O – Open-Closed Principle - This Principle affirms that an entity allows its behavior to be extended but never by modifying its source code. Any class (or function) should be written in such a way that it can be used as is. It can be extended if need be, but it can never be modified.

L – Liskov Substitution Principle – This Principle confirms that objects should be replaceable by instances of their subtypes without affecting the functionality of the system.

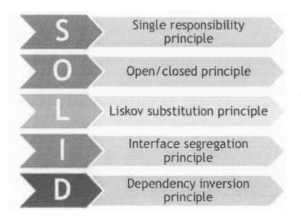

I – Interface Segregation Principle. – This Principle States that once an interface has become too large, it absolutely needed to split it into small interfaces that are more specific.

D – Dependency Inversion Principle. - This principle is primarily concerned with reducing dependencies amongst the code modules.

Build Automation	Build automation is the process of **automating the creation of a software build. It also includes the associated processes such as compiling computer source code into binary code, packaging binary code and running automated tests.**
	In the context of software development, build refers to the process that converts files and other assets under the developers' responsibility into a software product in its final or consumable form. The build may include: 1) Compiling source files 2) Packaging compiled files into compressed formats (such as jar, zip) 3) Producing installers 4) creating or updating of database schema or data The build is automated when these steps are repeatable, require no direct human intervention, and can be performed at any time with no information other than what is stored in the source code control repository.
	Build Automation is a necessary pre-condition for continuous integration and continuous testing.
	The advantages of build automation include: 1. Improving **Product Quality** by **making builds less error prone**. i.e eliminating a source of variation, and thus of defects; a manual build process containing a large number of necessary steps offers as many opportunities to make mistakes 2. Helps finds defects and configuration management issues. 3. Accelerating the compile and link processing, thus making more time for **feedback.** 4. Eliminating redundant tasks 5. Minimizing "bad builds" 6. Eliminating dependencies on key personnel. 7. Having history of builds and releases in order to investigate issues. 8. Providing assurance that defects and configuration management issues have not been introduced.
	Automated Software Build Development **allows frequent validation of the unit of software being worked on, ensuring it remains in a potentially shippable state.**
	Automated Software Build **Development supports Continuous Integration.**
	Automated Software Build Development process allows itself to be **clearly defined and scripted, making it easy, consistent and repeatable**.

	In case of Continuous integration Software Build Developments, the person **who broke the build will be responsible for fixing it**.
	Ideally, Automated Build should **trigger as soon as new code is checked in.** (or old code is changed).
	Automated Build should be followed by a set of selective Unit Test. Once it passes Unit test, it should then run through a set of comprehensive tests (Automated Test, Unit Test, Manual Test, Non-Functional Test). This would help identify bugs that the developers would fix before proceeding.
	Automating Software Build Process **does not speed up the Code Review Process.**
User Stories	A user story describes a new or changed functionality that will be valuable to an external stakeholder of a system or software. At the very least, User stories are composed of three aspects: • A **Written Description** of the story used for planning and development. • **Conversations** about the story that flush out the details of the story. • **Acceptance Criteria** that convey and document details, that can be used to determine when a story is complete.
	Scrum does not mandate the use of User Stories. Unless its mentioned in the Definition of Done, user stories don't need to be created or reported.
	According to the Scrum Guide, the Product Backlog lists all features, functions, requirements, enhancements, and fixes that constitute the changes to be made to the product in future releases. It lists all the work that is deemed necessary for the product. How Scrum Teams decide **to capture this work is entirely up to them. They can write User Stories, they can use a bunch of keywords, write use cases or even draw pictures.**

Continuous Integration

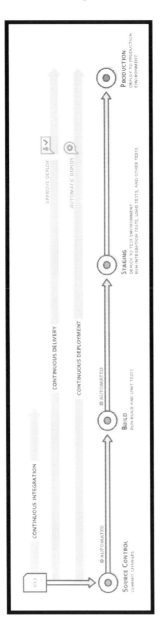

Continuous integration is a software development practice where **developers regularly merge their code changes into a central repository,** after which automated builds and tests are run.

Continuous Integration is a software development practice where members of a **Scrum team integrate and verify their work frequently,** often multiple times each day to detect integration errors as quickly as possible.

In the past, developers on a team **worked in isolation for an extended period of time,** only merging their changes to the master branch once their work was completed. This made merging code changes difficult and time-consuming. It also resulted in bugs accumulating for a long time without correction. These factors made it harder to deliver updates to customers quickly.

The purpose of Continuous Integration is to **avoid last minute integration surprises and find code issues right away.**

A Continuous Integration **service automatically builds and runs unit tests** on the new code changes to immediately surface any errors.

If code is continuously compiled and checked, **conflicts can be identified when they are easy to manage.** Other benefits of Continuous Integration are:

- Short and Less intense integrations
- Fast Feedback Loops
- Increase transparency and visibility enabling greater communication
- Detect and Correct issues early
- Invalid Builds are detected earlier.
- Code is kept in a **buildable** state.
- Less time spend debugging
- Building a solid foundation
- Less waiting to find out if a piece of code's going to work. One would find out as the code is checked in.
- Reduced integration problems allowing one to deliver software more rapidly.
- Causes Members to consider each other's work.

Note: Continuous Integration **does not improve the Readability of the Code.**

Continuous Delivery.	Continuous Delivery is a software delivery practice similar to Continuous Deployment **except a human action is required to promote changes into a subsequent environment along the pipeline.**
(!)	Continuous Delivery is the aim of keeping the system in "Production Ready" state (where it always able to release) to enable the release of a product to the end user on demand.
	Continuous Delivery **doesn't mean every change is deployed to production** ASAP. It means every change is proven to be deployable at any time.
	Continuous Delivery helps to move away from the activity of preparing and making software Ready. Instead the Scrum Team work in a way that the software is **always "Production Ready".**
	To support Continuous Delivery, the Scrum Team adds to the Definition of "Done": • "Deployed to Production" • "Ready to Release"
Continuous Deployment (!)	Continuous Deployment is a software delivery practice in which the release process is **fully automated** in order to have changes promoted to the production environment **with no human intervention.**
	Continuous Deployment **is deploying every change into production.** Once the change is released, it is available to the end user.

Bugs and Bug Reports	A software **bug is an error, flaw, failure, or fault that produces an incorrect or unexpected result.**
	Unless a company has specific guidance on fixing bugs, they represent work to be done and **should be ordered on the Product Backlog by the Product Owner.**
	If a Developer is unsure of what to do with a bug, he / she should talk to the Product Owner.
(!)	A bug should be resolved right away: 1) If the work to fix the bug (and test it) is less than the work to actually file it. 2) If the bug is so critical that it would be negligent to leave it unfixed.
	A bug report "should explain how exactly the product is broken." If bugs occur, the person finding the bug should be able to report (document & send) the bug to people in charge of fixing that error
	There are 4 key points that are essential for every bug report: A. The Problem. B. Steps to reproduce. C. Expected outcome D. Actual outcome
	Other information that good bug reports include are: A. The context of the bug report should be easily read by developers. B. Screenshot(s) of the problem should be presented. C. Log excerpts (encapsulated in the no format macro) D. Version of the plugin/platform. E. If it is a plugin bug, include the version of the platform (e.g. Confluence 5.6, JIRA 6.3)

Good Vs Bad Bug Reports	Good Bug Report:
(!)	1. A good bug report contains one Bug Per Report. 2. A good bug report contains the information needed to reproduce and fix problems. 3. A good bug report contains clear title and proper grammar in the report. 4. A good bug report is an efficient form of communication for both bug reporter and bug receiver. 5. A good bug report contains expected vs actual results. 6. A good bug report contains version of the plugin/platform. 7. A good bug report contains Screenshot(s) of the problem and Logs. 8. A good report should not assign Blame. Bad Bug Report 1. A bad bug report does not contain the information needed to reproduce and fix problems 2. A bad bug report is a lengthy, inefficient form of communication for everyone involved. 3. A bad bug report has generic titles 4. A bad bug report assigns Vague statements or untested assumptions. 5. A bad bug report assigns blames.
Code Conventions and Documentation (!)	The benefit of establishing naming standards for code is that it makes the code **more Readable**.
	Developers **writes tests in a Scrum Team.**
	Developers and Product Owners **can write Functional and Technical documentations if needed.**
	The Most reliable piece of Technical documentation is a documentation which is **similar to the Source Code itself.**

Code Metric / Code Health / Quality	Code Metric provides a **set of five measurements** that give an insight into code
	Class coupling: Class coupling is a **measure of dependencies a class has on other classes.** This dependency is measured through parameters, method calls and interface implementations.
Class Coupling	In Class Coupling, the higher this number, the more likely a change in one class will affect other classes. For class coupling, a low value is good, and a high value is bad.
	Depth of Inheritance: Depth of Inheritance indicates the number of different **classes that inherit from one another, all the way back to the base class.**
Depth of Inheritance	Depth of Inheritance is similar to class coupling however the difference is that in Depth of Inheritance, **a base class can affect any of its inherited classes.**
	For Depth of Inheritance, the higher the number, the deeper the depth of inheritance is. If the number if high, it's more likely for causing breaking changes in the code when modifying a base class. For Depth of Inheritance, a low value is good. (DIT Value = 4 in the diagram)
Lines of Code	Lines of Code **indicates the number of executable lines of code** in a method. This count is an approximate number, based on the Intermediate Language (IL) code.
	Lines of Code includes only executable lines of code, **so comments, braces, white space and member declarations are excluded.**
	For Lines of Code the more lines of code in your application, the more code there is to maintain. For Lines of Code, a low value is good, and a high value is bad.
	Line of code is not a metrics of code quality. E.g. Codebase A cannot be said to be of worse quality than codebase B on the grounds that its line-count is higher. The scope of work encompassed by codebase A might simply be far greater.

(Diagram: class inheritance tree — A at top, branching to B1 and B2; B1 branches to C1 and C2; B2 branches to C3; C3 to D1.)

Cyclomatic Complexity Maintainability Index 	Cyclomatic complexity is a software metric used to indicate the complexity of a program. It is a quantitative measure of the number of linearly independent paths through a program's source code. It represents **the number of unique paths in a code.**
	Cyclomatic complexity represents the **number of "if" statements, branching structures, nesting levels and switch cases in a code.**
	Code with a high cyclomatic complexity can be hard to test and maintain, as there are number of different paths through the code that must be tested. For Cyclomatic Complexity, a low value is good, and a high value is bad.
	The Maintainability Index is a combination of several metrics, including Cyclomatic Complexity and Average Lines of Code, as well as computational complexity, based off the Halstead Volume function. The maintainability index is a value between 1 and 100. Unlike the other four code metrics discussed previously, for this metric, the higher the value, the easier your code will be to maintain. There are three rating levels for this index: GREEN: This is a rating between 20 and 100 and indicates code that should be maintainable. YELLOW: This is a rating between 10 and 19 and indicates the code may be semi-difficult to maintain. RED: This is a rating between 0 and 9 and indicates the code may be very difficult

Application Lifecycle Management	ALM (Application Lifecycle Management): Application Lifecycle Management **is a holistic view on the management of software applications and systems, accounting for all stages of the existence of a software product.**
	Designed for the execution of a software delivery project, Application Lifecycle Management solutions coordinate **people, processes, and tools in an iterative cycle of integrated software development activities. ALM** includes: • Planning and change management • Requirements definition and management • Architecture management • Software configuration management • Build and deployment automation • Quality management.
	Application Lifecycle Management (ALM) **incorporates the specification, design, development and testing of a software application**. ALM covers the entire lifecycle from the idea conception, through to the development, testing, deployment, support and ultimately retirement of systems.
	Application Lifecycle Management (ALM) is really an umbrella term that covers several different disciplines that traditionally were considered separate, including project management, requirements management, development, testing and quality assurance (QA) as well as customer support and IT service delivery.
	ALM tools provide a standardized environment for communication and collaboration between Scrum teams and related departments, such as test and operations. They also automate the process of software development and delivery.

Branching	Branching is creating a logical or physical copy of code within a version control number **so that the copy might be changed in isolation**. Branching also implies the ability to later merge or integrate changes back onto the Parent branch.
	Branching models often differ between teams and typically depends upon how much work remains in a branch before getting merged back into master. Some of the common type of Branching's / Branching Strategies are: **Release branching**: Release branching refers to the idea that a release is contained entirely within a single branch. **Feature branching:** Feature Branching is an approach that uses a branch to work on a feature until it's complete. Once the Merge is complete the code is merged back into the trunk/master Branch. Feature branches are often coupled **with feature flags–"toggles" that enable or disable a feature within the product.** That makes it easy to deploy code into master and control when the feature is activated, making it easy to initially deploy the code well before the feature is exposed to end-users. **Task Branching**: Every organization has a natural way to break down work in individual tasks inside an issue tracker, like Jira Software. Issues then becomes the team's central point of contact for that piece of work. Task branching, also known as issue branching, **directly connects the issues with the source code**. Each issue is implemented on its own branch with the issue key included in the branch name. It's easy to see which code implements which issue by looking at the issue key in the branch name. With that level of transparency, it's easier to apply specific changes to master or any longer running legacy release branch.
	A Single Increment is needed at the end of the Sprint. **Regardless of the number of Teams or the Branch they work in**, the Scrum teams should merge their code to have one single "Valuable" Increment (one main branch) by the end of the Sprint.
	Multiple Scrum Teams can work on the Same Branch.
	Note: PSD Exam does not focus on the Types of Branching.
Single Responsibility Principle	The single responsibility principle is a computer programming principle that **states that every module, class, or function should have responsibility over a single part of the functionality provided by the software, and that responsibility should be entirely encapsulated by the class.** All its services should be narrowly aligned with that responsibility. Robert C. Martin expresses the principle as, "A class should have only one reason to change".

Clean Coding	Clean Code is defined as a software code that is expressed well, formatted correctly, and organized for later coders to understand. Clarity is preferred over cleverness. Clean Code should have the following features: • Descriptive Function Names • Small Functions • Few Comments • Few Arguments • Single Responsibility Principle • Necessary Code Only • Tested
Scout Rule	The practice of always **leaving the code base in a little better state than it was found before modifications,** is called the Scout Rule. Scout Rule is a mean to progress towards Clean Code.
Engineering Standards	Engineering Standards: A shared set of development and technology standards that a Scrum Team applies to create valuable Increments of software. The Scrum Team can inspect and adapt the product against the Engineering Standards.
Feature Toggle	Feature Toggle: Feature Toggle is a software development practice that allows dynamically **turning (parts of) functionality on and off without impacting the overall accessibility** of the system by its users.
Scrum Board	Scrum Board: a board to **visualize information** within the Scrum Team primarily, often used to **manage Sprint Backlog**. Scrum boards are an optional implementation within Scrum to make information visible and thereby increase transparency.

Coupling	Coupling is the **degree of interdependence between software modules.**
	Coupling is a measure of how closely connected two routines or modules are. It is a measure of the strength of the relationships between modules.
	In essence, coupling indicates the strength of relation between software modules. **When this coupling is high, we may assume that the software modules are interdependent, i.e., they cannot function without the other**. There are several dimensions of coupling: • Content coupling – In this type of coupling, **Module can access or modify the content of any other module.** In essence, when a component passes parameters to control the activity of some other component, there is a control coupling amongst the two components. • Common coupling – In this type of coupling. Multiple **modules** having **access to a shared global data**. • Stamp coupling – In this is a type of coupling, data structure is **used to pass information from one component in the system to another.** • Control coupling – In this is a type of coupling, one module can change the **flow of execution of another module.** • Data coupling -- in this type of coupling, two modules interact by exchanging or passing data as a parameter.
	Note: The PSD exam does not focus on the dimensions of Coupling.

Cohesion	
	Cohesion is a measure of the degree to which the responsibilities of a single module or a component form a meaningful unit. If a module performs one task and nothing else or has a clear purpose, the module has high cohesion. On the other hand, if the module tries to encapsulate more than one purpose or has an unclear purpose, our module has low cohesion. Modules with high cohesion tend to be preferable, simple because high cohesion is associated with several desirable traits of software including robustness, reliability, and understandability. Low cohesion is associated with undesirable traits such as being difficult to maintain, test, reuse, or even understand.

```
class A
checkEmail()
validateEmail()
sendEmail()
printLetter()
printAddress()
```

Fig: Low cohesion

```
class A
checkEmail()
```

```
class B
validateEmail()
```

```
class C
sendEmail()
```

```
class D
printLetter()
```

Fig: High cohesion

Quick Reference Guide & Exam Questions
Professional Scrum Master II (PSM II)

Cohesion is of the following types:

1. **Co-incidental cohesion** – This is an unplanned random cohesion that might be a result of breaking a module into smaller modules.
2. **Logical cohesion** -- This is a type of cohesion in which multiple logically related functions or data elements are placed in the same component.
3. **Temporal cohesion** -- This is a type of cohesion in which elements of a module are grouped in a manner in which they are processed at the same point of time. An example could be a component that is used to initialize a set of objects.
4. **Procedural cohesion** -- This is a type of cohesion in which the functions in a component are grouped in a way to enable them to be executed sequentially and make them procedurally cohesive.
5. **Sequential cohesion** -- in this type of cohesion the elements of a module are grouped in such a manner that the output of one of them becomes the input of the next -- they all execute sequentially. In essence, if the output of one part of a component is the input of another, we say that the component has sequential cohesion.
6. **Functional cohesion** -- This is the best and the most preferred type of cohesion in which the degree of cohesion is the highest. In this type of cohesion, the elements of a module are functionally grouped into a logical unit and they work together as a logical unit -- this also promotes flexibility and reusability.

A class or module is considered to be highly cohesive if it has a clear responsibility and all of the implementation of that responsibility is close together or in one place.

DevOps	DevOps is the **combination of cultural philosophies, practices, and tools** that increases an organization's ability **to deliver applications and services at high velocity**.
	DevOps is an organizational concept which serves to bridge the gap between development and operations. Gaps are filled with respect to skills, mind-set, practices and the silo-mentality.
	Under a DevOps model, **development and operations** teams are no longer "siloed." Sometimes, these two teams are merged into a single team where the engineers work across the entire application lifecycle (from development, test to deployment, operations). Developers develop a range of skills not limited to a single function. In some DevOps models, **quality assurance and security teams** may also become more tightly integrated with development (and operations) throughout the application lifecycle. These teams use practices to automate processes that historically are manual and slow. They use a **technology stack and tooling which help them operate and evolve applications quickly and reliably.** These tools also help engineers independently accomplish tasks (for example, **deploying code or provisioning infrastructure**) that normally would have required help from other teams thus further increases a team's velocity.
Advantages of DevOps	The Advantages of DevOps are: • **Speed**: The DevOps model enables developers and operations teams to achieve the needed results faster. Example, microservices and continuous delivery let teams take ownership of services and then release updates to the clients quicker. Note: The **microservices architecture is a design approach to build a single application as a set of small services.** • **Rapid Delivery**: The DevOps model enables Increase in the frequency and pace of releases so one can innovate and improve the product faster. Continuous integration and continuous delivery are practices that automate the software release process, from build to deploy.

	• **Reliability:** The DevOps model ensures the quality of 'application updates' and infrastructure changes are up to the needed standard, so one can reliably deliver at a more rapid pace while maintaining a positive experience for end users. • **Scale:** The DevOps model enables managing infrastructure and development processes at scale. • **Improved Collaboration:** Building more effective teams under a DevOps cultural model is possible as it emphasizes values such as ownership and accountability. Developers and operations teams collaborate closely, share many responsibilities, and combine their workflows. This reduces inefficiencies and saves time (e.g. reduced handover periods between developers and operations, writing code that considers the environment in which it is run). • **Security:** The DevOps model moves quickly while retaining control and preserving compliance. One can adopt a DevOps model without sacrificing security by using automated compliance policies, fine-grained controls, and configuration management techniques. For example, using infrastructure as code and policy as code, one can define and then track compliance at scale.
Things which are not Mandatory in Scrum	The following things are not mandatory or required by Scrum: 1) User Stories and EPIC's 2) Release Burn-Up 3) Burn Down Charts 4) Different Types of Test (Regression Test, Unit Test etc.) 5) Critical Part analysis 6) Refactoring 7) Build Automation

Professional Scrum Developer Questions and Answers

Please go through these questions and check the answers as you go along. The Assessments **online** (https://www.scrum.org/open-assessments) are the best way to assess your knowledge. The Questions and Answers below will ensure you understand the concepts and help you help you prepare for the PSD exam. Go through the answers regardless of whether you answered the questions correctly or not. Focus on understanding the answers and the concepts. As you go through these questions, make your own notes to the Quick reference tables.

Question 1	Correct answer: B

A company is trying to reduce the amount of time it puts in manual testing. The new guideline states that the developers should automate the unit test cases, going forward. This is not possible because Unit Testing cannot be Automated.
 	
   A. True
   B. False
	Unit Test: **A Unit test** is a way of testing a unit **(the smallest piece of code)** that can be logically isolated in a system. In most programming languages, that is a function, a subroutine, a method or property. A Unit test can be automated.
	
	Unit testing, also known as component testing, is a level of software testing where individual units / components of a software are tested. The purpose is to validate that each unit of the software performs as designed.

Question 2
 	
Which practice (based on Scrum) focuses on high quality of the code?
 	
   A. Functional testing.
   B. Scrum Architecture Rules and Regulations.
   C. Extreme Programming.
   D. Scrum Methodology.
	Correct answers: C
	
	Extreme Programming takes the engineering practices to an extreme, in order to create and release high quality code. Extreme (XP) is highly complementary to the Scrum framework.

Question 3
 	
The Order followed in Test Driven Development is:
 	
   A. Write Enough Code and Execute Test Case.
   B. Execute Test Cases, Write Enough Code, Refactor.
   C. Execute Test Cases, Write Enough Code and Release.
	Correct answers: B
	
	"Test-driven development" refers to a style of programming in which three activities are tightly interwoven: Testing (in the form of writing unit tests), Coding and design (in the form of refactoring).
	
	It can be succinctly described by the following set of rules:
	• Write a **"single" unit test describing** an aspect of the program.
	• **Run the test, which should fail** because the program **lacks** that feature.
	• **Write "just enough" code, the simplest possible**, to make the test pass.
	• "Refactor" the code until it conforms to the **Simplicity Criteria.**
	• Repeat, "accumulating" unit tests over time.

Question 4
 	
Continuous Delivery is:
   A. Delivering the developed items to the clients continuously in form of a release.
   B. Delivering to the clients continuously, provided it's the end of the Sprint.
   C. The aim of keeping the system "Production Ready" during development to enable the release of a product (to the end user) on demand.
   D. None of the above.
	Correct answers: C
	
	Continuous Delivery is the aim of keeping the system "Production Ready" during development to enable the release of a product to the end user on demand.

Question 5
 	
Code Coverage is a measurement indicating the amount of code that is exercised by tests.
 	
   A. True
   B. False
	Correct answer: A
	
	Code Coverage is a measurement indicating the **amount of product code** that **is exercised by tests.**

Question 6

A company has been practicing Scrum for years. This company works closely with clients who give their test requirements as well. The company typically practices expressing these requirements as acceptance tests. The company is practicing:

- A. Acceptance Test Driven Development.
- B. Behavior Driven Development.
- C. Application Lifecycle Management.
- D. Branching.

Correct answer: A

Acceptance Test Driven Development is a Test-First software development practice in which acceptance criterias for new functionality are created before the implementation actually begins. These acceptance tests are supported by examples and other necessary information.

Acceptance Test Driven development is the practice of expressing requirements as acceptance tests. Acceptance Test Driven Development (ATDD) involves team members with different perspectives (customer, development, testing) collaborating to write acceptance criteria in advance of implementing the corresponding functionality.

Test case creation is moved to the beginning of the cycle thus reducing defects and bug fixing effort as project progresses. Advanced practices of test-driven development can lead to Acceptance Test-driven development (ATDD) where the criteria specified by the customer are automated into acceptance tests. This then drive the traditional unit test-driven development (UTDD) process.

Question 7

The benefits of code refactoring are:

- A. Makes resolving bugs easier because the source code is easy to read.
- B. Improve readability and maintainability.
- C. Helps packaging the code on demand.
- D. Executing the software faster at runtime.

Correct Answer: A, B

There are two general categories of benefits of refactoring.
Maintainability. It is easier to fix bugs because the source code is easy to read, and the intent of its author is easy to grasp. This might be achieved by reducing large monolithic routines into a set of individually concise, well-named, single-purpose methods. It might be achieved by moving a method to a more appropriate class, or by removing misleading comments.
Extensibility. It is easier to extend the capabilities of the application if it uses recognizable design patterns, and it provides some flexibility where none before may have existed.

Question 8	Correct answers: A, C
A Technical Debt (Select 2): A. Misleads the Product Owners, Scrum Masters and even the developers with their assumptions about the "Current state" of the System. B. Makes the Product more stable. C. Makes the Product more unstable. D. Enhances Transparency.	A Technical debt reduces Transparency. It **misleads** the Product Owners, Scrum Masters and even the developers with their assumptions about **the "Current state" of the System**. For example, if Product Backlog item A is assumed to be completed in a day, it might take three days for it to complete, because of unseen bad code or Technical Debt. The **Product becomes more unstable**, as more functionality / features added over bad code (or existing technical debt). For example, suppose that the team decided to delay some important refactoring to facilitate an early release. Technical debt starts to accrue at that point, and it may not map cleanly to specific items on the Product Backlog. It is far more likely to impact components which cross-cut a range of features. Moreover, if the necessary refactoring is significant it could impact the entire product, and it could affect features in uneven ways.
Question 9 Who is responsible for the Product Architecture? A. Software architect. B. Domain architect. C. Developers in the Scrum Team. D. Product Owner.	Correct answer: C Developers in the Scrum **Team are responsible for creating the architecture. The** architectural and technical design discussions start as early as sprint planning and continue throughout the sprint as the design is being implemented (i.e. coding/construction).
Question 10 A story or task aimed at answering a question or gathering information, rather than at producing shippable product is called: A. EPIC B. Burndown chart C. Bug D. Spike	Correct answer: D A Spike is a story or task aimed at **answering a question or gathering information, rather than at producing shippable product.** In practice, the spikes teams take on are often proof-of-concept types of activities. The definition above says that the work is not focused on the finished product. It may even be designed to be thrown away at the end. This gives your product owner the proper expectation that you will most likely not directly implement the spike solution.

Question 11	Correct answers: A, B, C
The Benefits of DRY (Don't Repeat Yourself) are: (Choose all that Apply): A. It saves time and effort B. It is easy to maintain C. It reduces the chances of bugs. D. It helps merge code easily.	DRY Benefits are: (Choose all that Apply): 1. It saves overall development time and effort 2. Code is easy to maintain 3. It reduces the chances of bugs.
Question 12 Which of the following should uses a ubiquitous language that can be understood by the developers and stakeholders? A. Test First Development B. Behavior Driven Development C. Application Lifecycle Management D. Branching	Correct answer: B Behavior Driven Development is a variation / extension of Test-Driven Development methodology, where the main focus is on: 1) Behavioral specifications of the product or application (or its features). 2) User and System Interactions. Behavior Driven Development uses Ubiquitous language that can be understood by the developers and stakeholders. When Behavior Driven Development is adapted in a project, the technical nitty-gritty aspects of the requirements and implementation are outlined in a business-oriented language.
Question 13 Extreme Programming does not allow the Sprint iteration to be more than: A. 1 week or 2 weeks. B. 3 weeks. C. A Month. D. A Year.	Correct answers: A Extreme Programming does not allow the iteration to be more than one or two weeks.

Question 14	Correct answers: A
Pair programming configuration could be two developers working with one machine or a programmer and a tester working together, on the same machine. A. True B. False	Pair programming is an agile software development technique in which two programmers work together at one workstation. One of the developers (the driver) writes code while the other (the observer or navigator) reviews each line of code as it is typed in. The two programmers switch roles frequently. Scrum Team practicing Extreme Programming will pair programmers throughout the Sprint. Pair programming is a micro feedback loop. Pair programming is about live code review. Using Pair Programming, dirtiness in a code can be caught earlier by having a live code review. Pair programming is about two people collaborating to solve a problem together because two heads are better than one. Scrum Team practicing Extreme Programming will put pair programming in the definition of "Done". Pair programming configuration may be two developers working with one machine or a programmer and a tester working together. The Advantages of Pair Programming are: 1) Fewer Coding Mistakes and thus good Code Quality. 2) An effective way to share knowledge 3) Solve Problems Faster and Quicker 4) Train New People Joins 5) Improve Interpersonal and Social Skills.

Question 15
 	
The System's architecture is finalized in the beginning of the Project.
 	
  A. True
  B. False
	Correct answer: B
	
	The System's architecture is decided throughout the project, as **understanding emerges and the Scrum Team learns more about the project.**

Question 16
 	
A Unit test can be dependent on other unit tests.
 	
  A. True
  B. False
	Correct answer: B
	
	Each Unit test should be independent of other unit tests.

Question 17
 	
Using Test-First Development, a developer must first write a test that fails before they write new functional code.
 	
  A. True
  B. False
	Correct answer: A
	
	Test-First Development is an evolutionary approach to programming where agile software developers must first write a test that fails before they write new functional code.

Question 18
 	
Which of the following statements are true about Technical debt?
 	
  A. Technical debt is a concept in software development that reflects the implied cost of rework caused by choosing an quicker solution "now" instead of using a better approach that would take longer.
  B. A large accumulation of Technical Debt (bad code) can impact future maintainability of the product.
  C. It misleads the Product Owners, Scrum Masters and Developers about the "Current state" of the System.
  D. The Product becomes more unstable, as more functionality is added over bad code (or existing technical debt).
  E. Technical Debt is a result of a bad technical decision taken in order to save time effort.
	Correct answer: A,B,C,D,E,F,G
	
	Technical debt (also known as design debt or code debt) is a concept in software development that reflects the implied cost of rework caused by choosing an easy solution "now" instead of using a better approach that would take longer. Like any other debt, a large accumulation of Technical Debt (bad code) can impact future maintainability of the product. The downsides of Technical Debt are as follows:
	
	1. It misleads the Product Owners, Scrum Masters and Developers about the "Current state" of the System. For example, if Product Backlog item A is assumed to be completed in a day, it might take three days for it to complete, because of unseen bad code or Technical Debt.
	
	2. The Product becomes more unstable, as more functionality is added over bad code (or existing technical debt). It is far more likely to impact components which cross-cut a range of features.

F. Technical debt causes a greater percentage of the product's budget to be spent on maintenance of the product. G. The velocity at which new functionality can be created is reduced when you have technical debt.	Moreover, if the necessary refactoring is significant it could impact the entire product, and it could affect features in uneven ways. Technical Debt is a result of a bad technical decision taken in order to save time effort. Technical debt causes a greater percentage of the product's budget to be spent on maintenance of the product. The velocity at which new functionality can be created is reduced when you have technical debt.
Question 19 Continuous Integration is a software development practice where members of a special integration team (Nexus or other integration teams) integrate the increments and verify work frequently, often multiple times each day to detect integration errors as quickly as possible. A. True B. False	**Correct answers: B** Continuous Integration is a software development practice where **developers** integrate and verify their work frequently, often multiple times each day to detect integration errors as quickly as possible.
Question 20 Regression Testing is: A. Extensive Testing to make sure that every functionality works as expected. B. Testing the existing software to make sure that a change or addition (of code) hasn't broken existing functionality. C. Testing which cannot be automated. D. All of the above.	Correct answer: B Regression Test: Whenever developers change or modify their software, even a small tweak can have unexpected consequences. **Regression testing is testing existing software applications to make sure that a change or addition hasn't broken any existing functionality.**

Question 21	Correct answer: A
One of the drawbacks to code coverage is that one has to make sure that the developers do not simply write useless test cases in order to increase code coverage. A. True B. False	One of the drawbacks of code coverage could be that there might be incentives to write tests that simply increase code coverage, rather than tests that find bugs without increasing coverage.
Question 22 Extreme Programming is based on 5 values. Extreme Programming **values** are: A. Communication, Simplicity, Feedback, Courage, Respect. B. Communication, Simplicity, Focus, Courage, Respect. C. Communication, Simplicity, Focus, Curiosity, Respect. D. Communication, Simplicity, Feedback, Courage, Release Management Skills.	Correct answers: A XP is based on 5 values. Extreme Programming **values** are: 1. Communication 2. Simplicity 3. Feedback 4. Courage 5. Respect. Just like Scrum, EXTREME PROGRAMMING values Courage and Respect.

Question 23	**Correct answers: A,B,C,D,E,F,G**
Which of the following statements are true about application architecture? A. Developers in the Scrum Team are responsible for creating the architecture. B. The architectural discussions start as early as sprint planning and continue throughout the sprints. C. Defects, Non-functional testing (such as performance, reliability, usability testing) and Design issues may result to underlying application architecture changes. D. The Applications architecture is not designed upfront. E. The System's architecture is decided throughout the project as the understanding of the project increases. F. Developers in the Scrum Team should have a set of Guiding Architecture Principles that every Developer understands and follows when writing code. G. There is no assigned Role (e.g. a software architect) whose job it is to makes sure a consistent architecture is developed. Developers in the Scrum team makes sure that the architecture evolves based on the needs.	Developers in the Scrum Team are responsible for creating the architecture. The architectural and technical design discussions start as early as sprint planning and continue throughout the sprints as the design is implemented (i.e. coding/construction). Defects, Non-functional testing (such as performance, reliability, usability testing) and Design issues may result to underlying application architecture changes. The Applications overall architecture is not designed upfront. The emergence of the Architecture is based on guidelines and agreed principles. The System's architecture is decided throughout the project as the understanding of the project increases. Developers in the Scrum Team should have a set of Guiding Architecture Principles that every Developer understands and follows when writing code. There is no assigned Role (e.g. a software architect) whose job it is to makes sure a consistent architecture is developed. Developers in the Scrum team makes sure that the architecture evolves based on the needs. The Scrum Team plans some time each Sprint to discuss the architecture needed for the features planned in that Sprint.
Question 24 The benefits of Test First Development are: (Choose all that Apply) A. It promotes good code design. B. It improves quality and reduces bugs. C. It causes the developer to construct a test harness that can be automated. D. It speeds the overall development process.	**Correct answers: A, B, C, D** Benefits of TDD: • It promotes good design and separation of concerns. • It improves quality and reduces bugs. • It causes you to construct a test harness that can be automated. • It speeds the overall development process.

Question 25	Correct answer: B
A Spike should not be timeboxed. A. True B. False	Spikes should be time boxed, so the developer should do just enough work to get the value required.
Question 26 **A Unit test** is a way of testing a unit (**the smallest piece of code**) which cannot be logically isolated from other Units. A. True B. False	Correct answer: B **Unit Test: A Unit test** is a way of testing a unit (**the smallest piece of code**) that can be logically isolated in a system. In most programming languages, that is a function, a subroutine, a method or property. A Unit test can be automated.
Question 27 Which of the following are the examples of a Technical Spike? A. Evaluation of potential performance or load impact of a new user story. B. Evaluation of specific implementation technologies that can be applied to a solution. C. Team needs to develop a more confident understanding of a desired approach. D. An activity to learn about technical elements of a solution. E. Mockups and Wireframes.	Correct answer: A, B, C, D A technical spike may be used for evaluation of potential performance or load impact of a new user story, evaluation of specific implementation technologies that can be applied to a solution, or for any reason when the team needs to develop a more confident understanding of a desired approach before committing new functionality to a timebox. Mockups and wireframes are a spike however can be categorized under Functional Spikes.

Question 28	Correct answer: A
A Company has team members with different perspectives (customer, development, testing) collaborating to write acceptance tests in advance of implementing the corresponding functionality. This company is practicing: A. Acceptance Test Driven Development B. Behavior Driven Development C. ALM D. Branching	Acceptance Test Driven Development is a test-first software development practice in which **acceptance criteria for new functionality are created as automated tests.**
Question 29	**Correct answer: B**
An Applications overall architecture is designed upfront during Sprint 0. A. True B. False	The Applications overall architecture is not designed upfront, as the actual implementation of it emerges. The emergence of the Architecture is based on guidelines and agreed principles. The System's architecture is decided throughout the project, as understanding emerges and the Scrum Team learns more about the project. Also Scrum also does not acknowledge anything called as Sprint 0.
Question 30	**Correct answers: C**
The Practice of grouping the programmers to use one computer to code throughout the Sprint is called: A. Dual Programming B. Multiple Review C. Pair Programming D. Code Review	Pair programming is an agile software development technique in which two programmers work together at one workstation. One, the driver, writes code while the other, the observer or navigator, reviews each line of code as it is typed in. The two programmers switch roles frequently. While reviewing, the observer also considers the "strategic" direction of the work, coming up with ideas for improvements and likely future problems to address. This is intended to free the driver to focus all of their attention on the "tactical" aspects of completing the current task, using the observer as a safety net and guide.

Question 31	**Correct answer: B**
A company is trying to reduce the amount of time it puts in towards manual testing. It does instruct its testing team to automate the functionals test cases going forward. This is not possible because Functional Testing cannot be Automated. A. True B. False	Functional Test: **Functional testing is a form of testing that deals** with how applications functions. Traditionally, functional testing is implemented by a team of testers, independent of the developers. Functional tests can be automated.
Question 32 Extreme Programming is complementary to the Scrum framework. A. True B. False	**Correct answers: A** Extreme programming (XP) is highly complementary to the Scrum framework.
Question 33 Which of the following statements are true about Spike? A. Spikes are used to discover risk and uncertainty in a project. B. Spike allows the team an understanding of the upcoming Product Backlog items complexity. C. Spikes may be used for basic research to familiarize the team with a new technology or domain. D. The team may use a spike to analyze the implied behavior, so they can split the story into estimable pieces. E. Teams may have to do some research or prototyping (spikes) to gain confidence in a technological approach that will allow them to commit the user story to some future timebox. F. While the intent of the story may be understood, it's may not be clear on how the system would need to interact with the user to achieve the benefit implied, for which a spike might be used.	**Correct answers: A,B,C,D,E,F** Spikes are special type of stories that are used to discover risk and uncertainty in a project. A Spike is a great way to mitigate risks early and promotes fluid iterations later in the project. Spike allows the team an understanding of the upcoming Product Backlog items complexity. The team may not have knowledge of a new domain, and spikes may be used for basic research to familiarize the team with a new technology or domain. Product backlog items may be too big to be estimated appropriately, and the team may use a spike to analyze the implied behavior, so they can split the story into estimable pieces. Product backlog items may contain significant technical risk, and the team may have to do some research or prototyping (using spikes) to gain confidence in a technological approach that will allow them to commit the user story to some future timebox. Product backlog items may contain significant functional risk. While the intent of the story may be understood, it's may not be clear on how the system would need to interact with the user to achieve the benefit implied, for which a spike might be used.

Question 34	**Correct answer: B**

A company is trying to reduce the amount of time it puts in manual testing. It does instruct its testing team to automate the regressions test cases going forward. This is not possible because Regression Testing cannot be automated.
 	
  A. True
  B. False
	Regression Test: Whenever developers change or modify their software, even a small tweak can have unexpected consequences. **Regression testing is testing existing software applications to make sure that a change or addition hasn't broken any existing functionality.** Its purpose is to catch bugs that may have been accidentally introduced into a new build or release candidate, and to ensure that previously eradicated bugs continue to stay dead. By re-running testing scenarios that were originally scripted when known problems were first fixed, you can make sure that any new changes to an application haven't resulted in a regression or caused components that formerly worked to fail. A Regression test can be automated.

Question 35	**Correct answers: B**

A Developer has decided to adjust code within the code base without impacting the behavior of that code. This act is called:
 	
  A. Coding.
  B. Code Refactoring.
  C. Code Correction.
  D. Code Renewal.
	Code Refactoring is an agile software development practice popularized by Extreme Programming **in which code is adjusted within the code base without impacting the external, functional behavior of that code.**

Question 36	**Correct answers: B**

Automated Software Build Development does not support continuous integration.
 	
  A. True
  B. False
	Build automation is the process of **automating the creation of a software build. It also includes the associated processes such as compiling computer source code into binary code, packaging binary code and running automated tests.**
	Automated Software Build Development supports continuous integration.

Question 37	Correct answers: A

Which of the following statement about DRY is true?
  A. Every piece of knowledge must have a single, unambiguous, authoritative representation within a system.
  B. Every piece of knowledge must have multiple representations within a system.
	The DRY principle is stated as "Every piece of knowledge must have a single, unambiguous, authoritative representation within a system". The principle has been formulated by Andy Hunt and Dave Thomas in their book The Pragmatic Programmer.

Question 38
 	
Extreme Programming does not require the customer on-site to test the stories with the team.
 	
  A. True
  B. False
	Correct answers: B
	
	While Scrum does not require the customer to be on-site, **Extreme Programming requires the customer to be on-site and continuously test with the team**. For Scrum Team practicing EXTREME PROGRAMMING, during Sprint Review the customer, Product Owner and Developers will review the product that is already in production. The Sprint Review will not be the first time the Product Owner and the customer would be seeing the product. Scrum Team will assess what is possible for the next week Sprint based on what has already been delivered to production and what the customers recommend.

Question 39
 	
Which of the following are true statements about Whole Team in Scrums? (Choose all that apply)
  A. All skills that are required to turn the selected stories into a valuable software must be on the team.
  B. Anyone who is qualified to perform a role can undertake it. The roles are not reserved for people who specialize in one particular area.
  C. Whole Team means every single team member in the team should have all the skills needed.
  D. All of the above.
	Correct answers: A, B
	
	Scrum and XP values whole team approach. Whole Team means:
	1) All skills that are required to turn the selected stories into avaluable software must be on the team.
	2) Anyone who is qualified to perform a role can undertake it. The roles are not reserved for people who specialize in one particular area.

Question 40	Correct answers: A, B, C, D

Pair programming supports: (Choose all that apply)
    A. Fewer Coding Mistakes and thus good Code Quality.
    B. An effective way to share knowledge
    C. Solve Problems Faster and Quicker
    D. Train New People and Improve Interpersonal and Social Skills.
	Pair programming is an agile software development technique in which two programmers work together at one workstation. One, the driver, writes code while the other, the observer or navigator, reviews each line of code as it is typed in. The two programmers switch roles frequently.
	While reviewing, the observer also considers the "strategic" direction of the work, coming up with ideas for improvements and likely future problems to address. This is intended to free the driver to focus all of their attention on the "tactical" aspects of completing the current task, using the observer as a safety net and guide. Scrum Team practicing Extreme Programming will put pair programming in the definition of "Done". Pair programming configuration may be two developers working with one machine or a **programmer and a tester** working together.
	The Advantages of Pair Programming are:
	1) Fewer Coding Mistakes and thus good Code Quality.
	2) An effective way to share knowledge
	3) Solve Problems Faster and Quicker
	4) Train New People and Improve Interpersonal and Social Skills.

Question 41
The number of "if" statements, loops and switch cases in a code is represented by:
 	
    A. Depth of Inheritance
    B. Lines of Codes
    C. Cyclomatic Complexity
    D. None of the Above.
	Correct answers: C
	
	Cyclomatic complexity is a software metric used to indicate the complexity of a program. It is a quantitative measure of the number of linearly independent paths through a program's source code. It represents the number of unique paths in a code.
	Cyclomatic complexity represents the number of "if" statements, branching structures, nesting levels and switch cases in a code.
	Code with a high cyclomatic complexity can be hard to test and maintain, as there are number of different paths through the code that must be tested. For Cyclomatic Complexity, a low value is good, and a high value is bad.

Question 42	Correct answer: A
Which of the following test should use a language that can be understood by the customers? A. Acceptance Test Driven Development B. Customer Written Java Code C. ALM D. Branching	Acceptance Test Driven Development should be readable and focused for customers.
Question 43 Functional testing can be implemented by a team of testers, independent of the developers. A. True B. False	Correct answer: A Traditionally, functional testing is implemented by a team of testers, independent of the developers. Functional tests can be automated.
Question 44 Ten-minute builds result to faster client feedback loops. A. True B. False	Correct answers: A Ten Minute Build is another Extreme Programming practice that Scrum Teams find valuable. Extreme Programming requires the code to be integrated continuously and the build run for under ten minutes. Ten Minute Build is non-negotiable rule from Extreme Programming. When the build runs more than ten minutes, developers get more reluctant to continuously integrate their code. When developers don't continuously integrate their code, they lose the opportunity to get feedback. Extreme Programming highly values feedback. Faster build means faster feedback.
Question 45 Code Refactoring is the process of simplifying the design of existing code. The behavior of the system might or might not change. A. True **B.** False	Correct answers: B Code Refactoring is the process of clarifying and simplifying the design of existing code, without changing its behavior

Question 46	Correct answers: B
Whole Team means that:	Whole Team means that all skills that are required to turn the selected stories into a releasable software must be on the team, present across all the team members.
A. All Team members should have all the skills needed to turn the selected stories into a releasable software.	
B. All skills that are required to turn the selected stories into a releasable software must be on the team (across Members) as a whole.	
C. Team is complete and less than 9 Members.	
D. All of the above.	
Question 47	Correct answers: B
A unit test is:	**Unit Test: A Unit test** is a way of testing a unit (**the smallest piece of code**) that can be logically isolated in a system. In most programming languages, that is a function, a subroutine, a method or property. A Unit test can be automated.
A. A method to ensure that the system satisfies the unit requirements.	
B. A test that isolates and verifies individual units of source code.	
C. A test in which Units / Teams of programmers ensure their code works.	
D. A technique for ensuring that units of servers test together.	
Question 48	Correct answer: B
Code coverage **ensures that the most important or highest risk areas of the code are being exercised by tests**.	Code Coverage is a measurement indicating the amount of product code that is exercised by tests. Code Coverage is a measure which describes the degree to which the source code of the program has been tested.
A. True	
B. False	Code Coverage is a form of white box testing which shows the areas of the program exercised by a set of test cases.
	Measuring Code Coverage can help increase software quality by identifying untested parts of codes in a product / application.
	Code Coverage is NOT a metric of code quality. Code Coverage shows the ratio between the tested and untested code. Code Coverage does

not tell you anything about the quality of the tests being run.

Some Advantages of Code Coverage are:
1) It offers a Quantitative Measurement.
2) It defines the degree to which the source code has been tested.

Some shortcomings of Code Coverage as a measurement are:

1) Code Coverage does not ensure that the most important or highest risk areas of the code are being exercised by tests.
2) Code Coverage does not necessarily provide functional coverage.

3) Code Coverage could create incentives to write tests that simply increase code coverage, rather than tests that find bugs without increasing coverage.

Note:

1) There are always parts of code that are hard to test (e.g. I/O, multi-threaded and network code) and the benefits of testing them might not always worth the costs.

2) Writing unit tests for every new feature or change (preferably before writing production code, by practicing Test Driven Development) helps achieve Code Coverage automatically.

Code coverage **does not ensure that the most important or highest risk areas of the code are being exercised by tests**. It just addresses "How much" code not "Which" code.

Question 49	**Correct answer: A, B, C, D**
A Spike can be used when: (Choose all that apply) A. There is less knowledge about the technology used. B. To size and split a Big Story. C. Gain confidence on a technological approach. D. To capture how the user would interact with a designed system.	Spikes may be used for a number of reasons: • The team may not have knowledge of a new domain, and spikes may be used for basic research to familiarize the team with a new technology or domain. • The story may be too big to be estimated appropriately, and the team may use a spike to analyze the implied behavior, so they can split the story into estimable pieces. • The story may contain significant technical risk, and the team may have to do some research or prototyping to gain confidence in a technological approach that will allow them to commit the user story to some future timebox. • The story may contain significant functional risk, in that while the intent of the story may be understood, it's not clear how the system needs to interact with the user to achieve the benefit implied.
Question 50	**Correct answer: C**
Which test case is an approach between developer and tester to create well written unit of code (module, class, function)? A. Developers Test Driven Development. B. Acceptance Test Driven Development. C. Test Driven Development. D. Branching.	TDD is a Developer approach between developer and tester to create well written unit of code (module, class, function).
Question 51	**Correct answers: A**
One of the benefits of continuous integration is that Broken builds are detected quickly. A. True B. False	One of the benefits of continuous integration is that Broken builds are detected quickly.

Question 52
 	
In Test First Development, the developer writes the Code before the test cases.
 	
   A.   True
   B.   False
	Correct answers: B
	
	Test first development, also known as Test Driven Development (TDD) is a development style in which you write the unit tests before you write the code to test

Question 53
 	
Don't repeat yourself (DRY) is a principle of software development aimed at reducing :
 	
   A.   Repetition of software patterns.
   B.   Reducing repetition of similar hardware.
   C.   Reducing repetitive skills within the Scrum Team.
   D.   **All of the above.**
	Correct answers: A
	
	Don't repeat yourself (DRY, or sometimes do not repeat yourself) is a principle of software development aimed at reducing repetition of software patterns, replacing it with abstractions or using data normalization to avoid redundancy.

Question 54
 	
A Company is trying to reduce the amount of time it puts towards manual testing. It does instruct its testing team to automate the integration test cases going forward. This is not possible because Integration Testing cannot be automated.
 	
   A.   True
   B.   False
	Correct answer: B
	
	Integration Test: Integration testing, also known as integration and testing (I&T), is a type of testing in which program units are combined and **tested as groups in multiple ways.** Integration test can be automated.

Question 55
 	
TDD and ADD ensures that there are no defects in the code.
 	
   A.   True
   B.   False
	Correct answers: B
	
	TDD and ADD help is reducing the defects in code. However, they do not reduce the defects completely.

Question 56	Correct answers: D
What is the Acronym for design principle intended to make software design more understandable, flexible and maintainable? A. YOGA B. TDD C. Acceptance Test Driven Development D. SOLID	SOLID principles help software developers to achieve scalability and avoid that your code breaks every time you face a change. Ok, so let's start with the basics. S.O.L.I.D. stands for: S – Single-Responsibility Principle - This principle states that an object/class should only have one responsibility and that it should be completely encapsulated by the class. O – Open-Closed Principle- This Principle affirms that an entity allows its behavior to be extended but never by modifying its source code. Any class (or whatever you write) should be written in such a way that it can be used as is. It can be extended if need be, but it can never be modified. L – Liskov Substitution Principle – This Principle confirms that objects should be replaceable by instances of their subtypes without affecting the functioning of your system from a client's point of view. I – Interface Segregation Principle. – This Principle States that once an interface is becoming too large/fat, we absolutely need to split it into small interfaces that are more specific. D – Dependency Inversion Principle. - this principle is primarily concerned with reducing dependencies amongst the code modules.
Question 57 Code coverage represents the quality of a Unit Test. A. True B. False	**Correct answer: B** Code coverage **does not represent or talk about the quality of the code which is being exercised**. It just addresses "How much" code not "Which" code.

Question 58	**Correct answers: A, B, C and D**
The absolute essential for every bug report are (Select 4 only): A. The Problem Description. B. Steps to reproduce. C. Expected outcome. D. Actual outcome. E. Screenshots of the Issue F. Log / Version of the Platform.	There Key essential for every bug report are: A. The Problem Description. B. Steps to reproduce. C. Expected outcome. D. Actual outcome. Screenshots and Versions are good to have but not mandatory.

Question 59
 	
John, a developer is discussing with Sam (Product Owner) about the advantages of automating the software build process. The reasons to automate the software build process are? (Choose 3)
 	
A. Automation builds improves the Product by allowing creation of an increment with less errors.
B. Automation accelerates the compile and link processing, thus quickening the delivery to the clients and making more time for feedback.
C. Automating software build is a mandate in every software industry.
D. Code reviews are much faster if you automate your build.
E. Helps find defect and configuration issues.
	Correct answers: A, B, E
	
	Build automation is the process of automating the creation of a software build. It also includes the associated processes such as compiling computer source code into binary code, packaging binary code and running automated tests. In the context of software development, build refers to the process that converts files and other assets under the developers' responsibility into a software product in its final or consumable form. The build may include:
	
	1) Compiling source files
	2) Packaging compiled files into compressed formats (such as jar, zip)
	3) Producing installers
	4) creating or updating of database schema or data.
	The advantages of build automation to software development projects include:
	   1. A necessary pre-condition for continuous integration and continuous testing.
	   2. Helps find defect and configuration issues.
	   3. Improve product quality.
	   4. Accelerate the compile and link processing, thus get more feedback.
	   5. Eliminate redundant tasks
	   6. Minimize "bad builds"
	   7. Eliminate dependencies on key personnel
	   8. Have history of builds and releases in order to investigate issues

	Code Reviews frequency is impacted by the build process. Code review itself is not typically impacted by the build process.
Question 60 Which technique focuses on the behavior aspects of the functionality but still practices writing test before code? A. Acceptance Test Driven Development B. Behavior Driven Development C. ALM D. Branching	**Correct answer: B** Behavior Driven Development focuses on the behavioral aspect of system for customer and developer but still practices writing test before code.
Question 61 WET solutions make it difficult to manage the code. if the logic changes, then changes would have to be made in all the places where the code is repeated, thereby wasting everyone's time. A. True B. False	**Correct answers: A** Violations of DRY are typically referred to as WET solutions. Wet Solutions which stands for either "write everything twice", "we enjoy typing" or "waste everyone's time". It is difficult to manage such code and if the logic changes, then developers have to make changes in all the places where they have written the code, thereby wasting everyone's time.
Question 62 Which testing is used to make sure that a build is stable enough to proceed with further testing? A. Smoke Testing. B. Black Box Testing. C. Build Complete Testing. D. Stabilization Testing.	**Correct answer: A** **Smoke Testing:** Smoke testing, also known as **"Build Verification Testing",** is a type of software testing **that comprises of a non-exhaustive set of tests** that aim at ensuring that the most important functions work. The result of this testing is **used to decide if a build is stable enough to proceed with further testing.**

Question 63	**Correct answer: D**
Which of the following statements are true about pair programming? A. Pair programming is an agile software development technique in which two programmers work together at one workstation. Scrum Team practicing Extreme Programming will pair programmers throughout the Sprint. B. Pair programming is about live code review. Using Pair Programming, dirtiness in a code can be caught earlier by having a live code review. C. Pair programming configuration may be two developers working with one machine or a programmer and a tester working together. D. All of the above.	Pair programming is an agile software development technique in which two programmers work together at one workstation. One of the developers (the driver) writes code while the other (the observer or navigator) reviews each line of code as it is typed in. The two programmers switch roles frequently. Scrum Team practicing Extreme Programming will pair programmers throughout the Sprint. Pair programming is a micro feedback loop. Pair programming is about live code review. Using Pair Programming, dirtiness in a code can be caught earlier by having a live code review. Pair programming is about two people collaborating to solve a problem together because two heads are better than one. While reviewing, the observer also considers the "strategic" direction of the work, coming up with ideas for improvements and likely future problems to address. This is intended to free the driver to focus all of their attention on the "tactical" aspects of completing the current task, using the observer as a safety net and guide. Scrum Team practicing Extreme Programming will put pair programming in the definition of "Done". Pair programming configuration may be two developers working with one machine or a programmer and a tester working together. The Advantages of Pair Programming are: • Fewer Coding Mistakes and thus good Code Quality. • An effective way to share knowledge • Solve Problems Faster and Quicker • Train New People and Improve Interpersonal and Social Skills.

Question 64

A Good Bug Report has which of the following in it? (Choose all that apply)

A. A good bug report contains multiple bugs and clear descriptions
B. A good bug report contains detailed information needed to reproduce and fix problems.
C. A good bug report contains clear title and proper grammar in the report.
D. A good bug report is an efficient form of communication for both bug reporter and bug receiver.

Correct answers: B, C, D

A bug report "should explain how exactly the product is broken." If bugs occur, the person finding the bug should be able to report (document & send) the bug to people in charge of fixing that error or failure. There are 4 key points that are essential for every bug report:

E. The Problem.
F. Steps to reproduce.
G. Expected outcome.
H. Actual outcome

A Good Bug Report:

1. A good bug report contains one Bug Per Report
2. A good bug report contains the information needed to reproduce and fix problems
3. A good bug report contains clear title and proper grammar in the report,
4. A good bug report is an efficient form of communication for both bug reporter and bug receiver.
5. A good bug report contains expected vs actual results.
6. A good bug report contains version of the plugin/platform.
7. A good bug report contains Screenshot(s) of the problem and Logs.
8. A good report should not assign Blame.

Question 65	**Correct answers: D**
A Scrum team creates and manages User stories. The Product Owner and the Developers manage the user stories every morning. According to Scrum, User stories should be documented: A. Every Day B. Every Week C. At least before Sprint End. D. Only If they are part of Definition of Done.	**Scrum does not mandate the use of User Stories. Unless its mentioned in the Definition of Done, user stories don't need to be created or reported.** According to the Scrum Guide, the Product Backlog lists all features, functions, requirements, enhancements, and fixes that constitute the changes to be made to the product in future releases. It lists all the work that is deemed necessary for the product. How Scrum Teams decide to capture this work is entirely up to them. They can write User Stories, they can use a bunch of keywords, write use cases or even draw pictures.
Question 66 Lines of Code indicates: A. The number of total lines of code in a method. B. The number of executable lines of code in a method. C. The total number of executable lines, functions and procedures of code in a method. D. All of the above.	**Correct answers: B** Lines of Code indicates the total number of executable lines of code in a method. This count is an approximate number, based on the Intermediate Language (IL) code.
Question 67 It is recommended that the developers should be given **a set of guiding architecture principles** that every member understands and follows when writing code. A. True B. False	**Correct answers: A** Since the Architecture is always an ongoing process and subject to change, Developers should **have a set of Guiding Architecture Principles** that every member understands and follows when writing code.
Question 68 In Scrum, there is an assigned Role (e.g. a software architect) who makes sure a consistent architecture is developed. A. True B. False	**Correct answers: B** There is no assigned Role (e.g. a software architect) who makes sure a consistent architecture is developed. Developers in the Scrum Team make sure that the architecture evolves based on the needs.

Question 69	Correct answers: B
Continuous Deployment is a software delivery practice similar to Continuous Delivery except a human action is required to promote changes into a subsequent environment along the pipeline. A. True B. False	Continuous Delivery is a software delivery practice similar to Continuous Deployment except a human action is required to promote changes into a subsequent environment along the pipeline. Continuous Deployment is a software delivery practice in which the release process is fully automated in order to have changes promoted to the production environment with no human intervention.
Question 70 Developers should participate in the Product Refinement: A. Only if called for in the Refinement Meetings. B. As soon as possible and anytime during the Sprint. C. They should not Participate. It's the Product Owners responsibility to understand the requirements and convert them into Product Backlog items. D. Once grooming and decomposition begins in the Daily Scrum meetings.	**Correct answers: B** Developers should participate in the Product Refinement as soon as possible. Planning of which Product Backlog items will be selected, and their completion dates happens during Sprint Planning. Product Backlog refinement is the act of breaking down and further defining Product Backlog items into smaller more precise items. During Sprint planning, decomposing, designing (flow charts, logic Diagrams etc.) of the Sprint Backlog items are done. Through discussion with the Product Owner, the Developers select items from the Product Backlog to include in the current Sprint. The Scrum Team may refine these items during this process, which increases understanding and confidence. Thus the developers should be involved in the refinement sessions as soon as possible.
Question 71 A company is trying to reduce the amount of time it put in manual testing. It does instruct its testing team to automate the exploratory test cases going forward. This is not possible because Exploratory Testing cannot be Automated. A. True B. False	**Correct answer: A** Exploratory Test: Exploratory testing is all about discovery, investigation, and learning. It **emphasizes personal freedom and responsibility** of the individual tester. It is defined as a type of testing where Test cases are not created in advance, but testers check system on the fly. They may note down ideas about what to test before test execution. The focus of exploratory testing is more on testing as a "thinking" activity. Exploratory test cannot be automated.

Question 72	Correct answers: A
One of the benefits of continuous integration is that software is generally kept in a buildable state. A. True B. False	One of the benefits of continuous integration is that software is generally kept in a buildable state.
Question 73 Depth of Inheritance indicates: A. The number of different classes that inherit from one another, all the way back to the base class. B. The number of different functions that inherit from one another, all the way back to the base function. C. Depth of Inheritance is similar to class coupling, there is no difference. D. The number of users inheriting the company policies.	**Correct answers: A** Depth of Inheritance indicates the number of different classes that inherit from one another, all the way back to the base class.
Question 74 Which testing is also known as Behavioral Testing? A. Smoke Testing. B. Black Box Testing. C. Build Complete Testing. D. Stabilization Testing.	**Correct answer: B** **Black Box Testing:** Black Box testing, also known as Behavioral Testing, is a software testing method in which the **internal structure / implementation of the item being tested is not known to the tester.** Black Box Testing, either functional or non-functional, is a testing which has no reference to the internal structure of the component or system.
Question 75 There is an assigned Role (such as Quality Analyst) who develops and executes the Test Cases. A. True B. False	**Correct answers: B** There is no assigned Role (e.g. QA) who conducts the Test Cases. Developers are responsible for writing and executing the Test Cases.

Question 76	**Correct answers: C**
A Bug report is: A. A List of Bugs reported using a specific criterion. B. A Report generated for all the existing bugs in the System. C. A Single Bug explanation of how exactly the product is broken. D. A collection of errors, flaws, failures, or faults that produces an incorrect or unexpected result.	A software bug is an error, flaw, failure, or fault that produces an incorrect or unexpected result. If bugs occur (which they certainly do), the person finding the bug should be able to report (document & send) the bug to people in charge of fixing that error or failure. **A bug report "should explain how exactly the product is broken."**
Question 77 Code coverage **provides the measure of functional coverage.** A. True B. False	**Correct answer: B** Code coverage does not necessarily **provide functional coverage**.
Question 78 Which technique focuses on bringing the customer in design phase to review or help with the Test case creation. A. Acceptance Test Driven Development B. Behavior driven development. C. Brain storming. D. Branching	**Correct answer: A** ATDD Tests should be readable and focused for customers. ATDD Focus on capturing requirements in acceptance criteria and use to drive the development. ATDD technique encourages bringing the customer in design phase.
Question 79 A low priority bug is encountered by the developer. The Developer should: A. Resolve it right away. B. Create a Bug Report and Put in the Product Backlog. C. Notify the manager right away. D. Ignore the Bug.	**Correct answers: B** Unless your company has specific guidance on fixing bugs, they represent work to be done and **should be ordered on the Product Backlog by the Product Owner**.

Question 80
 	
When should a developer resolve the Bug right away?
 	
   A. Always.
   B. Never.
   C. if the work to fix the bug is less than the work to actually file and test it.
   D. if the bug is so critical that it would be negligent to leave it unfixed
	Correct answers: C, D
	
	A bug should be resolved right away if:
	   1) if the work to fix the bug is less than the work to actually file it.
	   2) if the bug is so critical that it would be negligent to leave it unfixed

Question 81
 	
Test Driven Development represents a test in form of requirement which should be satisfied.
 	
   A. True
   B. False
	Correct answers: A
	
	The Test exists before the code is written thus making it act as a requirement. As soon as the Test is passed, the requirement is met.

Question 82
 	
Which testing is a software testing method in which the **internal structure/design/implementation of the item being tested is not known to the tester?**
 	
   A. Smoke Testing
   B. Black Box Testing
   C. Build Complete Testing
   D. Stabilization Testing.
	Correct answer: B
	
	Black Box Testing, either functional or non-functional, is a testing which has no reference to the internal structure of the component or system

Question 83

Which of the following statements are true about code refactoring?

A. Code Refactoring is an agile software development practice in which code is adjusted (within the code base) without impacting the functional behavior of that code.

B. Readability and Maintainability is a benefit of code refactoring. It is easier to fix bugs because the source code is easy to read, and the intent of its author is easy to grasp.

C. Code Refactoring could involve reducing large monolithic routines into a set of individually concise, well-named, single-purpose methods.

D. Code Refactoring could involve moving a method to a more appropriate class, or by removing misleading comments.

Correct answer: A,B,C,D

Code Refactoring is an agile software development practice in which code is adjusted (within the code base) without impacting the external, functional behavior of that code. Code Refactoring is the process of clarifying and simplifying the design of existing code, without changing its behavior. Agile teams extend their code a lot from iteration to iteration with the help of code refactoring.
There are two general benefits to the activity of refactoring:

Readability and Maintainability. It is easier to fix bugs because the source code is easy to read, and the intent of its author is easy to grasp. Code Refactoring involves:
• Reducing large monolithic routines into a set of individually concise, well-named, single-purpose methods.
• Moving a method to a more appropriate class, or by removing misleading comments.

Extensibility. It is easier to extend the capabilities of the application if the code uses recognizable design patterns.

Question 84

Which of the following are the examples of a functional Spike? (Choose all that apply)

A. Mockups
B. Wireframes
C. Page flows
D. Techniques to collect functional feedback from customers
E. Evaluation of technical elements for a proposed solution

Correct answer: A, B, C, D

Functional spikes are often best evaluated through some level of prototyping, whether it be user interface mockups, wireframes, page flows, or whatever techniques is best suited to get feedback from the customer or stakeholders. Evaluation of technical elements for a proposed solution is a technical spike.

Question 85	**Correct answer: A, B, C, D**
Which of the following statements are true? (Choose all that apply) A. Test Driven Development (TDD) is technical in nature and is written in the same language the feature is implemented in. If the feature is implemented in Java, JUnit test cases are written. Whereas Behavior Driven Development (BDD) & Acceptance Test Driven Development (ATDD) are written in simple English language. B. The Test-Driven Development (TDD) approach focuses on the implementation of a feature. Behavior Driven Development (BDD) focuses on the behavior of the feature, and Acceptance Test Driven Development (ATDD) focuses on capturing the requirements (in form of acceptance criterias). C. TDD, BDD and ATDD basically talk about the "test-First" approach, unlike the "test-last" approach used in traditional development methodologies. D. When Behavior Driven Development is adapted in a project, the technical nitty-gritty aspects of the requirements and implementation are outlined in a business-oriented language.	1) Test Driven Development (TDD) is technical in nature and is written in the same language the feature is implemented in. If the feature is Implemented in Java, JUnit test cases are written. Whereas Behavior Driven Development (BDD) & Acceptance Test Driven Development (ATDD) are written in simple business language. 2) The Test-Driven Development (TDD) approach focuses on the implementation of a feature. Behavior Driven Development (BDD) focuses on the behavior of the feature, and Acceptance Test Driven Development (ATDD) focuses on capturing the requirements (in form of acceptance criterias). 3) TDD, BDD and ATDD basically talk about the "test-First" approach, unlike the "test-last" approach used in traditional development methodologies. When Behavior Driven Development is adapted in a project, the technical nitty-gritty aspects of the requirements and implementation are outlined in a business-oriented language.

Question 86	**Correct answers: A**
Developers within a company have been spending too much time debugging. A scrum masters makes a suggestion to implement and improve various continuous integration strategies and process. One of the benefits of continuous integration is that developers spend less time debugging and more time adding features. A. True B. False	The benefits of Continuous Integration are: • Short and Less intense integrations • Increase visibility enabling greater communication • Catching issues early • Spend less time debugging and more time adding features • Building a solid foundation • Less waiting to find out if your code's going to work • Reduced integration problems allowing one to deliver software more rapidly
Question 87	**Correct answers: A**
A Technical debt is a result of Poor Technical decisions. A. True B. False	A Technical debt represents results which are a consequence of poor technical choices.
Question 88	**Correct answers: A**
A Scrum team developer is working on Product Backlog item and encounters a bug. The developers should: A. Discuss it with Product Owner and ask for his suggestion to resolve it now or in the future. B. Work on it in the current Sprint as the Dev team owns quality. They should go ahead, create a task, and fix it within this sprint.	Talking with the Product Owner is the right thing to do. There needs to be an understanding of what the impact of the bug is, especially if it already exists. Perhaps some of the new development will cause more people to use the functionality and stumble across the bug. The existence of workarounds and how burdensome or effective those workarounds are also has an impact. Maybe the existence of the bug would make the resulting Increment not viable for use.

Question 89
 	
Automated Build should ideally trigger as soon as new code is checked in. (or old code is changed).
 	
  A. True
  B. False
	Correct answers: A
	
	Ideally, automated Build should trigger as soon as new code is checked in. (or old code is changed).

Question 90
 	
What is Class Coupling?
  A. Class Coupling is a measure which reflects the number of classes in a code.
  B. Class Coupling is a measure which reflects the strength of each class & its impact in a code.
  C. Class coupling is a measure of the dependencies a class has on other classes.
  D. Class coupling reflects the number of methods calls in a code.
	Correct answers: C
	
	Class coupling is a measure of the dependencies a class has on other classes.

Question 91
 	
A new Scum Team is demanding for a separate Quality Team / Testing Team as they cannot get enough time developing. A lot of development still needs to be completed. The Scrum Master should tell the Scrum Team:
  A. That testing functions needs to be a part of the scrum team and a separate team cannot be formed. They can internally hire more Testing specialist as Developers
  B. Split the Team into Developers and Testers. Hire resources as needed.
  C. Ask the CEO if this can be done.
  D. Raise this as an Impediment.
	Correct answer: A
	
	Remember, all the test cases and testing is performed by Members of the Scrum Team. Scrum does not approve roles such as Quality Analyst or Sub Teams (Testing Team, Business Team etc.).

Question 92	Correct answers: B
Continuous Delivery is a software delivery practice in which the release process is fully automated in order to have changes promoted to the production environment **with no human intervention**. A. True B. False	Continuous Delivery is a software delivery practice similar to Continuous Deployment except a human action is required to promote changes into a subsequent environment along the pipeline. Continuous Deployment is a software delivery practice in which the release process is fully automated in order to have changes promoted to the production environment with no human intervention.
Question 93 Which testing is a type of software testing **that comprises of a non-exhaustive set of tests** that aim at ensuring that the most important functions work? A. Regression Testing B. Smoke Testing C. Black Box Testing D. Exploratory Testing	**Correct answer: B** **Smoke Testing:** Smoke testing, also known as **"Build Verification Testing",** is a type of software testing **that comprises of a non-exhaustive set of tests** that aim at ensuring that the most important functions work. The result of this testing is **used to decide if a build is stable enough to proceed with further testing.**
Question 94 Which of the following statement is true about automated software builds? A. Automated Software Build Development allows frequent validation of the unit of software being worked on, ensuring it remains in a potentially shippable state. B. Automated Software Build Development supports Continuous Integration. C. Automated Software Build Development process allows itself to be clearly defined and scripted, making it easy, consistent and repeatable. D. In case of Continuous integration Software Build Developments, the person who broke the build will be responsible for fixing it. E. Ideally, Automated Build should trigger as soon as new code is checked in. (or old code is changed).	**Correct answer: A,B,C,D,E** Automated Software Build Development allows frequent validation of the unit of software being worked on, ensuring it remains in a potentially shippable state. Automated Software Build Development supports Continuous Integration. Automated Software Build Development process allows itself to be clearly defined and scripted, making it easy, consistent and repeatable. In case of Continuous integration Software Build Developments, the person who broke the build will be responsible for fixing it. Ideally, Automated Build should trigger as soon as new code is checked in. (or old code is changed). Automated Build should be followed by a set of selective Unit Test. Once it passes Unit test, it should then run through a set of comprehensive tests (Automated Test, Unit Test, Manual Test,

	Non-Functional Test). This would help identify bugs that the developers would fix before proceeding.
	Automating Software Build Process does not speed up the Code Review Process.
Question 95 John was working on the Continuous integration Software Build and it did not compile (Broke) because of a code he had written. John is responsible for fixing it since he broke the build. A. True B. False	**Correct answers: A** In case of Continuous integration Software Build Developments, the person who broke the build will be responsible for fixing it.
Question 96 A software code that is expressed well, formatted correctly, and organized for later coders to understand is called: A. Cleared Code B. Subscribed Code C. Clean Code D. System Code	**Correct answers: C** Clean Code is defined as a software code that is expressed well, formatted correctly, and organized for later coders to understand.

Question 97	**Correct answers: B**
The deeper the depth of inheritance, the less potential there is for causing breaking changes in the code when modifying a base class. A. True B. False	The deeper the depth of inheritance, the more potential there is for causing breaking changes in the code when modifying a base class.
Question 98	**Correct answers: A**
Cyclomatic complexity represents the number of unique paths through your code. A. True B. False	Cyclomatic complexity represents the number of unique paths through your code.
Question 99	**Correct answer: D**
Which testing is a software testing method in which the internal structure/design/implementation of the item being tested is known to the tester? A. Smoke Testing B. Black Box Testing C. Build Complete Testing D. White Box Testing.	**White Box Testing**: White Box testing, also known as Clear Box Testing, Open Box Testing, Glass Box Testing, Transparent Box Testing, Code-Based Testing or Structural Testing, is a software testing method in which **the internal structure/design of the item being tested is known to the tester.**
Question 100	**Correct answers: A**
Depth of Inheritance is similar to class coupling however the difference is that in depth of Inheritance, a base class can affect any of its inherited classes. A. True B. False	Depth of Inheritance is similar to class coupling however the difference is that in Depth of Inheritance, a base class can affect any of its inherited classes.
Question 101	**Correct answers: A**
Cohesion is a measure of the degree to which the responsibilities of a single module (or a component) form a meaningful unit. A. True B. False	Cohesion is a measure of the degree to which the responsibilities of a single module (or a component) form a meaningful unit.

Question 102	**Correct answers: B**

What is Application Lifecycle Management? (Choose the best answer)
  A. An application that manages only specific stages in a Lifecycle for a given Product.
  B. A holistic view on the management of software applications and systems, accounting for all stages of the existence of a software product.
  C. A mandatory software used in Scrum.
  D. A management practice which is used only for Software development.
	ALM (Application Lifecycle Management): is a holistic view on the management of software applications and systems, accounting for all stages of the existence of a software product.

Question 103	**Correct answers: A, B,C,D,E**

Which of the following statements are true? (Choose all that apply)
  A. Test Driven Development is a development style in which one writes the unit tests before writing the code.
  B. Test Driven Development is a Predictable, Incremental and Emergent Software development approach / technique which relies on Automated Test.
  C. "Test-Driven Development" refers to a style of programming in which three activities are tightly interwoven: Writing Test, Coding and Refactoring.
  D. A test written with Test-Driven Development represents a technical requirement that must be satisfied.
  E. Test-Driven Development is easier to implement in applications designed to unit test.
	Test First Development is also known as Test Driven Development (TDD). Test Driven Development is a development style in which one writes the unit tests before writing the code. Test Driven Development is a Predictable, Incremental and Emergent Software development approach / technique which relies on Automated Test. "Test-Driven Development" refers to a style of programming in which three activities are tightly interwoven: Writing Test, Coding and Refactoring. Example: Test Driven Development for a feature / aspect of a program can be concisely described by the following:
	
	• Write a "Single" Unit Test describing an aspect of the program.
	• Run the test, which should fail because the program lacks that feature.
	• Write "just enough" code to make the test pass.
	• "Refactor" the code until it conforms to the Simplicity Criteria.
	• Repeat, "Accumulating" unit tests over time.
	
	A test written with Test-Driven Development represents a technical requirement that must be satisfied.
	Test-Driven Development is easier to implement in in applications designed to unit test.

Question 104	Correct answers: A
A company has multiple teams working on a single product with a single Product Backlog. Is it a good idea for each member of the teams to frequently commit their code back to the main trunk, rather than each team managing their own branch? A. True B. False.	Continuous Integration (to trunk) is a great state to aim for.
Question 105 Smoke Testing consist of a set of exhaustive tests that aim at ensuring that the all the functions work. A. True B. False	**Correct answer: B** Smoke Testing: Smoke testing, also known as "Build Verification Testing", is a type of software testing that comprises of a non-exhaustive set of tests that aim at ensuring that the most important functions work. The result of this testing is used to decide if a build is stable enough to proceed with further testing.
Question 106 The approach to use a branch to work on a feature until it's complete, then merge into the trunk/master Branch is called: A. Release Branching B. Spin off Branching C. Feature Branching D. Task Branching	**Correct answers: C** Feature branching: Feature Branching is an approach is to use a branch to work on a feature until it's complete, then merge into the trunk/master Branch. Feature branches are often coupled with feature flags–"toggles" that enable or disable a feature within the product. That makes it easy to deploy code into master and control when the feature is activated, making it easy to initially deploy the code well before the feature is exposed to end-users.

Quick Reference Guide & Exam Questions
Professional Scrum Master II (PSM II)

Question 107	Correct answers: B, C

Developers of a Scrum team express concerns around the integration of their stories into the master branch, each sprint. These developers work within their own branch and towards the end of the sprint they all merge into one master branch. How can they reduce this burden and make it easier for the code to be merged? (Choose All that Apply)
 	
  A. One developer (usually the same one) should be left with the task of making sure everything has integrated well with another dev's code.
  B. Each developer should be pulling from the main branch into their own feature branch so that they ensure they don't go too far from the current baseline.
  C. Merging should happen more often. They can do that daily, so that tasks that take more than a couple days stay in sync and merge issues are resolved while they are still small.
  D. Make all changes in the main branch so no integration is needed.
  E. Reserve some time at the end of the Sprint for Merging.
	Each developer should be pulling from the main branch into their own feature branch so that they ensure they don't go too far from the current baseline. Conflicts with the Main branch are seen when developers rebase more than needed.
	
	Merging should happen more often. They can do that daily, so that tasks that take more than a couple days stay in sync and merge issues are resolved while they are still small. Continuous and Frequent Merges are always recommended.

Question 108 Which of the following are qualities of a bad bug report? (Choose all that apply) A. A bad bug report does not contain the important information needed to reproduce and fix problems. B. A bad bug report has generic titles. C. A bad bug report assigns vague statements or untested assumptions. D. A bad bug report assigns blames.	**Correct answers: A, B, C, D** Bad Bug Report has the following attributes: 1. A bad bug report does not contain the information needed to reproduce and fix problems 2. A bad bug report is a lengthy, inefficient form of communication for everyone involved. 3. A bad bug report has generic titles 4. A bad bug report assigns Vague statements or untested assumptions. 5. A bad bug report assigns blames.
Question 109 Continuous Delivery makes sure that team is always working towards a "Production Ready" software. A. True B. False	**Correct answers: A** Continuous Delivery helps to move away from the activity of preparing and making software Production Ready. Instead the Scrum Team makes sure that the software is **always "Production Ready"**.
Question 110 While counting the Lines in Lines of Code - Code Matrix it is recommended that the braces, white space and member declarations are excluded. A. True B. False	**Correct answers: A** Lines of Code include only executable lines of code, so comments, braces, white space and member declarations are excluded.
Question 111 Which of the following features should Clean Code should have? (Choose all that Apply): A. Descriptive Function Names B. Small Functions C. Few Comments D. Few Arguments E. Single Responsibility Principle F. Necessary Code Only G. Less Commas	**Correct answers: A, B, C, D, E, F** Clean Code should have the following features: • Descriptive Function Names • Small Functions • Few Comments • Few Arguments • Single Responsibility Principle • Necessary Code Only • Tested

Question 112	Correct answers: A, B, C, D, E, F

Application Lifecycle Management Includes (Choose All that Apply):
  A. Planning and change management
  B. Requirements definition and management
  C. Architecture management
  D. Software configuration management
  E. Build and deployment automation
  F. Quality management.
	Designed for the execution of a software delivery project, Application Lifecycle Management solutions coordinate people, processes, and tools in an iterative cycle of integrated software development activities. ALM includes:
	  • Planning and change management
	  • Requirements definition and management
	  • Architecture management
	  • Software configuration management
	  • Build and deployment automation
	  • Quality management.

Question 113
 	
If the code is continuously compiled and checked:
  A. Code conflicts can be identified earlier when they are easy to manage.
  B. Code conflicts will be increase due to the increased frequency.
  C. Team will be spending more time towards software integration rather than focusing on the software development.
  D. Lot of team members would need spend time towards build automation which would take away from the teams development time.
	Correct answers: A
	
	The purpose of Continuous Integration is to **avoid last minute integration surprises and find code issues right away.** If code is continuously compiled and checked, conflicts can be identified when they are easy to manage.

Question 114
 	
A Team is gathering requirements by using realistic examples from past experience instead of functional behavior requirements. The Team is acknowledging:
 	
  A. Experience requirement gathering.
  B. Specification by behavior.
  C. Specification by example.
  D. All of the above.
	Correct answers: C
	
	Specification by Example calls for using realistic examples from past experience instead of untested or abstract statements in the description of the desired functional behavior.

Question 115 Which of the following statements about code Coverage are true? (Select 3) A. Code Coverage offers a Qualitative Measurement. B. Code Coverage ensures that the most important or highest risk areas of the code are being exercised by tests. C. Code Coverage does not necessarily provide functional coverage. D. Code Coverage could create incentives to write tests that simply increase code coverage, rather than tests that find bugs without increasing coverage. E. Code Coverage is NOT a metric of code quality.	**Correct answers: C,D,E** Code Coverage is a measure which describes the degree to which the source code of the program has been tested. Code Coverage is a form of white box testing which shows the areas of the program exercised by a set of test cases. Measuring Code Coverage can help increase software quality by identifying untested parts of codes in a product / application. Code Coverage is NOT a metric of code quality. Code Coverage shows the ratio between the tested and untested code. Advantages of Code Coverage are: • It offers a Quantitative Measurement. • It defines the degree to which the source code has been tested. Some shortcomings of Code Coverage as a measurement are: • Code Coverage does not ensure that the most important or highest risk areas of the code are being exercised by tests. • Code Coverage does not necessarily provide functional coverage. • Code Coverage could create incentives to write tests that simply increase code coverage, rather than tests that find bugs without increasing coverage.
Question 116 John is a Developer and is been asked to Practice Test First Development. John does not understand the benefits of implementing the Test First Development right away. Jack is a Scrum Master and explains that the benefits of TDD are: (Choose all that Apply) A. It prevents them from avoiding the difficult task of writing code. B. It ensures that their code is always defect free. C. It reduces the questions from management on whether the code has been tested properly. D. It reduces the re-work developers would have to do and gives them the courage to refactor.	**Correct answers: D** Advantage of Test First Development are: • It promotes good design and separation of concerns. • It improves quality and reduces bugs. • It causes you to construct a test harness that can be automated. • It speeds the overall development process. • It reduces the re-work developers would have to do and gives them the courage to refactor.

Question 117

You are a team member on a software development project and have been asked to follow TDD process. The sequence of activities you would undertake is:

A. Write code, write test, refactor
B. Write test, refactor, write code
C. Write test, write code, refactor
D. Write code, refactor, write test

Correct answers: C

"Test-Driven Development" refers to a style of programming in which three activities are tightly interwoven: coding, testing (in the form of writing unit tests) and design (in the form of refactoring). It can be succinctly described by the following set of rules:
• Write a "single" unit test describing an aspect of the program.
• Run the test, which should fail because the program lacks that feature.
• Write "just enough" code, the simplest possible, to make the test pass.
• "Refactor" the code until it conforms to the Simplicity Criteria.
• Repeat, "accumulating" unit tests over time.

Question 118

The practice of always leaving the code base in a little better state than it was found before modifications, is called:

A. Scout Rule
B. Jerry's Rule
C. Clean Code Rule
D. James Rule

Correct answers: A

The practice of always leaving the code base in a little better state than it was found before modifications, is called the Scout Rule. Scout Rule is a mean to progress towards Clean Code.

Question 119

A measure of how closely connected two routines or modules are, is called:

A. Coupling.
B. Cohesion.
C. Transparency.
D. Dependency.

Correct answers: A

Coupling is the degree of interdependence between software modules; a measure of how closely connected two routines or modules are; the strength of the relationships between modules.

Question 120	**Correct answers: A**
John is a Developer. He is getting ready to create a Spike. The purpose of a spike would be: A. Reduce uncertainty in a feature, technology, or process. B. Increase the velocity from one iteration to another. C. Reduce work for the developers. D. Skip developing the need of writing Requirements.	Spike is a story or task aimed at **answering a question or gathering information, rather than at producing shippable product.** In practice, the spikes teams take on are often proof-of-concept types of activities. The definition above says that the work is not focused on the finished product. It may even be designed to be thrown away at the end. This gives your product owner the proper expectation that you will most likely not directly implement the spike solution.
Question 121	**Correct answers: A**
Branching Strategy that focuses on each issue and implements it as its own branch (with the issue key included in the branch name) is called: A. Task Branching B. Release Branching C. Bug Branching D. Jira Branching	**Task Branching**: Every organization has a natural way to break down work in individual tasks inside of an issue tracker, like Jira Software. Issues then becomes the team's central point of contact for that piece of work. Task branching, also known as issue branching, directly connects those issues with the source code. Each issue is implemented on its own branch with the issue key included in the branch name.
Question 122	**Correct answers: B**
It is a good practice to have a special technical Sprint which consists of only removing the technical debt without implementing any new functionality. Such technical sprints however should only be implemented once in a release. A. True B. False	Scrum does not acknowledge: 1) Hardening Phases. 2) Sprint 0. 3) Technical Sprints that consists only of tasks which help reduce the technical debt and do not add any functionality to the Product.
Question 123	**Correct answers: B**
Is it recommended to have a "hardening" Sprint to remove all technical debt and prepare the Product for upcoming release? A. True B. False	Scrum does not acknowledge: 1) Hardening Phases. 2) Sprint 0. 3) Technical Sprints that consists only of tasks which help reduce the technical debt and do not add any functionality to the Product.

Question 124	Correct answer: C

What is code coverage?
   A. The number of developers in the team covering the code.
   B. The percent of code being covered by the developers.
   C. The degree to which the system has been exercised by tests.
   D. Code being covered from issues and bugs.
	Code coverage is a measure which describes the degree of which the source code of the program has been tested. It is one form of white box testing which finds the areas of the program which have been exercised by a set of test cases.

Question 125 Burn down chart displays the following attributes on their axes: A. X axis = points remaining; Y axis = calendar time B. X axis = estimated time remaining; Y axis = calendar time C. X axis = calendar time; Y axis = Sum of Task Remaining. D. X axis = calendar time; Y axis = calendar time	Correct answers: C Burn-down chart shows the evolution of remaining effort against time. A burn down chart is a graphical representation of work left to do versus time. That is, it is a run chart of outstanding work. • X-Axis on the Burn-down chart shows he project/iteration timeline • Y-Axis on the Burn-down chart the work that needs to be completed for the project. • The Lines on the Graph show the **Actual Task Remaining Vs the Ideal Task Remaining.**

Question 126
 	
A group of developers are looking at the code they have developed so far. They have a few analyses which show the code coupling matrix across different feature modules. Which of the following is false?
 	
   A. When code coupling is high, the team may assume that the software modules are interdependent, i.e., they cannot function without the other.
   B. When Code Coupling is high, the team may assume that the software modules are less interdependent, i.e., they can function without each other.
	Correct answers: B
	
	When code coupling is high, the team may assume that the software modules are interdependent, i.e., they cannot function without the other.

Question 127	**Correct answers: A**
Scrum Teams with excellent technical practices will likely be more successful with Scrum then without it. A. True B. False	While technical practices aren't specifically included as a part of Scrum, the rapid pace of development using Scrum often requires that good technical practices are utilized by Developers in order to be successful.
Question 128	**Correct answers: B**
Test Driven Development is a technique which does not rely on automated test. A. True B. False	Test Driven Development is an incremental and emergent Software development approach / technique which relies on automated test.
Question 129	**Correct answers: B**
Continuous Delivery means every change is deployed to production ASAP. A. True B. False	Continuous Delivery doesn't mean every change is deployed to production ASAP. It means every change is proven to be deployable at any time.
Question 130	**Correct answers: B**
When would the scrum team typically add "Deployed to Production" or "Ready to release" to the Definition of "Done" of Product Backlog item? A. Right before the Release, all the Product backlog items are changed to add "Deployed to Production" or "Ready to release" to the Definition of "Done". B. When the team supports Continuous Integration. C. Both of the above. D. None of the above.	To support Continuous Delivery, the Scrum Team would add the following to the Definition of "Done": • "Deployed to Production" • "Ready to Release"

Question 131

A team is getting ready to write all of its logic to a database. The team decides to segregate the logic into multiple classes, each single class having one single purpose. Other modules would refer to the needed class if the same logic is needed. They would not copy the logic in its own class, rather just refer to it. This is an example of:

A. Coupling
B. Cohesion
C. Transparency
D. Dependency

Correct answers: B

Cohesion is a measure of the degree to which the responsibilities of a single module or a component form a meaningful unit.

If a module performs one task and nothing else or has a clear purpose, the module has high cohesion. On the other hand, if our module tries to encapsulate more than one purpose or has an unclear purpose, the module has low cohesion.

Modules with high cohesion tend to be preferable, simple because high cohesion is associated with several desirable traits of software including robustness, reliability, and understandability.

Low cohesion is associated with undesirable traits such as being difficult to maintain, test, reuse, or even understand.

This question is an example of Cohesion. Cohesion makes the software easier to understand, reduces the effects a change on one part of the system has on the rest of the system, and it allows us to reuse code within our application.

Examples:

1. **Logical cohesion** -- This is a type of cohesion in which multiple logically related functions or data elements are placed in the same component.
2. **Procedural cohesion** -- This is a type of cohesion in which the functions in a component are grouped in a way to enable them to be executed sequentially and make them procedurally cohesive.

Question 132 Continuous Deployment means automatically deploying every change into production. A. True B. False	**Correct answers: A** Continuous Deployment is deploying every change into production automatically.
Question 133 Developers in the Scrum Team tracks the total work remaining at least every: A) Sprint Review. B) Sprint Retrospective. C) Sprint Planning. D) Daily Scrum Call.	**Correct answer: D** Developers in the Scrum Team tracks this total work remaining at least for every Daily Scrum to project the likelihood of achieving the Sprint Goal.
Question 134 Which of the following Statements about Regression testing is true? (Choose all that apply) A. Regression testing is testing existing software applications to make sure that a code change or addition hasn't broken any existing functionality. B. One Regression testing is run successfully, originally scripted tests are discarded and not run again. C. The purpose of Regression Test is to catch bugs that may have been accidentally introduced into a new build or release candidate. D. The purpose of Regression test is to ensure that previously eradicated bugs continue to stay dead. E. Regression test suites tend to decrease with each found defect.	**Correct answer: A,C,D** Regression Test: Whenever developers change or modify their software, a small tweak can have unexpected consequences. Regression testing is testing existing software applications to make sure that a code change or addition hasn't broken any existing functionality. The purpose of Regression Test is to catch bugs that may have been accidentally introduced into a new build or release candidate. Its purpose is to ensure that previously eradicated bugs continue to stay dead. During Regression Test, by re-running testing scenarios that were originally scripted when known problems were first fixed, one can make sure that any new changes to an application haven't resulted in a regression or caused components that formerly worked to fail. As software is updated or changed, emergence of new faults and/or re-emergence of old faults is quite common. Sometimes re-emergence occurs because a fix gets lost through poor revision control practices (or simple human error in revision control). Therefore, it is considered good coding practice, to record a test that exposes the bug and re-run that test regularly after subsequent changes to the program. Thus

	regression test suites tend to grow with each found defect, test automation is frequently involved.
Question 135 Product Backlog refinement includes "Programming" and "Testing" the Product Backlog items as well. A. True B. False	**Correct answers: B** Refinement includes **Analyzing, Designing and Decomposing the Product Backlog items**. Programming and Testing does not happen during refinement. It happens during the actual Sprint.
Question 136 When should the programmers, developers and testers participate to understand the Requirements? A. During Refinement, as soon as possible and throughout the Sprint. B. Requirement meetings C. Sprint Retrospectives D. They should simply read the stories.	**Correct Answer: A** The Developers should participate and understand the stories as soon as possible. This can happen during the refinement phase. They can start Decomposing them after Sprint Planning.
Question 137 Only the Product Owner can refine Product Backlog items. A. True B. False	**Correct Answer: B** The Product Owner and the Developers Members refine the Product Backlog items together.
Question 138 Who writes write test cases and documentations in Scrum? A. Developers B. Product Owner C. Scrum Master D. Documentation and Quality analysis	**Correct Answer: A** Developers do write tests and documentations in Scrum. There are no special designated Testers or Documenters in a Scrum Team. Members of the Scrum teams are responsible for writing test and documentation.

Question 139	Correct Answer: A
The benefit of naming standards is that it: A. Makes the code more readable. B. Makes the code more communicable. C. Identifies Developers. D. All of the above.	The benefit of establishing naming standards for code is that it makes the code more Readable.
Question 140 Test Driven Development does **test the existing test cases / software** before developing new functionality. A. True B. False	**Correct Answer: B** Test Driven Development does not test the existing test cases / software before developing new functionality. It only tests the test cases writing for the new functionality which needs to be developed.

Question 141	Correct answer: A
Three Scrum Teams are working on the Same Product. Developers must merge their code before the Sprint Ends. A. True B. False	A Single Increment is needed at the end of the Sprint. Regardless of the number of Teams, the Scrum teams should merge their code to have one single "Valuable" Increment by the End of the Sprint.
Question 142	Correct answer: A
A Good Definition of Done provides guidance on specific patterns to be implemented in Code. It also informs the Scrum team about the quality of standard needed. A. True B. False	A Good Definition of Done provides: • Guidance on the specific Patterns to be implemented in Code. • Communicates to the Scrum Team about the Quality Standard needed.
Question 143	Correct answer: A
Dry Refers to the existence of minimum duplication in a code. A. True B. False	Dry Refers to the existence of minimum duplication in a code.

Question 144	**Correct answer: A,B,C,D,E,F**
Which of the following statements about a Unit testing is true? A. A Unit test is a way of testing a unit (the smallest piece of code) that can be logically isolated in a system. B. Unit testing, also known as component testing, is a level of software testing where individual units / components of a software are tested. The purpose is to validate that each unit of the software performs as designed. C. A Unit test can be automated. D. Unit Test is a test that Isolates and Verifies Individual units of source code. E. Unit test executes fast. F. Code in each Unit test is as small as possible. Unit test help maintaining readability of the code. G. Each Unit test can and may depend on other unit tests. H. Each Unit test can make assertions about more than one logical concepts.	Unit Test: A Unit test is a way of testing a unit (the smallest piece of code) that can be logically isolated in a system. Unit testing, also known as component testing, is a level of software testing where individual units / components of a software are tested. The purpose is to validate that each unit of the software performs as designed. A Unit test can be automated. Unit Test is a test that Isolates and Verifies Individual units of source code. Unit test executes fast. Code in each Unit test is as small as possible. Unit test help maintaining readability of the code. Each Unit test should independent of other unit tests. Each Unit test can make assertions about only one logical concept.

Question 145

Which of the following are good Criterias to include in the Definition of Done?

- A. Unit tests passed.
- B. Code reviewed Completed.
- C. Acceptance criteria met / Acceptance test passed.
- D. Functional tests passed
- E. Non-Functional requirements met.
- F. Integrated into a clean build.
- G. Automated regression tests pass.
- H. Feature level functional tests passed.
- I. Meets compliance requirements.

Correct answer: A, B, C, D, E, F, G, H, I

The entire Scrum Team must define a Definition of "Done":

1) Developers have the knowledge and skills to do the work to create useable Increments, so they should bring this expertise into the Definition of Done.
2) Product Owners often have inputs related to quality from the business perspective.
3) Scrum Masters helps facilitate improvements to a Definition of Done as part of their accountability for the Scrum Team's effectiveness. A Scrum Master can help create greater transparency for the Scrum Team to identify where quality needs to improve.

The entire Scrum Team would need to work together to change the definition of "Done". If more than one Scrum teams use the same definition of "Done", then those Scrum teams should be involved in changing the Definition of Done as well.

The Developers are required to conform to the Definition of Done. The Scrum Team plans ways to increase product quality by adapting and improving the Definition of "Done" as appropriate. So, Definition of Done changes with time.

A good time to change the Definition of Done is at the Retrospective right before the next Sprint. However, this is not mandatory.

A Good Definition of Done provides:

1) · Guidance on the specific patterns to be implemented in code.
2) Communicates about the Quality Standard needed.
3) Unit tests passed.
4) Code reviewed Completed.

	5) Acceptance criteria met / Acceptance test passed. 6) Functional tests passed 7) Non-Functional requirements met. 8) Integrated into a clean build 9) Automated regression tests pass 10) Feature level functional tests passed 11) Meets compliance requirements

Question 146
 	
Integration test is a test of multiple units of functionality.
 	
  A. True
  B. False
	Correct answer: A
	
	Integration testing is performed **on the modules that are unit tested first** and then integration testing defines whether the combination of the modules give the desired output or not.

Question 147
 	
A Developer is unsure of a bug priority however based on his analysis it's seems to be impacting multiple features. In such situations the developers should:
 	
  A. Talk to the Product Owner to check if he should resolve the bug right away.
  B. Resolve the bug right away as he is responsible for the quality of the Product.
	Correct answer: A
	
	Unless a company has specific guidance on fixing bugs, they represent work to be done and **should be ordered on the Product Backlog by the Product Owner**. If a Developer is unsure of what to do with a bug, he / she should talk to the Product Owner.

Question 148 Developers in the Scrum Team only listen to and understand during refinements. They can ask questions if they have doubts however they do not give any inputs. A. True B. False	**Correct answer: B** Developers gives input on technical dependencies during refining a Product Backlog item. During refinement, Developers also clarifies and expands on the intent of the Product backlog item, if needed.

Question 149	**Correct answer: A**
Branching is: A. Creating a logical or physical copy of code within a version control number **so that the copy might be changed in isolation**. B. Modifying the main branch or physical code with a version control number **so that the code is locked and changed in isolation**.	Branching is creating a logical or physical copy of code within a version control number **so that the copy might be changed in isolation**. Branching also implies the ability to later merge or integrate changes back onto the Parent branch.
Question 150 Automated Build does not really need Test to be run after it. A. True B. False	**Correct answer: B** Automated Build should be followed by a set of selective Unit Test. Once it passes Unit test, it should then run through a set of comprehensive tests (Automated Test, Unit Test, Manual Test, Non-Functional Test). This would help identify bugs that the Scrum Team would fix before proceeding.
Question 151 The Advantages of Pair Programming are: A. Fewer Coding Mistakes B. An effective way to share knowledge C. Less cost to the company D. Project becomes Less Risky	**Correct answer: A, B** The Advantages of Pair Programming are: • Fewer Coding Mistakes • An effective way to share knowledge • Solve Problems Faster and Quicker • Train New People Joins • Improve Interpersonal and Social Skills.

Question 152	**Correct answer: A, B, C, D, E**
Example of some Cross – Cutting concerns in Application Architecture are: (Choose All that Apply) A. Performance & Scalability B. Layering/partitioning Quality and validation C. Reusability, Reliability, Availability, Serviceability, and Performance D. Concurrency E. Security	Cross – Cutting concerns (concerns across different layers / modules / classes within the application) should also be addressed. Example of some concerns are: • Performance & Scalability • Layering/partitioning Quality and validation • Reusability, Reliability, Availability, Serviceability, and Performance • Concurrency • Security • Maintenance • Error Handling • Logging • Caching and Transaction Management
Question 153 Who represents the desires of stakeholders using the Product Backlog? A. Scrum Master B. Developers C. Product Owner D. Scrum Team	**Correct answer: C** A Product Owner may represent the desires of stakeholders using the Product Backlog.
Question 154 During Sprint Planning, the Sprint Backlog should be completely defined. A. True B. False	**Correct answer: B** During Sprint Planning, the Sprint Backlog should be groomed / defined enough **so the Developers in the Scrum Team can create its best forecast of what it can do and start the first several days of the Sprint.**

Question 155
 	
Static analysis is a method of computer program debugging that is done by examining the code by executing the program.
 	
   A.   True
   B.   False
	Correct answer: B
	
	Static analysis, also called static code analysis, is a method of computer program debugging that is done by examining the code without executing the program.

Question 156
 	
90% of Unit test cases passed with 70% Code Coverage. This Means:
 	
   A.   70% of your code is without errors.
   B.   30% of your code is without errors
   C.   10% of Unit Test Cases Failed. Only 30% of your code is checked.
   D.   10% of Unit Test Cases Failed. Only 70% of your code is checked.
   E.   None of the Above.
	Correct answer: D
	
	10% of Unit Test Cases Failed. Only 70% of your code is checked and 30% of your code remains to be checked. / validated using unit or other kind of test.

Question 157
 	
Behavior Driven Development is a variation / extension of Test-Driven Development methodology, where the main **focus is on:**
   A.   Behavioral specifications of the product or how an user would interact / behave with the features provided.
   B.   Users Interactions with the system.
   C.   Both of the above.
   D.   None of the Above.
	Correct answer: C
	
	Behavior Driven Development is a variation / extension of Test-Driven Development methodology, where the main **focus is on:**
	   1) **Behavioral specifications of the product or application (or its features).**
	   2) **User and System Interactions.**

Question 158	Correct answer: A
A dynamic analysis test will only find defects in the part of the code that is actually executed. A. True B. False	Dynamic analysis involves the testing and evaluation of a program based on its execution. Static and dynamic analysis, considered together, are sometimes referred to as glass-box testing. Dynamic program analysis tools may require loading of special libraries or even recompilation of program code. Dynamic analysis is capable of exposing a subtle flaw or vulnerability too complicated for static analysis alone to reveal and can also be the more expedient method of testing. A dynamic test will only find defects in the part of the code that is actually executed.
Question 159 Refactoring does "not" mean: A. Rewriting the entire code. B. fixing bugs. C. improve observable aspects of software such as its interface. D. All of the above	**Correct answer: D** Refactoring does "not" include: A. Rewriting the entire code B. Fixing bugs C. Improving observable aspects of software such as its interface D. All of the above

Question 160	**Correct answer: D**
The benefits of Layered Architecture are: A. Simplicity – The concept is very easy to learn and visible in the project at first grasp. B. Maintainability – Layering increases maintainability of a system by isolating functional responsibilities C. Consistent across different projects – the layers and so the overall code organization is pretty much the same in every layered project. D. All of the above	**Layered Architecture benefits include:** • Simplicity – The concept is very easy to learn and visible in the project at first grasp. • Maintainability – Layering increases maintainability of a system by isolating functional responsibilities • Layering makes it easier to reuse functions • Consistent across different projects – the layers and so the overall code organization is pretty much the same in every layered project. • Guaranteed separation of concerns – it is very easy to separate the concerns and the associated code organization with respect to the concern submitted. • Browsability from a technical perspective – when one wants to change something in some/all objects of a given kind, it's very easy to find and they're kept all together.
Question 161 Modeling increases the following in a Scrum Team: A. Understanding B. Communication C. Documentation D. All of the above	**Correct answer: D** "Agile Modeling" is a set of practices one can use in Agile teams for **effective modeling and documentation**. This method aligns with the Agile values and principles and still helps benefit from the power of modeling. The emphasis is on **models for conversation, not for handovers.**

CHAPTER 4: Scrum with Kanban

This chapter contains a lot about product management and specific metrics information used in Scrum. This chapter is designed to help you take a learn / revise / take a second look at a broader set of Kanban concepts.

1. **Read the Kanban Guide.**
2. Go through the **Kanban Guide Reference Table** mention in this book. Go through the questions and answers mentioned in the Book. These questions are compiled very carefully. Go through the answers and make sure you understand the concepts.
3. **Do the Kanban Open assessment (https://www.scrum.org/open-assessments) until you score close to 100% 3 times in a row.**

Kanban Reference Table

Kanban Definition	Kanban is a strategy which optimizes **the flow of value** through a process that uses a **visual, work-in-progress limited, pull system.**
	Kanban is a **visual system** for managing work as it **moves** through a process. **Kanban visualizes both the process (the workflow) and the actual work passing through that process.**
	Kanban is a method that uses a work-in-process limited pull system as the core mechanism to expose operation (or process) problems and to stimulate collaborative improvement efforts.
	The flow-based perspective of Kanban can enhance and **complement the Scrum framework** and its implementation. Teams can add complementary Kanban practices whether they are just starting to use Scrum or have been using it all along.
	When Kanban practices are applied to Scrum: 1. The Kanban practices provide a focus on improving the flow through the feedback loop. 2. The Kanban practices help optimizing transparency and the frequency of inspection and adaptation for both the product and the process.
	Kanban practices can help Scrum Teams improve flow and create an environment where decisions are **made just-in-time throughout the Sprint based on inspection and adaptation.** In this environment, Scrum Teams rely on the Sprint Goal and close collaboration within the Scrum Team to optimize the value delivered in the Sprint.
Kanban Values / Core Principles	Kanban practitioners follow a set of core principles that guide the way in which the Kanban practices are applied. These principles are: 1. **Start with what you do now**: Kanban's flexibility allows it to be overlaid on existing workflows, systems and processes without disrupting what is already successfully being done. 2. **Respect the current process, roles, responsibilities, and titles**: Kanban recognizes that existing processes, roles, responsibilities, and titles have value and are, generally, worth preserving. 3. **Agree to pursue incremental, evolutionary change**: The Kanban methodology is designed to meet minimal resistance and thus encourages continuous small incremental and evolutionary changes to the current process.

Kanban Work Flow	Kanban Workflow is the movement of **Value** through the **Product Development System**.
	Kanban optimizes flow by improving the efficiency, effectiveness, and predictability of a process.
	Kanban Work allows **creation of tables with consecutive lists of activities (Stages) where work items (Cards) flow from one Column (Stage) to another**. Using the Kanban Workflow, it's easy to know: 1. Which stage of the Process each of the Work Item is in? 2. Who is Performing the Work Item? 3. Other details about the Work Item's Execution.
Value Stream ⓘ	The **Scrum Team** should make sure it **monitors the flow** of Product Backlog items from idea identification, through refinement, analysis, design, coding, testing, and deployment; all the way to "Done." This is what Kanban teams call the **Value stream**.
	It is not enough to simply visualize the Sprint Backlog through the Kanban Workflow. Visualizing the flow **throughout the value stream** means the Scrum Team should mainly visualize the **flow of Product Backlog items (PBIs) rather than tasks**.
	There are times when multiple tasks might be completed however none of them might have created something of value for the customer.
	Value is created, and the feedback loop is closed only when a Product Backlog item is
	Kanban's goal when improving flow is to tighten the Feedback/Value loop.

Workflow Structure and	The Scrum Team's Definition of Workflow represents the Scrum Team members' explicit understanding of what their policies are. This shared understanding improves transparency and enables self-management.
Workflow Definition	Each Scrum Team must **create its definition of "Workflow"** containing the following elements (See Diagram Below): **A.** Defined points at which the Scrum Team considers work to have **Started** and to have **Finished.** **B.** A definition of the **Individual units** of **Customer value** that are flowing through the Scrum Team's system (most likely Product Backlog Items (PBIs)). **C.** A definition of the **workflow states that the PBIs flow** through from start to finish (of which there must be at **least one active state).** **D.** **Explicit policies** about how workflows through each state (which may include items from a Scrum Team's definition of "Done" and pull policies between stages). **E.** Policies for limiting Work in Progress (WIP).

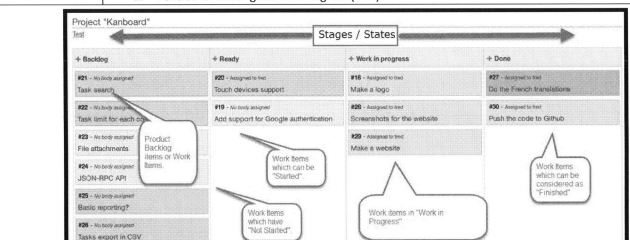

	A Kanban "Workflow" definition must include: 1. A **shared understanding** within the Scrum Team of how work is defined (work items) and what their policies are. 2. Definition of the **start state** of the process. 3. Definition of the **active states** for the work items. 4. Definition of the **finished state** of the process. 5. A definition of how Work in Progress (WIP) will be limited. 6. A set **Service Level Expectation (SLE)** that communicates a forecast of how long it should take to complete work items.

	The scope of the Definition of Workflow may span beyond the Sprint. For instance, a Scrum Team's Definition of Workflow may encompass flow inside and/or outside of the Sprint.
	Scrum Team's definition of "Workflow" may include states that are **upstream, downstream, inside, or outside of the Sprint Backlog.**
	A few elements, the Scrum Team must incorporate in the definition of Workflow are: • Identifying work items that **are not yet in an active state as "not started."** • Identifying work items **entering the active state ("started") as Work in Progress (WIP).** • Identifying work items that have passed through all of the active states planned for that item as **"finished."**
	The **States** in the definition of "Workflow" **may not coincide** with the states defined by a Sprint Backlog. **Example:** • The States of Product Backlog item in a Sprint Backlog could be: Ready → Developed → Tested → Completed. • The States of the same Product Backlog item on the Kanban Workflow could be: Ready → Work in Progress → Development Completed → Documented → Data Backup → Training.
	In a Kanban Workflow, a particular work item **might not flow** through all of the active states, and a work item might not even flow sequentially through the active states. **Example**: You might have a stage called "External Vendor / Dependencies" where only work dependent on external vendors would flow. Not all the work would depend upon external vendors and thus not all the work would flow through this Column / Stage.
	In a Kanban Workflow, the work items moving through the workflow **may not correspond** to Product Backlog Items or other parts of the Sprint Backlog or Scrum. **Example** in multiple companies, parts of the delivery cycle are to execute user studies, train support staff, notify users of upcoming downtime, ensure a backup is done prior to the deployment etc. These type of "states / stages " might not be a part of the process for the Scrum Team to provide a potentially valuable increment but are definitely needed for delivery. Since Kanban is focused on the entire workflow from idea to use, one would expect to see "states / stages" before and after the actual steps to build (Development). These additional stages would thus have more things to do. Thus the work items moving through the workflow **will not always correspond** to Product Backlog Items or other parts of the Sprint Backlog or Scrum.
	Items on the Kanban Dashboard **can and should be split any time** before they are considered finished from a Definition of Workflow perspective.
	Items on the Kanban Dashboard should rarely move backward in a flow. The only good reason to do so is if the exit criteria were missed earlier in the workflow.

	Work Items on a Kanban board can be color coded to represent: • The Team who is performing the work • Type of work • Work for a particular product
	The creation and adaptation of the definition of "Workflow" **may impact or be impacted by existing artifacts.**
	Kanban system **can extend beyond the Sprint boundaries** to include activities across the entire value stream such as discovery activities, refinement of PBIs, and production support.
	Kanban Workflow can and should change as Scrum Team's empirically discover better ways of flowing work.
Pull System	**Work in Kanban is pulled** rather than pushed. Scrum Team starts work on an item only when there is a clear signal that it has time to do so. **When the WIP drops below a defined limit, that is the signal to start new work.**
Push System	Push system demands that work start on an item whenever it is requested. Remember: "Push type" means "make-to-stock," in which the production is not based on actual demand. (a push production creates products without having a specific customer request). "Pull type" means "make-to-order," in which the production is based on actual demand.
Service Level Agreement Forecast **OR** **Service Level Expectation**	A Service Level Agreement forecasts **how long it should take** a given item to **flow from start to finish** within a workflow.
	SLEs are used by Scrum Teams to set **flow expectations to themselves. SLE is an aspiration** yet realistic and reliable.
	SLE enables the Scrum Team to forecast a finished date at a certain confidence level once the item has been started.
	SLE Can be used in **Sprint Planning** to provide Product Owners and stakeholders with **"an idea" of when** the service can be expected from the teams. That **doesn't include providing a specific date** for each Product Backlog Item in the Sprint Backlog.
(!)	SLE's are used by teams to focus **their own** flow inspection and adaptation effort. SLE's are analyzed • During the Sprint in the **Daily Scrum.** • Following the Sprint in the **Sprint Retrospective.** • They can also be shared (in **the Sprint Review)** with the stakeholders that care about the team's cycle time.
	The Service Level Expectation **is just an expectation** set by the team to themselves answering the question "**What Cycle Time do we expect to see for an item of this type, and what is our confidence level for this?**".

The Service Level Agreement itself has two parts:
1) **A period of elapsed days** in which the work would be completed.
2) The probability of work getting completed associated with that period.

SLE Example : 85% of work items will be finished in eight days or less OR 8 Days with 85% confidence / probability.

How should a Scrum Team come up with their SLE?
The SLE is based on a Scrum Team's **Historical Cycle Time**. If no historical cycle time data exists, the Scrum Team should make its **best guess** and then replace that guess once there is enough historical data to do a proper SLE calculation.

How is SLE Used?
- The team would compare active in-flight work items age to their SLE and look for items that are at risk of missing the SLE.
- As work ages without completing, it becomes more and more likely this work item would not meet the team's SLE.

Example: Once a work item reaches a point where its age is now at the point where half of the team's work items have already completed, it's a clear indication that there's more risk for this item than the typical item.
SLE can also be used in Sprint Planning to provide Product Owners and stakeholders with an idea towards the service level that can be expected from the team. **That doesn't include providing a specific date for each PBI.** The SLE enables the Scrum Team to **forecast** a finished date at a certain confidence level once the item has been started.

What happens when a item exceeds SLE?
When an item exceeds SLE, the teams should discuss what actions could be taken to get the item flowing properly again. Stopping the work would be the last thing a team would want.

SLE once calculated, should be posted on the Kanban board, on the Work Item.

With each day that passes in which a work item doesn't finish, the probability that a work item will not meet its SLE, **increases.**

The Scrum Team uses its SLE to find active flow issues and to inspect and adapt in cases of falling below those expectations.

A Service Level Expectation (SLE**) is based on cycle time scatter plot percentile lines.**

Kanban Practices	Scrum Teams achieve flow optimization by using the following four practices:
	1) **Visualization** of the Workflow
	2) **Limiting Work in Progress**
	3) **Active Management** of Work Items in Progress
	4) **Inspecting and Adapting** the definition of "Workflow" by:
	   a. Making Process Explicit
	   b. Implementing Feedback Loops
	   c. Improving Collaboratively and Evolving Experimentally (using models and the scientific method)

	The four Kanban practices are enabled by the Scrum Team's Definition of Workflow. 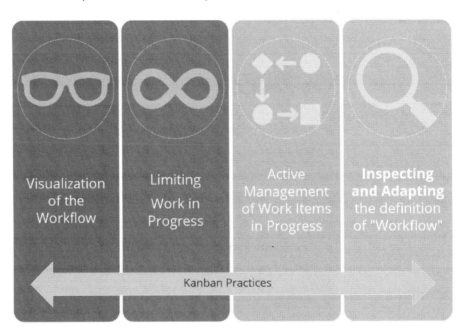

1 Visualization of the workflow / Kanban Board	**Visualization** using the **Kanban board** is the way the Scrum Team makes its workflow transparent.
	Kanban board's presentation should prompt the right conversations at the right time and proactively suggest opportunities for improvement.
	As mentioned about, Visualization should include the following (which is a part of the Definition of Workflow): 1. Defined points at which the Scrum Team considers work to have started and to have finished. 2. A definition of the work items - the individual units of value (stakeholder value, knowledge value, process improvement value) that are flowing through the Scrum Team's system (most likely Product Backlog items (PBIs)). 3. A definition of the workflow states that the work items flow through from start to finish (of which there must be at least one active state). 4. Explicit policies about how workflows through each state (which may include items from a Scrum Team's Definition of Done and pull policies between stages). 5. Policies for limiting Work in Progress (WIP).
	A basic Kanban board has a three-step workflow: **To Do, In Progress, and Done.** However, depending on a team's size, structure, and objectives, the workflow can be mapped to meet the unique process of any particular team. The Kanban methodology relies upon full transparency of work and real-time communication of capacity; therefore the Kanban board should be seen as the **single source of truth for the team's work.**
2 Limiting WIP	Work in Progress (WIP) refers to **the number of work items** the Scrum Team has started but has not yet finished.
	Work in progress limits set the maximum amount of work that can exist in each status of a workflow. Limiting the amount of work in progress makes it easier to identify inefficiency in a team's workflow.
	Scrum Teams using Kanban must explicitly limit the number of these work items in progress. A Scrum Team can explicitly limit WIP however they see fit but should stick to that limit once established.
	The primary effect of limiting WIP is **that it creates a pull system**. It is **called a pull system because the team starts work (i.e. pulls) on an item only when it is clear that it has the capacity to do so.**

What happens when the team is below the WIP Limit for a given stage?

When the WIP drops below the defined limit, that is **the signal to start new work.**

Scrum Teams using Kanban must **explicitly control the in-progress work items** from the time they consider them "started" until the time they consider them "finished."

The Control is usually represented as a number or numbers on a Kanban board. Those numbers are called **"WIP Limits."**

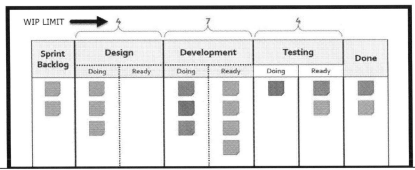

Once the Scrum Team has established a WIP Limit, **it refrains from pulling** more than that number of work items mentioned in the limits into a given part of the workflow.

WIP limits help create **focus by reducing multitasking which can in fact increase productivity.** A lower WIP limit which increases focus can result in **higher productivity.**

Limiting WIP helps flow and improves the Scrum Team's self-management, focus, commitment, and collaboration.

Kanban WIP **limit is the gatekeeper** that makes sure you start only as much work as you finish throughout the organization. This prevents the accumulation of unfinished work, which otherwise would flood your processes.

The Specified WIP limits in different stages of work (e.g. design, coding, testing, deploying, etc.) are listed on the Top of the Board.

What happens once the WIP Limit is reached?
Once the limit is reached in one stage, instead of starting a new PBI, members of the Scrum Team **help others deal with the current PBIs already in progress**. This can mean helping others in their own area of expertise or helping others in their areas of expertise (e.g. coders help testers, testers help business analysts, etc.)

A WIP Limit can include work items in a single column, several grouped columns, or a whole board.

Limit What? Tasks or Product Backlog Items?

With WIP Limits, the number of tasks is not necessarily limited, rather the amount of value-generating work items (PBI) are limited.
The goal of the WIP Limit is to reduce the amount of actual work which **has value in process (WIP).**

Who Own the Definition of the Workflow and the WIP Limits?

Who owns the **definition of Workflow depends** on the scope/context of the workflow:

1) If the team is using Kanban to improve the Sprint flow by visualizing and managing flow in the **Sprint Backlog, Developers in the Scrum Team** would own the workflow and specifically the WIP limits.
2) If the team is using Kanban from **a holistic perspective**, starting from the Product Backlog, refinement and Sprint Backlog, **the Scrum Team** that would own the workflow and therefore the WIP limits.
3) If the Dev Team actually wants to involve the Product Owner in their Sprint flow (to review and accept a story during the Sprint before it goes through testing), **the Scrum Team** that would own the workflow and therefore the WIP limits.

No **one outside of the Scrum Team should tell the Scrum Team how to define their Workflow.**

Should WIP Limit be comfortable enough?
WIP **limits should introduce pain**-- meaning that they push beyond what the team is comfortable with and used to. The team would want to channel this pain towards ways of improving the team's process and policies so that in the future, the flow will be better and the WIP limit will be less painful.

Improving engineering practices, using techniques such as acceptance test-driven development (ATDD), reducing batch/PBI size, cross-training, or any other technique are all ways to make the WIP Limit more comfortable. Over time, as team capabilities improve, the WIP limit can be tightened to catalyze even more improvement in capabilities. Limiting WIP is an effective way to drive deep collaboration at the team level.

Should WIP limits be changed to deal with mid-sprint high-priority work?

Let's assume a team is mid-Sprint and there's an important valuable item the Product Owner wants to add to the Sprint Backlog. It is aligned with the Sprint Goal. The team is currently at their WIP Limit. Could they add this item?

Step 1) First a decision needs to be made whether to pull this item into the Sprint Backlog. It is up to the team to agree to pull a new item into the Sprint Backlog. The Sprint Goal can be used to assess how aligned this item is with the current focus. If the item is really important, the work item could be pulled in the Sprint Backlog.

Step 2) In case the item is pulled into the Sprint Backlog, then the Dev Team needs to figure out whether they can actually start it right away. This depends on the WIP limits and the current WIP. If the team is at their WIP limit they shouldn't pull in that new item until some room frees up. If their backlog **items are pretty small, an empty WIP slot will free up pretty quickly.**

Step 3) Expedite this Work Item which needs to be pulled. Expediting is going beyond the current WIP limits and pushing this item along on top of the existing flow. The typical way to do this is **NOT to change the WIP limit** definition but to go above WIP and note a WIP exception. These exceptions can then be a topic for inspection and adaptation come time to retrospect.

When should the WIP limits be inspected and adapted?

Scrum Teams **should** adjust WIP limits during **the Sprint Retrospective**. However, **it is not mandatory** to do so.

WIP Limit can be set:
1) Per person.
2) Per the entire team throughout their workflow.
3) By time i.e. 10 Items Per Week.
4) Per Stage or for Multiple Stages.
5) Across the Board / Across All Stages.

The Sprint itself is a WIP Limit. A Sprint limits **the number of Product Backlog Items that Developers in a Scrum Team can forecasts it can complete during a fixed period.**

Applying WIP limits allows you to create a smooth workflow and use team's work capacity at optimal levels by:
- Preventing overloading of your work processes.
- Helping to locate blockers and to alleviate **bottlenecks** in your workflow
- Giving you the opportunity to deliver value to end customers as fast as possible
- Preventing a constant context switching between work items

3 **Active Workflow management / Manage Workflow** 	Active management of workflow can take several forms, including but not limited to the following: • Making sure that work items are **only pulled into the workflow at about the same rate that they leave the workflow.** • Ensuring work items aren't left to age unnecessarily. • **Responding** quickly to blocked work items. • **Responding** quickly to work items that are exceeding the team's expected Cycle Time levels (Service Level Expectation - SLE). • Unclogging work that piles up in a column or columns.
	It is the Scrum Team's responsibility to ensure the continuous proactive, active, and reactive management of work items in progress.
4 **Inspect and Adapt the Definition of the Workflow / Policies** 	Policies are the **"rules of the game"** for the Scrum Team's **"Workflow".** Small changes to those policies can have a material impact on how the Scrum Team performs overall.
	The Scrum Team uses the existing Scrum events to inspect and adapt its Definition of Workflow (or policies) thereby helping to improve empiricism and optimizing the value the Scrum Team delivers.
	The following are aspects of the Definition of Workflow the Scrum Team might adopt: • **Visualization policies** - for example, Workflow states - either changing the actual Workflow or bringing more transparency to an area in which the team wants to inspect and adapt. • **How-we-work policies** - these can directly address an impediment. For example, adjusting WIP limits and SLEs or changing the batch size (how often items are pulled between states) can have a dramatic impact.
	When applying Kanban, The Scrum Team will want to supplement The Scrum Guide with more explicit policies for its process.
	Policies will be captured in a Scrum Team's definition of "Workflow".
	The **Scrum Guide provides a minimum set of explicit policies** as well as instructions for how to figure out some context-specific policies (e.g. Scrum Team's definition of "Done"). Explicit means that these policies are written down or visualized somehow and that the whole Scrum Team understands them.
	The Kanban board should display all relevant policies or direct Scrum Team members where to find them.

	Example of Explicit Policies.
	1) **The Scrum Guide** (Scrum Events, Rules etc) is an explicit policy that a Scrum Team implements.
	2) **Scrum's definition of "Done"** is an excellent example of an explicit policy.
	3) **The Scrum framework itself is an example of an explicit policy.** The Scrum Guide is an explicit policy that a Scrum Team implements.
	4) Kanban teams add explicit policies such as the **WIP limit** for each lane or each person, escalation/ class of service policies, how to visualize and deal with blockers, how to prioritize work.
	5) **Workflow** can be thought of as the "Team's policy" for how to get work to "Done".
	6) Scrum Team definition of when items go from not started to start and from in-progress to finished.

Basic Metrics of Flow	The four-basic metrics of flow that Scrum Teams (using Kanban) will need to track, are as follows: 1) Work in Progress. 2) Cycle Time. 3) Work Item Age. 4) Throughput.
WIP	Work in Progress (WIP): Work in Progress can be defined as the **total number of work items started but not finished (according to the Scrum Team's definition of "Workflow").**
	The team can use the **WIP metric (in daily Sprints) to provide transparency into their progress towards reducing their WIP and improving their flow.** **Example:** The Team worked on Work items all day and the WIP has reduced from 10 to 6.
	Cumulative Flow Diagram(CFD) shows the amount of work arriving, at various stages of in progress, and done. Most people use the Cumulative Flow Diagram to visualize the WIP. Cumulative Flow Diagram (CFD) shows the amount of work arriving, at various stages. 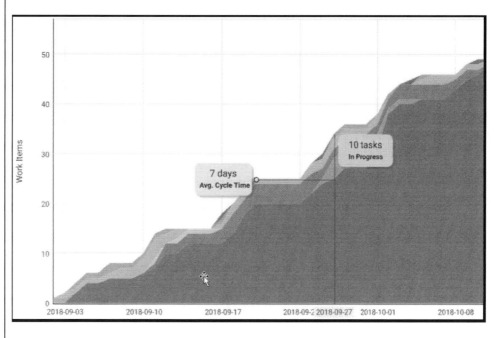

Cumulative Flow Diagram is a stacked area chart showing, at each time interval, the number of items in each stage of the process. As time goes by, the chart shows the flow of items through the process.

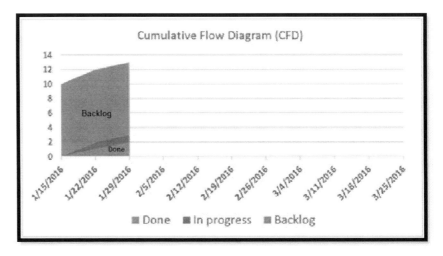

X Axis: Time Scale
Y Axis: Total Number of Work Items. (One item counts as 1 on the Y axis)
Differently colored bands = Different Phases

CFD Helps with: Visualizing the amount of **Work in Progress (WIP)** at each interval. The vertical height of each band is the **Number of items (WIP) in that stage.**

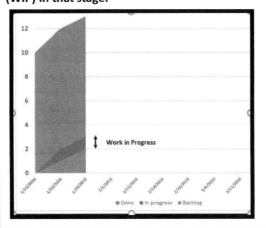

The horizontal height of each band exposes the **Average cycle time.**

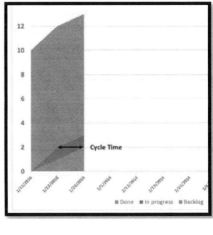

	Note: WIP Limit (which is different from WIP) is a policy which the Scrum Team uses as a "constraint" to help them shape the flow of work
	Example: The Team worked on Work items all day and the WIP has reduced from 10 to 6. The WIP Limit is 12 so the team is getting ready to pull 6 new items which have not started yet.
	Bottlenecks/systemic constraints are typically identified by looking at the queues on the board as well as charts like the Cumulative Flow Diagram.
	** In the CFD diagram: **The Top line** = The entry point of tasks in the respective stage of the Kanban board . **The Bottom Line** = The Leaving point of tasks in the respective stage of the Kanban board .
	If a line **becomes flat**, it means nothing is arriving in the corresponding stage or nothing is leaving it.
Stable Band ⚠	You can spot whether your process is stable by looking at how the top and bottom line of each band in your cumulative flow diagram are progressing.
Narrow Band ⚠	If a band on your CFD is continuously **narrowing that means that the throughput of the stage it represents is higher than the entry rate.** This is a sign that you've got more capacity than you really need at this stage and you should relocate it in order to optimize the flow.

Wide Band	If a band on your CFD is continuously **broadening, it means the number of cards that enter the corresponding stage on the Kanban board is higher than the number of assignments that are leaving it. This is a sign that the team has got less capacity for the work undertaken.**
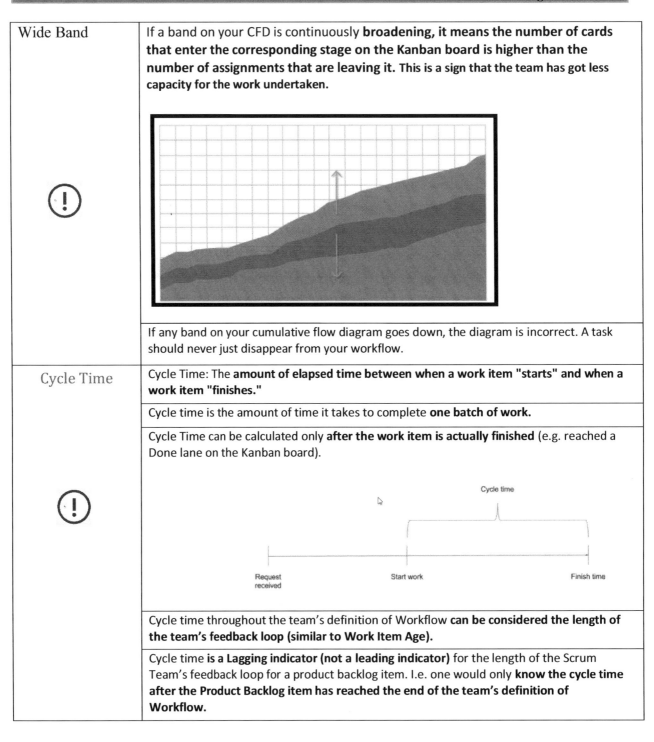	
	If any band on your cumulative flow diagram goes down, the diagram is incorrect. A task should never just disappear from your workflow.
Cycle Time	Cycle Time: The **amount of elapsed time between when a work item "starts" and when a work item "finishes."**
	Cycle time is the amount of time it takes to complete **one batch of work.**
	Cycle Time can be calculated only **after the work item is actually finished** (e.g. reached a Done lane on the Kanban board).
	Cycle time throughout the team's definition of Workflow **can be considered the length of the team's feedback loop (similar to Work Item Age).**
	Cycle time **is a Lagging indicator (not a leading indicator)** for the length of the Scrum Team's feedback loop for a product backlog item. I.e. one would only **know the cycle time after the Product Backlog item has reached the end of the team's definition of Workflow.**

Cycle Time is used to:
1) Drive improvement work .
2) Establish internal/external expectations as to the team's turnaround time on specific items.

"Cycle Time" depends on the context of the flow definition, that is, the definitions of the start and end defined by the owners of that part of the process. For example:
1) **Developers in a Scrum Team can measure the "Cycle Time"** since entering the Sprint.
2) **A Product Owner can measure the "Cycle Time" since starting the Refinement** of a Product Backlog item (PBI) or since the PBI enters the Product Backlog.

Average Cycle time: Different tasks within a sprint may have different cycle times. In a two-week sprint, one task may be completed within one day, while another task might take 13 days to complete. **Average cycle time is different than the cycle time**. If you look at the example below, the cards that made it in the Done column took 5, 3, and 7 days. The Average Cycle Time is 5 days, which is the average length of the time each card took to get delivered on this Kanban board.

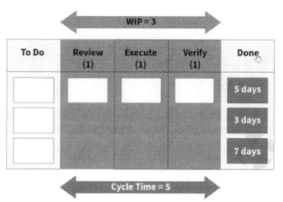

Can cycle time for "a" Product Backlog item be longer than the Sprint length? "Yes"
Yes. Sprint Length is a WIP Limit and yes Product backlog items (at times) may take longer than a Sprint. This could absolutely happen. Thus the cycle time (and not the average cycle time) for a Product Backlog item can be longer than the Sprint Length.

Can the "Average" cycle time be longer than the Sprint length? "No"
The average cycle time should be quite a **bit shorter** than the sprint length. If you have a few items go above the sprint length, its fine, the average cycle time will stay below the Sprint Length. However, the average cycle time should not exceed the sprint length. If it does, it means most of your Product backlog items are not getting completed in a single Sprint.

Version 32.0 "© 2019 Sid Bathia. All rights reserved."

The main chart/report used to visualize and analyze Cycle Times is the **Cycle Time Scatterplot** where teams can understand their Cycle Time trends, distributions, look at anomalies. A leader practicing Lean management may use the **cycle time scatter plot** to:

- Visualize Clearly the Cycle Times of Multiple Assignments of a Kind
- Compare How Much Time Different Work Types Take by Coloring the Dots of Each One in a Distinguishable Color
- Forecast the Cycle Time on Future Assignments

In the **Cycle Time Scatterplot:**

- The horizontal axis (X-Axis) of the chart visualizes a selected time frame by dates.
- The vertical axis (Y-Axis) represents the cycle time of the tasks that were completed during this period calculated in days.
- Each dot that you see scattered across the chart is a marker representing a task within a card on your Kanban board. The positions of the dots are determined by the date of completion and how long it required for the Kanban card to reach the done column.

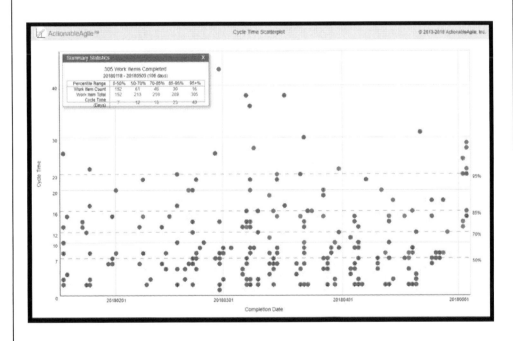

One of the greatest benefits of using a cycle time scatter plot for Lean management is that it gives you the ability to **forecast the outcome of future tasks.**

Example 1: Let's say that you've got 100 tasks that were completed in 50 days. If 50 of them were finished in 7 days or less, while all the others took longer, you've got 50 percent chance to finish any future task within 7 days.

	Example 2: Let's say that 70 tasks (out of the 100 task) which were completed within 12 days. This means that you've got 70 percent chance to finish any future task within 12 days.
	The **higher the percentile**, the higher the chance to complete a future task within this time frame.
	Calculating Cycle times requires the Scrum Team to (at a minimum) **track the start date and finished date of each item.**
Work Item Age	Work Item Age is defined as **the amount of elapsed time between when a work item "started" and the current time.**
	Work Item Age shows how **long ago has each item has been pulled into WIP,** on the Kanban Board.
	Work Item Age provides transparency to which items are flowing well and which are sort of "stuck" even if not formally blocked.
	Work Item Age can be compared with the Service Level Expectation (SLE) so that the team can focus on the items that are at most risk of missing the team's expectations/SLE.
(!)	Work Item Age is a **leading indicator** only relevant for: 1) The length of the Scrum Team's feedback loop for that (in progress) item. 2) Non-finished items Only. (VS) Cycle Time is a **lagging indicator** only relevant for **finished items**. I.e. One would only know the cycle time after the PBI reached the end of the team's definition of Workflow.
	If an **item that hasn't started**, best bet is to look at Historical Cycle Times.
	If an item is aging quite a bit, it is **certainly an indication that it's cycle time will be high.**
	Better results get attained if work in progress items are not allowed to age.
	Calculating Work item age requires the Scrum Team to (at a minimum) track the start date of each item.

Aging Work in Progress chart gives us a lot of just-in-time data about how predictable Work items which are in-progress are. The "Aging Work in Progress" chart below provides information:

- To help **identify specific items that are struggling and require attention.**
- For each item on the Kanban board **how long ago has it been pulled into WIP.**
- The Stage active items are currently in the workflow
- What the typical cycle times for this team are, and based on that which items are indications of flow risks

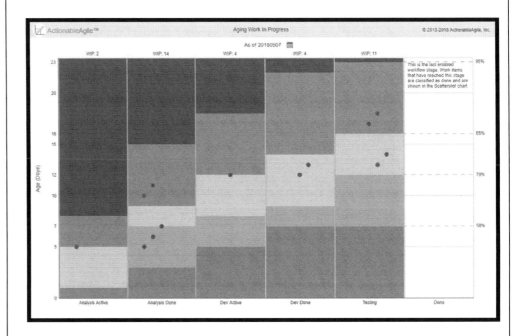

The Aging Work in Progress chart shows:
1) At the bottom of the horizontal axis (X-Axis), all the stages of the workflow are represented.
2) Above each column, there is a WIP indicator that shows how many tasks are in progress in every stage
3) A calendar icon that indicates the basis date for which the information is displayed.
4) The vertical axis (Y-Axis) visualizes how long each task (dots in the chart) has spent in that section, in days.

The data in the **Aging Work in Progress chart** lets you easily get an idea of how your team was performing in **similar contexts in the past.**

The higher the task / **dot, the longer the task** will take to complete and the higher the chances of a delay.

The Percentile lines that run alongside the vertical axis indicate the percentage of tasks that were previously completed.

Example 1: (See Diagram Below): if a task is climbing past the 50th percentile line, it means it is already taking more time to complete **than half of previous tasks.**

Example 2: (See Diagram Below) There is a 70% certainty your team can handle any task in less than 11 days. Equally, you could commit to delivering a task within 7 days but there's a 50/50 chance of achieving that goal.

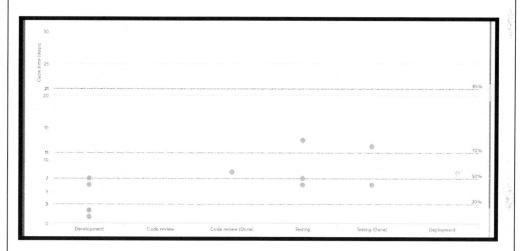

Throughput	Throughput can be defined as the **number of work items "finished" per unit of time.**
	The measurement of throughput is the exact count of work items, **without any compensation for item size.**
	Throughput is measured at a certain step in the workflow, typically at the finish line of the workflow.
	Throughput can also be used as part of release or **Sprint Planning/road-mapping** discussions, especially when combined with Monte-Carlo simulations provide some better visibility/confidence into "What can be done by when?".
	Throughput can be visualized via a separate run chart or by looking at the angle of curves on a Cumulative Flow Diagram.
	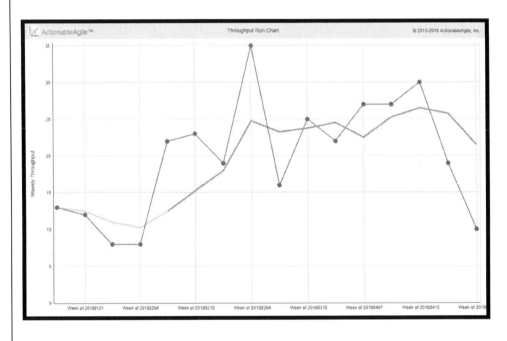

Metrics Summary Table ⚠

Metrics & Meetings	Description	X and Y Axis	Helps with?
Work in Progress **Daily Sprints** **Sprint** **Retrospective**	Cumulative Flow Diagram: Cumulative Flow Diagram (CFD) shows the amount of work arriving, at various stages of in progress, and done.	• X- AXIS: Time Scale • Y-AXIS: Cumulative Number of Work items • Areas with different Colors: Stages	WIP Helps with: • Knowledge of the Number of WIP Items • Average Cycle Time • Throughput • Bottlenecks
Work Item Age Chart **Daily Sprint** **Sprint Planning**	Aging Work in Progress Chart shows for each item on the Kanban board **how long ago has it been pulled into WIP.**	• X Axis: The columns of the chart show team's workflow steps • Y Axis: Items age in time (usually days). • Pace Percentiles (right vertical axis) • Tasks (dots in the chart)	Work Item age shows how **long ago has each item has been pulled into WIP,** on the Kanban Board.
Cycle Time Scatterplot **Sprint Review** **Sprint** **Retrospective**	**Cycle Time Scatterplot** where teams can understand their Cycle Time trends, distributions, look at anomalies.	• X- axis = Selected time frame by dates. • Y- axis = Cycle time of the tasks that were completed during this period calculated in days. • Each dot scattered across the chart = A task within a card on your Kanban board. .	A leader practicing Lean management may use the cycle time scatter plot to: • Visualize Clearly the Cycle Times of Multiple Assignments of a Kind • Compare How Much Time Different Work Types Take by Coloring the Dots of Each One in a Distinguishable Color • Forecast the **Cycle Time on Future Assignments** • Ability to forecast the outcome of future tasks.
Throughput separate run chart **Sprint Planning** **Sprint Review** **Sprint** **Retrospective**		• X- AXIS: Time Scale • Y-AXIS: Cumulative Number of Work items	Throughput can also be used as part of release or **Sprint Planning/road-mapping** discussions, especially when combined with Monte-Carlo simulations provide some better visibility/confidence into "What can be done by when?".

Batch Size	Batch size is **the size, measured in work product, of one completed unit of work**. Requirements, designs, code, tests, and other work items that move through the system, all can be weighed in terms of batch sizes.
	Batch size, risk and cycle time are all directly proportional. As any grows larger, so do the others. The amount of risk we create is equal to our batch size and cycle time, i.e. our total work in
	Each activity in the Scrum Team's definition of Workflow can have its own batch size. For example, the team might deploy each PBI and then their deployment batch size would be 1.
	Batch size is not **the same as Sprint length.**
	By limiting our WIP or batch size, we achieve the following beneficial properties or impacts: 1. Improved efficiency due to faster feedback loops. 2. Higher motivation due to seeing work get done and deliver value earlier. 3. Lower efficiency due to overhead / transaction costs in case the batch size is too small. 4. Highlight a need to work to improve processes/infrastructure to reduce the pain of frequent costly overhead. 5. Minimum queue size 6. Minimum iteration length and cycle time 7. Maximum speed to completion (Minimum time to market) 8. Minimum technical risk 9. Minimum personnel risk 10. Minimum documentation 11. Fast hypothesis testing, rapid learning 12. Minimum cost of ownership per increment of completed work **13.** Reduce the number of blind assumptions that fuel our decisions

Flow Based Events / Kanban Events

Flow Based Events Introduction (!)	Kanban in a Scrum context does not **require any additional events** to those outlined in The Scrum Guide. However, using a flow-based perspective and metrics in Scrum's events strengthens Scrum's empirical approach. Adding Kanban to Scrum provides a technique to help the Scrum Team focus on driving a continuous flow of activity but does not negate value provided by the Scrum Events, Artifacts, Roles, or Rules. However, flow-based metrics/charts & forecasts may get added to Scrum events as per the Kanban Guide for Scrum Teams. E.g. the Scrum Team cannot choose to skip conducting a Sprint Retrospective when using Kanban with Scrum. **Are Kanban Events and Roles Mandatory?** Kanban is, at its heart, a just-in-time and continuous flow approach to work. Instead of having a Sprint cadence that starts with a Sprint Planning, has a Daily Scrum every day, and ends with a Sprint Review and Sprint Retrospective, Kanban can be considered a process where you plan when you need to, meet when you need to, collaborate with key stakeholders when you need to, and inspect and improve your way of working when you need to. In Kanban, similar events happen as in Scrum, but at different regularities or schedules that may or may not be consistent over time. **So if it's Kanban by itself, Scrum Events, roles and Candance are not mandatory.** **When Kanban is layered on top of Scrum (or used with Scrum), the Scrum Events and Roles become mandatory.**
Flow Based Sprints	The Kanban complementary practices don't invalidate the need for Scrum's Sprint.
	The Sprint and its events provide opportunities for inspection and adaptation of: • Product which is being worked on. • Process used to create the Product.
	Teams using Scrum with Kanban use the Sprint and its events **as a feedback improvement loop** by collaboratively inspecting and adapting their Definition of Workflow and flow metrics.
Flow Based Sprint Planning	A flow-based Sprint Planning meeting uses **flow metrics as an aid for developing the Sprint Backlog.**
	The Scrum Team uses **historical Throughput** (of previous Sprints) to understand the Scrum Team's capacity for the next Sprint. A Scrum Team's SLE might influence the work planned for the first days of the Sprint.
	When planning a Sprint, the main **interest is to figure out how many backlog items to pull** into the Sprint. **Throughput of previous Sprints** is the most useful in figuring this out. An advanced technique would be to use **Monte Carlo** simulation using this throughput data in order to figure out confidence-levels for various amounts of items in the Sprint Backlog.

	Key benefits of Sprint Planning in Kanban are: 1. Sprint Planning identifies a reasonable amount of work thus avoiding spreading team too thinly. In other words, it is a form of limiting WIP. Good Kanban teams limit WIP already albeit in a different way. 2. Teams come together in Sprint Planning to craft a Sprint Goal.
Flow-Based Daily Scrums	A flow-based Daily Scrum **focuses on ensuring the Scrum Team is doing everything it can to maintain consistent flow every day.**
	While the goal of the Daily Scrum remains the same as outlined in The Scrum Guide, the meeting itself takes place around the Kanban board and focuses on where flow is lacking and on what actions the Developers can take to get it back.
	WIP aging is especially useful during the Daily Scrum to help surface flow issues regarding specific Product Backlog items.
	The Scrum Guide use to suggests that Developers explain what they did yesterday, what they are focusing on today, and what their impediments are. Kanban teams typically focus on **the flow of work instead of the people doing the work.** They work the board right to left (Not always) focusing on flow problems.
	One **Daily Scrum aspect** that the Scrum Guide **emphasizes is the focus on the Sprint Goal** to make sure that tactical decisions are best aligned with the overall mission. Kanban teams would benefit from this higher-level focus beyond the immediate flow of specific work.
	The Daily Scrum meeting itself takes place around the Kanban board and focuses on: • Where is the **flow lacking**? • What **actions** the Scrum Team can take to get work flowing again?
⊙	Some additional things to consider during a flow-based Daily Scrum are as follows: • What work items are blocked and what can the Scrum Team do to get them unblocked? • What is the **Work Item Age of each item in progress?** What work is flowing slower than expected? • What work items **have violated or are about to violate their SLE** and what can the Scrum Team do to get that work completed? • Are there any things that may impact the Scrum Team's ability to complete work today that is not represented on the board? • Have we learned anything new that might change what the Scrum Team has planned to work on next? • Have we broken our WIP limit? And what can we do to ensure we can complete the work in progress?

	Reading the Kanban board from right to left (not always), team members might collectively ask themselves: <ul><li>How can we remove impediments, so the work does not continue to age and incur further flow debt?</li><li>What else is in progress, and how can we bring each item to completion?</li><li>Who among us can help to finish this work according to the workflow policies we have established?</li><li>What new items can we potentially start, having taken all steps to assure that work in progress will be finished?</li></ul>
Flow-Based Sprint Review	Flow based Sprint Reviews are essentially an example of a feedback loop.
	Inspecting Kanban flow metrics as part of the review can create opportunities for new conversations about **monitoring progress towards the Product Goal.**
	Kanban teams could potentially just do Sprint Reviews on demand. However, experience **shows that having a cadence typically makes it easier to get the right stakeholders in the room and is overall more efficient and effective.**
	Inspecting Kanban flow metrics as part of the Sprint Review creates opportunities for new conversations about monitoring progress towards a goal.
⚠	**Reviewing Throughput** might provide some additional information when the Product Owner discusses likely target and delivery dates. Reviewing a Scrum Team's SLE may cause the Product Owner to revise the Product Backlog.
Flow-Based Sprint Retrospective	A flow-based Sprint Retrospective adds the inspection of flow metrics and analytics to help determine **what improvements the Scrum Team can make to its processes,** including the Sprint Retrospective itself.
	The Scrum Team using Kanban also inspects and adapts the **Definition of Workflow** to optimize the flow in the next Sprint.
	The Scrum Guide dictates that the Sprint Retrospective **take place after the Sprint Review and before the next Sprint Planning.** This **does not change** when using Kanban. However, flow-based retrospective opportunities need not coincide within the boundaries of a Sprint. They can occur "just in time".
⚠	Using reports such as **Cycle Time Control Charts and Cumulative Flow diagrams**, Scrum Teams can gain deeper insights into the flow of work, thus driving improvement experiments that typically don't surface as a result of a classic Sprint Retrospective.
	As part of the Sprint Retrospective, Scrum Teams should consider adding the use of models and the scientific methods to guide their evolution empirically.
	Retrospectives are the **place to design experiments** based on ideas of how something might improve the team's capabilities. In the next Retrospective, the team can review the results and decide whether another round of experimentation is necessary (pivoting) or whether the team can deploy the change as a standard operating policy.

	Changes to a team's definition of "Workflow" may happen at any time, however, as these changes will have a material impact on how the Scrum Team performs, changes made during the regular cadence provided by the Sprint Retrospective event will reduce complexity and improve transparency.
	Sprint Retrospective is all about inspecting and adapting the process and the workflow. Therefore, it is the place to look at WIP, Cycle Times, Throughput from a perspective of looking for areas to improve.
	While the Sprint Retrospective is indeed the recommended time to inspect and adapt the workflow, any **workflow policy including WIP limits can be changed at any point.** There aren't many reasons to change WIP limits throughout the Sprint though. Changing WIP should be a process improvement strategy rather than a tactical way to deal with ongoing daily impediments.
	Using a cumulative flow diagram to visualize a Scrum Team's WIP, approximate average Cycle Time and average Throughput can be valuable.

Flow Metrics in Scrum Event Chart Summary

The following table summarizes the use of flow metrics in different Scrum Events.

Metrics	Daily Sprint	Sprint Retrospective	Sprint Review	Sprint Planning
SLE	SLE is used during Daily Sprint to monitor the progress of each work item. Teams makes sure that the work items move from one stage to another before the SLE is exceeded.	The "Surprise" or "Anomaly" of missing SLE can drive an improvement discussion.	SLE can be used in the Sprint Review when the team is working with stakeholders that care about the team's cycle time and want to compare the cycle time with what was expected.	SLE can also be used in Sprint Planning to provide Product Owners and stakeholders with an idea of when the service level can be expected from the team. That doesn't include providing a specific date for each PBI. The SLE enables the Scrum Team to forecast a finished date at a certain confidence level once the item has been started.
Work Item Age	** One of the things to consider during a flow-based Daily Scrum is the **Work Item Age of each item in progress.** Comparing the WIP Age with the SLE would let the team focus on the items which are close to or already have violated the SLE. WIP Age especially useful during the Daily Scrum to help surface flow issues regarding specific PBIs.			During Sprint Planning, the Work Item Age **might be** relevant when some items are left over from the previous Sprint and the team want to decide what to do about them.
Work in Progress (WIP)	The focus of Daily Scrum is the ongoing flow within the Sprint so naturally what the team cares about is what's currently going on. Therefore, Current WIP and Work Item Age are the most important metrics in the Daily Scrum.	Sprint Retrospective is all about inspecting and adapting the process and the workflow. Therefore, it is the place to look at WIP, Cycle Times, Throughput from a perspective of looking for areas to improve.		

Metrics	Daily Sprint	Sprint Retrospective	Sprint Review	Sprint Planning
Throughput		Sprint Retrospective is all about inspecting and adapting the process and the workflow. Therefore, it is the place to look at WIP, Cycle Times, Throughput from a perspective of looking for areas to improve.	Sprint Review includes a review with stakeholders of both the Increment as well as overall flow behavior of the team - trends Reviewing Throughput might provide some additional information when the Product Owner discusses likely target and delivery dates.	** When planning a Sprint, the main interest is to figure out how many backlog items to pull into the Sprint. Throughput of previous Sprints is the most useful in figuring this out. During Sprint Planning, the Scrum Team uses **historical Throughput** (of previous Sprints) to understand the Scrum Team's capacity for the next Sprint. An advanced technique would be to use Monte Carlo simulation using this throughput data in order to figure out confidence-levels for various amounts of items in the Sprint Backlog.
Cycle Time		Sprint Retrospective is all about inspecting and adapting the process and the workflow. Therefore, it is the place to look at WIP, Cycle Times, Throughput from a perspective of looking for areas to improve.	Sprint Review includes a review with stakeholders of both the Increment as well as overall flow behavior of the team - trends in Cycle Times and Throughput are interesting.	

Flow Based Roles and Artifacts

Please read the Scrum Guide Reference Table Roles and Artifacts before this session.

Kanban Developers	Kanban Developers are a group of people using Kanban who agree on explicit policies that enable members to **make decentralized, self-organized decisions** around work. The team also self-organizes to improve collaboratively rather than having somebody "manage the improvement" for them.
	Each person/team working in a Kanban system is **held accountable** for contributing to **great flow** and high-quality value delivery not just in their area of the Kanban but from a whole **value stream perspective**.
	Kanban **doesn't prescribe restructuring to cross-functional** teams spanning the value stream. Having said that, many organizations implementing Kanban realize that creating an autonomous cross-functional team is better for work/value flow.
Kanban Scrum Master	From a Kanban perspective, identifying **an "process coach" for** the team is a useful practice whether you call that person a Scrum Master, Kanban Flow Manager, or Agile Coach. In Lean, managers are expected to be process leaders. Although not prescribed in Kanban, many managers/leaders take on the "**Process Leader**" role. Scrum is officially neutral on the role managers should take.
Kanban Increments	Kanban doesn't explicitly mention having a potentially shippable Increment. The options Kanban teams have here are: • Use a Scrum-like Sprint Increment. • Have an increment upon completion of higher level that is marketable e.g. at the "feature" level. • Have an increment upon completion of every product backlog item/card. • Have a continuously available increment based on highly mature continuous integration/continuous deployment capabilities. This is harder but enables smoother flow throughout the Sprint boundaries.
Product Backlog	The different queues Kanban teams maintain to the left of their boards can be seen as a visualization of a Product Backlog. **Kanban teams limit the Product Backlog size and depth.** Having a limited Product Backlog wouldn't mean maintaining another backlog of the backlog items that don't fit the Product Backlog. It means actively ensuring the **Product Backlog is relevant and actionable** and not a complete list of everything ever asked for.
Sprint Backlog	Kanban teams might have 1) A **content-based Sprint backlog** for the entire Goal they are focusing on OR 2) A timebox-oriented backlog similar to Scrum.

Product Backlog Refinement	**Kanban teams** decide how to refine the backlog. They may **do this just in time when the inventory of ready stories goes below a threshold, or they can use a cadence.**
On Demand Kanban Teams	Teams On-Demand - Whenever pulling a new Feature for work, the relevant people might be temporarily associated with it. They will deliver that feature, and after a few weeks return to their home teams. This approach provides lots of flexibility, but typically has relatively high coordination costs. It also doesn't really benefit from the improved communication bandwidth among the team members that you get from persistent teams.

Little's Law	Average Cycle Time = Average Work in Progress / Average Throughput.
	$$\text{average cycle time} = \frac{\text{average work in progress}}{\text{average throughput}}$$

WIP = Throughput * Lead Time

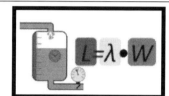

Where
- WIP = Average Number of items in process
- Throughput = Average Arrival / Departure rate
- Cycle Time / Lead Time = Average time an item spends in the system

WIP (Work in Progress) is the number of items being worked on by the team. In software development the unit of measure could be cards, user stories, scenarios, or something else.

We can put Throughput into the formula because Little's Law assumes a stable system. Throughput is the departure rate and in a stable system it is the same as the arrival rate of Little's original formula. **An example of Throughput is five user stories per week.**

Cycle Time / Lead Time is the elapsed time an item spends in the system. For example, if it takes 20 days for a user story to go through the system the **Lead Time on that item was 20 days.**

Cycle time can also be defined as a measure of the amount of time that has passed as an item on the Kanban board moves from the start through the end stage in a value stream.

Teams monitor aging/staleness on an ongoing basis (e.g. during the Daily Scrum) to identify stalled/struggling PBIs and find ways to help them along. Here, the team's focus is on the healthy flow of work. It may start using cumulative flow diagrams, which add information about the queues within the system to a burnup chart. The Scrum Team may also identify opportunities to decrease the amount of time it takes to get work to production. For development work inside a Sprint, Scrum directs teams to have that work be "Done" by the end of the Sprint, but if teams want to increase their flow, they should look for ways to release the work as soon as it's ready. There's nothing in the Scrum Guide that says you have to wait until the end of the Sprint.

	Little's Law reveals that in general, for a given process with a given throughput, **the more things that you work on at any given time (on average), the longer it is going to take to finish those things (on average).**
	To **Reduce Cycle** Time, one should: • Increase throughput. • Reduce WIP.
	Little's Law also shows us how **flow theory relies on empiricism by using flow metrics and data to gain transparency into historical flow and then using that data to inform flow inspection and adaptation experiments.**
	In order to get more stuff done faster, you need to work on less at a time. (again, on average).
	Little's Law is concerned with **looking backward over a time period** that has completed. It is not about looking forward; that is, is not meant to be used to make deterministic predictions.
	Little's law cannot predict the future. For example, the effect of reducing WIP limits cannot be predicted - it depends on whether the Scrum Team can achieve effective flow with lower WIP limits.
	Little's Law only applies when you are looking back over historical data.
	Little's Law is a **relationship of averages**.
	In Little Law, work items size does not matter because the law does not necessarily care about each item individually. It cares about what all items look like on average.
ScrumButs	ScrumButs are reasons why teams can't take full advantage of Scrum to solve their problems and realize the full benefits of product development using Scrum.
	ScrumButs mean that Scrum has exposed a dysfunction that is contributing to the problem but is too hard to fix. A ScrumBut retains the problem while modifying Scrum to make it invisible so that the dysfunction is no longer a thorn in the side of the team.
	ScrumBut Examples: 1. "(We use Scrum, but) (we can't build a piece of functionality in a month,) (so our Sprints are 6 weeks long.)" 2. "(We use Scrum, but) (Retrospectives provides no value,) (so we don't do them.)"

Kanban Guide Questions and Answers

Please go through these questions and check the answers as you go along. The Kanban Assessments online (https://www.scrum.org/open-assessments) are the best way to assess your knowledge. The Questions and Answers below will ensure you understand the concepts and help you help you prepare for the PSK exam. Go through the answers regardless of whether you answered the questions correctly or not. Don't try to time yourself. Focus on understanding the answers and the concepts. As you go through these questions, make your own notes to the Quick reference tables.

Question 1	Correct answer: B
The states of product backlog items in the definition of "Workflow" always coincide with the states defined by a Sprint Backlog. A. True B. False	Kanban Work Flow is the movement of Customer Value through the Product Development System. Kanban Work allows **creation of tables with consecutive lists of activities (Stages) where work items (Cards) flow from one Column (Stage) to another.** Using the Kanban Work Flow it's easy to know: 1. Which stage of the Process each of the Work Item is in. 2. Who is Performing the Work Item. 3. Other details about the Work Item's Execution. The States in the definition of "Workflow" do not always coincide with the states defined by a Sprint Backlog. Example: The states of Product Backlog item in a Sprint Backlog could be: Ready → Developed → Tested → Completed. The State of the same Product Backlog item on the Kanban Workflow could be: Ready →Work in Progress → Development Completed → Documented → Data Backup → Training. Scrum Team's definition of Workflow may include states that are upstream, downstream, inside, or outside of the Sprint Backlog. Similarly, the work items moving through the workflow may not correspond to Product Backlog Items or other parts of the Sprint Backlog or Scrum.

Question 2	**Correct answer: D**

Kanban Work Flow is the movement of _____ through the product development system.
 	
   C.   Customer Requirements
   D.   Work Flow Processes.
   E.   Rules.
   F.   Customer Value.
	Central to the definition of Kanban is the concept of "flow." Flow is the movement of customer value throughout the product development system.

Question 3
 	
Who creates the definition of "Workflow"?
 	
   A.   Process Owner.
   B.   Scrum Master.
   C.   Work Manager.
   D.   Scrum Team.
	Correct answer: D
	
	The work of all Kanban teams revolves around a Kanban board, a tool used to visualize work and optimize the flow of the work among the team. While physical boards are popular among some teams, virtual boards are a crucial feature in any agile software development tool for their traceability, easier collaboration, and accessibility from multiple locations.
	
	Regardless of whether a team's board is physical or digital, their function is to ensure the team's work is visualized, their workflow is standardized, and all blockers and dependencies are immediately identified Based on the Kanban Guide: The Scrum Team must create its definition of "Workflow".

Question 4	**Correct answer: B**
In a Kanban Workflow, a particular work item must **flow** through all of the active states, and a work item must flow sequentially through the active states. A. True. B. False.	A hallmark of the Kanban board are the columns. Each column represents a specific Stage that together compose a "workflow". Work flow through the workflow until completion. Workflows can be as simple as "To Do," "In Progress," "Complete," or much more complex. As Per the Kanban Guide, a particular work item **might not flow** through all of the active states, and a work item might not even flow sequentially through the active states. Example: You might have a stage called "External Vendor / Dependencies" where only work dependent on external vendors would flow. Not all the work would depend upon external vendors and thus not all the work would flow through this Column / Stage.
Question 5 Scrum Team's definition of "Workflow" may include states that are outside of the Sprint Backlog. A. True B. False	**Correct answer: A** Scrum Team's definition of "Workflow" may include states that are upstream, downstream, inside, or outside of the Sprint Backlog. Remember: Scrum Team's definition of Workflow may include states that are upstream, downstream, inside, or outside of the Sprint Backlog. Similarly, the work items moving through the workflow may not correspond to Product Backlog Items or other parts of the Sprint Backlog or Scrum.
Question 6 The creation and adaptation of the definition of "Workflow" does not **impact the Spring Backlog or the Product Backlog.** A. True B. False	Correct answer: B Kanban is all about visualizing your work, limiting work in progress, and maximizing efficiency (or flow). Kanban teams focus on reducing the time it takes to take a project (or user story) from start to finish. They do this by using a Kanban board and continuously improving their flow of work. The creation and adaptation of the definition of "Workflow" **thus may impact or be impacted by existing artifacts.**

Question 7	Correct answer: C
An SLE (Service Level Expectation) forecasts shows: A. How long it should take a given item to flow from start to finish within a Product Backlog. B. How long it should take a given item to finish based on the developers estimates. C. How long it should take a given item to flow from start to finish within a workflow. D. All of the above.	An SLE forecasts how long it should take a given item to flow from start to finish within your workflow. The Service Level Agreement itself has two parts: 1) A period of elapsed days in which the work would be completed. 2) The probability of work getting completed associated with that period.
Question 8	**Correct answer: B**
A Scrum Master liked to post the SLE (Service Level Expectation) on the Kanban board after its calculated. However, It is not recommended to post the SLE on the Kanban board after its calculated. A. True B. False	Based on the Scrum Guide: SLE (Service Level Expectation) once calculated, should be posted on the Kanban board.
Question 9	**Correct answer: A**
Different Scrum Teams having different Sprint Backlogs can have different definitions of "Workflow". A. True B. False	The main purpose of having a Workflow is to allow team members to track the progress of work through its workflow in a highly visual manner. Kanban board feature critical information about that particular work item, giving the entire team full visibility into who is responsible for that item of work, a brief description of the job being done, how long that piece of work is estimated to take, and so on. Each Scrum Team has its own Sprint Backlog and its own way of managing the items within the Backlog. Thus, different Scrum Teams having different Sprint Backlogs can have different definitions of "Workflow". Based on the Kanban Guide: Each Scrum Team must create its definition of "Workflow".

Question 10	Correct answer: A, C, D, E
Scrum Teams achieve flow optimization by using the following four practices: (Choose all that apply) A. Visualization of the workflow. B. Updating the States. C. Limiting WIP. D. Active management of work items in progress. E. Inspecting and adapting their definition of "Workflow". F. Managing the Sprint Backlog dependencies.	Scrum Teams achieve flow optimization by using the following four practices: 1) Visualization of the workflow. 2) Limiting WIP. 3) Active management of work items in progress. 4) Inspecting and adapting their definition of "Workflow".
Question 11 A Kanban "Workflow" definition includes a shared understanding within the Scrum Team of how work is defined (work items). A. True B. False	**Correct answer: A** A Kanban "Workflow" definition must include: 1. A shared understanding within the Scrum Team of how work is defined (work items). 2. The start state of the process. 3. The active states for the work items. 4. The finished state of the process. 5. A definition of how Work in Progress (WIP) will be limited. 6. A set Service Level Expectation (SLE) that communicates a forecast of how long it should take to complete work items.
Question 12 A basic Kanban board has which three-step workflow? A. To Do / Ready to Start. B. In Progress. C. Completed / Done. D. Work Pended.	**Correct answer: A, B, C** A basic Kanban board has a three-step workflow: To Do, In Progress, and Done. However, depending on a team's size, structure, and objectives, the workflow can be mapped to meet the unique process of any particular team.

Question 13	Correct answer: D
Scrum Teams using Kanban must explicitly control the in-progress work items from the time they consider them "started" until the time they consider them "finished." These work items are called: A. Started Work items. B. Sprint backlog items. C. Moving backlog items. D. Work in Progress (WIP) items.	In agile development, work in progress (WIP) limits set the maximum amount of work that can exist in each status of a workflow. Limiting the amount of work in progress makes it easier to identify inefficiency in a team's workflow. Work in Progress (WIP) refers to the work items the Scrum Team has started but has not yet finished. Scrum Teams using Kanban must explicitly control the in-progress work items from the time they consider them "started" until the time they consider them "finished."
Question 14 In a Kanban Workflow, the work items moving through the workflow **will always correspond** to Product Backlog Items or other parts of the Sprint Backlog or Scrum. A. True B. False	**Correct answer: B** In the Kanban Workflow, the work items moving through the workflow **may not correspond** to Product Backlog Items or other parts of the Sprint Backlog or Scrum. Example in multiple companies, parts of the delivery cycle are to execute user studies, train support staff, notify users of upcoming downtime, ensure a backup is done prior to the deployment etc. These type of "states / stages " might not be a part of the process for the Scrum team to provide a potentially releasable increment but are definitely needed for delivery. Since Kanban is focused on the entire workflow from idea to use, one would expect to see "states / stages" before and after the actual steps to build (Development). These additional stages would thus have more things / work items.Thus, the work items moving through the workflow **will not always correspond** to Product Backlog Items or other parts of the Sprint Backlog or Scrum.

Question 15	Correct answer: D

Who owns the definition of "Workflow"?
 	
  A. Process Owner.
  B. Scrum Master.
  C. Work Manager.
  D. Scrum Team.
	Scrum board is always owned by one Scrum team. A Scrum team is a cross-functional group of employees whose background contains all the skills required for successful completion of all the tasks during this Sprint. Kanban board doesn't need to be owned by a specific team since it's mostly devoted to a workflow.

Question 16
 	
Active management of workflow can take several forms, including (Choose all that Apply):
 	
  A. Responding quickly to blocked work items (seen on the workflow).
  B. Making sure that work items are only pulled into the workflow at about the same rate that they leave the workflow.
  C. Ensuring work items aren't left to age unnecessarily and are completed according to an established SLE.
  D. Unclogging work that piles up in a column or columns.
  E. Updating the Sprint Backlog.
	Correct answer: A, B, C, D
	
	It is the Scrum Team's responsibility to ensure the continuous proactive, active, and reactive management of work items in progress. Active management of workflow can take several forms, including but not limited to the following:
	
	• Responding quickly to blocked work items.
	• Making sure that work items are only pulled into the workflow at about the same rate that they leave the workflow.
	• Ensuring work items aren't left to age unnecessarily and are completed according to an established SLE.
	• Unclogging work that piles up in a column or columns.

Question 17
 	
The Kanban board should display all relevant policies or direct Scrum Team members.
 	
  A. True.
  B. False.
	Correct answer: A
	
	As per the Kanban Guide, the Kanban board should display all relevant policies or direct Scrum Team members where to find them.

Question 18	Correct answer: A
Consider you are a Member of Kanban Team. You are looking at the Kanban Board and notice the WIP Limits. Having too high WIP limits means that probably your team is working on multiple tasks, switching context all the time and not meeting the deadlines. Having really low limits on the other side means that when a given item is pending, and your members have to wait, they are static. A. True. B. False.	What these two scenarios have in common is that your team is unproductive and inefficient. In order to escape from this paradox, you have to carefully monitor your KPIs when you either increase or decrease your limits. If you change your team's WIP limits and your KPIs go in the opposite direction of what you'd expect, then you're probably a victim of the paradox and you have to examine your team's operations closer in order to ensure smoother flow.
Question 19	**Correct answer: B**
It is the Product Owners responsibility to ensure the continuous proactive, active, and reactive management of work items is in progress within the Kanban Workflow. A. True. B. False.	In the Kanban Workflow, it is the Scrum Team's responsibility to ensure the continuous proactive, active, and reactive management of work items in progress.
Question 20	**Correct answer: D**
A Scrum Master is talking to a member of a Developer. The Scrum Master does ask him "What Cycle Time do we expect to see for an item of this type, and what is our confidence level for this?". The Scrum Master is asking for: A. Work in Progress (WIP). B. Cycle Time. C. Work Item Age. D. Service Level Expectation.	Service Level Expectation address the questions "What Cycle Time do we expect to see for an item of this type, and what is our confidence level for this?". Example 1) 85% of work items will be finished in eight days or less OR 8 Days with 85% confidence / probability. 2) 3 out of 5 items are expected to be finished in the coming Sprint.

Question 21	Correct answer: A, C, D, E
The basic metrics of flow that Scrum Teams using Kanban will need to track are as follows: A. Work in Progress (WIP). B. Burndown charts. C. Cycle Time. D. Work Item Age. E. Throughput. F. Velocity.	The basic metrics of flow that Scrum Teams using Kanban will need to track are as follows: A. Work in Progress (WIP): The number of work items started but not finished (according to the Scrum Team's definition of "Workflow"). B. Cycle Time: The amount of elapsed time between when a work item "starts" and when a work item "finishes." C. Work Item Age: The amount of elapsed time between when a work item "started" and the current time. D. Throughput: The number of work items "finished" per unit of time. Note the measurement of throughput is the exact count of work items.
Question 22	Correct Answer: B, C
Calculating which metrics of flows requires the Scrum Team to (at a minimum) track the start date of each item. (Choose all that Apply) A. Work in Progress (WIP). B. Cycle Time. C. Work Item Age. D. Throughput.	Calculating Cycle times and Work item age requires the Scrum Team to (at a minimum) track the start date and finished date of each item.
Question 23	Correct answer: A
The SLE forecast is based on a Scrum Team's historical cycle time. A. True B. False	The SLE is based on a Scrum Team's historical cycle time. If no historical cycle time data exists, the Scrum Team should make its **best guess** and then replace that guess once there is enough historical data to do a proper SLE calculation.

Question 24	Correct answer: D

A flow-based **Sprint Planning** meeting (driven by Kanban practices) uses which metrics as an aid for developing the Sprint Backlog?
 	
  A. Work in Progress (WIP).
  B. Cycle Time.
  C. Velocity.
  D. Throughput.
	Throughput can be defined as the number of work items "finished" per unit of time. A flow-based Sprint Planning meeting uses historical Throughput to understand the Scrum Team's capacity for the next Sprint.
	
	Refer to the **Flow Metrics in Scrum Event Chart Summary** and **Metrics Summary Table**, if you get confused on such exam questions.

Question 25	Correct answer: A

For a Team practicing Kanban, which meeting always takes place around the Kanban board and focuses on getting the work flow going smooth again?
 	
  A. Daily Scrum.
  B. Sprint Planning.
  C. Sprint Retrospective.
  B. All of the above.
	Per the Kanban Guide, A flow-based Daily Scrum takes place around the Kanban board and focuses on Where flow is lacking and on what actions the Scrum Team can take to get work flowing smooth again.

Question 26	Correct answer: C,E
A flow-based **Daily Meeting** uses which metrics as an aid for tracking the Flow of work daily? (Select 2) A. Velocity Chart. B. Cycle Time. C. Work Item Age. D. Throughput. E. Work in Progress (WIP).	Work Item Age is defined as the amount of elapsed time between when a work item "started" and the current time. Work Item Age shows how long ago has each item has been pulled into WIP, on the Kanban Board. Things consider during a flow-based Daily Scrum are as follows: • What work items are blocked and what can the Scrum Team do to get them unblocked? • What is **the Work Item Age** of each item in progress? • What work items have violated or are about to violate their SLE and what can the Scrum Team do to get that work completed? • Are there any things that may impact the Scrum Team's ability to complete work today that is not represented on the board? Refer to the **Flow Metric in Scrum Event Chart Summary Table** and **Metrics Summary Table**, if you get confused on such exam questions.

Question 27	**Correct answer: D,E**

A flow-based **Sprint Review** uses which metrics as an aid for tracking the Flow of work daily? (Choose two)
 	
   A.   Work in Progress (WIP):
   B.   Team Velocity
   C.   Work Item Age
   D.   Throughput.
   E.   Cycle Time.
	Throughput can be defined as the number of work items "finished" per unit of time. During Sprint Reviews, reviewing Throughput might provide some additional information when the Product Owner discusses likely target and delivery dates. Reviewing a Scrum Team's SLE may cause the Product Owner to revise the Product Backlog.
	
	Cycle Time could also be useful when inspecting the overall flow of the sprint.
	
	Refer to the **Flow Metrics in Scrum Event Chart Summary** and **Metrics Summary Table**, if you get confused on such exam questions.

Question 28	**Correct answer: B**

A Brand-new team who has just started implementing Scrum is on its third Sprint. The team has an average WIP of 20 work items, an average Cycle Time of 5 days and an average Throughput of 4 items per day. The Team predicts that it can increase average WIP to 40, keep average Cycle Time constant at 5 days and the Throughput will increase to 8 items per day. They may increase the number of team members if needed.
 	
   A.   True.
   B.   False.
	This questions is taking about Little's law (WIP = Throughput * Lead Time) . Remember **Little's law cannot predict the future**. One cannot assume that Little's Law will make a prediction. It will not be true even if you add staff to the keep the WIP to staff ratio. All Little's Law says is that an increase in average WIP will result in a change to the average Cycle Time and average Throughput.
	
	In this scenario the teams are very new as well. However, once we start to trust our data, one can start to use something like Monte Carlo simulation on historical data to make forecasts.

Question 29	**Correct answer: B**
Kanban is a method that uses a work-in-process limited push system to expose operation (or process) problems and to stimulate collaborative improvement efforts. A. True B. False	Be careful with the Pull and Push Questions. Kanban is a method that uses a work-in-process limited pull system as the core mechanism to expose operation (or process) problems and to stimulate collaborative improvement efforts.
Question 30 Kanban practitioners follow a set of core principle / principles which are: A. Start with what you do now. B. Respect the current process, roles, responsibilities, and titles. C. Agree to pursue incremental, evolutionary change. D. All of the above.	**Correct answer: D** Kanban practitioners follow a set of core principles that guide the way they apply the Kanban practices. These principles are: A. Start with what you do now: Kanban's flexibility allows it to be overlaid on existing workflows, systems and processes without disrupting what is already successfully being done. B. Respect the current process, roles, responsibilities, and titles: Kanban recognizes that existing processes, roles, responsibilities, and titles have value and are, generally, worth preserving. C. Agree to pursue incremental, evolutionary change: The Kanban methodology is designed to meet minimal resistance and thus encourages continuous small incremental and evolutionary changes to the current process.

Question 31	**Correct answer: A**
Individual units of customer value that are flowing through the Scrum Team's system are a part of the "Definition of Workflow." A. True B. False	Each Scrum Team must **create its definition of "Workflow"** containing the following elements (See Diagram Below): **A.** Defined points at which the Scrum Team considers work to **have started and to have finished.** B. A definition of the **individual units of customer value** that are flowing through the Scrum Team's system (most likely Product Backlog Items (PBIs)). C. A definition of the **workflow states that the PBIs flow** through from start to finish (of which there must be at least one active state). D. Explicit policies about how work flows through each state (which may include items from a Scrum Team's definition of "Done" and pull policies between stages).
Question 32	**Correct answer: C**
One of the keys to effective visualization for a Scrum Team is to make sure it sees the flow of Product Backlog items from idea identification, through refinement, analysis, design, coding, testing, and deployment; all the way to "Done." This is what Kanban teams calls: A. Sprint Refinement. B. Backlog grooming. C. Value stream. D. Product Backlog grooming.	One of the keys to effective visualization for a Scrum Team is to make sure it sees the flow of Product Backlog items from idea identification, through refinement, analysis, design, coding, testing, and deployment; all the way to "Done." This is what Kanban teams call value stream. It is not enough to simply visualize the Sprint Backlog. It is important to make the flow of work into and out of the Sprints visible as well because many teams have difficulty with this aspect. Visualizing the flow throughout the value stream means we should mainly visualize the flow of Product Backlog items (PBIs) rather than tasks.

Question 33	**Correct answer: B**

A Scrum Team learns from their cycle time scatterplot that 85% of their work items finish in 8 days or less and 50% of the items actually finish within 4 days. They have an item A that has been active for 5 days already and an item B that has been active for 3 days. Which of these items should the team feel more confident they can finish within their 8 days or less SLE?
 	
  A. Item A
  B. Item B
  C. Both of them
  D. Depends on the Team
	Without further information about where each of the items is in their workflow, the team should feel more confident about item B that aged less. Item A has already been active more than it takes for 50% of the cards to finish, so it's quite a strong signal that there's a flow risk to it. Basically, with each day that passes in which a work item doesn't finish, the probability that a work item will not meet its SLE increases.

Question 34	**Correct answer: A**

What is not considered a Flow in Kanban?
 	
  A. Movement of Tasks from one state to another.
  B. Movement of PBI from one state to another.
  C. Movement of Customer Value from one state to another.
  D. All of the above.
	Kanban does not acknowledge movement of Tasks from one state to another.

Question 35	**Correct answer: D**

What is not true with respect to Work in Progress Limit?
 	
   A. Different WIP Limits can be applied on different stages.
   B. WIP Limits across stages can be combined.
   C. WIP Limit is associated with Littles LAW.
   D. WIP Limit can be changed at the retrospective only.
   E. A Sprint itself is a WIP Limit.
	Scrum Teams **should** adjust WIP limits during the Sprint Retrospective. However, it is not mandatory to do so.

Question 36	**Correct answer: A**

WIP Limits should be low enough that they introduce pain / challenge, to the implementing Scrum Members.
 	
   A. True.
   B. False.
	WIP limits should be low enough that they introduce pain-- meaning that they push beyond what the team is comfortable with and used to. The team would want to channel this pain towards ways of improving the team's process and policies so that in the future, the flow will be better and the WIP limit will be less painful.
	
	 Improving engineering practices, using techniques such as acceptance test-driven development (ATDD), reducing batch/PBI size, cross-training, or any other technique are all ways to make the WIP Limit more comfortable. Over time, as team capabilities improve, the WIP limit can be tightened to catalyze even more improvement in capabilities. Limiting WIP is an effective way to drive deep collaboration at the team level.

Question 37	**Correct answer: A**
In Kanban, Value is created, and a feedback loop is closed only when:	**Value is created, and the feedback loop is closed** only **when a Product Backlog item is complete.**
A. A Product Backlog item is completed. B. All Tasks within a Sprint backlog are completed. C. Most of the Stories within a Sprint backlog are completed. D. The originator of the feedback loop is satisfied. E. All of the Above.	Kanban's goal when improving flow is to tighten the feedback/value loop - so flow improvement techniques such as Limiting WIP can be applied to the valuable items i.e. the Product Backlog Items. **Stories and Tasks in the Sprint backlog might or might not generate Value. A Product backlog item always does.**
Question 38	**Correct answer: A**
Explicit Policies about how work flows through each state are part of the "Definition of Workflow." A. True B. False	Each Scrum Team must **create its definition of "Workflow"** containing the following elements (See Diagram Below): **A.** Defined points at which the Scrum Team considers work to **have started and to have finished.** B. A definition of the **individual units of customer value** that are flowing through the Scrum Team's system (most likely Product Backlog Items (PBIs)). C. A definition of the **workflow states that the PBIs flow** through from start to finish (of which there must be at least one active state). D. Explicit policies about how work flows through each state (which may include items from a Scrum Team's definition of "Done" and pull policies between stages).

Question 39

A Scrum Master has decided to share the Service Level expectation (SLE) for all the items on the Kanban Board to external Stake holders. Although SLE's are used by Scrum Teams to set flow expectations / aspirations for themselves, they can shared with stakeholders who care about them.

A. True
B. False

Correct answer: A

A Service Level Expectation is just an expectation set by the team to themselves answering the question "What Cycle Time do we expect to see for an item of this type, and what is our confidence level for this?". SLE Example : 85% of work items will be finished in eight days or less OR 8 Days with 85% confidence / probability. With each day that passes in which a work item doesn't finish, the probability that a work item will not meet its SLE, increases. The team would compare active in-flight work items age to their SLE and look for items that are at risk of missing the SLE. As work ages, it becomes more and more likely that the work item would not meet the team's SLE.

Can SLE be shared with external stakeholders? Yes they can be shared with the Stakeholders.

Bottom line – SLEs are used by Scrum Teams to set flow expectations to themselves. SLEs are ideally created based on actual historical cycle time data. They are then used by teams to focus their flow inspection and adaptation effort – during the Sprint in the Daily Scrum and following the sprint in the Sprint Retrospective. They can also used in the Sprint Review when the team is working with stakeholders that care about the team's cycle time.

Question 40

WIP limits help create focus by reducing multitasking which can in fact increase productivity.

A. True
B. False

Correct answer: A

During development, it's easy to think "I'll pause on this one issue while I begin work on another." Having two issues open means context switching between two different things or transferring work between teammates. It's almost always better to work through the original issue rather than starting and not completing new work. In other words, WIP limits discourage us from impeding the teams internal flow.
WIP limits help create **focus by reducing multitasking which can in fact increase productivity**. A lower WIP limit which increases focus can result in higher productivity.

Question 41	**Correct answer: D**
A newly formed Scrum Team is using Kanban to improve the Sprint flow by visualizing and managing flow in the **Sprint Backlog.** Who owns the workflow and specifically the WIP limits? A. The Scrum Team. B. The Product Owner. C. The Scrum Master. D. Developers.	Who owns the definition of Workflow depends on the scope/context of the workflow: 1) If the team is using Kanban to improve the Sprint flow by visualizing and managing flow in the **Sprint Backlog, Developers in the Scrum Team** would own the workflow and specifically the WIP limits. 2) If the team is using Kanban from **a holistic perspective**, starting from the Product Backlog, refinement and Sprint Backlog, **the Scrum Team** that would own the workflow and therefore the WIP limits. 3) If the Dev Team actually wants to involve the Product Owner in their Sprint flow (to review and accept a story during the Sprint before it goes through testing), **the Scrum Team** that would own the workflow and therefore the WIP limits.
Question 42	**Correct answer: A**
Who is responsibility to ensure the continuous proactive, active, and reactive management of work items in progress? A. The Scrum Team. B. The Product Owner. C. The Scrum Master. D. Developers.	**It is the Scrum Team's responsibility** to ensure the continuous proactive, active, and reactive management of work items in progress.

Question 43	**Correct answer: A**
In a newly formed Scrum Team, Developers wants to involve the Product Owner in their Sprint flow. The Product Owners role will be to review and accept a story during the Sprint before it goes through testing. In such a situation who owns the workflow and specifically the WIP limits? A. The Scrum Team. B. The Product Owner. C. The Scrum Master. D. Developers.	Who owns the definition of Workflow depends on the scope/context of the workflow: 1) If the team is using Kanban to improve the Sprint flow by visualizing and managing flow in the **Sprint Backlog, Developers in the Scrum Team** would own the workflow and specifically the WIP limits. 2) If the team is using Kanban from **a holistic perspective**, starting from the Product Backlog, refinement and Sprint Backlog, **the Scrum Team** that would own the workflow and therefore the WIP limits. 3) If the Dev Team actually wants to involve the Product Owner in their Sprint flow (to review and accept a story during the Sprint before it goes through testing), **the Scrum Team** that would own the workflow and therefore the WIP limits.
Question 44 The total number of work items started but not finished (according to the Scrum Team's definition of "Workflow") are called: A. WIP Limit. B. Work in Progress (WIP). C. Sprint Backlog Items. **D.** Velocity.	**Correct answer: B** Work in Progress (WIP) is nothing but **the number of work items started but not finished (according to the Scrum Team's definition of "Workflow").**
Question 45 Depending on a team's size, structure, and objectives, the workflow can be mapped to meet the unique process of any particular team. A. True. B. False.	**Correct answer: A** A basic Kanban board has a three-step workflow: To Do, In Progress, and Done. However, depending on a team's size, structure, and objectives, the workflow can be mapped to meet the unique process of any particular team.

Question 46
 	
In which meeting does the Scrum Team tracks the blocked work items and actions to get them unblocked?
 	
    A.   Flow Based Sprint Planning.
    B.   Flow Bases Sprint Retrospective.
    C.   Flow Based Daily Sprint.
    D.   Flow Based Sprint Review.
	Correct answer: C
	
	Things consider during a flow-based Daily Scrum are as follows:
	
	• What work items are blocked and what can the Scrum Team do to get them unblocked?
	• What is the Work Item Age of each item in progress?
	• What work items have violated or are about to violate their SLE and what can the Scrum Team do to get that work completed?
	• Are there any things that may impact the Scrum Team's ability to complete work today that is not represented on the board?

Question 47
 	
A Scrum Team's SLE might influence the work planned for the first few days of the Sprint.
 	
    A.   True.
    B.   False.
	Correct answer: A
	
	A flow-based Sprint Planning meeting uses historical Throughput to understand the Scrum Team's capacity for the next Sprint. A Scrum Team's SLE might influence the work planned for the first days of the Sprint.

Question 48
 	
Cumulative Flow Diagram helps with: (Choose all that Apply)
 	
    A.   Visualizing the amount of Work in Progress (WIP) at each interval.
    B.   Average Cycle time.
    C.   Average Velocity.
    D.   Average SLE.
	Correct answer: A, B
	
	CFD's help with visualizing the amount of **Work in Progress (WIP)** at each interval. The vertical height of each band is the **Number of items (WIP) in that stage**'s and the horizontal length of each stage expose the **Average cycle time.**

Question 49	Correct answer: A
If a band on your CFD is continuously narrowing that means: A) That the throughput of the stage it represents is higher than the entry rate. B) That the throughput of the stage it represents is lower than the entry rate. C) That the WIP is High. D) That the WIP is Low. 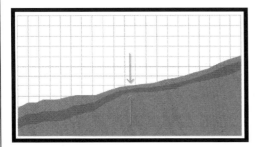	If a band on your CFD is continuously narrowing that means that the **throughput of the stage it represents is higher than the entry rate.** This is a sign that you've got more capacity than you really need at this stage and you should optimize the flow.
Question 50 A Kanban "Workflow" definition does not include the finished state of the process. A. True. B. False.	Correct answer: B A Kanban "Workflow" definition must include: 1. A shared understanding within the Scrum Team of how work is defined (work items). 2. The start state of the process. 3. The active states for the work items. 4. The finished state of the process. 5. A definition of how Work in Progress (WIP) will be limited. 6. A set Service Level Expectation (SLE) that communicates a forecast of how long it should take to complete work items.

Question 51	Correct answer: A

While calculating SLE, if no historical cycle time data exists, the Scrum Team should:
 	
   A. Make its **best guess** and then replace that guess once there is enough historical data to do a proper SLE calculation.
   B. Look at other similar team's cycle time.
   C. Let's the manager of the Scrum Team decide based his / her experience.
   D. Let's the Scrum Master decide.
	While calculating SLE, if no historical cycle time data exists, the Scrum Team should make its **best guess** and then replace that guess once there is enough historical data to do a proper SLE calculation.

Question 52
 	
If a band on your CFD is continuously broadening that means:
 	
  A) That the throughput of the stage it represents is higher than the entry rate.
  B) That the throughput of the stage it represents is lower than the entry rate.
  C) That the WIP is High.
  D) That the WIP is Low.
 	
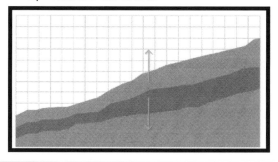
	Correct answer: B
	
	If a band on your CFD is continuously broadening that means, the number of cards that enter the corresponding stage on the Kanban board is higher than the number of assignments that are leaving it. **This is a sign that the team has got less capacity for the work undertaken.**

Question 53	Correct answer: B

A new Scrum team is trying to calculate the amount of elapsed time between when a work item "started" and when a work item "finished." The Scrum Team is trying to calculate the work item's _____?
 	
   A. Work Item Age.
   B. Cycle time.
   C. WIP.
   D. Throughput.
	Cycle Time: The **amount of elapsed time between when a work item "starts" and when a work item "finishes."**

Question 54
 	
Cycle time and Work item age (throughout the team's definition of Workflow) can be considered as the length of the team's feedback loop?
 	
    A. True.
    B. False.
	Correct answer: A
	
	Cycle time throughout the team's definition of Workflow **can be considered the length of the team's feedback loop (similar to Work Item Age).**
	
	Work item age: This gives daily feedback on the age of an item. This is very important during Daily Scrum.

Question 55
 	
A WIP Limit can include work items across the all the stages on the Board.
 	
    A. True.
    B. False.
	Correct answer: A
	
	A WIP Limit can include work items in a single column, several grouped columns, or a whole board.

Question 56
 	
The average cycle time can be longer than the sprint length.
 	
    A. True.
    B. False.
	Correct answer: B
	
	Cycle Time: The amount of elapsed time between when a work item "starts" and when a work item "finishes." Cycle Time can be calculated only after the work item is actually finished (e.g. reached a Done lane on the Kanban board). Cycle time is a Lagging indicator (not a leading indicator) for the length of the Scrum Team's feedback loop for a product backlog item. I.e. one would only know the cycle time after the Product Backlog item has reached the end of the team's definition of Workflow. Sprint Length is a WIP Limit and yes Product backlog items (at times) may take longer than a Sprint. This could absolutely happen. Thus the cycle time (and not average cycle time) for a Product Backlog item can be longer than the Sprint Length.
	
	The average cycle time should be quite a bit shorter than the sprint length. If you have a few items that go above the sprint length, its fine, the average cycle time will stay below the Sprint Length. However, the average cycle time should not exceed the sprint length. If it does means most of your Product backlog items are not getting completed in a single Sprint.

Question 57 One of the greatest benefits of using a cycle time scatter plot for Lean management is that it gives you the ability to **forecast the outcome of future tasks.** A. True B. False	**Correct answer: A** One of the greatest benefits of using a cycle time scatter plot for Lean management is that it gives you the ability to **forecast the outcome of future tasks.**
Question 58 You've got 100 tasks that were completed in 50 days. If 50 of them were finished in 7 days or less, while all the others took longer, you've got 50 percent chance to finish any future task within 7 days. This is an Example of: A. Work Item Age. B. Cycle time. C. WIP. D. Throughput.	**Correct answer: B** Cycle Time: The **amount of elapsed time between when a work item "starts" and when a work item "finishes."** Cycle time is a Lagging indicator (not a leading indicator) for the length of the Scrum Team's feedback loop for a product backlog item. I.e. one would only know the cycle time after the Product Backlog item has reached the end of the team's definition of Workflow.
Question 59 70 tasks (out of the 100 task) which were completed within 12 days. This means that you've got 70 percent chance to finish any future task within 12 days. This is an Example of: A. Work Item Age B. Cycle time C. WIP **D.** Throughput	**Correct answer: B** Cycle Time: The **amount of elapsed time between when a work item "starts" and when a work item "finishes."** Calculating Cycle times requires the Scrum Team to (at a minimum) **track the start date and finished date of each item.**

Question 60	Correct answer: A
What is defined as **the amount of elapsed time between when a work item "started" and the current time?** A. Work Item Age. B. Cycle time. C. WIP. D. Throughput.	Work Item Age is defined as **the amount of elapsed time between when a work item "started" and the current time.**
Question 61 Work Item Age is a leading indicator only relevant for: (Choose all that apply) A. The length of the Scrum Team's feedback loop for that (in progress) item. B. Non-finished items Only. C. Items which have not started. D. All the Work Items.	Correct answer: A, B Work Item Age is a leading indicator only relevant for: A. The length of the Scrum Team's feedback loop for that (in progress) item. B. Non-finished items Only.

Question 62

The Graph below is a Aging Work in Progress chart. Looking at the Plot Diagram below, the Product owner can say which of the following (Choose all that apply)

    A.   There is a 70% certainty your team can handle any task in less than 11 days.

    B.   There is a 70% certainty your team can handle any task in less than 7 days.

    C.   Dev Team can commit to delivering a task within 7 days but there's a 50/50 chance of achieving that goal.

    D.   All of the above.

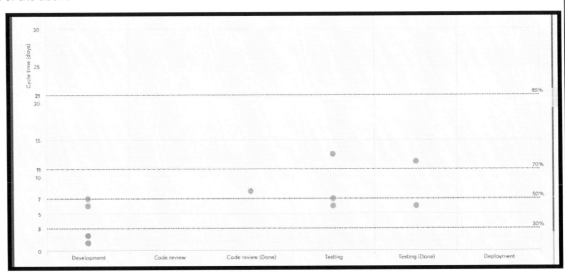

Correct answer: A, C

There is a 70% certainty your team can handle any task in less than 11 days. Equally, you could commit to delivering a task within 7 days but there's a 50/50 chance of achieving that goal.

Question 63	Correct answer: B
The Scrum Team can choose to skip conducting a Sprint Retrospective when using Kanban with Scrum. A. True B. False	**The Scrum Team cannot choose to skip conducting a Sprint Retrospective when using Kanban with Scrum.**
Question 64	Correct answer: D
During Sprint planning, a Scrum team is trying to figure out how many backlog items to pull into the Sprint. Which metrics is useful while doing so? A. Work Item Age. B. Cycle time. C. WIP. D. Throughput of the Previous Sprints.	When planning a Sprint, the main interest is to figure out how many backlog items to pull into the Sprint. Throughput of previous Sprints is the most useful in figuring this out. An advanced technique would be to use **Monte Carlo** simulation using this throughput data in order to figure out confidence-levels for various amounts of items in the Sprint Backlog.
Question 65	Correct answer: B
The Scrum Guide dictates that the Sprint Retrospective take place after the Sprint Review and before the next Sprint Planning. This can change when a team is using Kanban. A. True B. False	The Scrum Guide dictates that the Sprint Retrospective **take place after the Sprint Review and before the next Sprint Planning.** This does not change when using Kanban. However, flow-based retrospective opportunities need not coincide within the boundaries of a Sprint. They can occur "just in time".
Question 66	Correct answer: B
Changes to a team's definition of "Workflow" may happen only during Sprint Retrospective. A. True B. False	Changes to a team's definition of "Workflow" may happen at any time, however, as these changes will have a material impact on how the Scrum Team performs, changes made during the regular cadence provided by the Sprint Retrospective event will reduce complexity and improve transparency.

Question 67	**Correct answer: B**

Workflow policy including WIP limits can be changed only during Sprint Retrospective.
 	
   A. True
   B. False
	While the Sprint Retrospective is indeed the recommended time to inspect and adapt the workflow, any **workflow policy including WIP limits can be changed at any point.** There aren't many reasons to change WIP limits throughout the Sprint though. Changing WIP should be a process improvement strategy rather than a tactical way to deal with ongoing daily impediments.

Question 68	**Correct answer: A**

The **fundamental of Little's Law** states that in a given process, the more things that one work on, the longer it is going to take for each of those things to complete.
 	
   A. True
   B. False
	The **fundamental of Little's Law** states that in a given process, the more things that one work on, the longer it is going to take for each of those things to finish. (on average).

Question 69	**Correct answer: A, B**

To Reduce Cycle Time, one should:
   A. Increase throughput.
   B. Reduce WIP.
   C. Decrease throughput.
   D. Increase WIP.
	To Reduce Cycle Time, one should:
	   • Increase throughput.
	   • Reduce WIP.

Question 70	Correct answer: B

Little's law can be used to predict the future.
 	
   A. True.
   B. False.
	Little's law cannot predict the future. For example, the effect of reducing WIP limits cannot be predicted - it depends on whether the Scrum Team can achieve effective flow with lower WIP limits.

Question 71	Correct answer: A
ScrumButs are reasons why teams can't take full advantage of Scrum to solve their problems or realize the full benefits of product development using Scrum. A. True B. False	ScrumButs are reasons why teams can't take full advantage of Scrum to solve their problems and realize the full benefits of product development using Scrum. ScrumButs mean that Scrum has exposed a dysfunction that is contributing to the problem but is too hard to fix. A ScrumBut retains the problem while modifying Scrum to make it invisible so that the dysfunction is no longer a thorn in the side of the team.
Question 72 Work in Kanban is pulled rather than pushed. A. True B. False	Correct answer: A Work in Kanban is pulled rather than pushed. I.e. Scrum Team starts work on an item only when there is a clear signal that it has time to do so.
Question 73 Scrum Team (using Kanban) starts work on an item only when there is a clear signal that it is time to do so. Clear Signal to start work would be: A. Developers have no work or have completed the work assigned. B. The Project Plan Start date is crossed. C. When the WIP drops below a defined limit. D. When the throughput drops.	Correct answer: C Work in Kanban is pulled rather than pushed. Scrum Team starts work on an item only when there is a clear signal that it has time to do so.
Question 74 Using a flow-based perspective can enhance the Scrum events. A. True B. False	Correct answer: A Kanban is a strategy which optimizes the flow of stakeholder value through a process that uses a visual, work-in-progress limited pull system. Adding Kanban to Scrum provides a technique to help the Scrum Team focus on driving a continuous flow of activity but does not negate value provided by the Scrum Events, Artifacts, Roles, or Rules. However, flow-based metrics/charts & forecasts may get added to Scrum events as per the Kanban Guide for Scrum Teams.

Question 75	Correct answer: A, B, D, E

Scrum Teams achieve flow optimization by using the following (**Select 4 answers**)
 	
A. Inspecting and adapting their definition of "Workflow".
B. Active management of work items in progress.
C. Padding estimates to allow space in the Sprint Backlog
D. Limiting WIP.
E. Visualization of the workflow.
F. Grooming the workflow.
	Scrum Teams achieve flow optimization by using the following four practices:
	1) Visualization of the workflow.
	2) Limiting WIP.
	3) Active management of work items in progress
	4) Inspecting and adapting their definition of "Workflow"
	    d. Make Process Explicit.
	    e. Implement Feedback Loops.
	Improve Collaboratively, Evolve Experimentally (using models and the scientific method)

Question 76 Throughput is: A. The number of work items "finished". B. The number of work items "finished" per unit of time. C. The number of work items "started". D. The number of work items "started" and "finished".	Correct answer: B Throughput can be defined as the number of work items "finished" per unit of time.
Question 77 Work in Progress (WIP) is: A. Equal to the number of PBI's in the Sprint Backlog. B. The number of work items started but not finished. C. The total of all items in the Product Backlog. D. The number of PBI's being worked on actively by the Developers.	Correct answer: B Work in Progress (WIP) is **the number of work items started but not finished (according to the Scrum Team's definition of "Workflow").**

Question 78 A Service Level Expectation (SLE) is: A. Forecasts how long it should take a given item to flow from start to finish within your workflow. B. Defines agreed timings around fixing support issues. C. Defines a customer's expectation of the level of service to be supplied. D. Sets expectations around how the system will be supported.	**Correct answer: A** A Service Level Agreement forecasts **how long it should take** a given item to flow from start to finish within a workflow. The Service Level Expectation is just an expectation set by the team to themselves answering the question "What Cycle Time do we expect to see for an item of this type, and what is our confidence level for this?".
Question 79 **The definition of "Workflow" includes (Select 4 answers)** A. The active states for the work items. B. A shared understanding within the Scrum Team of how work is defined (work items) C. A definition of what customer value should be. D. The start state of the process E. The finished state of the process	**Correct answer: A, B, D, E** A Kanban "Workflow" definition must include: 1. A **shared understanding** within the Scrum Team of how work is defined (work items). 2. Definition of the **start state** of the process. 3. Definition of the **active states** for the work items. 4. Definition of the **finished state** of the process. 5. A definition of how Work in Progress (WIP) will be limited.
Question 80 WIP Limits are primarily applied to tasks in the Sprint Backlog? A. True B. False	**Correct answer: B** WIP Limits can be applied to every task in the Sprint Backlog that is not the primary concern of WIP Limits. Primarily WIP Limits are applied to entities that create value thus our Product Backlog items.
Question 81 A Kanban Flow is : (Choose the best answer) A. an undesirable effect of too much work being present in the system B. the movement of work between workflow stages C. a software development technique D. the movement of customer value throughout the product development system	**Correct answer: D** Kanban Work Flow is the movement of **Customer Value** through the product development system.

Question 82	**Correct answer: A**
Cycle time **is considered a Lagging indicator (not a leading indicator)** for the length of the Scrum Team's feedback loop for a product backlog item? A. True. B. False.	Cycle time **is a Lagging indicator (not a leading indicator)** for the length of the Scrum Team's feedback loop for a product backlog item. I.e. one would only **know the cycle time after the Product Backlog item has reached the end of the team's definition of Workflow.**
Question 83 If the team decreases their WIP Limit what is likely to happen to the teams cycle time? A. Cycle time is likely to decrease. B. Cycle time is like to increase.	**Correct answer: A** Little's Law principle applies here: Average cycle time = Average work in progress / average throughput
Question 84 Who (in a Kanban system) is held accountable for contributing to great flow and high-quality delivery? A. Process Manager. B. Product Owner. C. Each person/team working. D. Scrum Master.	**Correct answer: C** Each person/team working is held accountable for contributing to great flow and high-quality value delivery not just in their area of the Kanban but from a whole value stream perspective.
Question 85 Kanban doesn't prescribe restructuring to cross-functional teams spanning the value stream. A. True. B. False.	**Correct answer: A** Kanban doesn't prescribe restructuring to cross-functional teams spanning the value stream.

Question 86	**Correct answer: B**
In Scrum with Kanban we do not track progress towards the Sprint goal. The Daily Scrum is changed into tracking work items. A. True. B. False.	Remember Kanban does not replace anything in Scrum. However, the Daily Scrum has additional questions to consider regarding flow. The progress towards the Sprint Goal should be inspected and adapter as in the Scrum guide.
Question 87	Correct answer: A
Sprint Planning is a form of limiting WIP. A. True B. False	Sprint Planning identifies a reasonable amount of work thus avoiding spreading team too thinly. In other words, it is a form of limiting WIP. Good Kanban teams limit WIP already albeit in a different way.
Question 88	Correct answer: B
During Daily Sprints, the Scrum Guide suggests that the Developers explain what they did yesterday, what they are focusing on today, and what their impediments are. Kanban teams typically focuses: A. On the Work policies only. B. On the flow of work instead of the people doing the work. C. On the People doing the work. D. On the Project plan.	The Scrum Guide suggests that the Developers explain what they did yesterday, what they are focusing on today, and what their impediments are. Kanban teams typically focuses on the flow of work instead of the people doing the work. They work the board right to left focusing on flow problems.
Question 89	Correct answer: A, B
Kanban teams decide how to refine the backlog. They may do this (Choose all that apply): A. Just in time when the inventory of ready stories goes below a threshold. B. They can use a cadence. C. End of the release. D. When the Scrum Masters wants to do so.	Kanban teams decide how to refine the backlog. They may do this just in time when the inventory of ready stories goes below a threshold, or they can use a cadence.

Question 90	Correct answer: B
SLE CAN be used in **Sprint Planning** to provide Product Owner and stakeholders **with "an idea" towards** the service level that can be expected from the team. That includes providing a specific date for each Product Backlog Item in the Sprint backlog. A. True. B. False.	SLE CAN be used in **Sprint Planning** to provide PO and stakeholders **with "an idea" towards** the service level that can be expected from the team. That **doesn't include providing a specific date f**or each PBI in the SBL. The SLE enables the Scrum Team to forecast a finished date at a certain confidence level once the item has been started.
Question 91	Correct answer: A
Kanban system **can extend beyond the Sprint boundaries** to include activities across the entire value stream such as discovery activities, refinement of PBIs, and production support. A. True B. False	Kanban system **can extend beyond the Sprint boundaries** to include activities across the entire value stream such as discovery activities, refinement of PBIs, and production support.
Question 92	Correct answer: A
Kanban board should be seen as the **single source of truth for the team's work.** A. True B. False	The Kanban methodology relies upon full transparency of work and real-time communication of capacity, therefore the Kanban board should be seen as the **single source of truth for the team's work.**
Question 93	Correct answer: B
Once the WIP limit is reached in one stage, members of the scrum team should: A. Start on a new PBI. B. Help others deal with the current PBIs already in progress. C. Help others deal with the current PBIs already in progress, only in their own area of expertise. D. Wait for WIP to go down.	Once the limit is reached in one stage, instead of starting a new PBI, members of the Scrum team help others deal with the current PBIs already in progress. This can mean helping others in your area of expertise or helping others in their areas of expertise (e.g. coders help testers, testers help business analysts, etc.)

Question 94	Correct answer: A
Expediting is: A. Going beyond the current WIP limits and pushing this item along on top of the existing flow. B. Going beyond the current WIP limits and pushing this item along on bottom of the existing flow. C. Changing the WIP limit definition to include an important work item D. All of the above.	Expediting is going beyond the current WIP limits and pushing this item along on top of the existing flow. The typical way to do this is **NOT to change the WIP limit** definition but to go above WIP and note a WIP exception. These exceptions can then be a topic for inspection and adaptation come time to retrospect.
Question 95	Correct answer: A
Sprint 1 consist of 100 completed stories. Each story is 50 points. Sprint 2 consist of 100 completed stories. Each story however in sprint 2, is only 2 points. The throughput for both the Sprints is 100 / sprint. A. True B. False	The measurement of throughput is the exact count of work items, **without any compensation for item size.**
Question 96	Correct answer: G
A Kanban "Workflow" definition must include: A. A shared understanding within the Scrum Team of how work is defined (work items). B. The start state of the process. C. The active states for the work items. D. The finished state of the process. E. A definition of how Work in Progress (WIP) will be limited. F. A set Service Level Expectation (SLE) that communicates a forecast of how long it should take to complete work items. G. All of the Above.	A Kanban "Workflow" definition must include: 1. A shared understanding within the Scrum Team of how work is defined (work items). 2. The start state of the process. 3. The active states for the work items. 4. The finished state of the process. 5. A definition of how Work in Progress (WIP) will be limited. A set Service Level Expectation (SLE) that communicates a forecast of how long it should take to complete work items.

Question 97	**Correct answer: A, D**
The Service Level Agreement forecast consist of: (Choose all that apply) A. A period of elapsed days in which the work would be completed. B. The developer / developers (who are assigned) agreement to get the work items completed. C. The Deadline for a given work item. D. A probability of work getting completed associated within a period.	The Service Level Agreement itself has two parts: 1. A period of elapsed days in which the work would be completed. 2. A probability of work getting completed associated with that period.
Question 98 Cycle Time can be calculated only after the work item has reached a Done lane on the Kanban board. A. True. B. False.	**Correct answer: A** Cycle Time can be calculated only after the work item is actually finished (e.g. reached a Done lane on the Kanban board).
Question 99 A newly formed Scrum Team is using Kanban from **a holistic perspective**, starting from the Product Backlog, refinement and Sprint Backlog. Who owns the workflow and specifically the WIP limits? A. The Scrum Team B. The Product Owner C. The Scrum Master D. Developers	**Correct answer: A** If the team is using Kanban from **a holistic perspective**, starting from the Product Backlog, refinement and Sprint Backlog, **the Scrum Team** that would own the workflow and therefore the WIP limits.
Question 100 Which Metrix shows how **long ago has each item has been pulled into WIP,** on the Kanban Board. A. Work Item Age. B. Cycle time. C. WIP. D. Throughput.	**Correct answer: A** Work Item age shows how **long ago has each item has been pulled into WIP,** on the Kanban Board.

Question 101	Correct Answer: A
Below is a sample agile board with WIP limits used by a typical Scrum Team. In this board above, "Ready for dev" signifies that the story has been fully vetted by the product owner and team. The scrum team pulls work from "ready for dev" into "in progress" as they start on work items.	WIP limits improve throughput and reduce the amount of work "nearly done", by forcing the team to focus on a smaller set of tasks. At a fundamental level, WIP limits encourage a culture of "done." More important, WIP limits make blockers and bottlenecks visible.

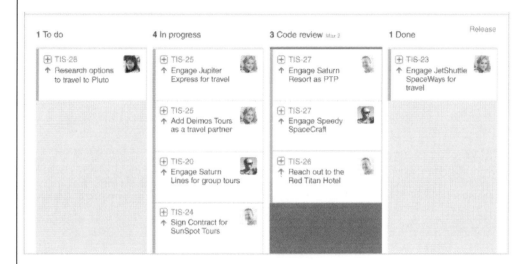

In the board above, the WP limit for "in progress" items is 7, and there are currently 4 items in that state. This tells the team that:

a) They've got capacity to take on more work and can move items in the In-Progress State.
b) They've got capacity to take on less work and should move items in the In-Progress State.

Question 102	Correct Answer: B
A team completes 95 out of 100 tasks within 10 days. This means that the forecast of a given work item has 95% chance to complete in 10 days. What metric of flow is used here? A. Work Item Age. B. Cycle time. C. WIP. D. Throughput. E. Work item age.	Remember SLE is not a Metric of Flow. Cycle Time is a lagging indicator for how long it takes for a Work Item from start to finish. If the question asked what does the Probability and Days in the question indicate, the correct answer would be SLE (assuming SLE was one of the given options).
Question 103 What does Scrum with Kanban add to increase team collaboration? (Choose Two) A. Velocity. B. Kanban Scrum Master. C. WIP. D. WIP Limit. E. WIP Push System. F. WIP Pull System.	**Correct Answer: D, F** WIP Limits improve collaboration because they force to help other team members when limits are reached. Pull system improves collaboration because it allows the team too 'pull' work whenever they have the capacity to do so.
Question 104 - A A Team implementing Scrum notices that it's been facing longer Cycle times. The Scrum Master and other Members are concerned. What should the Scrum Team do if cycle times are too long? A. The Scrum Team should increase the number of Work in Progress items. B. The Scrum Team should lower the number of Work in Progress items. C. The Scrum Team should increase the number of Scrum Team members and thus the velocity. D. The Scrum Team should increase the throughput by increasing more Team Members.	**Correct Answer: B** According to Little's Law WIP and cycle time are connected. Lowering WIP might lead to faster cycle times.

Question 104 - B
 	
A Scrum Team Member has got 10 tasks that were completed on average in 12 days.
 	
Which metric of flow is being described here?
 	
    A.   Work Item Age.
    B.   Cycle time.
    C.   WIP.
    D.   Throughput.
    E.   Work item age.
    F.   Service Level Expectation.
	Correct Answer: B
	
	Cycle Time according to the Scrum with Kanban guide:
	"The amount of elapsed time between when a work item starts and when a work item finishes"
	
	Why not SLE?
	
	To begin with SLE is not a Metric of flow. SLE is based on Cycle Time so it might look like we describe SLE here. The fundamental difference is that an SLE has a probability and an expectation.
	
	We could rewrite the sentence to become an SLE:
	We are 70% confident to complete these 10 tasks in 12 days.

Question 105
 	
Which roles become obsolete when using Scrum with Kanban?
 	
    A.   Scrum Master as the entire Scrum Team is now responsible for the Scrum Flow.
    B.   Product Owner.
    C.   D
    D.   All of the above.
    E.   None of the above.
	Correct Answer: E
	
	Kanban recognizes that existing processes, roles, responsibilities, and titles have value and are, generally, worth preserving. No **roles or Events** of Scrum are adjusted/removed/added when using Scrum with Kanban.

Question 106	Correct Answer: B
Which of the following statement is True? A. Kanban is a framework which optimizes the flow of stakeholder value through a process that uses a visual, work-in-progress limited, pull system. B. Kanban is a strategy which optimizes the flow of stakeholder value through a process that uses a visual, work-in-progress limited, pull system. C. Kanban is a process which optimizes the flow of stakeholder value through a process that uses a visual, work-in-progress limited, pull system. D. Kanban is a strategy which optimizes the flow of stakeholder value through a process that uses a visual, work-in-progress limited, push system.	Kanban is a strategy which optimizes the flow of stakeholder value through a process that uses a visual, work-in-progress limited, pull system.
Question 107 In Kanban, which of the following are considered as Explicit Policies? A. The Scrum Guide. B. Definition of Done. C. Scrum Framework. D. WIP Limit. E. All of the above.	**Correct Answer: E** Following are example of Explicit Policies. 1) **The Scrum Guide** is an explicit policy that a Scrum Team implements 2) **Scrum's definition of "Done"** is an excellent example of an explicit policy. 3) **The Scrum framework itself is an example of an explicit policy.** 4) Kanban teams add explicit policies such as the **WIP limit** for each lane or each person, escalation/ class of service policies, how to visualize and deal with blockers, how to prioritize work. 5) **Workflow** can be thought of as the "Team's policy" for how to get work to "Done". 6) Scrum Team definition of when items go from not started to start and from in-progress to finished.

Question 108	Correct Answer: B, C, D
Which metrics of flow can be used in the **Sprint Retrospective**? (Select three) A. Work Item Age. B. Cycle time. C. WIP. D. Throughput. E. Work item age. F. Service Level Expectation.	Sprint Retrospective is all about inspecting and adapting the process and the workflow. Therefore, it is the place to look at WIP, Cycle Times, Throughput from a perspective of looking for areas to improve. Remember, the basic metrics of flow that Scrum Teams using Kanban will need to track are as follows: A. Work in Progress (WIP): The number of work items started but not finished (according to the Scrum Team's definition of "Workflow").B. Cycle Time: The amount of elapsed time between when a work item "starts" and when a work item "finishes." C. Work Item Age: The amount of elapsed time between when a work item "started" and the current time. D. Throughput: The number of work items "finished" per unit of time. Note the measurement of throughput is the exact count of work items. SLE is used in Sprint retrospective but it's not really a basic metric of flow. Hope this helps. Refer to the **Flow Metrics in Scrum Event Chart Summary** and **Metrics Summary Table**, if you get confused on such exam questions.

Question 109	Correct Answer: C, D
At which Scrum Event can the Cycle Time Scatterplot be used? (Select 2) A. Daily Sprint. B. Sprint Planning. C. Sprint Retrospective. D. Sprint Review.	Cycle Time Scatterplot where teams can understand their Cycle Time trends, distributions, look at anomalies. They are thus used in Sprint Retrospective and Sprint Review. Refer to the **Flow Metrics in Scrum Event Chart Summary** and **Metrics Summary Table**, if you get confused on such exam questions.
Question 110	**Correct Answer: A,B**
At which Scrum Events can the Work Item Age Chart be used? (Select 2) A. Daily Sprint. B. Sprint Planning. C. Sprint Retrospective. D. Sprint Review.	One of the things to consider during a flow-based Daily Scrum is the Work Item Age of each item in progress. Comparing the WIP Age with the SLE would let the team focus on the items which are close to or already have violated the SLE. WIP especially useful during the Daily Scrum to help age surface flow issues regarding specific PBIs. During Sprint Planning, the Work Item Age might be relevant when some items are left over from the previous Sprint and the team want to decide what to do about them. Refer to the **Flow Metrics in Scrum Event Chart Summary** and **Metrics Summary Table**, if you get confused on such exam questions.

Question 111	**Correct Answer: A,C**
At which Scrum Event can the Cumulative Flow Diagram be used? A. Daily Sprint. B. Sprint Planning. C. Sprint Retrospective. D. Sprint Review.	Cumulative Flow Diagram: Cumulative Flow Diagram (CFD) shows the amount of work arriving, at various stages of in progress, and done. CFD used in Daily Sprint and Sprint Retrospective helps with: • Knowledge of the Number of WIP Items • Average Cycle Time. • Throughput. • Bottlenecks. Refer to the **Flow Metrics in Scrum Event Chart Summary** and **Metrics Summary Table**, if you get confused on such exam questions.
Question 112 Sprint backlog is a form of limiting WIP. A. True B. False	**Correct answer: A** Sprint Backlog it is a form of limiting WIP. Good Kanban teams limit WIP already albeit in a different way.
Question 113 What does one see in a typical Cumulative Flow Diagram? (Choose all that Apply). A. Total Number of work Items. B. Stage of Workflow. C. Cycle Time. (and Not Average Cycle Time). D. WIP items.	**Correct answer: A, B and D** Cumulative Flow Diagram: Cumulative Flow Diagram (CFD) shows the amount of work arriving, at various stages of in progress, and done. In a CFD one can see: • X- AXIS: Time Scale • Y-AXIS: Cumulative Number of Work items • Areas with different Colors: Stages The vertical height of each band is the Number of items (WIP) in that stage. The horizontal height of a CFD Helps with exposing the Average cycle time.

Question 114	Correct answer: A, D
How is Little's Law represented? (Select 2)	Average Cycle Time = Average Work in Progress / Average Throughput.
A. Average Cycle Time = Average Work in Progress / Average Throughput	WIP = Throughput * Lead Time
B. Average Cycle Throughput = Average Work in Progress / Average days.	Where
C. Cycle Time = Average Work in Progress / Average Throughput.	• WIP = Average Number of items in process
D. WIP = Throughput * Lead Time.	• Throughput = Average Arrival / Departure rate
	• Cycle Time / Lead Time = Average time an item spends in the system

Question 115	Correct answer: A
Let's assume a team is mid-Sprint and there's an important valuable item the Product Owner wants to add to the Sprint Backlog. It is aligned with the Sprint Goal. The team is currently at their WIP Limit. Could they add this item?	Let's assume a team is mid-Sprint and there's an important valuable item the Product Owner wants to add to the Sprint Backlog. It is aligned with the Sprint Goal. The team is currently at their WIP Limit. Could they add this item?
A. Yes	Step 1) First a decision needs to be made whether to pull this item into the Sprint Backlog. It is up to the team to agree to pull a new item into the Sprint Backlog. The Sprint Goal can be used to assess how aligned this item is with the current focus. If the item is really important, the work item could be pulled in the Sprint Backlog.
B. No	Step 2) In case the item is pulled into the Sprint Backlog, then the Dev Team needs to figure out whether they can actually start it right away. This depends on the WIP limits and the current WIP. If the team is at their WIP limit they shouldn't pull in that new item until some room frees up. If their backlog items are pretty small, an empty WIP slot will free up pretty quickly.
	Step 3) Expedite this Work Item which needs to be pulled. Expediting is going beyond the current WIP limits and pushing this item along on top of the existing flow. The typical way to

	do this is NOT to change the WIP limit definition but to go above WIP and note a WIP exception. These exceptions can then be a topic for inspection and adaptation come time to retrospect.
Question 116 Can cycle time for "a" Product Backlog item be longer than the Sprint length? A. Yes B. No	**Correct answer: A** Cycle Time: The amount of elapsed time between when a work item "starts" and when a work item "finishes." Cycle Time can be calculated only after the work item is actually finished (e.g. reached a Done lane on the Kanban board). Cycle time is a Lagging indicator (not a leading indicator) for the length of the Scrum Team's feedback loop for a product backlog item. I.e. one would only know the cycle time after the Product Backlog item has reached the end of the team's definition of Workflow. Sprint Length is a WIP Limit and yes Product backlog items (at times) may take longer than a Sprint. This could absolutely happen. Thus, the cycle time (and not average cycle time) for a Product Backlog item can be longer than the Sprint Length. The average cycle time should be quite a bit shorter than the sprint length. If you have a few items that go above the sprint length, its fine, the average cycle time will stay below the Sprint Length. However, the average cycle time should not exceed the sprint length. If it does means most of your Product backlog items are not getting completed in a single Sprint.

Question 117	Correct answer: A
The flow-based perspective of Kanban can enhance the Scrum framework and its implementation. A. True B. False	The flow-based perspective of Kanban can enhance and complement the Scrum framework and its implementation. Teams can add complementary Kanban practices whether they are just starting to use Scrum or have been using it all along.
Question 118 Which of the following are true statements? (Choose all that Apply) A. Kanban is a strategy which optimizes the flow of value through a process that uses a visual, work-in-progress limited, pull system. B. Kanban is a visual system for managing work as it moves through a process. C. Kanban visualizes both the process (the workflow) and the actual work passing through that process. D. Kanban is a method that uses a work-in-process limited pull system as the core mechanism to expose operation (or process) problems and to stimulate collaborative improvement efforts. E. The flow-based perspective of Kanban can enhance and complement the Scrum framework and its implementation. F. When Kanban practices are applied to Scrum they provide a focus on improving the flow through the feedback loop and help optimizing transparency and the frequency of inspection and adaptation for both the product and the process.	**Correct answer: A,B,C,D,E,F** Kanban is a strategy which optimizes the flow of value through a process that uses a visual, work-in-progress limited, pull system. Kanban is a visual system for managing work as it moves through a process. Kanban visualizes both the process (the workflow) and the actual work passing through that process. Kanban is a method that uses a work-in-process limited pull system as the core mechanism to expose operation (or process) problems and to stimulate collaborative improvement efforts. The flow-based perspective of Kanban can enhance and complement the Scrum framework and its implementation. Teams can add complementary Kanban practices whether they are just starting to use Scrum or have been using it all along. When Kanban practices are applied to Scrum, they provide a focus on improving the flow through the feedback loop and help optimizing transparency and the frequency of inspection and adaptation for both the product and the process.

Question 119
 	
What enables the four Kanban practices for teams practicing Scrum? (Choose the best answer).
 	
  A. Presence of Scrum Master in the Kanban Meetings.
  B. Kanban Board.
  C. Kanban tools.
  D. Scrum Team's definition of workflow.
	Correct answer: D
	
	The four Kanban practices are enabled by the Scrum Team's Definition of Workflow. This definition represents the Scrum Team members' explicit understanding of what their policies are for following the Kanban practices. This shared understanding improves transparency and enables self-management. Note that the scope of the Definition of Workflow may span beyond the Sprint and the Sprint Backlog. For instance, a Scrum Team's Definition of Workflow may encompass flow inside and/or outside of the Sprint.

Question 120
 	
Teams cannot add complementary Kanban practices when they have already started using Scrum or have been using it all along.
 	
  A. True
  B. False
	Correct answer: B
	
	The flow-based perspective of Kanban can enhance and complement the Scrum framework and its implementation. Teams can add complementary Kanban practices whether they are just starting to use Scrum or have been using it all along.

Question 121
 	
The scope of the Definition of Workflow may not span beyond the Sprint.
 	
  A. True
  B. False
	Correct answer: B
	
	The scope of the Definition of Workflow may span beyond the Sprint. For instance, a Scrum Team's Definition of Workflow may encompass flow inside and/or outside of the Sprint, having items beyond what the Sprint backlog captures. Scrum Team's definition of "Workflow" may include states that are upstream, downstream, inside, or outside of the Sprint Backlog.

Question 122	Correct answer: B

Experts outside the Scrum Team can build the Definition of workflow for the Scrum Team, if the Scrum Team agrees.
 	
   A. True
   B. False
	Remember:
	1) If the team is using Kanban to improve the Sprint flow by visualizing and managing flow in the Sprint Backlog, Developers in the Scrum Team would own the workflow and specifically the WIP limits.
	2) If the team is using Kanban from a holistic perspective, starting from the Product Backlog, refinement and Sprint Backlog, the Scrum Team that would own the workflow and therefore the WIP limits.
	3) If the Dev Team actually wants to involve the Product Owner in their Sprint flow (to review and accept a story during the Sprint before it goes through testing), the Scrum Team that would own the workflow and therefore the WIP limits.
	No one outside of the Scrum Team should tell the Scrum Team how to define their Workflow.

Question 122	**Correct answer: A, B,C,D**

During one of the team retrospectives, the scrum team is trying to inspect and adopt the of the Definition of Workflow. The team is likely to: (Choose all that apply)
   A. Inspect and adopt the Visualization policies for example, Workflow states. i.e. changing the actual Workflow or bringing more transparency to an area in which the team wants to inspect and adapt.
   B. Inspect and adopt the WIP limits.
   C. Inspect and adopt the SLEs.
   D. Change the batch size (how often items are pulled between states).
	The following are aspects of the Definition of Workflow the Scrum Team might adopt:
	• Visualization policies - for example, Workflow states - either changing the actual Workflow or bringing more transparency to an area in which the team wants to inspect and adapt.
	• How-we-work policies - these can directly address an impediment. For example, adjusting WIP limits and SLEs or changing the batch size (how often items are pulled between states) can have a dramatic impact.

Question 123	**Correct answer: B**
The Kanban complementary practices invalidate the need for Scrum's Sprint. . A. True B. False	The Kanban complementary practices don't invalidate the need for Scrum's Sprint. The Sprint and its events provide opportunities for inspection and adaptation of both product and process.
Question 124	**Correct answer: B**
Scrum teams can only deliver value to customers only once per Sprint. A. True B. False	It's a common misconception that teams can only deliver value once per Sprint. In fact, they must deliver value at least once per Sprint. Teams using Scrum with Kanban use the Sprint and its events as a feedback improvement loop by collaboratively inspecting and adapting their Definition of Workflow and flow metrics.
Question 125	**Correct answer: A**
A change to the Scrum Team's Definition of Workflow can be done: A. At any time. B. Only during Sprint retrospective. C. When the WIP Limit is crossed. D. Scrum Team's Definition of Workflow cannot change.	Changes to a Scrum Team's Definition of Workflow may happen at any time. Because these changes will have a material impact on how the Scrum Team performs, changes made during the regular cadence provided by the Sprint Retrospective event will reduce complexity and improve focus, commitment and transparency.
Question 126	**Correct answer: A**
The straight-line horizontal distance between the top line and the bottom line on a Cumulative Flow Diagram is known as: A. Average Cycle Time B. Exact Average Lead Time C. Exact Average Cycle Time D. Exact Lead Time E. Exact Cycle Time F. Total Work in Progress	CFD Helps with: Visualizing the amount of Work in Progress (WIP) at each interval. The vertical height of each band is the Number of items (WIP) in that stage. The horizontal height of each band exposes the Average cycle time.

Question 127	Correct answer: B
A Service Level Expectation is: A. A commitment B. A forecast C. An estimate D. All of the above	An SLE forecasts how long it should take a given item to flow from start to finish within your workflow. The Service Level Agreement itself has two parts: 1) A period of elapsed days in which the work would be completed. 2) The probability of work getting completed associated with that period.
Question 128	**Correct answer: E**
A Scrum Team is newly formed and has started using Kanban. They have designed a Scrum Board and all the column on the Kanban board has a Work In Progress limits defined. One of the Columns named **In-Progress** has 3 blocked items in that column and a WIP Limit of 5. Should these Blocked items count against the columns WIP limit of 5 ? A. They should count only if the Workflow contains a blocked column and the blocked items are in the blocked column. B. Never. Blocked items are usually the result of an external dependency and therefore should not count against an internal WIP limit. C. Only if there is no new work to start. Blocked items should never impair the ability to start new work. D. Always. Having a blocked item is never a good enough reason to exceed a Work In Progress limit. E. It depends on how policies are defined in the Kanban System's Definition of Workflow.	The correct action depends completely on what policies have been set in the Definition of the Workflow on how to handle blockers.

Question 129	Correct answer: F
The straight-line vertical distance between the top line and the bottom line on a Cumulative Flow Diagram is known as: A. Average Cycle Time B. Exact Average Lead Time C. Exact Average Cycle Time D. Exact Lead Time E. Exact Cycle Time F. Total Work in Progress	CFD Helps with: Visualizing the amount of Work in Progress (WIP) at each interval. The vertical height of each band is the Number of items (WIP) in that stage. The horizontal height of each band is the exposes the Average cycle time.
Question 130 In Kanban, work items can be split: A. During backlog refinement only. B. Only if the customer agrees to the split. C. Only before items are considered started. D. Any time before items are considered finished.	**Correct answer: D** Items can and should be split any time before they are considered finished from a Definition of Workflow perspective.

Question 131	Correct answer: E
On a Kanban Board, WIP Limits can be set : A. On every column B. On every swim lane C. Per Person D. For the whole Kanban board E. All of the above.	There are no rules as to how WIP Limits must be set on a Kanban Board. It is valid (though potentially not recommended depending on context) to have some columns on a Kanban board that are not WIP limited (e.g., upstream and downstream columns that are outside of a team's control). The point is that all Kanban requires is some notion of how WIP is controlled in the system between started and finished--that does not necessarily mean WIP is controlled on the whole board. In Kanban there is no prescribed way to limit WIP. Any scheme that controls how many things are in progress at a time is allowed. The only important thing is that WIP is explicitly controlled. WIP Limit can be set: 1) Per person. 2) Per the entire team throughout their workflow. 3) By time i.e. 10 Items Per Week. 4) Per Stage or for Multiple Stages. 5) Across the Board / Across All Stages.
Question 132	Correct answer: A
A New team has just started working using Kanban practices. The team's see's that the Work In Progress (WIP) items are 14 and the Cycle Time is 7, and your Throughput is 1. To reduce the Cycle Time to 2, the team should: A. Cannot be answered from the supplied information B. Reduce WIP to 2 C. Reduce WIP to 7 D. Increase Throughput to 7	Based on this information alone, it would be impossible to know what intervention would reduce Cycle Time to 2. If you were looking to apply Little's Law, remember that first Little's Law is a relationship of averages and average is not mentioned here. Second, Little's Law cannot be used to forecast how a change in one metric will deterministically affect another metric.

Question 133	**Correct answer: C,D**
Are the Scrum Events mandatory for Teams using Kanban practices? (Choose two)	Kanban is, at its heart, a just-in-time and continuous flow approach to work. Instead of having a Sprint cadence that starts with a Sprint Planning, has a Daily Scrum every day, and ends with a Sprint Review and Sprint Retrospective, Kanban can considered a process where you plan when you need to, meet when you need to, collaborate with key stakeholders when you need to, and inspect and improve your way of working when you need to. In Kanban, similar events happen as in Scrum, but at different regularities or schedules that may or may not be consistent over time. **So if it's Kanban by itself, Scrum Events and Candance are not mandatory.**
A. Yes. The Kanban complementary practices don't invalidate the need for Scrum's Sprint. The Sprint and its events provide opportunities for inspection and adaptation of both product and process.	
B. Yes. The flow-based perspective of Kanban can enhance and complement the Scrum framework and its implementation.	
C. No. If it's Kanban is used by itself (without Scrum), Scrum Events and Candance are not mandatory.	
D. Yes. Only when Kanban is layered on top of Scrum (or used with Scrum), Scrum Events become mandatory.	**When Kanban is layered on top of Scrum (or used with Scrum), the Scrum Events become mandatory.**
Question 134	**Correct answer: A,B**
Are the Scrum Roles / Accountabilities mandatory for Teams using Kanban practices? (Choose all that apply)	There are many processes and methods that don't have the Scrum Roles and Scrum Events. Kanban is, at its heart, a just-in-time and continuous flow approach to work. Instead of having a Sprint cadence that starts with a Sprint Planning, has a Daily Scrum every day, and ends with a Sprint Review and Sprint Retrospective, Kanban can be considered a process where you plan when you need to, meet when you need to, collaborate with key stakeholders when you need to, and inspect and improve your way of working when you need to. In Kanban, similar events happen as in Scrum, but at different regularities or schedules that may or may not be consistent over time. **So if it's Kanban by itself, Scrum Events, Roles and Candance are not mandatory.**
A. No. If it's Kanban is used by itself (without Scrum), Scrum roles are not mandatory.	
B. Yes. Only when Kanban is layered on top of Scrum (or used with Scrum), Scrum roles become mandatory.	
C. Scrum Roles / Accountabilities are always mandatory.	
D. Depends upon the Scrum Master,	**When Kanban is layered on top of Scrum (or used with Scrum), the Scrum Events and roles become mandatory.**

CHAPTER 5: Leadership Basics

PAL-I tests the experience of executives and leaders that use agile to bring more value to its businesses. This chapter is designed to help you take a learn / revise / take a second look at a broader set of Leadership concepts.

1. Go through the Leadership Learning Path on Scrum.org.
2. Go through the PAL Reference Table.

PAL Reference Table

Manifesto for Agile Software Development	The Agile Manifesto guides teams within an organization to consider projects from a value-based perspective. Team will need processes, tools, documentation, and plans for a project. Yet while dealing with these assets, teams should remember that focus must be on the people engaged, the product being building, cooperation, and flexibility. The Agile Manifesto acknowledges four important values: 1. **Individuals and interactions over processes and tools** This value reminds teams within an organization that while processes and tools will likely be necessary on the projects, we should try to focus the team's attention on the individuals and interactions involved. 2. **Working software over comprehensive documentation** This value reminds teams within an organization to focus on the purpose or business value which is being delivered rather than paperwork. 3. **Customer collaboration over contract negotiation** This value reminds teams within an organization to be flexible and accommodating rather than fixed and uncooperative. 4. **Responding to change over following a plan** This value reminds teams within an organization that one still need to plan, but also needs to acknowledge that initial plans are made when less was known about the project (at the beginning) and these plans will need to be updated as the work progresses.	
	Reference link: http://agilemanifesto.org/. Created by 17 visionaries in 2001, the Agile Manifesto was developed to look at the core principles and values for Agile software development.	
"Declaration of Interdependence" (DOI)	**"Declaration of Interdependence" (DOI)** are a set of six management principles intended for software development projects. The principles are: 1. We Increase return on investment by making **continuous flow of value** our focus. 2. We deliver reliable results by engaging customers in **frequent interactions and shared ownership.** 3. We **expect uncertainty** and manage for it through iterations, anticipation, and adaptation. 4. We unleash creativity and innovation by recognizing that **individuals are the ultimate source of value** and **creating an environment** where they can make a difference. 5. We boost performance through **group accountability** for results and shared responsibility for team effectiveness. 6. We improve effectiveness and reliability through situationally specific strategies, processes, and practices.	**Characteristics of Agile Mindset:** 1. Welcoming change 2. Working in small value-added increments 3. Using build and feedback loops 4. Learning through discovery 5. Value-driven development 6. Failing fast with learning 7. Continuous delivery 8. Continuous improvement
	Reference link: https://www.adventureswithagile.com/2014/08/19/declaration-of-interdependence/	Mike Griffin – PMI-ACP® Exam Prep Exam

Being Agile Vs Doing Agile	**Being Agile** is the correct way to adopt agile where teams 1) Start by internalizing the agile mindset (welcoming change, small increments, etc.), 2) Use the learned principles to guide selection and implementation of agile practices. Note: Teams start with a good understanding of why they are using the practices, which in turn helps them understand how to use them most effectively. 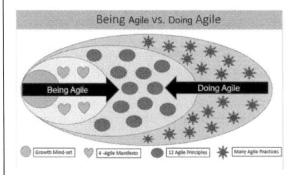 Doing Agile is **a way where teams decide to adopt agile practices (such as daily standup meetings and short iterations), without taking the time to understand what these practices are designed to accomplish.** Teams jump directly into the how of agile without first understanding the why. This is a common problem in agile adoption. Mike Griffin – PMI-ACP® Exam Prep, A Course in a Book® for Passing the PMI Agile Certified Practitioner (PMI-ACP)® Exam
Creating Organization Change	The Steps involved the process of creating Organization change are: 1) **Think**: Teams to need to focus on individually learning and internalizing agile principles. 2) **Do:** Doing is the practice of agile. Example: Visualizing work items, using short iterations, building in feedback and improvement steps. 3) **Encourage Others:** Persuading others to adopt the agile mindset and practices will magnify agile learning and effectiveness across the entire organization.
Agile Triangle	The Agile Triangle which is a reversal of the traditional triangle which means that agile teams allow **scope to vary** within the fixed parameters of cost and time. 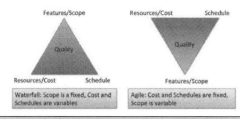 Reference : First edition of the DSDM Manual, published in 1994.

12 Agile Principles	The Agile Manifesto is based on 12 Agile Key Principles mentioned below: 1. The highest priority is to satisfy the customer through early and continuous delivery of valuable software. 2. Welcome changing requirements, even late in development. Agile processes harness change for the customer's competitive advantage. 3. Deliver working software frequently, from a couple of weeks to a couple of months, with a preference to the shorter timescale. 4. Business people and developers must work together daily throughout the project. 5. Build projects around motivated individuals. Give them the environment and support they need and trust them to get the job done. 6. The most efficient and effective method of conveying information to and within a Scrum team is face-to-face conversation. 7. Working software is the primary measure of progress. 8. Agile processes promote sustainable development. The sponsors, developers, and users should be able to maintain a constant pace indefinitely. 9. Continuous attention to technical excellence and good design enhances agility. 10. Simplicity--the art of maximizing the amount of work not done--is essential. 11. The best architectures, requirements, and designs emerge from self-organizing teams. 12. At regular intervals, the team reflects on how to become more effective, then tunes and adjusts its behavior accordingly. Reference: https://agilemanifesto.org/principles.html. The 12 Principles are based on the Agile Manifesto.
Definition of Agile and 7 Agile Principles -	Although the term "Agile" in the context of software development is quite well known, the definitions vary. The most common descriptions of Agile are: 1. Agile is a set of values and principles (Agile Manifesto) 2. Agile is a way of developing software that reminds us that although computers run the code, it's people who create and maintain it (The Agile Samurai). 3. Agile is the courage to be honest enough to admit that building software is complex, and it can't be perfectly planned since requirements change. The 7 principles of continuous Innovation described below come close to stating what Agile is all about. These principles are described in the book 'The Leader's Guide to Radical Management' by Steve Denning.

1. **Focus work on delighting the client**: It all begins by getting the goal right. The purpose of work is to delight clients, not merely to produce goods or services or make money for shareholders. The key to an enduring future is to have a customer who is willing to buy goods and services both today and tomorrow. It's not about a transaction: it's about forging a relationship.

2. **Self-Organizing Teams**: Do work through self-organizing teams. When team members work together with people who have different interpretations, perspectives, ways of solving problems, they are often able to solve problems that they wouldn't be able to solve alone. A complex problem, is best solved by a cognitively diverse group of people that is given responsibility for solving the problem, self-organizes, and works together to solve it.

3. **Client-Driven Iterations:** Through client-driven iterations companies are able to keep inventory and work in process as small as possible and customize their product not only to meet the customer's original perceived needs but also to adjust it to meet any changes in those needs. Client-driven iterations improve productivity for the organization by focusing work on the elements that really add value and eliminating work that doesn't add value. They also eliminate unproductive planning time and reduce risk by providing management not with unreliable progress reports, but with evidence of whether actual progress is made.

4. **Delivering Value to Clients in Each Iteration**: Client-driven iterations (and Radical Management) imply a mental revolution, a different way of thinking about work. The key to success is delivering value to clients at the end of each iteration.

5. **Radical Transparency**: Be totally open about impediments to improvement. Achieving the complex goal of client delight requires total openness about any impediments to the work: everyone levels with everyone else. Radical Management accepts the inevitability of failure and puts arrangements in place to learn rapidly from failure and so progress toward success.

6. **Continuous Self-Improvement**: Create a context for continuous self-improvement by the team. Continuous self-improvement is a deeply rooted set of values and attitudes focused on fixing problems as soon as they occur. Continuous self-improvement is fragile and therefore needs every day nurturing and attention. Continuous self-improvement is a top management responsibility.

7. **Interactive Communication**: Interactively share stories, questions, conversations. The modern organization cannot be an organization of 'boss' and 'subordinate': it must be organized as a team of associates. Traditional managers speak to employees as employees, and power is the currency of communication. The Radical Manager communicates as one human being. Hierarchy is present but in the background.

Reference: So What is Agile Really About? - Barry Overeem
https://www.scrum.org/resources/blog/so-what-agile-really-about

Waterfall Vs Scrum	Waterfall is a methodology for developing products that organizes work into large sequential steps. The process typically flows in one direction, which is forward – thus the term Waterfall. For example, the steps could be design, implementation, testing, deployment, and release.

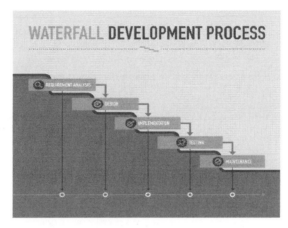

The sequential approach of Waterfall means taking big steps instead of a more iterative and incremental approach. Big steps are more likely to fail. For one reason, it requires you to predict outcomes sometimes months or years ahead of time. Surely, predicting the future is a challenge; bad predictions lead to bad products, and bad products lead to failed projects.

With deployment and release as the final steps of the Waterfall sequence, feedback from stakeholders is limited. You primarily get feedback at the beginning and end of a product development cycle. In between, there could be months, even years. You see the problem here: this lack of feedback over a sizable period leads to a disconnect from current customer requirements and causes you to deliver a product of low business value.

Scrum is a process framework for resolving complex problems iteratively and incrementally to a create a high-value solution that elates customers. Scrum directly addresses many of the shortcomings of Waterfall with project management. Scrum as opposed to Waterfall is:

- Empirical instead of predictive: Bases decisions on Experience and Experiment
- Iterative instead of sequential: Organizes work in smaller step.
- Concentrated on gathering continuous feedback instead of gathering in stages.
- Value-focused instead of deadline-focused.
- Self-organizing instead of control and command.

Calling All Industries: Your Process is Failing You - Donis Marshall
https://www.scrum.org/resources/blog/calling-all-industries-your-process-failing-you

Traditional Vs Agile Methodology	Characteristics	Agile approach	Traditional approach
	Organizational structure	Team based, combining different competencies, value delivery focus	Linear, Functional, Silo-based.
	Behavior	Collaboration and Team Work	Command and Control
	User requirements	Interactive input	Clearly defined before implementation
	Involvement of clients	High	Low
	Development model	Evolutionary delivery based on experiments and mistakes	Life cycle, Long Approval and need for Authorities approvals, Limited tolerance for mistakes
	Customer involvement	Customers are involved from the time work is being performed	Customers get involved early in the project but not once the execution has started
	Management Style	Servant Leaders focusing on providing service	Directive Managers
	Escalation management	When problems occur, the entire team works together to resolve it	Escalation to managers when problem arise
	Decisions	Empirical, Decision driven by data	Decisions driven by assumptions and forecast
	Reviews and approvals	Reviews are done after each iteration	Excessive reviews and approvals by leaders
	Model preference	Agile model favors adaption	Traditional model favors anticipation
	Product or process	Less focus on formal and directive processes	More serious about processes than the product
	Test documentation	Comprehensive test planning	Tests are planned one sprint at a time
	Effort estimation	Scrum master facilitates, and the team does the estimation	Project manager provides estimates and gets approval from PO for the entire project

Business Agility - Mehmet Yitmen
https://www.scrum.org/resources/blog/business-agility

Leadership Principles	Jeffrey Pinto, in Project Leadership (from Theory to Practice) offers the following great list of principles for leaders to follow:

- Learn the **team members 'needs**. Find out what motivates and demotivates people.
- Learn the project's requirements. Talk to the customers and sponsors; find out their priorities.
- Act for the simultaneous welfare of the team and the project. **Balance and promote** the needs and desires of both the team and the other project stakeholders.
- Create **an environment of functional accountability**. Make sure people know what success and failure look like and empower the team to self-organize to reach the goal. Be proud of accomplishments, but don't hide or shy away from failures—instead, examine them, learn from them, and adapt.
- Have a **vision** of the completed project. Create a "beckoning summit" to which others can chart their own course. When we are head-down in the weeds, it's good to know where we are trying to get to, so we can navigate our own course.
- Use the **project vision to drive your own behavior**. Model action toward the project goals.
- Serve as the central figure in successful project team development. Model desired behavior for the team.
- Recognize **team conflict** as a positive step. Unfiltered debate builds strong buy-in for well discussed topics.
- Manage with an eye toward **ethics**. Be honest and ethical, because people don't want to be associated with goals or missions they feel are unethical. Remember that ethics is not an afterthought, but an integral part of our thinking. You cannot add trust in later—like quality, it has to be a core ingredient.
- Take **time to reflect** on the project. Review, diagnose, and adapt; improve through progressive change and learning.
- Develop the trick of **thinking backwards**. This means imagining that we have reached the end goal and then working backwards to determine what had to happen to get there and what problems and risks we were able to avoid. So first discuss and decide what "done" will look like; then chart the path to get there, and plan how you will avoid any obstacles in your way.

Reference: Jeffrey Pinto, in Project Leadership (from Theory to Practice)

Leadership Tasks	Leadership Task's are as follows: • **Practice Transparency through Visualization** "Transparency" means being open and honest, not only about the progress and achievements, but also about team issues and setbacks. Agile teams demonstrate transparency by openly displaying their work, progress, and review findings for other stakeholders to see. • **Create a Safe Environment for Experimentation** When people believe that it's okay to try new approaches and they won't be criticized if they don't succeed the first time, they are more likely to have a go and try new things. Leadership should encourage trials and tests, not dwelling on experiments that have failed, and encouraging the generation of new ideas. • **Experiment with New Techniques and Processes** Short iterations offer the same short feedback cycles and provide ready-made test periods for new approaches. • **Share Knowledge through Collaboration** It's important for teams to share knowledge about the product they are working on and how things work within teams. Collaborative work—either through pairing workers or Adhoc knowledge transfer through co-location—has emerged as an agile best practice. • **Encourage Emergent Leadership via a Safe Environment** Emergent leadership is when a team member takes the initiative and tries a new approach after gaining team approval. Agile team members are not only empowered to make decisions but also to lead the charge on improvements.
	Mike Griffin – PMI-ACP® Exam Prep, A Course in a Book® for Passing the PMI Agile Certified Practitioner (PMI-ACP)® Exam
Agile Leaders Focus	Agile Leaders focus on three things: 1) They **create and nurture a culture** in which experimentation and learning are embraced 2) They **collaborate with employees** (at all levels in the organization) to find common values to create a greater goal for the company and the teams; 3) They **create an organizational structure** that reinforces and rewards the other two dimensions. 

Goals : Goals should be bold and audacious; both aspirational and inspirational. These motivational goals that leaders help teams to identify have some common characteristics:

1) They are motivating and inspiring, but they also are uncertain.
2) They force the team to stretch, to do things we have never done before.

Leaders help their employees to persist in the pursuit of their shared goals and values when times get rough and old behaviors want to take over.

Organization: There will always be things outside the scope of what agile teams do, even if they are only as mundane as payroll, accounting, tax compliance, legal, and investor relations. The role of management is to design, monitor, and correct this system to make sure that the organization achieves its goals. Even product development companies need to do more than simply developing the product. Where agile leadership comes into play in the management context is that they need to **make sure that the different parts of the organization, with different operating models, don't destroy each other.** Put more positively, agile leaders need to help the organization optimize for **flexibility and continuous improvement, making sure that improving customer outcomes always comes first,** and that the other parts of the organization support this mission.

Culture: The most important thing agile leaders do is to foster a culture that supports empiricism and learning, and that is constantly seeking better customer outcomes and better ways of achieving those outcomes. One can't control all factors, however, and an organization's culture emerges only partly as an expression of its leaders' aspirations; most of it comes from the people in the organization, how they treat each other and work together. But while leaders can't control and dictate this culture, they can encourage it and cause it to flourish by the examples they set and the behaviors that they model.

Agile leaders play an important, even essential, role in scaling agility in an organization. Larger the scope and scale of agility, the more agile teams need supportive leaders to:

1) Help them to frame the right goals
2) Make the organization work in support of agility and not against it,
3) Evolve the culture to embrace and reward learning, rather than merely tolerating it.

What organizations who are struggling to scale their agility are most often missing is strong, supportive agile leadership that helps them to build strong, cohesive agile teams.

Leadership Skills which help create mature Scrum Teams	Agile Leadership Tips for Creating Mature Scrum Teams:
	Focus on the people: As a leader one should have focus on helping the roles grow. Once people understand their role, they can take responsibility for the events & artifacts. Leaders should ask their Product Owners & Scrum Masters what they can do to help them grow in their role.
	Dare to let go: Scrum depends on the ability of teams to learn from mistakes and self-organize around difficult problems. A lot of the traditional leadership responsibilities (such as planning, quality and customer-communication) are needed at the level of the team. For a leader this means letting go of responsibilities and a possible re-definition of the traditional role. As a leader, one should be open to delegate responsibilities and create a plan on how to do so. Leaders should ask their Scrum Team what incentives could lead to a higher focus on customer value.
	Lead by example: The Scrum values are at the heart of Scrum: Commitment, Focus, Openness, Respect and Courage. Without these values, Scrum will not come to life. The reason why many teams might not show this behavior is because they are situated in an often-political environment where these values are missing. Leaders cannot expect a Scrum team to act according these values if they do not set the right example themselves. As a leader on4 need to create a safe environment where these values can flourish and where one ca continuously set the right example. To give the right example, leaders should play an active part in an Agile transformation (monitoring, guiding and regular evaluations)
	Growing in the same pace causes less tension: Leaders should create an environment where these roles can work together so they can mature in the same pace. As a leader, make sure that you support the entire Scrum team, so they are not limited by organizational limitations.
	References: 5 Agile Leadership Tips for Creating Mature Scrum Teams - Ron Eringa https://www.scrum.org/resources/blog/5-agile-leadership-tips-creating-mature-scrum-teams

Story Mapping	The story map is an excellent way to create a nice overview of all the features the Product Owner and his / her stakeholders can think of, which will be important to your product.

What is Story Mapping?

Story mapping is a method for arranging user stories to create a more holistic view of how they fit into the overall user experience and Roadmap. Arranged on a horizontal axis, the fundamental steps of the customer journey (sometimes labeled as epics, sometimes not) are arranged in chronological order based on when a user would perform the particular task relative to their overall workflow with the product.

Individual user stories are arranged beneath the larger steps they roll up under. When a story map is complete, one can see all of the ways a user might interact with a product in a single, logical view that progresses from the first interaction to the completion of the overall user objective.

Story mapping is usually done on a wall (or floor) using sticky notes or index cards and a whole lot of tape. Usually, the entire team takes part in identifying and agreeing on the primary steps of the user journey and then assigning user stories beneath them. Each story is discussed so there's no doubt about what a story actually is, its purpose and how it fits into the scheme of things.

Story map provides an overview of all the user activities that need to be covered by the system, which in turn enables one to create small and valuable user stories, which can be developed and delivered incrementally and iteratively.

Tips for Agile product roadmaps & product roadmap examples - Robbin Schuurman
https://www.scrum.org/resources/blog/tips-agile-product-roadmaps-product-roadmap-examples
https://www.productplan.com/glossary/story-mapping/
Jeff Patton is credited as the inventor of story mapping and he has literally written the book on it (User Story Mapping).

Feature Vs Component Teams	Feature team is a long-lived, cross-functional, cross-component team that completes many end-to-end customer features. A component team is a single component and cross-functional team that focuses on developing one or more components that can be used to develop only a part of an end-customer feature.

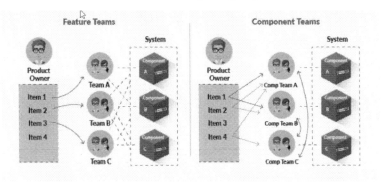

Feature Team	Component Team
A Modern way of organizing teams	A Traditional way of organizing teams
Responsible for the whole customer-centric feature	Responsible for only part of a customer-centric feature
Targets on multiple specializations	Targets on single specialization
Shared team responsibilities	Definite individual responsibilities
Focuses on system productivity	Focuses on increased individual productivity
Increases flexibility by reducing dependencies between teams	Dependencies between teams drive additional planning
Expert engineering practices are required	Works with poor engineering practices
Carries iterative development	Carries Waterfall development
Delivers maximum customer value	Delivers a maximum number of lines of code
Difficult to implement	Easy to implement

Evidence Based Management Reference Table

Evidence Based Management Definition	**What is Evidence-Based Management (EBM)?** Evidence-Based Management is a framework which organization can use to help them measure, manage, and increase the value they derive from their product delivery. EBM focuses on improving outcomes, reducing risks, and optimizing investments.
	Evidence-Based Management improves the quality of managerial decision-making through the integration of current best evidence with practical experience and human values. The gathering, appraisal and application of evidence permit to better forecast the likelihood of business success and of achieving company goals. It permits organizational optimizations through the ongoing discovery of better practices and the removal of dysfunctional practices.
	Evidence helps managers justify decisions about how to organize, structure, invest in and deliver services. Evidence increases the legitimacy of decisions in the organization and the value a manager represents for the organization.
	Evidence-Based Management requires managing knowledge, decision support systems, and artifacts to hold verifiable information. The possible sources of 'evidence' are diverse: • Internal: organizational data, metrics, internal research, reviews, surveys, measured, effectiveness of processes and procedures. Internal evidence requires an unbiased, scientific approach to gather it. • External: books, public research, studies, documented practices, experiments, benchmarks and industry comparison. External evidence needs appraisal to the organization's specific context and values. Evidence in the managerial domain primarily serves to support or to reject a managerial hypothesis, an assertion that certain organizational practices are beneficial to the organization, and that other practices hinder or limit the organization. The strength of evidence stretches between 2 extremities: • Direct evidence, or primary evidence, is the strongest type of evidence. It contains direct, clear and indisputable proof or contradiction of the truth or validity of an assertion. • Circumstantial evidence, or secondary, supportive evidence is much weaker. It might show consistency with an expected result but does not necessarily rule out other, possibly contradictory assertions. Circumstantial evidence might point to alternative explanations.

	Monitoring only the direct use of Agile practices **does not** provide the best evidence of their effectiveness. Example, tracking a Scrum Team's velocity says nothing about whether that team is actually delivering something that is useful to customers or users.

	Evidence-Based Management (EBM) is an empirical approach that
	   1) Provides organizations with the ability to measure the value they deliver to customers.
	   2) The means by which they deliver that value to the customers.
	   3) Use of measures to guide improvements on Business Outcomes.

	Evidence-Based Management (EBM) approach:
	   1) Measures value delivered as evidence of organizational agility.
	   2) Provides ways to measure and improve the ability to deliver value.

	Evidence-Based Management (EBM) approach enables organizations:
	   1) To make rational, fact-based decisions.
	   2) Elevates conversations from preferences and opinions to empirical evidence, logic, and insight.

Evidence Based Managers	Evidence-based managers of software organizations use evidence about the value the organization actually delivers, and its ability to deliver value and to innovate.
	Evidence-Based Management identifies the right internal evidence, at home, from the inside of the organization. Upon such evidence, informed management decisions are possible about the addition, revision and removal of organizational practices that will influence the organization's success, survival and prosperity.
	Evidence is captured at an organizational, departmental or product level. Evidence in software organizations is often and wrongly collected at individual team level.
	Empirical Management Explored - Gunther Verheyen

Key Value Areas	EBM looks at 4 Key Value Areas (KVAs). Defined measures will vary by organization, but all 4 areas contribute to an organization's ability to deliver business value. EBM consists of four Key Value Areas (KVAs).  1. Current Value: Measures value delivered to customer or user today 2. Unrealized Value: Measures value that could be realized by meeting all potential needs of the customer or user 3. Ability to Innovate: Measures the ability to deliver a new capability that might better serve a customer or user need 4. Time to Market: Measures the ability to quickly deliver new capability, service, or product The total organizational value is captured through these metrics
Current Value 	Current Value (CV) reveals the value that the product delivers to customers, as of today.
	The **Goal** of looking at CV is to maximize the value that an organization delivers to customers and stakeholders at the present time.
	Current Value considers only **what exists right now**, not the value that might exist in the future.
	Questions that organizations need to continually re-evaluate for current value are: 1. How happy are users and customers today? Is their happiness improving or declining? 2. How happy are your employees? Is their happiness improving or declining? 3. How happy are your investors and other stakeholders? Is their happiness improving

	Things which can improve CV
	   1) Usability.
	   2) Customer or user outcomes.
	   3) Workplace Happiness.

	Looking at CV from the perspectives of customers or users, as well as investors, is obvious, but considering employee attitudes recognizes that employees are ultimately the producers of value.
	Engaged employees that know how to maintain, sustain and enhance are one of the most significant assets of an organization, and happy employees are more productive.
Revenue per Employee	The Revenue Per Employee ratio (gross revenue / # of employees) is a key competitive indicator within an industry. This varies significantly by industry. It equals the company's total revenue divided by the number of employees for the period.
Product Cost Ratio	The Product Cost Ratio equals to the total expenses (Costs of building the system, operational costs, maintenance cost etc.) divide the compared to revenue.

Employee Satisfaction	Employee satisfaction is some form of sentiment analysis to help gauge employee engagement, energy, and enthusiasm.
Customer Satisfaction	Customer satisfaction is some form of sentiment analysis to help gauge customer engagement.
Customer Usage Index	Customer Usage Index is a measurement of usage, by feature, to help infer 1) The degree to which customers find the product useful 2) Whether actual usage meets expectations on how long users should be taking to use that feature.
Time-to-Market (T2M)	Time-to-Market (T2M) expresses the organization's ability to quickly deliver new capabilities, services, or products
	The Goal of looking at Time-to-Market is to minimize the amount of time it takes for the organization to deliver value. Without actively managing Time-to-Market, the ability to sustainably deliver value in the future is unknown.
	Questions that organizations need to continually re-evaluate for time to market are: 1. How fast can the organization learn from new experiments? 2. How fast can you learn from new information and adapt? 3. How fast can you deliver new value to customers?
	A variety of things can reduce the Time-to-Market: everything from removing internal communication bottlenecks to improving delivery pipeline automation to improving application maintainability and removing technical debt; anything that reduces time spent waiting or time spent performing work.
Build and integration frequency	The number of integrated and tested builds per time period. For a team that is releasing frequently or continuously, this measure is superseded by actual release measures.
Release Frequency	The number of releases per time period, e.g. continuously, daily, weekly, monthly, quarterly, etc. This helps reflect the time needed to satisfy the customer with new and competitive products.
Release Stabilization Period	The time spent correcting product problems between the point the developers say it is ready to release and the point where it is actually released to customers. This helps represent the impact of poor development practices and underlying design and code base.
Mean time to Repair	The average amount of time it takes from when an error is detected and when it is fixed. This helps reveal the efficiency of an organization to fix an error.

Cycle Time	The amount of time from when work starts on a release until the point where it is actually released. This measure helps reflect an organization's ability to reach its customer.
Lead Time	The amount of time from when an idea is proposed, or a hypothesis is formed until a customer can benefit from that idea. This measure may vary based on customer and product. It is a contributing factor for customer satisfaction.
Time-to-Learn	The total time needed to sketch an idea or improvement, build it, deliver it to users and learn from their usage.
Ability to Innovate	Ability to Innovate expresses the ability of a product development organization to deliver new capabilities that might better meet customer needs.
	The goal of looking at the A2I is to maximize the organization's ability to deliver new capabilities and innovative solutions.
	Organizations should continually re-evaluate their A2I by asking: 1. What prevents the organization from delivering new value? 2. What prevents customers or users from benefiting from that innovation?
	A variety of things can impede a team from being able to deliver new capabilities and value (thus reducing A2I): 1. Spending too much time fixing defects or reducing technical debt 2. Having to maintain multiple code branches or product versions 3. A complex or monolithic application architecture 4. Insufficient product-like environments to test on 5. Lack of operational excellence 6. poor code management practices 7. lack of decentralized decision-making 8. inability to hire and inspire talented 9. passionate team-members 10. hard to install software 11. lack of capabilities that would be compelling enough to warrant installing the software
	As low-value features and systemic impediments accumulate, more budget and time is consumed maintaining the product or overcoming impediments, reducing its available capacity to innovate.
Feature Usage Index	Measurement of features in the product that are frequently used. This helps capture features that are rarely or never used.
Innovation Rate	The percentage of effort or cost spent on new product capabilities, divided by total product effort or cost. This provides insight into the capacity of the organization to deliver new product capabilities.

Defect trends	Measurement of change in defects since last measurement. A defect is anything that reduces the value of the product to a customer, user, or to the organization itself. Defects are generally things that don't work as intended.
On-Product Index	The percentage of time teams spend working on product and value.
Installed Version Index	The number of versions of a product that are currently being supported. This reflects the effort the organization spends supporting and maintaining older versions of software. It also shows the percentage of customers who are able to take advantage of new features on the latest release.
Technical Debt	A concept in programming that reflects the extra development and testing work that arises when "quick and dirty" solutions result in later remediation. It creates an undesirable impact on the delivery of value and an avoidable increase in waste and risk.
Production Incident Trends	The number of times the Scrum Team was interrupted to fix a problem in an installed product. The number and frequency of Production Incidents can help indicate the stability of the product.
Active code branches, time spent merging code	These measures are like the Installed Version Index, since different deployed versions usually have separate code branches.
Time spent context switching	Number of meetings per day per person, and the number of times a day team member is interrupted to help people outside the team can give simple insight into the magnitude of the problem.

Unrealized Value	Unrealized Value suggests the potential future value that could be realized if the organization could perfectly meet the needs of all potential customers
	The goal of looking at Unrealized Value is for the organization to maximize the value that it realizes from the product over time.
	Questions that organizations need to continually re-evaluate for unrealized value are: 1. Can any additional value be created for our organization in this market or other markets? 2. Is it worth the effort and risk to pursue these untapped opportunities? 3. Should further investments be made to capture additional Unrealized Value?
	Considering both CV and UV provide organizations with a way to balance present and possible future benefits. For example, a product may have low CV, because it is an early version being used to test the market, but very high UV, indicating that there is great market potential. Investing in the product to try to boost CV is probably warranted, given the potential returns, even though the product is not currently producing high CV. Conversely, a product with very high CV, large market share, no near competitors, and very satisfied customers may not warrant much new investment; this is the classic cash cow product that is very profitable but nearing the end of its product investment cycle.
Market Share	The relative percentage of the market controlled by the product.
Customer or user satisfaction gap	The difference between a customer or user's desired experience and their current experience.

Time-to-Learn	"Time-to-Learn" is the **total time from the moment the work is started to the moment the team learns through feedback from the users.** 3 benefits of an improved T2L: 1. Upfront discussion on what needs to be achieved 2. Focus on learning more, and not on doing more 3. Faster learning is faster value

	Time to Learn **includes**
	    1) **Releasing it to market.**
	    2) **Gathering feedback.**
	    3) **Studying it in order to learn.**

	The T2L is a good indication of the agility of the organization as it provides clarity on the speed a company is able to react to new market opportunities, as well as how responsive it is to real customer feedback.
	Example: Let's have a look at an example. In the beginning of January, a team starts to refine, work out the first details and make the first implementation of a new feature. It's deployed to customers in May. The gathering of usage data and customer feedback takes 3 months. At the end of September, the lessons learned are presented, new ideas are added to the backlog, priorities are re-assessed, and some existing Product Backlog Items are removed. The total T2L is 9 months: from beginning of January until the end of September.
	How to start tracking the T2L Every sprint the Product Owner picks one or two important Product Backlog Items (PBIs) that are tracked throughout the next months. The date the work is started is recorded. Every sprint the team also spends time on learning from actual work it has done several sprints ago. The moment the learning is done, the date can be used to calculate the T2L of that individual Product Backlog Item. Using the data of multiple PBIs the average T2L is found. Tracking the development of the T2L is handy to see if the improvements really result in a better T2L. Start small and start simple but start thinking about how to instrument your backlog items to drive learning and capture when that learning happens.
	Agility indexTM', a speed indicator of an organization's current and future ability to deliver value.

Professional Agile Leadership Essentials Questions

Please go through these questions and check the answers you go along. The Scrum Assessments **online (https://www.scrum.org/open-assessments)** are the best way to judge where you stand. The Questions and Answers below will make sure you understand the concepts and help you help you prepare for the PAL-E. Go through the answers regardless of you answering the questions right or wrong. Don't try to time yourself. Rather focus on understanding the answers and thus the concepts.

1) Charles is an Agile Leader who manages 3 Scrum Teams. Charles prefers to delegate responsibilities depending on the maturity of his team and team members. It is a good practice to delegate responsibilities depending upon the team maturity even if it takes more time. A. True B. False	**Correct Answer: A** If Scrum is done well, a Scrum team self-organizes, creates value on a regular basis and is highly efficient. A. The Scrum Master serves the Scrum team and the organization in understanding the theory, practices, rules and values. He / she helps team members to grow and coaches his/her peers towards success. B. The Product Owner owns the product, optimizes the value of the product and manages the Product Backlog. He / she helps team members to collaborate with stakeholders and creates a vision that is aligned to the stakeholders' needs. C. Developers along with the rest of the team own the work and turns Product Backlog Items into valuable Increments. They are responsible for the quality of the product and have all the skills to organize their work. If Scrum is done well, a lot of traditional Management and Leadership responsibilities will move to the Scrum team. Depending on how mature the team is, Agile Leaders would start delegating to the Scrum Master, Product Owner and Developers.

2) You are a Developers of an Agile organization. As a team member, if you encounter a tricky problem during a development iteration, agile recommends that you: A. Stop what you're doing until you figure out a solution, using your individual expertise and ingenuity. B. Tell the Scrum Master about the problem and let him/her decide what to do about it, since it's their job to remove impediments to progress. C. Just keep moving ahead so your team's velocity isn't disrupted, since most problems eventually take care of themselves. D. Quickly bring the problem to your team members and ask for their help in solving it, since many heads are better than one.	**Correct answer: D** Agile teams rely on **collective problem solving** rather than individual ingenuity because problems are solved more quickly and effectively when diverse viewpoints are brought to bear, rather than when team members try to push through on their own. Although it is the Scrum Masters role to remove impediments to progress, that refers to road blocks. When it comes to development issues, in many cases only the team members have the expertise needed to resolve the issue, so those kinds of problems can't be delegated to the Scrum Master. Also, one thing we definitely don't want to do is to ignore a problem and hope it will go away; that's a sure-fire recipe for technical debt, if not project failure.
3) Which of the following is not a Key Value Area from the Scrum.org Evidence Based Management framework? A. Time to Market (T2M) B. Current Value (CV) C. Unrealized Value (UV) D. Desire to Innovate (D2I)	**Correct Answer: D** EBM looks at 4 Key Value Areas. Defined measures will vary by organization, but all 4 areas contribute to an organization's ability to deliver business value. 1. **Current Value**: Measures value delivered to customer or user today. 2. **Unrealized Value**: Measures value that could be realized by meeting all potential needs of the customer or user. 3. **Ability to Innovate**: Measures the ability to deliver a new capability that might better serve a customer or user need. 4. **Time to Market**: Measures the ability to quickly deliver new capability, service, or product.

4) Which of the following is not a principle from the Manifesto for Agile Software Development? A) Business people and developers must work together daily throughout the project. B) At regular intervals, the team reflects on how to become more effective, then tunes and adjusts its behavior accordingly. C) Our highest priority is to satisfy the customer through early and continuous delivery of valuable software. D) The most efficient and effective method of conveying information to and within a Scrum team is via comprehensive documentation.	**Correct Answer: D** The Agile Manifesto States: We are uncovering better ways of developing software by doing it and helping others do it. Through this work we have come to value: • Individuals and interactions over processes and tools • Working software over comprehensive documentation • Customer collaboration over contract negotiation • Responding to change over following a plan That is, while there is value in the items on the right, we value the items on the left more. Remember: The most efficient method of communications within a Scrum team is face-to-face communication.
5) Charles and John are two team members of the same Scrum Team. These two team members are having a difference of opinion about how to build the next user story. What should be done? A. The team coach should assess the level of conflict and intervene appropriately. B. The team should gather to discuss the issue and come up with a collective solution. C. The Scrum Master should resolve the issue, since it is becoming an impediment to progress. D. The Product Owner should be consulted.	**Correct answer: B** On an empowered agile team, it is up to the team members to resolve their technical disputes collectively. The coach, Scrum Master, or Product Owner is unlikely to have the knowledge required to make such decisions. Remember, if the team had issues understanding the story, then the Product owner would be consulted. However here there seems to be a technical issue with building the story.
6) The Current Value (CV) Key Value Area from the Scrum.org Evidence Based Management framework reveals: A) The market capitalization of the organization B) The profit and loss account of the organization for the past financial year C) The net worth of the organization D) The value that the organization delivers to customers, today.	**Correct Answer: D** Current Value: Measures value delivered to customer or user today.

7)	The Time to Market (T2M) Key Value Area from the Scrum.org Evidence Based Management framework reveals: A. The average time taken to carry out a release B. The organization's ability to quickly deliver new capabilities, services, or products C. The sum of velocities across all Scrum Teams in the organization. D. How fast the organization can develop Products.	**Correct Answer: B** Time-to-Market (T2M) expresses the **organization's ability** to quickly deliver new capabilities, services, or products.
8)	The most efficient and effective method of conveying information within a Scrum team is face-to-face conversation. **A.** True **B.** False .	**Correct answer: A** The Agile Manifesto is based on 12 Agile Key Principles mentioned below: 1. The highest priority is to satisfy the customer through early and continuous delivery of valuable software. 2. Welcome changing requirements, even late in development. Agile processes harness change for the customer's competitive advantage. 3. Deliver working software frequently, from a couple of weeks to a couple of months, with a preference to the shorter timescale. 4. Business people and developers must work together daily throughout the project. 5. Build projects around motivated individuals. Give them the environment and support they need and trust them to get the job done. 6. **The most efficient and effective method of conveying information to and within a Scrum team is face-to-face conversation.** 7. Working software is the primary measure of progress. 8. Agile processes promote sustainable development. The sponsors, developers, and users should be able to maintain a constant pace indefinitely.

	9. Continuous attention to technical excellence and good design enhances agility. 10. Simplicity--the art of maximizing the amount of work not done--is essential. 11. The best architectures, requirements, and designs emerge from self-organizing teams. 12. At regular intervals, the team reflects on how to become more effective, then tunes and adjusts its behavior accordingly.
9) Scrum is a process framework for resolving complex problems iteratively and incrementally to a create a high-value solution. Scrum directly addresses many of the shortcomings of Waterfall Agile method. Which of the following is true when you compare Scrum to Waterfall? A. Scrum is empirical instead of predictive: Bases decisions on experience and experiment B. Scrum is iterative instead of sequential: Organizes work in smaller step. C. Scrum is concentrated on gathering continuous feedback instead of gathering in stages. D. Scrum is value-focused instead of deadline-focused E. Scrum is self-organizing instead of control and command. F. All of the Above.	**Correct answer: F** Scrum is a process framework for resolving complex problems iteratively and incrementally to a create a high-value solution that elates customers. Scrum directly addresses many of the shortcomings of Waterfall with project management. Scrum as opposed to Waterfall is: • Empirical instead of predictive: Bases decisions on Experience and Experiment. • Iterative instead of sequential: Organizes work in smaller step. • Concentrated on gathering continuous feedback instead of gathering in stages. • Value-focused instead of deadline-focused. • Self-organizing instead of control and command.
10) The Unrealized Value (UV) Key Value Area from the Scrum.org Evidence Based Management framework reveals: A. The potential future value that could be realized if the organization was able to approximately meet the needs of the high revenue customers only. B. The planned revenue uplift expected in the next 12 months from scheduled new features to be delivered	**Correct Answer: C** Unrealized Value suggests the potential future value that could be realized if the organization could perfectly meet the needs of all potential customers.

C. The potential future value that could be realized if the organization was able to perfectly meet the needs of all potential customers D. Projected revenue for the next financial year E. The cash value of work currently in the development pipeline	
11) As the coach of an agile team, you expect the team members to: A. Come to you as soon as they encounter a problem. B. Report all their problems in the daily stand-up meeting. C. Solve most problems collectively as the work proceeds. D. Figure out the best solution on their own.	**Correct answer: C** Agile team members are expected to solve most of their technical problems collectively as the work proceeds. They don't try to figure out solutions on their own as the stakeholder feedback would be necessary for that. They also would not bring their problems to their coach, since those approaches would be solved by the team's collective technical expertise and diverse viewpoints. They also don't report all their problems in the daily stand-up meeting; the issues mentioned in that meeting are those that the team members can't resolve themselves and that pose impediments to their further progress.
12) Agile Maturity Is a result of Role Maturity A. True B. False	**Correct Answer: A** If Scrum is done well, a Scrum team self-organizes, creates value on a regular basis and is highly efficient: • The Scrum Master serves the Scrum team and the Organization in understanding the theory, practices, rules and values. He helps team members to grow and coaches his peers towards success. • The Product Owner owns the Product, optimizes the value of the product and manages the Product Backlog. He helps team members to collaborate with stakeholders and creates a vision that is aligned to the stakeholders' needs. • Developers along with the rest of the team owns the work and turns Product Backlog Items into valuable Increments. They are responsible for the quality of the product and have all the skills to organize their work. Agile Maturity is thus a result of team maturity.

13) You are a Scrum Master on an agile team. A team member becomes very sick halfway through an iteration. The team had committed to deliver 55 story points, however, is only able to deliver 20 story points. Which action is most appropriate? A. Make the remaining team work longer hours. B. Send work home to the sick team member. C. Start development yourself to assist the team. D. Deliver what you can within the sprint.	**Correct answer: D** In such a situation, the Scrum or Agile team delivers what they can within the sprint. Sending work home and working the team longer are counterproductive in the long term and don't adhere to the agile principle of maintaining a sustainable pace. Starting development work yourself would leave nobody to do the Scrum Master role. It Is better to just deliver what is possible within this iteration and explain the variance.
14) You are a manager in an Agile organization. 16 Scrum Teams fall under your responsibility. You need a way measure the value that each Scrum Team produces so that you can provide the information to investors and stakeholders. How do you go about measuring the value for these 16 Scrum teams? A. Consult with the Scrum Master of each Scrum Team. As the person who spends the most time with Developers, they are uniquely qualified to present information on the value that is provided. B. Consult with the Product Owners of the teams. As the person responsible of maximizing the value of the Scrum team's work, they are best suited to help provide you with the information you seek. C. Consult with the Product Owners of the teams. As the person responsible for managing the Scrum teams, they are best suited to help provide you with the information you seek. D. Compare the story point velocity of each Scrum Team. Those with the highest points completed per Sprint obviously produce the most value.	**Correct Answer: B** As the person responsible of maximizing the value of the Scrum team's work, the Product Owners are best suited to help provide the value that each Scrum Team produces. The value provided by each team can be seen by looking at the increment the team produces each sprint. It can also be seen by looking at the Product Backlog items in the Product Backlog.

15) You are leading a team with an average velocity of 85 points per iteration. Another team of the same size in your organization is working on a project with similar complexity. The other team's velocity is averaging 155 points per month. Your team should: A. Perform affinity estimating to check their estimates, since something is off. B. Work longer hours. C. Ignore the difference. D. Request additional resources to get more work done.	**Correct answer: C** Velocity is team-specific and unique to that team. In other words, a story point for one team probably wouldn't have the same value as a story point for another team. Therefore, it is not appropriate to compare velocities between teams. The best choice would be to ignore the difference.
16) You are a Scrum Master for a Scrum Team. Developers within the Scrum Team has some disagreements on the intended purpose of one of their tasks. Developers attempt to settle the disagreement themselves, but they still have questions. As A Scrum Master, what is your role in answering the team's questions? A. You should facilitate a meeting with the Product Owner so that the Product Owner can help clarify the requirements for the task. B. You should consult with customer stakeholders to understand the intent of the task. Since it is their product, they are in the best position to explain the intent. C. Developers within the Scrum Team is a self-organizing team and therefore they should have the ability to figure out how best to proceed. The Scrum Master should not be involved. D. You should instruct the team to make a best guess at the intended meaning of the task.	**Correct Answer: A** Remember, the Scrum team is a is a self-organizing team and therefore they should have the ability to figure out how best to proceed. However, if they do have questions about the Scrum Goal, requirements or any Product Backlog items, the Product Owner is responsible for helping them out. The Scrum Master should facilitate such meetings when opportunity arises.
17) Your team committed to delivering 20 story points this iteration, but it looks like they will only complete 8. You should: A. Extend the iteration. B. Add more resources to the team. C. Be transparent about the 8 completed points and put 12 back in the Product backlog. D. Be transparent about the 8 completed points and put 12 back in next Sprint backlog.	**Correct answer: C** Since iterations are timeboxed, the duration won't be changed. You also wouldn't change the iteration plan or expand the team. Instead, work that isn't completed within the iteration is returned to the Product backlog. Therefore, the choice of completing 8 points and returning 12 points to the backlog is the correct option.

18) What is the ideal type of Product Owner? A. The Product Owner isn't very important to the Scrum Team. There is no ideal type of Product Owner. B. A team with a Product Owner that constantly changes opinions provides a team with changing views of a product and thus enhanced perspectives. C. A former Project Manager is the ideal type of Product Owner. This helps them to better manage the team in the delivery of excellent products and gaining maximum value. D. A single long-serving Product Owner with subject matter expertise in the product that is being developed is the ideal type of Product Owner.	**Correct Answer: D** An ideal Product Owner would be a single long-serving Product Owner with subject matter expertise in the product that is being developed. A team with a Product Owner does not constantly changes opinions. He / she keeps up with the market changes and provides a single vision to the team using the Product Backlog and Product Goals.
19) Your lead engineer just came down with a health issue in the middle of a sprint. As team coach, what should you do? A. Call his functional manager and request a new lead engineer for your team. B. Ask the team how much of the planned work can be done. C. Ask everyone else to work overtime. D. Postpone the release date.	**Correct answer: B** This question tests your grasp of the agile principle of timeboxing. The correct answer is to discuss with the team how much of the planned work they will be able to complete within the timebox. We wouldn't request a new lead engineer, either temporarily or permanently, because swapping people in and out of the team would be likely to throw the team back to the Storming stage, lowering its productivity. The option of asking everyone to work overtime isn't consistent with the Agile principle of sustainable Development. Although postponing the release date might be necessary in some cases, we aren't given enough information to support the conclusion that this is the BEST answer.

20) You are an Agile leader. A customer has come to you with an item they want to see changed within the product your company is developing for them. His improvement ideas seem to be outside of the scope of the original product plan. What is your course of action? A. Facilitate a meeting between the Product Owner of the team working on the customer's product and the customer. You want to make sure the customer is satisfied with the outcome and you hope to find a satisfactory and mutually beneficial solution to the customer's request. B. Begin negotiations with the customer on adding this scope change to the project. You want to ensure that the value you provide to the customer can be increased so you handle these negotiations yourself. When you are finished, you have delighted the customer with your adaptability. C. Do nothing, let the Scrum Team deal with it. D. Facilitate a meeting between the Developers working on the product and the customer. Instruct the Developers that as an Agile organization it is part of their duty to ensure that the customer is satisfied. Recommend that the Developers complete the customer's request for the next Sprint.	**Correct Answer: A** New Requirements should always flow through the Product Owner. Regardless of the sources of the requirement (Customer, CEO etc.). a meeting between the Product Owner of the team should be facilitated so the Product Owner can understand the requirements and work with the Developers as needed. The Product owner would also make sure that the customer is satisfied with the outcome and find a satisfactory and mutually beneficial solution to the customer's request.

21) Developers in a Scrum Team believes that it will take 35 hours of effort to write the user guide for the new product they are building. How many hours of effort should they quote for that task? A. 35 hours. B. 40 hours, to add a buffer for distractions and availability issues. C. 30 hours since teams tend to overestimate how long a task will take. D. 35 to 40 hours.	**Correct answer: A** Agile teams estimate tasks in ideal time—how long it will take if there are no interruptions or distractions. In this case, they have decided that the effort will take 35 hours, so their estimate should also be 35 hours. Teams should avoid padding or buffering the estimates.
22) What are the primary benefits of an Agile approach when compared to a Waterfall approach? (Select two) A. To save the organization money through quicker product development practices. B. To deliver product incrementally (to improve the feedback loop) eventually the entire intended product as a result of the frequent feedback. C. An improved ability to deliver on-budget, on-time, and on-scope. D. Deliver business value by improving the customer's satisfaction with the outcome of doing business with your organization.	**Correct Answer: B, D** Primary Benefit of an Agile Approach is an increased delivery strategic business value (and thus customer satisfaction). This is often done by involving business stakeholders in the development process. By doing so, the team understands what's most important and can deliver the features that provide the most business value to their organization.
23) You are a manager at an Agile organization. One of your direct reports comes to you with questions regarding some of his work. How should you handle this situation? A. Work with the employee to help him / her find the answers to their questions from the Product Owner, Scrum Master or anyone else. B. Instruct the employee that they will be terminated if they cannot find the answers to their questions. There is no room for manager/employee collaboration a self-organizing Agile organization. C. Instruct the employee about the self-organizing principle in the Scrum philosophy. It is the employee's responsibility to find the answers themselves. D. Instruct the employee to consult with a consultant who would remove their impediments.	**Correct Answer: A** In Scrum, the Scrum team is self-organizing. However, they often will have questions about the requirements or impediments which is where they would need help. The Manager would need to work with the employees to make sure his / her questions are answered. The answers could come from the Product Owner or someone else. The Scrum Master would help removing the impediments.

24) Charles is very hands-on Product Owner. He writes the requirements and does test of the product himself once the development is complete. Charles has told the team how much work will need to be completed in the next iteration based on his vision, experience and skills. In this scenario: A. The iteration planning process is proceeding smoothly. B. Charles is overstepping his role. C. Charles is taking over the Scrum Master's responsibilities for planning. D. The team should claim more responsibility for planning in their next retrospective.	**Correct answer: B** During iteration planning, the Product Owner's role is to prioritize the backlog items. The team then decides how many of the top-priority items in the backlog can be completed in the next iteration timebox. So, this Product Owner is overstepping their role, since the amount of work that can be completed in the next iteration is decided by the team, not the Product Owner or the Scrum Master.
25) What is one direct benefit of an Agile approach? A. Ability to deliver more value. B. Elimination of all managers. C. Improved team structure. D. Cost reduction.	**Correct Answer: A** One direct Benefit of the Agile Approach is the ability to deliver more Value.
26) What does a trendline in a release burndown chart represent? A. When the all the technical backlog will be completed. B. What the Ideal Tasks remining would look like. C. When all the remaining tasks will be completed. D. All of the above. 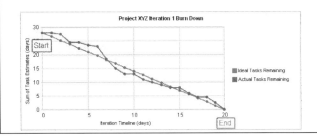	**Correct Answer: C** Trendline in burn down chart is a way to predict how many sprints the remaining work will take. The trendline is based on the team's average velocity and the projective completion to zero is also based on the team's velocity. The burndown chart is a helpful tool for Developers to self-manage BUT it is not mandatory as the teams will decide the best way to manage their own progress and promote transparency.

27) An agile team leader in your organization comes to you for advice. He is having trouble getting his team to take ownership of the project. He keeps finding himself making the needed decisions and directing their work. What do you advise him to do? A. At the stand-up meetings, assign a different person each day as the decision maker to get them all comfortable in the role. B. Implement an incentive plan and officially report any lack of participation to team members' functional managers. C. Meet them and work with the team to align everyone's expectations. Coach them if needed. D. Explain to them that agile teams self-select their work and tell them to get on with it.	**Correct answer: C** In this situation, the team leader should assume a coaching role to help the team members get to the point where they are comfortable selecting their own work. This will include meeting team members a half-step ahead, guaranteeing safety, partnering with their managers, and building positive regard. Assigning someone as a decisionmaker at stand-up meetings is incorrect since agile teams are consensus-driven, and decisions aren't made in stand-up meetings. Incentive plans can be useful, but what this team really needs is guidance, not rewards and punishments. Simply explaining that agile teams self-select their work isn't enough to get team members comfortable assuming more ownership of the project.
28) You are a leader in an Agile organization. You are trying to gain information regarding the future product and goals of the Scrum Team. How should you do this? A. Ensure that you are attending the Sprint Retrospective each Sprint so that you can question the Scrum Team on their planned goals and improvement activities. B. Consult with the Product Owner and ask about the Product Backlog, as the Product Backlog should contain the current state and current intended order of all future tasks to be worked on. C. Attend the Daily Scrum and ask the team each day to update you on the status of their tasks. D. Consult with the Scrum Master and ask about status changes to the team's goals. The Scrum Master should be tracking all the work that the Scrum Team performs and should be able to provide regular updates.	**Correct Answer: B** The Product backlog and the Sprint Backlog is the best way to know: 1) What work was done so far(Product Backlog) 2) What work is currently being worked on in the Sprint (Sprint Backlog) 3) What work is remaining (Product Backlog).

29) How does the Scrum Team prove its value to the organization? A. During each Sprint Review, the Product Owner provides value reports to stakeholders in attendance. B. By eliminating technical debt and reducing the probability of flaccid Scrum. C. Through the continuous reporting during the Daily Scrum. D. By consistent delivery of quality product at the end of each Sprint.	**Correct Answer: D** Value of a Team is tied to the work it does which can be seen in: 1) The Product and the Sprint Backlogs. 2) The Increment the team produces.
30) What are the main benefits of self-organization? A. Increase Compliance, Self-Accountability, Commitment. B. Increase Compliance, Self-Accountability, output. C. Increase Compliance, accuracy of estimates, Commitment. D. Increase Creativity, Self-Accountability, Commitment.	**Correct Answer: D** The preferred leadership style in Scrum is "servant leadership", which emphasizes achieving results by focusing on the needs of the Scrum Team. Some of the benefits of Self-organization are: • Team buy-in and shared ownership • Motivation, which leads to an enhanced performance level of the team • Innovative and Creative environment conducive to growth • Increased Self Accountability, & Commitment to achieving the goals of the Scrum Team.
31) "Vtech", a Toy company has stores and offices across the world. Vtech offices and Scrum teams across the world cannot implement the Scrum methodology as Scrum dictates that all the members of the Scrum team should be in the same office (co-located). A. True B. False	**Correct answer: B** Scrum can be implemented for both co-located and distributed teams. Work is more effectively when teams are collocated and thus co-location is recommended. However, it is not mandatory to be co-located in Scrum.

32) Developers in a Scrum Team (in an Agile organization) approach the Scrum Master and complain that all the team members feel that they are falling behind in keeping up with the new market trends and coding techniques. The developers feel that they are using old methods of coding and their self-development is impacted. Which of the following statements are true? (Select Two) A. The Scrum master should tell the Scrum Team that each one should approach their managers as the Managers are responsible for their self-development. B. The Scrum Master should work with each Individual and improve his / her coding technique. C. Developers themselves are responsible for their own Self Development. D. The Scrum Team as a whole is responsible for everyone's Personal Development.	**Correct Answer C, D** Personal development is a responsibility of everyone in the organization. While Scrum Masters and Managers typically facilitate team members to grow, the individual is still responsible for his / her own personal growth. Even if the organization (or more likely your department or team) is based on 100% Agile principles, as a manger you will still be responsible for peoples' development, but people will make their own decisions on how they develop themselves without the involvement of their manager\leader.
33) Which of the following sets of characteristics are displayed by High-performing agile teams? A. Consensus-driven, empowered, low trust. B. Self-organizing, plan-driven, empowered. C. Consensus-driven, empowered, plan-driven. D. Constructive disagreement, empowered, self-organizing.	**Correct answer: D** Through a process of elimination, we can determine that the correct answer is choice D. High-performing agile teams work in high-trust, rather than low-trust, environments, and they are consensus-driven, not plan-driven.
34) One of the software development company follows the waterfall software development method. The company realizes that the code development is progressing as expected (on time) however the cost of development has been more than what they had initially planned. The Management is considering adapting an Agile approach and believes adopting to the Agile approach will surely reduce cost. Adapting Scrum will definitely make Teams work more efficiently and deliver more value in less time, thus guarantying cost savings. Should the Management adapt the Agile approach to reduce cost? A. Yes B. No	**Answer: B** One benefit of an Agile approach is that it enables teams to build and deliver a product and get feedback so that they can adapt the product based on that feedback to deliver more value. Reducing cost by not building unrequired features, and improving practices based on feedback may reduce cost. Cost reduction may become a secondary benefit but reducing cost should not be viewed as a benefit of using an Agile approach.

35) The Tasks of an Agile Leader are: (Choose all that apply)

A. Practice Transparency through Visualization.
B. Create a Safe Environment for Experimentation.
C. Experiment with New Techniques and Processes.
D. Share Knowledge through Collaboration.
E. Encourage Emergent Leadership via a Safe Environment.

Correct Answer: A, B, C, D, E

Leadership Tasks are as follows:

- **Practice Transparency through Visualization**
  "Transparency" means being open and honest, not only about the progress and achievements, but also about team issues and setbacks. Agile teams demonstrate transparency by openly displaying their work, progress, and review findings for other stakeholders to see.

- **Create a Safe Environment for Experimentation**
  When people believe that it's okay to try new approaches and they won't be criticized if they don't succeed the first time, they are more likely to have a go and try new things. Leadership should encourage trials and tests, not dwelling on experiments that have failed, and encouraging the generation of new ideas.

- **Experiment with New Techniques and Processes**
  Short iterations offer the same short feedback cycles and provide ready-made test periods for new approaches.

- **Share Knowledge through Collaboration**
  It's important for teams to share knowledge about the product they are working on and how things work within teams. Collaborative work—either through pairing workers or Adhoc knowledge transfer through co-location—has emerged as an agile best practice.

- **Encourage Emergent Leadership via a Safe Environment**
  Emergent leadership is when a team member takes the initiative and tries a new approach after gaining team approval. Agile team members are not only empowered to make decisions but also to lead the charge on improvements.

36) A critical responsibility of an Agile leader is to create an environment where trials, test and failed experiments are encouraged. A. True B. False	**Correct Answer: A** When people believe that it's okay to try new approaches and they won't be criticized if they don't succeed the first time, they are more likely to have a go and try new things. Leadership should encourage trials and tests, not dwelling on experiments that have failed, and encouraging the generation of new ideas.
37) You are a manager in an organization which develops products for customers. John is a Development Lead and lately his enthusiasm level has been decreasing. While talking to John in a meeting, he expresses his concerns about the decisions that are made within the team without his consultation. What would you do? A. Move him to another team that would be more receptive of his opinions B. Ask John whether he has discussed the issue with the team himself and raise it as an issue with the Scrum Master. C. Ask the Scrum Master to teach the Scrum Value of respect. D. Schedule a meeting with the team to discuss your concerns and explain that they need to consider John's expertise.	**Correct Answer: B** One of the attributes of Scrum Teams is self-organization. A sign of a self-organizing team is the ability to resolve internal conflicts. One of the responsibilities of an Agile leader is to support the teams in self-organization and providing an environment where they are able to feel safe to make local decisions whether it is technical or how to best work together.
38) You have been assigned to lead a distributed agile team. To help them communicate, the best option would be to: A. Ask the team members to share photos of themselves. B. Document a common language for all project communications. C. Set up some initial face-to-face meetings for everyone to meet each other. D. Define common working hours so everyone can better communicate.	**Correct answer: C** If possible, setting up some initial face-to-face meetings for everyone to meet is an effective way of improving remote communications later in the project. Once people have met face-to-face, it is generally much easier to follow up with e-mail, phone calls, etc. Defining common working hours or a common language might appear to be helpful, but these actions might also be viewed as disrespectful. Sending photos is also unlikely to assist much, and it is certainly not the best option.

39) You are a newly joined Agile Leader in an organization. Over the course of several Sprints, you see that the Scrum Team is been distracted by unplanned support requests from other teams. These requests have caused the team to regularly fail in meeting their Sprint Goals and deliver the Increment on time. As a manager, you should: A. Extend the Sprint Time box so the teams can finish the unplanned work towards the end of the Sprint. B. Add additional sprints to the project to compensate for interruptions C. Allocate Additional people to the team D. Work with the Product Owner, Scrum Master and Developers in the Scrum Team to find ways to reassign the unplanned work to people outside the Scrum Team. E. Add buffer of Product backlog items to include the unplanned work.	**Correct Answer: D** It's very common to get work which was not planned during the Sprint. The Sprint Goal and Sprint Backlog items help the team focus only on the items which need to be completed during the Sprint. Any other work beyond this would need to be discussed with the Product Owner to be considered. The Product Owner would decide on the criticality and work with the developers to change the Sprint backlog, if needed. The Sprint Goal however should not be impacted and be achieved at the end of the Sprint.
40) There are 20 different Stakeholders involved in giving feedback to a Healthcare Software. These Stakeholders have different priorities and want different enhancements for the Product. The Stakeholders however can't seem to come on an agreement on prioritizing the enhancements. The Product Owner should: (Choose all the Apply) A. Work with all the stakeholders so that they agree on what provides the most value for the Product. The Product Owner should then create Product backlog items based on the final list given by the stakeholders. B. Work with the stakeholders however prioritize based on what Product Owner thinks is the best for the Product. C. Ask the Scrum team to work directly with the Stakeholders. D. Ask the Product Owner to raise this as an impediment.	**Correct Answer: B** The Product Owner is responsible for gathering the input of Stakeholders, but it is not the stakeholder's job to come to an agreement. The Product Owner is responsible for prioritizing the enhancements based on what provides most value to the product.

41) Benefits of Agile Approach are: (Choose All that Apply) A. Quick feedback, quickly adapting change, resulting into more customer satisfaction. B. Short increments reducing complexity. C. Short increments increasing predictability. D. All of the above.	**Correct Answer: A, C** One benefit of an Agile approach is that it enables teams to build and deliver a product and get feedback so that they can adapt the product based on that feedback to deliver more value. Delivering in short increments does not decrease the complexity of the project or make it 100% predictable; however, it does increase the probability of delivering value. Customer feedback may result in significant changes from plans. The goal of becoming agile is not to improve predictability or eliminate complexity. The goal of Agile is recognizing that a complex project will never be 100% predictable.
42) A company located in Boston has very small conference rooms. If it isn't possible to locate all your team members in the same room, they are likely to experience: A. More communication challenges. B. Higher levels of conflict. C. More privacy. D. Less difficulty reaching convergence.	**Correct answer: A** Team members who are co-located are likely to have lower levels of conflict. If team members don't work in the same room, it doesn't necessarily mean they will have more privacy; it just means they won't all be together. The most likely outcome of this scenario is more communication challenges.
43) The Agile Manifesto recommends comprehensive documentation over working software. A. True B. False	**Correct answer: B** The Agile Manifesto recommends working software over comprehensive documentation. This value reminds teams within an organization to focus on the purpose or business value which is being delivered rather than paperwork.
44) In Agile Leadership, a lot of traditional Leadership responsibilities are delegated to the members of the Scrum Team. A. True B. False	**Correct answer: A** Scrum depends on the ability of teams to learn from mistakes and self-organize around difficult problems. A lot of the traditional leadership responsibilities (such as planning, quality and customer-communication) are needed at the level of the team. For a leader this means letting go of responsibilities and a possible re-definition of the traditional role. As a leader, one should be open to delegate responsibilities and create a plan on how to do so. Leaders should ask their Scrum Team what incentives could lead to a higher focus on customer value.

45) As an Agile leader, your most important responsibility is to define the product goals for the team and hold everyone accountable for meeting the goals. A. True B. False	**Correct Answer: B** During the exams, you will need to make sure you read the questions correctly. Is holding people accountable the most important job? No. The most important function of an Agile leader is to provide an environment that supports localized decisions made by the members and help remove impediments that may hinder them.
46) How is risk related to value delivery? A. Risk is an inherent part of delivering value. B. Risk increases as value decreases. C. Risk is factored into value. D. Risk reduces value delivery.	**Correct Answer: D** Risk can be considered the opposite of value, or anti-value, since risks or threats to the project have the potential to erode, remove, or reduce value if they occur. The other options are made up ideas.
47) A software company has multiple software products. These products are released to 1000's of different clients. Some products are dependent on each other's releases. The Scrum Master has made it mandatory that all the Product teams should adhere to the same release schedule. This will guarantee increased value to the customer/user. A. True B. False	**Answer: B** While using a common release schedule could increase team synchronization, it is the role of the Product Owner to set common goals and help the teams to deliver value. Having the same release schedule might be a good recommendation but it does not guarantee increased value and it should not be coming from the Scrum Master. The increase of value delivery is an often a result of applying Scrum in combination with empirical principles (transparency, inspection and adaptation) and the Scrum Values (Commitment, Focus, Openness, Respect, Courage).

48) The relationship between leadership and management in agile methods is: A. Leadership replaces all aspects of management. B. Leadership is subsidiary to management. C. Management and leadership are used together. D. Management and leadership are incompatible.	**Correct answer: C** Agile methods employ a combination of management and leadership. Leadership neither totally replaces nor is subsidiary to management—and since the two approaches can be used together, they aren't incompatible.
49) The CEO of the company has asked you to prepare a report on the "Health" of the Project. If Scrum is followed in the company: A. The Scrum Master can provide this information as he / she is responsible for managing the team and tracking the project status B. The Product Owner can provide this information as he / she is responsible for managing the team and tracking the project status. The Product Owner maintains a weekly report anyways. C. The CEO should attend Sprint Retrospectives to gain insights into how the team is working together and provide feedback on what needs to be improved. D. The CEO should pay attention to the improvement items that come from the Sprint Retrospective and stay informed about the Product Backlog items.	**Correct Answer: D** One of the pillars of empiricism is Transparency. The Product Backlog provides the most insights about the project and Retrospectives provides improvements to the team's internal process.
50) Developers in the Scrum Team have the freedom to choose how they work in a sprint. There are no Scrum restrictions at all. A. True B. False	**Correct Answer: B** The basic Scrum rules apply to all the roles including the Developers. Organizational standards and policies, as well as the maturity level of the team, will put guard-rails on what a team is allowed to do. More mature teams may be given more authority than less mature teams, but even for the most mature teams, every organization has some rules that everyone must follow.

51) As a Scrum Master, you assess that the market has shifted and the product which the team is building is no longer viable. What should you do? A. Request that the Product Owner immediately re-prioritize the backlog. B. Ask the Product Owner if the viability of the project has changed. C. Cancel the project. D. Alert the team that they can expect to be assigned to a new project soon.	**Correct answer: B** In reading the scenario, you should have noticed that it implies the Scrum Master is stepping outside of their role, since that role doesn't include assessing the value of the project. The Scrum Master can't cancel the project because they don't make those kinds of decisions. They also wouldn't direct the Product Owner what to do when. The only person on a Scrum team who has the information needed to assess the viability of the project is the Product Owner. So, the correct answer is "ask the Product Owner if the viability of the project has changed."
52) What outcomes would you expect for a newly formed team or from a Team where the team members keep changing? (Choose two best answers). A. Changing Team members will result into an increased productivity as they come with new energy and enthusiasm to work. B. The team will likely have communication and knowledge sharing challenges that will require help to resolve. C. Having the right collaboration tools can make a distributed team as productive. D. Cost of delivering the product will be significantly high. E. Velocity of the team will decrease.	**Correct Answer: B, E** In a short term the productivity will decrease because the new teams will spend time to get up to speed with the Product. The old team will spend a lot of time communicating with the new teams. Adding More Members to a Team or adding more teams would **lead to immediate decrease in Productivity as communication and coordination time between the Scrum Teams increase**.

53) A company has 3 Products with 3 different Scrum Teams. The company is planning to have a rotation policy where the Product Owners will work on a Product for only 3 months. After 3 months they will be swapped by another Product Owner. These will decrease the dependency teams have on one Person / Product Owner. Product Owners can be interchanged across Scrum Teams, without any impacts on the team or velocity, as the Product Owner do not develop the code. A. True B. False	**Answer: B** While an experienced Product Owner may be able to effectively work Developers in the Scrum Team, the importance of the Product Owner having subject matter expertise, or strong relationships with the stakeholder community cannot be overlooked. In complex value chains it often takes a long time before the Product Owner can become effective.
54) As an agile team leader, you want to avoid: A. Prioritizing team goals over individual goals. B. Help with setting the Product Goals. C. Finding out what motivates the team members individually. D. Rewarding individual goals at the expense of project goals.	**Correct answer: D** As an agile team leader, it might be helpful to focus on any of the activities listed here except for rewarding individual goals at the expense of project goals. An effective team leader understands the team members' individual goals and leverages them for the good of the project, rather than the other way around.
55) Charles is one of the sponsors for your product. Charles wants to know if the product you're building will be ready to demo at an upcoming conference. What do you tell Charles? A. It will be ready when it's ready. B. We'll try our best get the demo ready. It should have the high priority functionalities. We have prioritized the work. Based on the velocity we should have the minimum functionality needed done by then. C. We'll let you know as soon as our velocity has stabilized. D. That depends on your budget.	**Correct answer: B** This question tests your grasp of agile concepts in an indirect way. In this case, you need to know that agile teams will typically fix time and cost and allow scope to vary, as reflected in the agile triangle. When balancing constraints, the agile approach is to get the highest-priority product functionality done by the customer's deadline.
56) Your team is tasked with developing a medical device. The team does not know what the final product will look like. How would you advise them to proceed? A. Try the most promising approaches in short iterations and learn as you go. B. Perform a risk-based spike. C. Ask the customer for more detailed information about the product. D. Follow the project charter as closely as possible.	**Correct answer: A** In the uncertain environment of knowledge work projects, the agile method is to try the most promising approaches in short iterations and learn as we go. (This is a key agile theme that is emphasized throughout the book.) A risk-based spike and gathering more information might be good ideas, but they are not the best answers. Agile charters usually don't provide much detail or technical guidance for the team.

57) A company is going to start a project to develop a new software. The Product is huge and has 1000's of features. The company has decided to implement Scrum. The company should Invest additional time (1 or 2 Sprints) upfront just for planning, before beginning the development work. The planning will help them be more organized and thus increase the chance of success. A. True B. False	**Correct Answer B.** When addressing complex adaptive problems or products, the level of uncertainty is highest at the beginning of the project and reduces when more information emerges as the work being done progresses. While upfront planning helps, Scrum requires at least one feature delivered every Sprint. Scrum also does not recommend sprints just for Planning or Tech debt. Note: This doesn't mean we don't Plan in Scrum. Planning can be done in parallel, while the Sprints are on ongoing and people are implementing new features.
58) You are an Agile leader your organization. Several customers have been complaining about a missing feature in the product. The Product Owner is aware of the missing feature however he feels that the features which are currently planned are more important for the business. You believe that he may not have enough information to make the right decision. As the Agile Leader what should you do? A. Hire a new Product Owner who is more aligned with the clients. B. Hire more people who can get the work done as the feature is important and will provide increased product value. C. Work directly with the Developers and get the missing features completed. D. Ask the Product Owner if he would like to connect with the customer to understand the problems they have been facing and complaining about. Make sure he is informed; however, he would still make the final call of including or excluding the missing feature.	**Correct Answer: D** For the Product Owner to succeed, the entire organization must respect his or her decisions. The Product Owner is responsible for maximizing the value of the product resulting from the work of the Scrum Team.
59) At least one representative of the management leaders should attend all the Scrum Events (and meetings) to make sure they are going as expected. A. True B. False	**Answer: B** Transparency and openness of the Scrum team may be negatively impacted if the management team is "always" present. Management Team should let the Scrum Teams operate by themselves as long as they meet the needed Goals.

60) The primary benefit of an Agile approach is to make it easier to deliver on-time and within budget. A. True B. False	**Answer: B** The primary benefit of an Agile approach is to enable a team to inspect and adapt their results by delivering a working product.

61) What is most important for your agile team to continuously focus on? (Choose the best answer) A. Getting the right answers. B. Understanding their tasks. C. Defining their tasks. D. Measuring their performance.	**Correct answer: B** This question tests your high-level understanding of knowledge work versus industrial work. Getting the right answers, defining tasks, and measuring performance are emphasized more in industrial work than knowledge work. Knowledge workers focus instead on understanding their tasks. Although all of these activities are performed on an agile project, notice that the question asks what the team should "continuously focus on." This is a clue that the question is looking at the team's high-level process, not specific parts of their work.
62) A company is planning to transition from waterfall to Scrum. For the first phase the management has decided to only change the organization's current terminology to fit Scrum. Proper understanding and support of Scrum (as defined in the Scrum Guide) will be a part of Phase 2. Doing this will: A. Result into very few changes as the vocabulary in Scrum is specifically defined to implement Scrum. B. Teams won't realize the benefits of Scrum. C. Result into more chaos in understanding as there will be a mix of terms and methods from different frameworks. D. All of the above.	**Answer: D** The defined terminology in Scrum was selected, designed, and defined specifically for supporting the Scrum Framework. Understanding the differences between traditional methods and the Scrum Framework will help move teams in the right direction in Scrum adoption.

63) Which of the following shows that the Scrum Team is doing well? A. Team working at the expected velocity. B. Team has a releasable product every release. C. Team is meeting the Sprint Goals. D. Team works over the weekends.	**Answer: C** Consistent achievement of Sprint Goals shows that the Scrum Team is working well together, that they are able to agree on the Sprint Goal, and they are able to work together to achieve that goal. Read the choices carefully. A valuable (and not necessarily releasable) product every Sprint (and not every release) shows the team is doing well.
64) Stakeholders are only allowed to meet with the Scrum Team at Sprint Review. A. True B. False	**Correct Answer: B** Getting feedback from Stakeholders is a crucial activity in Scrum. Working with stakeholders frequently ensures the team to focus on the right things to build. Although it is required to have Stakeholders at Sprint Review, they can also engage with the Scrum Team during Product Backlog Refinement, Sprint Planning or during the Sprint if the Scrum Team requires it.
65) A Project Manager has raised concerns about a Scrum Team's productivity and progress it has made towards the objectives. He needs a report about the "Status" of the project. Which is the best way to respond to the Project Managers concerns? A. Ask the Scrum Master to provide a report to the Project Manager. B. Scrum does not support Project Managers as there are no accountability in Scrum such as a Project Manager. C. Share the Product Backlog and Sprint Backlog details with the Project Manager. D. Share the last stakeholder report with the Project Manager.	**Correct Answer: C** One of the key pillars that support the empirical process control is Transparency. Transparency will help manage stakeholder expectations and allow the teams to effectively adapt if and when needed. The Product Backlog and Sprint Backlog should be managed, transparent and exposed to all the needed stakeholders.
66) The Agile Manifesto recommends responding to change over following a plan. A. True B. False	**Correct answer: A** **The Agile Manifesto recommends Responding to change over following a plan.** This value reminds teams within an organization that one still need to plan, but also needs to acknowledge that initial plans are made when less was known about the project (at the beginning) and these plans will need to be updated as the work progresses.

67) Velocity measures: A. The value of the work done by the Team in a Sprint. B. The amount of work done by Team in a Sprint. C. The coding speed of the developers. D. None of the above.	**Correct Answer: B** Velocity tells you only how many units of work were completed, not whether that work was valuable. Instead of focusing on productivity, look at the business value that the team is delivering. To improve their ability to deliver business value, focus on removing impediments.
68) A company is in the beginning stages of adapting the Scrum Framework. Three Scrum teams need to be formed. The Scrum Master should spread the team members across the teams so that they can maintain high utilization of resources, be able to respond quickly and remain productive when impediments occur. A. True B. False	**Correct Answer: B** Spreading people across multiple teams virtually guarantees that the teams will increase the amount of time they spend waiting while a team member is off doing something else. Utilization of resources (people) should not be the objective; the objective should be delivering value. To improve throughput and speed delivery, dedicate people to a single team.
69) In a Team Retrospective meeting, Developers in the Scrum team are complaining about the re-work they have to do because of the biweekly Sprint Review sessions. The Sprint Review causes around 28% of the code to be rewritten. The Scrum Master explains to the team that re-work, when it results from feedback given by customers or stakeholders, is both expected and beneficial. A. True B. False	**Correct Answer: A** Acknowledgment that organizations and teams cannot predict every possible outcome or desire when working with complex products is a core requirement of adopting an Agile approach. The adoption of Scrum forces teams to inspect and adapt at frequent intervals providing opportunity to correct course before veering too far in a direction that may not deliver the value intended.
70) You've been asked to recommend how a team should transition to using agile. How would you reply? A. Try out some agile structures and practices first to see if they are helpful in your situation. B. Hire the best Scrum Master you can afford and make that person accountable for the transition. C. Identify a successful agile team and copy what they are doing. D. Learn agile values and principles. Use them to guide which practices to adopt in your situation.	**Correct answer: D** We need to first understand and integrate the mind set behind agile practices before we can use them effectively. Therefore, the best way to transition using agile is to learn agile values and principles and use them to guide which agile practices to adopt in your situation.

71) The risk of delivering the wrong product to your customer increases the longer you wait to receive feedback about that product. Agile product delivery aims to deliver a working product to the customer, early and in smaller increments, allowing teams to correct course as needed. A. True B. False	**Answer: A** Agile product delivery approaches help a team manage risk more effectively than a traditional approach. In addition, delivering working product on frequent intervals helps a team to manage and reduce technical risk.
72) A company is facing issues with its releases. The Release dates are always delayed by a few months due to the bugs found. These bugs are always discovered during the last few months of the release. To improve the product's time to market, the team should: A. Reduce the number of features. B. Commit team members to only one team, at a time. C. Co-locate team members. D. All of the above.	**Answer: D** All of these practices will contribute to delivering a product to market faster. Reducing features in a release shortens the effort and complexity of a release (thus reducing bugs), committing team members to only one team at a time, and collocating them improves the ability of the team to focus, and continuous integration practices reduce manual effort and improve consistency.
73) The Teams at the Toyota factory have been implementing Scrum for two decades. They have now mastered and implemented Scrum perfectly. Since they have mastered Scrum, they no longer need Managers. A. True B. False	**Correct Answer: B** When applied correctly many leadership responsibilities move to the roles in the Scrum Team. This might lead to a lower demand for the number of managers. Experience teaches that the role of the manager is to create and maintain an environment where Scrum teams can become and stay successful.

74) A client is concerned with the security of an existing Product. The Product seems to have the functionalities asked for and the team is successfully able to demo the same during the Sprint Reviews. However, there are some minor security gaps which are seen every now and then. What should one do next? A. Create special test documentation for the client. B. Ask the client to do acceptance and security testing before accepting the Product. C. Improve work processes and adapt new Definition of Done during Sprint Retrospective.	**Correct answer: C** The Scrum Team plans ways to increase product quality by improving work processes or adapting the definition of "Done", if appropriate and not in conflict with product or organizational standards". Thus, it would be best to wait for the Sprint Retrospective and improve the terms of quality in the Definition of "Done" for the product.
75) During the 4th Sprint Review, the stakeholders are upset because the product being built is not what they expected and will incur additional costs and time. What may have led to this? (Choose all that apply) A. The Scrum Master must have not sent the Daily, Monthly or Weekly Reports to the Stakeholders. B. The Scrum Master must not have ensured that the project is transparent. C. The Product Owner must have not made the stakeholders aware of project progress. D. The stakeholders may not be attending the Sprint Reviews.	**Correct answer: B, C, D** Scrum requires significant aspects of the process to be visible to those responsible for the outcome. This includes transparency with internal and external stakeholders.
76) Whose responsibility is it to create an environment where agility is supported and also help remove impediments to delivering "done" products? A. Agile Leader B. Product Owners C. Developers D. Project Managers E. Scrum Master	**Correct Answer: A** Agile leaders are primarily serving leaders who help their teams improve by supporting good agile working practices and, most importantly, interceding on their behalf when they need help to remove impediments. Shipping/Delivering a valuable product should be the metric used to measure success.

77) What would be the main benefits of self-organization? A. Increase Compliance, Self-Accountability, Commitment. B. Increase Compliance, Self-Accountability, output. C. Increase Compliance, accuracy of estimates, Commitment. D. Increase Creativity, Self-Accountability, Commitment.	**Correct Answer: D** The preferred leadership style in Scrum is "servant leadership", which emphasizes achieving results by focusing on the needs of the Scrum Team. Some of the benefits of Self-organization are: • Team buy-in and shared ownership • Motivation, which leads to an enhanced performance level of the team • Innovative and Creative environment conducive to growth • Increased Self Accountability, & Commitment to achieving the goals of the Scrum Team.
78) Having a Product Owner and Scrum Master in a Scrum Team is mandatory. A. False. A Scrum Master is not needed. B. True. Each Scrum Master and Product Owner should work full time with the Scrum Team. C. True. Their participation and availability will impact the outcome of the Product. D. False. Project Manager can take over the Scrum Masters role.	**Correct Answer: C** A Product Owner or Scrum Master can be dedicated to one team OR participate as a member on more than one team. How much time they spend with each team will directly impact effectiveness of the team.
79) In an existing organization, the head of product development has asked managers to compare the Scrum Teams. The head of product wants to identify the best agile teams so that they can reward them with additional bonus. Which of the following statements is true? A. Comparing performance between teams results to unhealthy team behavior. B. Standardize the use of story points across teams in order to extract performance based on completed Story Points. C. Look at Velocity and Technical debt to Judge the best team. D. Team with the highest velocity is the best team.	**Correct Answer: A** An important responsibility of an organization is to support and provide an environment that maximizes the effectiveness of each team rather than competing against each other. Our highest priority is to satisfy the customer through early and continuous delivery of valuable software. Comparing performance between teams typically results to unhealthy team behavior.

80) An organization has just started implementing Scrum. 11 Scrum Masters have been hired to make sure that the existing work continues while implementing the new Scrum framework. To make the transition successful, should the Scrum Masters shield Scrum Teams from change and uncertainty created by those who do not yet understand Agile yet? A. True B. False	**Correct Answer: B** Change and uncertainty are part of life. Instead of resisting these influences, an Agile Leader should serve teams into building the capability to deal with change and uncertainty. Agile Leaders should support the teams in collaborating with their environment, so that people share a common goal in the value chain.
81) As an agile leader, what would be your highest priority? A. Resolving conflicts and disagreements B. Keeping the team members healthy. C. Making sure the team members understand what the project is trying to accomplish D. Controlling the team's performance	**Correct answer: C** When faced with a tricky question, try to rule out the incorrect answers first. "Keeping the team members healthy" wouldn't be the leader's responsibility. "Resolving conflicts and disagreements" and controlling the team's performance" are done by an agile leader as needed, but are they really the leader's HIGHEST priority? Probably not. (Also, the term "controlling" implies a command-and-control approach rather than servant leadership.) That leaves "making sure the team members understand what the project is trying to accomplish" If you think about it, this is simply another way of stating one of the primary duties of a servant leader, to "communicate and re-communicate the project vision." So, this is the correct answer.

82) Developers in a Scrum Team are requesting to extend the Sprint by an extra 5 days in order to complete the Product Backlog items in the Sprint Backlog. They are worried that management will be upset if they are not able to finish all of the items before the end of the Sprint. As a Product Owner, what should you do?

A. Remind the Developers, that once they have selected Product Backlog items in the Sprint Backlog, they have to complete it.
B. Ask the Developers to work over the weekend to complete the work.
C. Do not extend the Sprint. Work with the stakeholders and explain the reasons for the delay. Transparency and Openness are important in an empirical Process.
D. Its ok to extend the Sprint. The Scrum team can self-manage and have the freedom to work and deliver as needed.

Correct Answer: C

Time-boxes helps everyone focus on the same problem at the same time and encourages the people who are closest to the problem to create the best possible result in the time allotted, give the current context. The Sprint Backlog is a forecast of functionality that will be developed during the Sprint if completed would achieve the Sprint Goal. If Developers in the Scrum team determine that they have too much or too little work, they may renegotiate the selected Product Backlog items with the Product Owner in order to produce a Valuable Increment and achieve the Sprint Goal.

83) A Teams Definition of "Done" requires creating or updating technical documentation in order to maintain the product and/or features in the future. The team's technical writer will be on vacation during the Sprint. What should the team do? A. Scrum Master should update the documentation. B. Developers in the Scrum Team should update the documentation. C. Product Owner should update the documentation. D. Wait for the Technical Writers to return.	**Correct Answer: B** All Product Backlog items selected for the Sprint are owned by the Scrum Team as a whole. Although individual members may work on specific tasks, the Scrum Team is still accountable for doing the work to deliver a valuable Increment.
84) You are Agile Leader responsible for developing the product. A sales executive comes to the Product Owner (who reports to you) requesting for a specific feature to be added to the product in order to sign a deal with one of her customers. The Product Owner understands the need but believes that there are more valuable items on the Product Backlog that will lead to more long-term value to the business. Disappointed, the sales executive comes to you asking you to intervene. As the manager of the development department, how do you respond? A. Ask the Product Owner to implement the feature B. Work directly with the Developers to accommodate the specific features. C. Negotiate with the Product Owner to see which Product Backlog items can be removed to add this item. D. Support the Product Owners decision to focus on the long-term needs.	**Correct Answer: D** For the Product Owner to succeed, the entire organization must respect his or her decisions. The Product Owner is responsible for maximizing the value of the product resulting from the work of the Developers.

85) You are an Agile manager at an organization that develops and provides products and services for customers. One of the stakeholders feels that the Scrum Team, developing the product, lacks the domain expertise and thus will not be able to meet expectations. What do you do? A. Hire more domain experts and add them as members of the Scrum Team. B. Have the Stakeholder discuss his concerns with the Scrum Master and leave the final actions to the Scrum Team. C. Work with other Scrum Teams to help balance the expertise needed. D. Hire temporary consultants and add them to the team so they can fill up the gap in expertise.	**Correct Answer: B** Having the Stakeholder discuss directly with the team is more efficient and effective than going through a manager. The team can then address the concerns and decide on the best actions. As a manager in an agile environment, support the team on removing impediments that would hinder the team's progress.
86) When using an Agile approach, it is both expected and beneficial to receive feedback from customers or stakeholders that results in changes to the plan. A. True B. False	**Correct Answer: A** In adopting an Agile approach, it is acknowledged that organizations and teams cannot predict every possible outcome or desire when working with complex products. The adoption of Scrum forces teams to inspect and adapt at frequent intervals to provide opportunities to adjust course before deviating too far in a direction that may not deliver the value that is intended. Thus it is both expected and beneficial to receive feedback from customers or stakeholders that results in changes to the plan.
87) A company is transforming from Waterfall (Traditional Process) to Agile Culture. Which practices can make it difficult? A. Individuals working in a specific functional team and doing work related to their expertise only. B. Measuring Individual performances more than team performances. C. Committing to a fixed schedule and scope. D. All of the Above.	**Correct Answer: D** The primary benefit of an Agile approach is enabling a team to inspect their results and adapt their plan by frequently delivering working product increments.

88) You are a Scrum Leader of an organization. The Scrum Master has come to you asking for advice concerning the lack of availability of their team's Product Owner. The Product Owner has other responsibilities outside of the Scrum Team and cannot dedicate all of his time to the team. The Scrum Master has discussed this issue with the Product Owner, but the team is still struggling to meet their goals without more guidance from the Product Owner. As a manager, what is the best way for you to help the Scrum Master? A. Hire another Product Owner. Ask the Product Owners to split the workload between them. Two Product Owners on the same Product will make it more efficient. B. Work with the Product Owner to make sure that his availability is high for the Scrum Team. C. Add additional Team members such as Project Managers and Business Analyst, who can take over the Product Owners responsibility. D. Ask the developers in the Scrum team to take over the Product Owners Job.	**Correct Answer: B** The value delivered by the Developers in the Scrum Team is affected by the Product Owner's participation and availability. Replacing the PO or delegating his responsibilities may not fix the root cause.
89) What does the Customer Usage Index indicate? (Choose all that applies). A. Customer Usage Index is an index which shows the number of customers and their UX usage. The index can be further broken down by Scrum Team. B. Customer Usage Index is a measurement of usage, by feature, to help infer the degree to which customers find the product useful. C. Customer Usage Index is a measurement of usage, by feature, to help infer whether actual usage meets expectations on how long users should be taking to use that feature. D. All of the above.	**Correct Answer: B, C** Customer Usage Index is a measurement of usage, by feature, to help infer 3) The degree to which customers find the product useful. 4) Whether actual usage meets expectations on how long users should be taking to use that feature.

90) Which of the below activities will help the Scrum team deliver an Increment by the end of the Sprint? (Choose three) A. Synchronizing release schedules across all the Teams. B. Product Backlog Refinement. C. Automating the delivery process. D. Reducing dependencies between teams.	**Correct Answer: B, C, D** Scrum Teams should release early and often, regardless of whether their releases are synchronized or not. Synchronizing release schedules does not guarantee improved productivity. Decreasing dependencies between teams, automating the delivery pipeline, and a healthy Product Backlog will improve autonomy and localized decision making.
91) Synchronizing release schedules across multiple teams will: A. Increase the frequency of delivery. B. Increase productivity. C. Reduce dependency. D. Help deliver the increment on time. E. None of the above.	**Correct Answer: E** Synchronizing release schedules does not guarantee improved productivity. Decreasing dependencies between teams will improve autonomy and localized decision making.
92) Your organization has 4 Scrum Teams. Over the past several Sprints it has come to your observation that one of the teams is only averaging 10-15 story points per Sprint whereas the other teams are averaging 25-30 story points. Both the Teams have the same number of Members. Is this something to be worried about? A. No. The number of Team Members assigned to a Team keep changing and so the velocity will keep changing. B. No. Velocity of a team can change based on the Product Backlog items considered in a Sprint. Velocity also depends upon the way stories are sized. C. Yes. More resources should be hired to get the average of the teams to be around 25-30. D. Yes. The team's individual resources and their performances should be looked at and improved.	**Correct Answer: B** Velocity is a localized measurement and helps the team forecast what they believe they can achieve in the Sprint rather than its performance. Having a high or low velocity does not reflect in the value of the work being done.

93) The amount of time from when an idea is proposed, or a hypothesis is formed until a customer can benefit from that idea is called: A. Development Time. B. Implementation Time. C. Lead Time. D. Time to Learn.	**Correct Answer: C** Lead time is the amount of time from when an idea is proposed, or a hypothesis is formed until a customer can benefit from that idea. This measure may vary based on customer and product. It is a contributing factor for customer satisfaction. Lead Time is a measure of the time it takes to go from having an idea to the point where a customer experiences the benefit of that idea, and customer acceptance feedback has been gathered. This means that Lead Time is a way to measure business agility. Delivering working software frequently and satisfying the customer through early and continuous delivery helps maximize opportunity for the business to deliver value.
94) Currently, the development departments in your organization are component based. I.e. they are organized by function (Example: design, front-end, back-end, database, and testing). You are a Project Manager. What would you consider when moving away from component teams towards feature teams? A. You cannot begin Scrum without have having feature teams. All Feature teams should have an equal number of team members, and should follow separate Daily Scrum, Sprint Reviews etc. B. Moving from component teams to feature teams could reduce productivity in the initial stages.	**Correct Answer: B** The initial phase of forming a new team could cause short-term disruption as they need time to discover how to best work together. Because all the skills and competencies are inside the team the communication overhead is reduced. Having an environment that supports the Scrum values reduces complexity. **Feature team is a long-lived, cross-functional, cross-component team that completes many end-to-end customer features. A component team is a team whose primary area of concern is restricted to a specific component.**
95) The total time needed to sketch an idea or improvement, build it, deliver it to users, and learn from their usage is called: A. Development Time. B. Implementation Time. C. Lead Time. D. Time to Learn.	**Correct Answer: D** Time to Learn is total time needed to sketch an idea or improvement, build it, deliver it to users, and learn from their usage.

| 96) The primary benefit of an Agile approach is to enable a team to inspect and adapt the results before delivering a working product.

A. True
B. False | **Correct Answer: A**

Complex products require experimentation as the cause and effect can only be deduced in retrospect. There's no singular method that leads to guaranteed success when addressing complex adaptive problems. Next steps can be best decided when the results of earlier experiments are determined. |

97) Which of the following are true statements about the Product Owner? The Product is: (Select all that Apply)

A. **The Visionary**: The Product Owner clearly communicates the product vision, strategy, business goals and objectives with all the relevant parties. A visionary Product Owner tends to focus on the future, on changing the status quo and helping people to see what could be, instead of what is.

B. **The Collaborator**: The Product Owner is involved with closely working together with the various stakeholders and Developers. A collaborative Product Owner tends to support people in their own discovery process, whether it's about defining goals, clarifying PBIs or analyzing customer needs.

C. **The Customer Representative**: The Product Owner is focused on helping others (Dev. Team or others) to understand what customers need, what their challenges are, what pains and gains they have. Acting from this stance, the Product Owner tends to explain how our work affects customers, users and business processes.

D. **The Decision Maker**: The Product Owner helps the stakeholders and Scrum Team to keep time-to-market short, by keeping decision making time short. All sorts of decisions have to made on a daily basis. Some can be delegated to the Scrum Team or stakeholders, some the Product Owner has to take him-/herself.

E. All of the Above.

Correct Answer: E

The preferred Stances are:

1. **The Visionary**: The Product Owner clearly communicates the product vision, strategy, business goals and objectives with all the relevant parties. A visionary Product Owner tends to focus on the future, on changing the status quo and helping people to see what could be, instead of what is.

2. **The Collaborator**: The Product Owner is involved with closely working together with the various stakeholders and Developers. A collaborative Product Owner tends to support people in their own discovery process, whether it's about defining goals, clarifying PBIs or analyzing customer needs.

3. **The Customer Representative**: The Product Owner is focused on helping others (Dev. Team or others) to understand what customers need, what their challenges are, what pains and gains they have. Acting from this stance, the Product Owner tends to explain how our work affects customers, users and business processes.

4. **The Decision Maker**: The Product Owner helps the stakeholders and Scrum Team to keep time-to-market short, by keeping decision making time short. All sorts of decisions have to made on a daily basis. Some can be delegated to the Scrum Team or stakeholders, some the Product Owner has to take him-/herself.

5. **The Experimenter**: The Product Owner helps by stating hypothesis, explaining what we know AND what we don't know, by seeing a lot of the work we do as experiments, rather than 'set-in-stone' work packages. The Experimenter understands the need of trying out new things, exploring, innovating and therefore; experimenting.

6. **The Influencer**: The Product Owner helps the stakeholders to align around the product vision, strategy, goals and objectives. Influencing the stakeholders and Scrum Team is a hard but very important job. The Influencer uses effective

---

	communication, negotiation and influencing skills to get people to join the cause.
98) A Scrum Team which has remote team members, typically spends time before the Daily Scrum to go through architectural designs, code designs, code reviews, high priorities bugs, concerns etc. How should the Scrum Master handle this situation? A. Ask the Scrum Team to discuss everything needed in the Daily meetings. Meetings outside the Scrum Events are not allowed. They are a waste of time. B. Allow the Developers to self-manage and decide for themselves. C. Inform the Management about such meetings. Try and reduce such meetings as much as possible so the Scrum team can get more time to develop. D. Get involved and start facilitating such meetings.	**Correct Answer: B** As members of a self-organized Scrum team, they will decide for themselves how to best manage communication between team members. The Scrum Master will only act if requested or if he/she observes that there is a potential problem.
99) Sid is a new Product Owner on a newly formed Scrum Team. Sid has projected a product release date based on an estimated velocity of 40 completed points per Sprint. After the first 3 Sprints, the team has determined that their maximum velocity is 25 points and they are unable to create a shippable increment by the projected release date. What is the best way for the team to proceed? A. Increase the number of work hours to make sure that the velocity goes up from 25 to 40. B. Add more resources to make sure that the velocity goes up from 25 to 40. C. Ask the Scrum Master to coach the developers and Product Owner so such estimating issues don't happen again. D. Inform Sid that the Projected completion date is not correct. Sid will need to calculate a new Projected date based on the velocity changes.	**Correct Answer: D** Velocity is a measure of the amount of work a Team can tackle during a single Sprint and is the key metric in Scrum. Velocity is calculated at the end of the Sprint by totaling the Points for all fully completed User Stories. Team velocity has nothing to do when it comes to which items are selected in the Sprint Backlog. Velocity of the team is based on the empirical data. Note that in this case the team are new. Also based on the work done in each Sprint, the velocity is more like to vary each Sprint. The Product Owner should explain to the stakeholders the new release dates along with the reasons of delay.

100) John (a Developer) has notified the Scrum Master of a potential risk which could delay the release of the Product. What action should the Scrum Master take? A. Inform the Management to give them a heads up. B. Work with the entire Scrum Team, discuss the risk and possible solutions. C. Add the risk as a Product Backlog item in the current Sprint Backlog so that its resolved. D. Wait for the Sprint Review and Sprint Retrospective meetings to bring up this issue.	**Correct Answer: B** It is best to coach the Developers to collaborate on issues regardless of severity. They may consult the Scrum Master of Product Owner if needed. Impediments encountered during the release may cause delays. Being transparent about it and working together with the Scrum Team is the key to success.
101) A Product Owner approaches a Scrum Master for guidance on Product Backlog item Story Points. What guideline should the Scrum Master provide if the Product Owner asks how estimations should be made in Scrum? (Choose only one answer) A. Estimates should always be made in story points. B. Product Owner should provide the initial estimates based on his / her experience and the Developers can correct them if needed. C. The Development Lead will provide the estimates. D. Developers / People doing the work are responsible for the estimates.	**Correct Answer: D** The people who will perform the work make the final estimates.
102) Which of the following Statement is true? A. Agile Leaders understand the value of the Product more than anyone else. B. All Agile Projects have certain level of unpredictability and unexpected things can occur. The best approach is to accept the changes and adapt. C. If an Agile Project is not predictable, then it's not planned enough. D. A good Agile Leader always gets all the work completed on time.	**Correct Answer: B** Complex contexts are often unpredictable, and the best approach here is to "Probe – Sense – Respond." Rather than trying to control the situation or insisting on a plan of action, it's often best to be patient, look for patterns, and encourage a solution to emerge.

103) During the 8th Sprint, Developers of a Scrum Team realize that they have not completed designing the entire software architecture yet. What is the most appropriate action for the Scrum Master to take? A. Stop the ongoing Sprint and get the architecture complete first. B. Consider the architecture as technical debt and only focus on the functionality which needs to be build. C. Coach the team that the architecture will be build overtime. D. The Scrum Master should ask the Developers to resolve this issue themselves.	**Correct Answer: C** The Applications overall architecture **is not designed upfront**, as the actual implementation of it emerges. The emergence of the Architecture is based on guidelines and agreed principles. Functionality and architecture in a software product go hand in hand / are built in parallel.
104) Developers in the Scrum Team wants to move the Sprint Retrospective to every other Sprint instead of every Sprint. What is the most appropriate action for the Scrum Master to take? A. The Scrum Master should support the decision made by the developers in the Scrum Team who are self – organizing B. The Scrum Master should raise this as an Impediment. C. The Scrum Master should try to understand why the Scrum Team is trying to move the Sprint Retrospectives. The Scrum Master should work with the team to improve the outcomes of the meeting. D. The Scrum Master should hire development leads to guide the process better.	**Correct Answer: C** Scrum recommends **using all the Scrum components** and rules (not just the ones which suit the project). **Example 1**: A Team cannot just decide that Sprint Retrospective Meeting would not be implemented since it is not needed. **Example 2:** Developers cannot just choose to skip the Daily Scrum Meetings because they might be busy with writing code or developing the Product.
105) What are the downsides of having multiple Product Owners for the Same Product? A. With multiple Product Owners on the same product, the Product Owners focus will be on detailed stories instead of value creation. B. With multiple Product owners on the same Product, there will be lack of domain expertise as the domain knowledge will be concentrated with the Product Owners. C. Multiple Product Owners bring unclear responsibility and ownership.	**Correct Answer: E** Downsides of having multiple Product Owners: 1. With multiple Product Owners, the Product Owners become the people that spell out all the detailed specs (user stories). This setup leads to Product Owner focusing on story readiness, negotiating the level of story detail instead of focusing on value creation. This is a well-known pattern known as the "contract negotiation game". Note : A Product Owner can write the stories as needed, however his / her focus should be on value creation at all times.

D. Multiple Product Owners stimulates part-time jobs, by adding the Product Owners work to someone's existing workload. E. All of the Above.	2. Another effect of multiple Product Owners is the growing absence of domain expertise in the teams. Domain knowledge is concentrated in the Product Owners, which makes the team stick to executing tasks (opposed to solving customer problem), which re-enforces the need for more Product Owners. Multiple Product Owner per team setup reduces opportunities for learning and self-organization. 3. Multiple Product Owners bring unclear responsibility and ownership. One Product Owner means that one person is accountable for the ROI on the product under development. With multiple Product Owners, accountability, responsibility and ownership are oblique. 4. Multiple Product Owners stimulate part-time jobs, by adding the Product Owners work to someone's existing workload. This introduces a conflict of interest. With multiple people working part-time on one product the situation does not get any better. Volunteers come to the rescue, thinking "if nobody takes care of this, then I will" and change backlog item priority, add items or even create their own backlog, creating more complexity.
106) How can the Scrum Master ensure communication between the Product Owner and Developers within the same Scrum Team? A. Ask the Developers to copy the Scrum Master on all important emails. B. Ask the Developers to copy the Product Owner on all the communication. C. Facilitate discussions in the needed meetings. D. Teach the Product Owner to use the technical terms.	**Correct Answer: C** One of the primary responsibilities of a Scrum Master is the ability to facilitate regardless of the context or setting. The other options can work as a short-term solution for selected issues however they are not long term solutions. Keeping the Scrum Team and Product Owner copied on all email would not be a sustainable option.

107) A Scrum Master, besides being the leader who impacts the effectiveness of the Scrum Team, also plays a role of : (Choose all that Apply). A. **An Impediment Remover** that helps resolve issues that are blocking the team's progress, considering the self-organizing capabilities of the Scrum Team. B. **A Facilitator** that sets the stage and provides clear boundaries in which the team can collaborate. This includes facilitation of the Scrum events to ensure they'll achieve the desired outcome and - most importantly - that the empirical process is optimized. C. **A Coach** that helps individuals and groups to continuously improve in how they deliver valuable outcomes as a team or as an organization; D. **A Teacher** that ensures that Scrum and relevant events, techniques are well-understood and enacted. E. All of the Above.	**Correct Answer: E** 1. **An Impediment Remover** that helps resolve issues that are blocking the team's progress, considering the self-organizing capabilities of the Scrum Team; 2. **A Facilitator** that sets the stage and provides clear boundaries in which the team can collaborate. This includes facilitation of the Scrum events to ensure they'll achieve the desired outcome and - most importantly - that the empirical process is optimized; 3. **A Coach** that helps individuals and groups to continuously improve in how they deliver valuable outcomes as a team or as an organization; 4. **A Teacher** that ensures that Scrum and relevant techniques are well-understood and enacted; 5. **A Servant Leader** that creates environments where teams can work effectively with stakeholders to create valuable outcomes; 6. **A Manager** that is responsible for managing (true) impediments, eliminating waste, managing the process, managing the team's health, managing the boundaries of self-organization, and managing the culture; 7. **A Change Agent** that helps to enable a culture in which Scrum Teams can flourish - on every level of the organization. 8. **A Mentor** that transfers agile knowledge and experience to the team.
108) As a Scrum Master, you observe that the Product Owner is not collaborating with the Developers effectively. What actions would you take? A. Hire another Product Owner. B. Act as a liaison between the Scrum Master and the Product Owner. C. Ask the Product Owner to copy you on all communication going forward so you can facilitate. D. Find a Proxy Product Owner E. Coach the Product Owner.	**Correct Answer: E** A Scrum Master coaches those inside and outside the team on the values of Scrum and incremental delivery. A Scrum Master also would make sure that the communications amongst the team members are effective.

109) One of the Scrum teams has requested hiring additional team members in order to improve their ability to deliver. As the department's manager, what is your best response? A. Let the Scrum Team know what the budget is. Let the Scrum Team find, interview and hire the new Team member. They can work with the hiring department, if they need more help. B. The HR department should gather requirements of the type of resources needed. You should conduct the interview and hire an appropriate candidate. C. You should hire the New Team Member for the team. You can call consultants outside the team to do the work. D. None of the above.	**Correct Answer: A** Self-organized teams choose how best to accomplish their work, rather than being directed by others outside the team. As a leader, provide the team with guidelines and assistance. Allow the team members to decide who would best fit their current team within the provided guidelines and provide the support needed.
110) A new Organization has 10 Scrum Teams working on the same product. You are the Scrum Master. You would need to make sure: (Choose all that Apply). A. Each Team has its own unique Product Owner. B. There is only one Product Owner across all the teams as only one Product Owner per Product is recommended. C. There is only one Product Backlog. D. All 10 teams are working through the same Sprint Backlog.	**Correct Answer: B, C** **Only One Product Backlog and Only One Product Owner can exist for** a Product (Regular Scrum framework or in Nexus). Multiple Scrum Teams work on the Same Product Backlog. Different Scrum Teams working on the same Product (in Nexus) can: • Have different Sprint Lengths. • Have different Scrum Masters. • Have only one Product Owner. • Have only one Product Backlog.
111) What are the reasons for keeping the same Scrum Team together for a long time? (Choose all that Apply): A. Efficient collaboration B. Consistent forecasting C. Improving focus D. Increased knowledge sharing E. High Utilization	**Correct Answer: A, B, C, D** High utilization is not always a result when teams are kept together. Better reasons for keeping a team together would be improving collaboration, consistent forecasting, improving focus, and increased knowledge sharing.

112) Which metric expresses the organization's ability to quickly deliver new capabilities, services, or products? A. Current Value B. Unrealized Value C. Time to Market D. Lead Time	**Correct Answer: C** Time-to-Market (T2M) expresses the organization's ability to quickly deliver new capabilities, services, or products
113) You are an Agile Leader in an organization. For years you have been working directly with a Scrum Team. The Scrum Master recently reaches out to you. He wants to act as a liaison between you and the Scrum Team. All the communication going forward needs to be channeled through him. What would you do? A. Tell him its fine. There might be situations where you would need to talk to the team directly to clear their doubts. B. Say No and continue to work with the team directly. You are responsible for what the team delivers.	**Correct Answer: A** The Scrum Master is a leader for the Scrum Team. The Scrum Master helps those outside the Scrum Team understand which of their interactions with the Scrum Team are helpful and which aren't. The Scrum Master helps everyone change these interactions to maximize the value created by the Scrum Team.
114) Benefits of having a cross-functional Team are: A. Team Members step outside their comfort zone to do their best. B. Less dependency on Individual Members. C. Reduces external dependencies. D. Increases the opportunity of delivering value to the users. E. Team Members will develop and grow their individual skills (Learning from others etc.) F. All of the Above.	**Correct Answer: F** Benefits of having a Cross Functional Team are: 1) Team Members step outside their comfort zone to do their best. 2) Less dependency on Individual Members. 3) Reduces external dependencies. 4) Increases the opportunity of delivering value to the users. 5) Team Members will develop and grow their individual skills (Learning from others etc.)

115) A performance review process rewards individual team members based on the measure of their annual performance. As a result of this, some team members are receiving larger bonuses than others. A few team members are unhappy as they feel that the way bonuses are currently distributed is unfair as everyone contributes to their team's overall success. As their manager, what would be the best approach? A. Expose everyone performance and ratings on a notice board. Explain how and why the bonuses were distributed. Transparency is very essential in Scrum. B. Let the Scrum Team suggest how to best distribute the bonuses and rewards.	**Correct Answer: B** Self-organized teams choose how best to accomplish their work and self-manages. They would know how best to distribute the bonuses and rewards and allow them to take ownership of the decision.
116) You're a Product Owner who has just been hired. During a meeting (conducted to gather requirements) you observe that the stakeholders are unable to come to an agreement on the primary objective of a few requirements. They are also unsure of the final list of the functionalities needed from the product. As a Product Owner, what should you do? A. Inform the stakeholders that the development would not start till they all agree on the objectives and functionalities of the product. B. Ask the Developers to work on technical debt and automation till the stakeholders sign off on the requirements. C. Gather Market Insights, start building the product iterative and incrementally, delivering selective elements of the Product. Keep sharing the requirements with the Stakeholders. D. All of the above.	**Correct Answer: C** Complex products require experimentation as the cause and effect can only be deduced in retrospect. There's no singular method that leads to guaranteed success. The outcomes of earlier experiments play a crucial role in making product decisions and deciding on the direction. Short feedback loops from having an idea to gathering user feedback will improve business agility. Ultimately, the market response will define the value of the work being done.

117) You are an Agile Leader in an organization. Members from other Scrum Teams continuously interrupt your teams by requesting for customer support on products they have worked on / completed in the past. The Scrum Master has reached out to you. What is the best approach for the team to address the unplanned work and interruptions? (Choose two) A. Leave it to the Scrum Team. They should be able to manage such issue themselves. B. Work with your Scrum Team to transfer the needed knowledge to another team who can support the request and issues. C. Inform the Scrum Master and ask him to raise this as an Impediment. Work with the entire Scrum Team to come up with different solutions and help them implement the same. D. Increase the Sprint Length. This will create more buffer and time which will allow the Scrum team to resolve such issues. E. Dedicate a few days within the Sprint for such support.	**Correct Answer: B, C** As a leader, one should support the teams by removing impediments that may hinder their progress. Help them maintain focus and empower other teams to resolve issues.

118) You are an Agile Leader. One of the Scrum Team requires a new environment. This environment would replicate the production environment and help the team perform security testing. Current company policy dictates that new environments are only available for actual production purposes and not for any testing. Security testing is the last stage before making the completed work shippable. Which would be the best two strategies to manage such a situation? A. As a Leader you are responsible for supporting the team in what they need. You should work with the senior Management and get the environment approved. B. The Team should do the security testing in their existing development environment trying to replicate Production environment as much as possible. Work with the Scrum team to make sure that they don't face any issues upfront. C. Add additional time at the end of the Sprint to focus on Security testing. This way an environment for security would not be needed. D. Ask the Developers to come up with different alternate solutions resolve this issue themselves. You as a Leader will make sure you support them as needed.	**Correct Answer: B, D** The team should try to find a way to work with the current limitations if an external solution is not possible. Help the team collaborate with other people to help come up with a solution. Adding additional time or budget takes focus away from solving the core problem which is creating potentially shippable increments.

119) You are a Scrum Master who has just joined a Scrum Team in an organization. One of the developers notify you that they will need full-time help of an external technical specialist in the upcoming two Sprints. What concerns should the Scrum Master take into account? A. The Team velocity will increase as the specialist will be added to the Team for the next two Sprints. B. The Team velocity will decrease as the specialist will be doing some work in the next two Sprints. External resources velocity is not considered in the Team velocity. C. The Team is not cross-functional enough to do the work themselves. A Scrum Team should be self-supporting. D. All of the above.	**Correct Answer: C** Scrum Teams should be Cross-functional teams that they should all the competencies needed to accomplish the work without depending on others outside the team.
120) Customer satisfaction should be measured: A. Every Day. B. At least Every Sprint Review. C. When issues arrive. D. Frequently.	**Correct Answer: D** Customer satisfaction should be measured frequent enough to ensure the team is building the right thing at the right time but not so frequent it hinders the team from the work.
121) Developers of a Scrum Team are having conversations about different technical approaches that would help them resolve a bug. The team members are not able to come to an agreement nor compromise on a solution. The Team approaches you as you are the team's manager. How would you recommend the team to proceed? A. Don't get involved as a Leader. The Scrum team is supposed to solve such issues themselves. B. Look at the different approaches and you select one. C. The Scrum Team should vote and select the approach accordingly.	**Correct Answer: D** Complex products require experimentation as the cause and effect can only be deduced in retrospect. There's no singular method that leads to guaranteed success. The outcomes of experimentation will validate the assumed value or benefit of the different approaches.

D. Ask the Developers to do a Spike. Based on the results they should be able to select an approach.	
122) Joseph Rogers is the director of the product development. Joseph needs to know how each product is doing periodically. What would be the best approach for understanding the current status of different products? A. All Product Owners should send a Status report to Joseph Rogers periodically. B. Joseph Rogers should work with every team. He should go through the Product Backlogs and Sprint Backlogs, to understand the status of the different Products. C. All Scrum Masters and Product Owners should send a Status report to Joseph Rogers end of every Sprint. D. Ask the Scrum Master of each Product to send a Weekly Report.	**Correct Answer: B** Agile teams are structured and empowered by the organization to organize and manage their own work. Self-organized teams are responsible for applying the most appropriate practices to provide transparency in order to optimize value, control risk, and manage expectations.
123) You are a Scrum Master in an organization. Developers in the Scrum Team are having a disagreement on a functionality and how it is going to be used by the system users. Developers are unable to come to an agreement on the requirement. Some Developers have questions on whether the functionality is necessary at all as there are other similar functionalities in the system. As a Scrum Master, which would be the best approach? A. Developers should understand the requirements from the Product Owner. You as a Scrum Master should not get involved. B. Developers should vote and decide. C. The functionality should be moved to the Next Sprint till a final decision is made. D. You should facilitate a meeting between the Product Owner and the Developers so that the requirements are clarified.	**Correct Answer: D** The Scrum Master is a leader for the Scrum Team. The Scrum Master helps members of the Scrum Team understand which of their interactions are helpful and which aren't. The Scrum Master helps everyone change these interactions to maximize the value created by the Scrum Team. The Scrum Master is responsible for helping everyone understand Scrum theory, practices, rules, and values. The Scrum Master is responsible for facilitating when needed and helping the team remove impediments blocking their progress.

124) You are an Agile leader. A customer has come to you requesting a new feature for a product your company is developing for them. This feature is however not a plan of original product plan. What would be your best approach?

A. Facilitate a meeting between the Product Owner and the customer. You want to make sure that the client is satisfied with the Product and the Product Owner has all the requirements from the clients, so he can maximum product value.
B. Tell the customer to submit a change request with all the details documented. The team will consider it if they have the bandwidth.
C. Ask the customer to directly deal with the Scrum Team.
D. Facilitate a meeting between the Developers and the customer. You as Leader can work on the pricing changes.

Correct Answer: A

The Product Owner is the sole person responsible for managing the Product Backlog to ensure the value of the product resulting from the work of the Developers is maximized. Connecting the Product Owner with the customer will help him/her make the best decision for the customer and his/her company.

125) You are a manager in an Agile organization. You need a way to measure how much business value each Scrum Team is producing. How do you go about measuring the value produced by each team?

A. Velocity of each team across time would show how much value they produced and will produce in the future.
B. Consult with the Product Owner of the teams. The Product Owners are responsible for maximizing the value of the Product. The increment produced each sprint is a good reflection of the value produced as well.
C. Consult with the Product Owner of the teams. They work with the most with the Developers.
D. Consult with the Scrum Master of each Scrum Team.

Correct Answer: B

The Product Owner is the sole person responsible for managing the Product Backlog to ensure the value of the product resulting from the work of the Developers is maximized. How this is done may vary widely across organizations, Scrum Teams, and individuals so directly consulting with them will provide the most accurate information on value produced and projected value that will be worked on.

126) How does a Scrum Team produce value for the organization? A. Team value reports created by the Scrum Master can show the value of each Scrum Team B. Teams with lowest technical debt have the highest value. C. Scrum Teams deliver high values by consistently delivering Products at the end of each sprint.	**Correct Answer: C** Each Sprint consist of 1. A goal of what is to be built 2. A design and flexible plan that will guide building it 3. The work done to build the increment 4. The resultant product increment
127) The primary benefit of an Agile approach is to make projects more predictable through execution in short increments. A. True B. False	**Correct Answer: A** One of the primary benefits of an Agile approach is to make projects more predictable through planning and executing in short increments.
128) The Agile Manifesto recommends that the highest priority is to satisfy the customer. If the Product owner need to build features of less or no value in the Product, that's fine as well, as longs as it provides value to the customers. A. True B. False .	**Correct Answer: B** The Agile Manifesto is based on 12 Agile Key Principles mentioned below: • **The highest priority is to satisfy the customer through early and continuous <u>delivery of valuable software.</u>** • Welcome changing requirements, even late in development. Agile processes harness change for the customer's competitive advantage. • Deliver working software frequently, from a couple of weeks to a couple of months, with a preference to the shorter timescale. • Business people and developers must work together daily throughout the project. • Build projects around motivated individuals. Give them the environment and support they need and trust them to get the job done. • The most efficient and effective method of conveying information to and within a Scrum team is face-to-face conversation.

	- Working software is the primary measure of progress.
	- Agile processes promote sustainable development. The sponsors, developers, and users should be able to maintain a constant pace indefinitely.
	- Continuous attention to technical excellence and good design enhances agility.
	- Simplicity--the art of maximizing the amount of work not done--is essential.
	- The best architectures, requirements, and designs emerge from self-organizing teams.
	- At regular intervals, the team reflects on how to become more effective, then tunes and adjusts its behavior accordingly.

129) A company has two products. Which of the following is an acceptable way of forming Scrum teams? Choose all that apply.
 	
A. There must be a single Product Owner for each product.
B. There can be a single Product Owner across two products however a Single Product cannot have more than one Product Owner.
C. There should be one Product Owner supported by a Junior Product Owner
D. There should be a Chief Product Owner and one Product Owner for each product
	Correct answers: A, B
	Only One Product Backlog and Only One Product Owner can exist for a Product (Regular Scrum framework or in Nexus). Multiple Scrum Teams work on the Same Product Backlog. Thus, the same Product Owner would participate in the Nexus Sprint Planning sessions and Team Specific Sprint Planning sessions, as needed. Different Scrum Teams working on the same Product (in Nexus) can:
	
	    • Have different Sprint Lengths.
	    • Have different Scrum Masters.
	    • Have only one Product Owner.
	    • Have only one Product Backlog.
	A Product owner can act as Product Owner for more than one Products however this is not recommended. Remember:
	A) For a given Product, there should be only one Product Owner. E.g. Charles and John both cannot be Product Owners for the same Product (Product XYZ) in an Organization. One Product can only have one Product Owner.
	B) The same person can be a Product Owner for more than one Products. This might not be recommended, however is still allowed in Scrum. For e.g. Charles can be a Product Owner for Product A and Product B, at the same time. Thus, Both A and B are true.

130) You work in a company as a Director of Product Management. A Scrum Team comes to you with a concern about the amount of work they have. They talk about the number of hours they have been spending to complete the work and meet the deadline. The Team requires five more resources in order to increase their capacity to get the work done on time. The need for the resource seems very compelling. As a part of the Product Management team you should: (Choose the best answer) A) Give the appropriate resources within the Scrum team budgetary boundaries. You should allow them to hire the needed five people. B) You should do the initial screening and pass along good candidates to the team, who conduct their own interviews and make the final decision. This will make sure that the Scrum team is not aware of the salaries. C) Let the Scrum team hire candidate however you make the final hiring decisions. D) Hire external consultants.	**Correct answers: A** Providing the proper guidelines will help promote self-management, creativity, and problem solving. The decisions on who and how to work together in order to deliver a valuable increment is best decided by the Scrum team and team members involved with doing the work.
131) An agile team leader in your organization comes to you for advice. He is having trouble getting the developers in the team to take ownership of the project. He keeps finding himself making decisions and directing their work. What do you advise him to do? (Select two best answers). A. At the stand-up meetings, assign a different person each day as the decision maker to get them all comfortable in the role. B. Implement an incentive plan and officially report any lack of participation to team members' functional managers. C. Meet them and work with the team to align everyone's expectations. Coach them if needed. D. Explain to them that agile teams self-select their work and tell them to get on with it. E. Help the team create a shared and compelling Product vision and Product Goals. F. Setup Bonus structures to motivate the team.	**Correct answer: C,E** In this situation, the team leader should assume a coaching role to help the team members get to the point where they are comfortable leading their own work. This will include meeting team members a half-step ahead, guaranteeing safety, partnering with their managers, and building positive regard. Assigning someone as a decisionmaker at stand-up meetings is incorrect since agile teams are consensus-driven, and decisions aren't made in stand-up meetings. Incentive plans can be useful, but what this team really needs is guidance, not rewards and punishments. Simply explaining that agile teams self-select their work isn't enough to get team members comfortable assuming more ownership of the project.

132) Charles manages the product delivery for 6 products in his organization. His manager has asked him to create a document which lays out the delivery plan for the next 2 years. The plan should have a list of features the Scrum Team will deliver. What is the best way to proceed?

A. Charles should use his past knowledge and create a rough plan. He can later negotiate its scope and implementation with the Scrum Team.

B. Charles should work with specialists from each team to build an estimated 2 year backlog that translate the same into charts.

C. Charles should work with the Product Owner(s) to analyze the priority or important of the PBI's items as of today. He should also analyze the current team's velocity, then use that data to build a probabilistic forecast that would show a picture of what could be achieved.

D. Charles should ask each Scrum Team to stop working on current backlog and make a plan based on the story points previously delivered.

Correct answer: C

Managers should not make a guess. They should work with the Scrum teams to understand:

1) The existing Product Backlog along with the priorities of the Product Backlog items.
2) The velocity of the Scrum team.

Based on the above, Managers should be able to make appropriate guesses. For example, if Team A has velocity of 40 per Sprint, then it should be able to deliver Items X and Z (20 points each) in the coming Sprint. Remember predicting items which can be complete in the future is always subject to change and should not be understood as a commitment.

Professional Scrum Master II Questions and Answers

Please go through these questions and check the answers you go along. The Scrum Assessments **online** (**https://www.scrum.org/open-assessments**) are the best way to judge where you stand. The Questions and Answers below will make sure you understand the concepts and help you help you prepare for the PSM II. Go through the answers regardless of you answering the questions right or wrong. Don't try to time yourself. Rather focus on understanding the answers and thus the concepts.

Question 1	Correct answers: A,C

Charles, the Scrum Master, works in a company which makes software's for video games. Each game is typically assigned a Scrum Team and is interactive with other games. Charles is informed by a Developer that they plan on not completing the integration testing for all of the work they have performed so far (as mentioned in the Definition of Done). They have discussed this with the Product Owner and decided to remove integration testing from the Definition of Done. Which two actions are the most appropriate for Charles to take? (Choose the best two answers.)
 	
   A. Ask the Developers and the Product Owner about the problem they are trying to solve by altering the Definition of Done and removing integration testing from it. Ask them if this decision will impact transparency and quality?
   B. Reject the decision as the maintainability of the product will be negatively impacted by modifying the Definition of Done.
   C. Ask the Developers and the Product Owner if they are still able to produce potentially valuable product increment by altering the Definition of Done.
   D. Accept the decision as a mutual agreement has been made between the Developer and the Product Owner.
	The Scrum Master is accountable for the Scrum Team's effectiveness. A Scum team's effectiveness can be measured by the quality of increment they produce. The Scrum Master facilitates conversations through open ended questions in order to help the team members make the best possible decisions according to what is known at the time. He/she should not approve or reject team decisions just because they are approved by the Developers and the Product Owner. The Scrum Master should also ensure that the team does not compromise on the quality of the increment which is being created.
	
	"Reject the decision as the long term maintainability of the product will be negatively impacted by modifying the Definition of Done" is not the right answer. Definition of done typically grows in time and helps improve the quality of the product rather than negatively impacting it.
	
	Simply accepting the decision as a mutual agreement has been made between the Developer and the Product Owner is not the correct approach either. Decisions made in the Scrum Team are not just facilitated by the Scrum Master. They are guided and driven by the Scrum Master.

Question 2	Correct answers: A,C
Sid works in a company's budget approval team. He has just joined the company and is new to Scrum. Sid wants to know more about how budgeting and financial forecasting is performed in Scrum. Which statements below are true? (Choose the best two answers.) A. A single development release may be funded by the sponsors. The release may contain several Sprints where every Sprint is producing a valuable increment. B. Budgeting in Scrum is not necessary. The only funding necessary is the operational costs of the Scrum Teams. C. Frequently inspect the outcomes of the delivered Sprint Increments to understand how much value is being produced per investment spent. D. Budgeting and Financial forecasting are managed outside Scrum.	Every agile organization must determine its own cadence for releasing features to its customers. Some choose to release every sprint. Others group the results of multiple sprints into one release. Still others release as soon as each feature is completed, a practice often referred to as continuous deployment or continuous delivery. Whichever cadence an organization chooses, most find some amount of longer-term, release planning to be useful. If the term release planning doesn't fit well with your organization's practices, replace the terminology with longer-term planning or milestone-driven planning. Whatever you choose to call it, release planning in Scrum targets a future state when important variables such as date, scope, and budget need to be balanced. The basic timing, participants, and process remain the same regardless of the name. Release planning (not an official Scrum Event) in Scrum happens every sprint, either as part of the sprint review or in the normal course of preparing for the subsequent sprint. Release planning in Scrum consists of several activities: 1. Review and update the release constraints of scope, date, and budget. 2. Product backlog grooming. 3. Review and update the minimum releasable features (MRFs) 4. Product a sprint map (optional). A release is a combination of multiple Sprints. Each Sprint is an opportunity to inspect the investment (money invested, time, effort, etc.) against the returned value (customer satisfaction, revenue, product value).The cost of developing, delivering, and sustaining products can impact product value is managed throughout the life of a product. Calculating costs on a fixed-date release can be done as follows : 1. Determine who is on the team. 2. Determine the sprint length, in hours or days.

	3. Multiply personnel cost (per hour or per day) by sprint length to get a cost per sprint. For a fixed-date release, multiply the number of sprints in the release by the cost per sprint.
Question 3 A company is building a healthcare software. At the end of the 15th Sprint, few of the sponsors are upset with the progress made by the Scrum Team. The current state of the product is not as expected and will require additional Sprints (and more budget) than originally anticipated at the start of the project. What factors may have led to this? (Choose the best two answers.) A. The Stakeholders have not been using the Daily Scrum effectively to track the Scrum Team's progress. B. The Product Owner has not been engaging with sponsors frequently enough and has not been aware of the overall progress of the project. C. The project plan proposed to the sponsors at the start of the project was not followed stringently. D. The scope changes may have not been tracked adequately and the change request process might not been followed properly. E. The sponsors haven't been using the Sprint Reviews to actively engage and inspect and evaluate progress.	**Correct answers: B, E** In order to manage Stakeholder's expectation, there must be open communication throughout the project cycle and work together. Scrum Events such as Sprint Reviews help continuous feedback from the client. This event maximizes alignment and expectations between the client and stakeholders, helps with making business decisions, and reduces risk. Scrum Teams can collaborate with the needed stakeholders' multiple times in the Sprint to help inspect and adopt, if needed. If not multiple times, then at least once during the Sprint Review. Also the Product Owner accountability: 1. Communicates regularly with the Stakeholders. 2. Creates new items in the Product Backlog. 3. Revises the priority of Product Backlog items 4. Work with the **Developers on Product Backlog refinement**. 5. Answers questions about the Product Backlog items and makes sure that everyone **has the right understanding** of Product Backlog items. 6. Checks the completed items with the Developers to ensure they are Done based on the "Definition of Done". 7. Collaborate with stakeholders, user communities, and subject matter experts.
Question 4 An organization wants to apply Scrum to build a new product and has hired Charles to be the Scrum Master for three new teams that will build the first release. The organization is new to Scrum and asks Charles for advice on how to start. Which two things should Charles first advise? (Choose the best three answers.) A. Hire three Product Owners, one for each Scrum Team. B. There should be one Product Backlog to represent all of the known work needed to	**Correct answers: B,D,F** Only One Product Backlog and Only One Product Owner can exist for a Product. This is true in Regular Scrum framework or in Nexus. Multiple Scrum Teams work on the Same Product Backlog. Different Scrum Teams working on the same Product (in Nexus) can: • Have different Sprint Lengths. • Have different Scrum Masters. • Have only one Product Owner. • Have only one Product Backlog. • Have a shared Definition of Done.

be done for the product. (including bugs, enhancements, technical debt etc)

C. Each Scrum Team should have its own Product Backlog with items only their team will be working on.

D. The Product should have one Product Owner to be accountable for maximizing the flow of value throughout the development process and provide transparency on the overall progress.

E. The three Scrum teams should have the exact same definition of done.

F. The three Scrum teams should have a shared definition of done.

When multiple teams are working on the same project, there can be more than one Definition of "Done" for all of them. Each team might be working on a different part of the product (e.g. desktop application, mobile application, web application), or simply have different styles of work. If there are multiple Scrum Teams working together on a product, they must mutually define and comply with a shared Definition of Done. They can add their own specific criteria on top of this Definition of "Done" Criteria.

When different teams are working on the same product, they must observe a common Definition of Done which qualifies for the integrated increment.

The Definition of Done observed by an individual team should reinforce and not contradict any shared Definition for a product increment. For example, a team may incorporate a shared DoD as a subset of their own.

Question 5	Correct answers: A

Question 5

A Product Owner of a company is technical savvy and often does the testing of the Product backlog items himself. He has started attending the Daily Scrum. Beyond the sprint's progress, he has asked for the Developers to report their individual work progress to him every day as he also is interested in tracking what every individual is working on. He wants a better hold on the number of hours they work every day. What is the best thing for the Scrum Master to do in this situation?

A. Coach the Product Owner and Developers on the purpose of Scrum events. Teach them the advantages and disadvantages of little and excessive reporting. Teach them the Scrum Values. After coaching, Scrum team as a whole should collaborate and do what is best for the Product.

B. Ask the Product Owner to stop attending the Daily Scrum as the meeting is for Developers.

C. Let the Product Owner join the Daily Scrum and let him continue to track individual progress. The Product Owner is responsible for the Product after all.

Correct answers: A

The Product Owner should not micromanage the Developers. Without trust, team members would have difficulties acting and behaving in the ways that reflect the Scrum values. He should teach them the advantages and disadvantages of little and excessive reporting. He should teach them the Scrum Values. The Scrum Master should coach the Product Owner and Developers on the purpose of Scrum events. After coaching, Scrum team as a whole should collaborate and do what is best for the Product. Lets take this opportunity to quickly read the Scrum Values again:

Different Scrum values are:

1. **Commitment**: The Scrum Team members personally commit to achieving the Scrum Goals and to supporting each other.

2. **Courage:** The Scrum Team members have courage to do the right thing and work on tough problems.

3. **Focus**: Everyone focuses on the work of the Sprint and the best possible progress made toward the goals of the Scrum Team.

4. **Openness** (No Hiding): The Scrum Team and its stakeholders agree to be open about all the work

D. Start attending the Daily Scrum along with Product Owner. Whenever the Developers has a conflict with the Product Owner, the Scrum Master can take over and resolve the conflict.	and the challenges with performing the work. This enable trust. 5. **Respect**: Scrum **Team members respect each other to be capable, independent people.** Scrum Team members are respected by the people with whom they work

Question 6
 	
A company in Texas has hired a few Scrum Team members who works in Japan. The Scrum Team has a total of nine members, seven members who work full time in the office and two members who work part time at home. The Scrum Team is complaining that it is too difficult to synchronize every day (at the same time) because of the country time differences and work schedules. The team has suggested having the Daily Scrum every other day instead. What would be three key concerns if the Daily Scrum is held less frequently? (Choose the best three answers.)
  A. The Scrum Master will lose the ability to update the burndown chart adequately.
  B. The Product Owner cannot accurately inspect utilization of the individual team members.
  C. Opportunities to inspect and adapt the Sprint Backlog would be reduced.
  D. Less information about the progress will be shared causing the Sprint plan to become inaccurate. It will also reduce transparency reflecting less of the progress made toward the Sprint Goal.
  E. Impediments would be raised and resolved more slowly.
	Correct answers: C, D, E
	
	The Daily Scrum is an internal meeting for the Developers to inspect progress toward the Sprint Goal and to inspect how progress is trending toward completing the work in the Sprint Backlog. The Daily Scrum increases the probability for the Developers to meet the Sprint Goal. Every day, Developers within the Scrum Team should understand how it intends to work together as a self-organizing team to accomplish the Sprint Goal and create the anticipated Increment by the end of the Sprint. Daily Scrum is an opportunity to inspect and adapt every day, a change to get feedback and insight from the team members every day and a change to correct the increment every day. Reducing the frequency of the event will increase the length of the feedback loop and adds risk if the team deviates too far off course.

Question 7	**Correct answers: C, D**
A newly formed Scrum Team is trying to understand the concept of Scrum and the boundaries defined in Scrum. What two boundaries in Scrum would give guidance for teams to effectively self-organize? (Choose the best two answers.) A. Clearly defined functional teams within the Scrum Team to define handoff phases during development. B. Having a mixture of different levels of skills and experience to promote domain knowledge sharing. C. Timeboxing the events in Scrum to allow for regular inspection and adaptation thus creating opportunities to adjust as needed D. Creating an integrated and potentially valuable Increment by the end of each Sprint.	The Sprint and the events within your sprint are boundaries within the Team. Rules within which the team members have to work can be defined as a boundary. Time-boxing promotes regularity and focus for self-organized teams. Having valuable Increments end of the sprint allows teams to collaboratively make decisions on what needs to be done next.
Question 8	**Correct answers: D**
James is a Scrum Master and has been working in an organization for 8 years. He is assigned to a new project and has been asked to assist in creating seven new Scrum Teams that will be working to build a highly anticipated product. He talks with the Scrum teams about the importance of being able to integrate their Increments by the end of their Sprints. This includes integrating their product in the first Sprint as well. The product is very important to both the end users and the organization. A few Team members provide a few choices to keep the Product integrated. Which one should James encourage? A. Each Scrum Team delivers functionality at the end of each Sprint. New Product Backlog items will then be added to the next Sprint Backlog to integrate their functionality with the other teams to create a unified Increment. B. Each Scrum Team delivers Increments in its own code branch. After in-depth UAT is performed on each individual branch, the branches should be merged. No further testing would be needed on the final merged branch.	When a Product Backlog item or an Increment is described as "Done", everyone must understand what "Done" means. If there are multiple Scrum Teams working on the system or product release, the Scrum Teams must mutually define the definition of "Done" to have a shared understanding of what it means for work to be complete, to ensure transparency. Each Increment is additive to all prior Increments thoroughly tested, ensuring that all Increments work together. Scrum encourages increments to be integrated as soon as possible. Integrating just in time at the end of the sprint often causes merge issues. Continuous integration and continuous deployment are essential, but they can be built over time.

C. Wait until enough of the infrastructure and architecture is in place before starting the first Sprints. Once continuous integration and continuous deployment is in place, integration will be easy. This will increase the success of delivering integrated Increments in Sprint 1.

D. All Scrum Teams should start with a mutual understanding of 'done' that defines all work necessary to deliver a valuable Increment that includes all previous Increments delivered for the product.

Question 9	Correct answers: D
A Scrum Master is working with Developers in different geographical locations. The Team meets in a variety of meeting rooms. They do a lot of work logistically (for example, set up conference calls, book the place) before the Daily Scrum. What action should the Scrum Master take in this situation? A. Ask the Developers to alternate who is responsible for meeting setup. This will make them accountable for the logistical work. B. The Scrum Master should set up the meeting and an assign a developer for the logistical work. C. Since only the Daily Scrum events need to be conducted in the same place, coach the Scrum Team on conducting this event in the same conference room if possible. Allow the Scrum Team to self-manage and determine for itself what to do. This will make the team more self-organizing. D. Coach the Scrum Team that all the Scrum events (including the Daily Sprint) should be conducted in the same place, if possible. This would enforce consistency. Allow the Scrum Team to self-manage and determine for themselves on what to do. E. Inform management and ask them to solve it as it is an impediment.	Scrum Teams are structured and empowered by the organization to organize and manage their own work. The resulting synergy optimizes the Scrum Team's overall efficiency and effectiveness. They are self-managing. Remember that the new Scrum guide states that all the Scrum events (including the Daily Sprint) should be conducted in the same place if possible. This would enforce consistency. Allow the Scrum Team to self-manage and determine for themselves on what to do.

Question 10	Correct answers: A,B

Sid is the Product Owner for a newly formed Scrum Team. To keep the team members on track, he has been giving rewards to individual Developers who have moved their work to 'done' during the Daily Scrum. Sid wants to ensure the team sticks to the Sprint Backlog commitments they made during Sprint Planning. What would be two valid actions for Charles, the Scrum Master, to take? (Choose the best two answers.)
  A. Chares should talk to Sid about the disadvantages of having a reward system in place and how it can demotivate other team members.
  B. Charles should tell Sid that Spring Planning enables the developers to make an estimate of work which will be delivered. The Sprint backlog is an estimate and not a commitment.
  C. Charles should coach Sid on different ways to report or reflect the work done to stakeholders.
  D. Charles should do nothing. Sid is optional at the Daily Scrum and it is the responsibility of the Developers to decide how to best run it.
	Incentive plans can be useful, but what the team really needs is guidance, not rewards and punishments. The Scrum Master is responsible for promoting and supporting Scrum as defined in the Scrum Guide. Scrum Masters do this by helping everyone understand Scrum theory, practices, rules, and values.
	
	The Sprint Backlog is highly visible, real-time picture of the work that the Developers plan to accomplish during the Sprint in order to achieve the Sprint Goal.
	The Sprint Backlog is updated throughout the Sprint as more is learned. Developers keep adding tasks during the Sprint, so, the Sprint Backlog keeps getting updated. The Sprint Backlog is the Developers plan for the current Sprint. This plan is not detailed upfront.

Question 11	Correct answers: A, E

An organization has 17 Products managed across 3 Product Owners. A Scrum Team has requested a hardening Sprint to test the work produced across different servers and databases before releasing. What scenarios have likely occurred? (Choose the best two answers.)
  A. Developers are having difficulties with the ability to regularly release during a Sprint. They are keeping up with the deadlines by marking the Product backlog items as complete, ignoring parts of the Definition of 'Done'.
  B. Sprint Length is too short.
  C. Scrum has not been customized in a suitable manner to make the previous work releasable.
  D. Hardening Sprints are supported by the Scrum framework, so this is acceptable.
  E. The team's shared Definition of Done is weak or incomplete causing buildup of technical debt.
	At the end of a Sprint, the new Increment must be 'Done', which means it must be in useable condition and meet the Scrum Team's Definition of Done. The entire Scrum Team would need to work together to create the definition of "Done". If more than one Scrum teams use the same definition of "Done", then those Scrum teams should be involved in changing the Definition of Done as well. .The Developers are required to conform to the Definition of Done.
	
	A Hardening Sprint is defined as a sprint focused on "catching up" on technical test debt and readying a Scrum-produced release. In this case, it typically focuses on completing testing activities such as integration, system, and full regression testing. Frequently it includes some final defect repairs as well. In Core Scrum, the notion of a sprint or iteration is a general-purpose construct. It is intended to take a set of product backlog items (PBI's) and produce a

"valuable product increment" at the end of each sprint. This intent, producing an valuable increment, is central to the essence of Scrum. The hardening sprint conceptually disrupts this. It is a periodic thing that is specially focused toward repairing / adding to the previously produced content.

If you take a pure LEAN view to things, the team has a responsibility for "hardening" the software within the sprint itself based on the definition of "done", so deferring work to hardening is considered wasteful.

Technical debt (also known as design debt or code debt) is a concept in software development that reflects the implied cost of rework caused by choosing an easy solution "now" instead of using a better approach that would take longer. Like any other debt, a large accumulation of Technical Debt (bad code) can impact future maintainability of the product. The downsides of Technical Debt are as follows:

1. It misleads the Product Owners, Scrum Masters and Developers about the "Current state" of the System. For example, if Product Backlog item A is assumed to be completed in a day, it might take three days for it to complete, because of unseen bad code or Technical Debt.

2. The Product becomes more unstable, as more functionality is added over bad code (or existing technical debt). It is far more likely to impact components which cross-cut a range of features. Moreover, if the necessary refactoring is significant it could impact the entire product, and it could affect features in uneven ways.

Question 12	Correct answers: C,D

Question 12

Uber has just hired Charles as a new Scrum Master to help them transform their teams from their current traditional process to Scrum. The teams are currently structured to specialize in a single function. I.e. A team would only address a single layer (i.e. design, frontend, backend, testing, etc.). Charles has introduced the concept of cross-functional feature teams where all the skills needed to produce a single business functionality, (end to end) are inside a single team. What should Charles keep in mind when transitioning from single function (aka component teams) to cross-functional feature teams? (Choose the best two answers.)

A. Without cross functional feature teams, one cannot do Scrum. Postpone Scrum adoption until the teams are reorganized as feature teams.

B. It is easier to compare the performance between cross-functional features teams in order to identify to which teams to assign tasks and which teams need additional coaching.

C. Newly formed cross functional feature teams will need time to stabilize before reaching their peak performance. During the initial stages of forming, performance will suffer, and productivity may be low, although even then delivery of business value is still likely to increase. Teams will spend a lot of time initially coaching and communicating internally.

D. People from the different layers and components will need time to become accustomed to working and delivering unified functionality together as one Scrum Team thus productivity may suffer in the beginning.

Correct answers: C,D

Forming a team takes time, and members often go through recognizable stages as they change from being a group of individuals to a team with common goals. Forming, Storming, Norming, and Performing model describes these stages by Bruce Tuckman. When you understand it, you can help your new team become effective more quickly. Feature team is a long-lived, cross-functional, cross-component team that completes many end-to-end customer features.

A component team is a team whose primary area of concern is restricted to a specific component.

Component team	Feature team
Can be implemented in a Scrum Framework	Can be implemented in a Scrum Framework
More Communication Overhead	Less Communication Overhead
Optimized for delivering the maximum number of lines of code	Optimized for delivering the maximum customer value
Focus on increased individual productivity by implementing 'easy' lower-value features	Focus on high-value features and system productivity (value throughput)
Dependencies between teams leads to additional planning	Minimizes dependencies between teams to increase flexibility
Focus on single specialization	Focus on multiple specializations
individual/team code ownership	Shared product code ownership
Clear individual responsibilities	Shared team responsibilities

Question 13	**Correct answers: C,D**
A Sprint Planning meeting is just about to end. At the end of the Sprint Planning meeting, Developers were not able to forecast the Product Backlog items they would need to complete in the upcoming Sprint. The Product Owner, however, was able to clearly define the Sprint Goal. Which of the following two actions would you support? (Choose the best two answers.) A. Extend the Spring planning meeting, If all the participants agree that they can extend the Sprint Planning until the Developers can forecast enough Product Backlog items. B. Allow the Developers as much time as needed to review the Product Backlog items based on the goal and reconvene with the Product Owner when they are confident enough to make a forecast for the Sprint again. Another Sprint Planning meeting can be scheduled to go through the remaining items. C. Developers in the Scrum Team should forecasts the most likely Product Backlog items to meet the Sprint Goal and create a Sprint Backlog based on a guess. Once the time-box for the Sprint Planning meeting is over, they can start working on the Product Backlog items, analyze and decompose, create the functionality during the Sprint. The Product owner can inspect and developers' team can adopt throughout the Sprint as needed. D. The Scrum Team should discuss in the upcoming Sprint Retrospective why this happened and what changes will make it less likely for it to occur again.	All events are time-boxed events, such that every event has a maximum duration. Developers modify the Sprint Backlog throughout the Sprint, and the Sprint Backlog emerges during the Sprint. This emergence occurs as the Developers works through the plan and learns more about the work needed to achieve the Sprint Goal. Remember a team does not need to finalize all the Product backlog items which need to be completed during Sprint Planning. They make a best guess. A Sprint backlog is merely an estimate of what could be done. The entire sprint could be used to inspect and adopt (add, remove Product backlog items as needed).

Question 14

Charles is a Scrum Master for three different teams who are building a single Product from the same Product Backlog. Developers from each team have approached Charles requesting that their teams need Jane, an external specialist, to commit full time for their next Sprint. Which solutions would Charles consider acceptable? (Choose the best two answers.)

- A. Have the Developers work with the Product Owner to re-order the Product Backlog so Jane can serve each team, one after another, as needed.
- B. People from the Scrum Teams with the same skills as Jane's could take on Jane's work.
- C. Create a different team with Jane and people from this team can act as specialist and temporarily work to serve the existing teams.
- D. For Sprints that require Jane's expertise for more than one team, combine the teams into one and separate when they no longer need to share her services.
- E. Ask Jane for a plan to hire and train additional people in her domain, and in the meantime work with the Product Owner and Developers to re-prioritize the work so that tasks does not depend on Jane.

Correct answers: A,B

Dependencies in Scrum may be broadly classified as:

1. Inter Story: Dependencies between user stories within the same team.
2. Inter Team: Dependencies between teams.
3. Inter Product/Release: Dependencies across products or releases of the same product.
4. External: Vendors, Third parties, Customer dependencies, People.

Official Scrum classifies the dependencies as follows:

1. Product structure dependencies: The degree to which different concerns are independently separated in the product will greatly affect the complexity of creating an integrated product release. The scope of the requirements may overlap if not separated as needed. The order in which these requirements are implemented may also affect each other. While ordering the Product Backlog and selecting the Product Backlog items in the Sprint Backlog, one should make sure that such dependencies are accommodated.

2. Communication structure dependencies: The way that people communicate within and between teams affects their ability to get work done; delays in communication and feedback reduce the flow of work.

Dependencies can be reduced by :
1) Decomposing Product backlog items to be less dependent on each other.
2) Ordering the Product backlog items in the Product backlog to avoid further dependencies.
3) Changing organizational design and forming cross-component cross-functional Scrum Teams (Feature Teams). This would reduce resource dependencies as well.
4) Using tools such as Kanban to visualize the dependencies well in advance,
5) Making the complicated architecture simpler, reducing the number of components.

Question 15	Correct answers: A,B,F
By the end of the Sprint, a Product Backlog item in the Sprint Backlog does not meet the team's Definition of Done. What three things should happen with the item? A. Do not include the item in the Increment for the Sprint. B. Do not demo the item in the Sprint Review. C. Split the item and add the estimation of the completed work to the current Sprint so not to impact the velocity and add the 'undone' work to the next Sprint. D. It will be inspected at the Sprint Review and if it is acceptable by the Stakeholders then include it in the Increment. E. Add the remaining work to the next Sprint backlog F. Estimate the remaining work needed to make it 'done' and add the Product Backlog item back to the Product Backlog for the Product Owner to decide what to do with it.	At the end of a Sprint, the new Increment must be 'Done', which means it must be in useable condition and meet the Scrum Team's definition of 'Done'. Scrum Team members must have a shared understanding of what it means for work to be complete, to ensure transparency. This is the Definition of Done for the Scrum Team and it is used to assess when work is complete on the product Increment. Work cannot be considered part of an Increment unless it meets the Definition of Done. The Definition of Done creates transparency by providing everyone a shared understanding of what work was completed as part of the Increment. If a Product Backlog item does not meet the Definition of Done, it cannot be released or even presented at the Sprint Review. Instead, it returns to the Product Backlog for future consideration.
Question 16 During Sprint Planning, the Definition of Done will help the Developers to forecast the amount of work deemed feasible to make 'done' by the end of the Sprint. Which two items best describes what 'done' means? (Choose the best two answers.) A. All the work done on the Increment should be ready for User Acceptance Testing. B. All the work done on the Increment should pass the written test cases. C. All the work done on the Increment should prepare the Increment for Integration Testing. D. All the work performed on the Increment should make the Increment meet the Definition of Done. E. Having an Increment of working software that is valuable to the end users.	**Correct answers: D,E** When a Product Backlog item or an Increment is described as 'Done', everyone must understand what 'Done' means. Although this may vary per Scrum Team, members must have a shared understanding of what it means for work to be complete, to ensure transparency. This is the "Definition of Done" for the Scrum Team and is used to assess when work is complete on the product Increment. The purpose of each Sprint is to deliver Increments of potentially value that adhere to the Scrum Team's current Definition of Done.

Question 17	Correct answers: B
During the implementation of an item in the Sprint Backlog, team members argue about a Product backlog item they are trying to implement. The team members debate about the work needed to make the item 'done'. Some say the remaining work which needs to be completed is a part of the Definition of Done and others say it isn't. Charles, the Scrum Master, observes a debate forming and members beginning to take sides. What is the best action for Charles to take? A. Bring the Scrum Team members together and interpret the Definition of Done for them so that there are no future conflicts on interpretation. B. Facilitate a session with all members on the Scrum Team to help them resolve the conflict, refine the Definition of Done, and become effective again. Tell the team that conflicts are a natural occurrence and coach them on the value of resolving conflicts. C. Immediately end the discussion before it becomes worse. Make the decision on what work is needed to make the item 'done' and teach the team about the importance of avoiding conflicts. D. Bring the Product Owner to the discussion and have him/her decide the work needed to make the item 'done.' It is the Product Owner's responsibility to manage the Developers.	The Scrum Master is a leader for the Scrum Team. The Scrum Master helps the Scrum Team understand which of their interactions are helpful and which are not. The Scrum Master helps everyone change these interactions to maximize the value created by the Scrum Team. The Scrum Master serves the Scrum Team in several ways, including: 1. Coaching the team members in self-management and cross-functionality. 2. Helping the Scrum Team focus on creating high-value Increments that meet the Definition of Done. 3. Causing the removal of impediments to the Scrum Team's progress; and, 4. Ensuring that all Scrum events take place and are **positive,** productive, and kept within the timebox. 5. Helping teams become more independent.
Question 18 How should the Scrum Master divide a 75 Developers into three Scrum Teams? A. Have the Resource Manager to assign people to different teams based on skills. B. Ask the Developers to divide themselves into teams. C. Create teams based on their functional layers. D. Ask the Product Owner to divide the teams up.	**Correct answer: B** Scrum Teams are self-organizing. Scrum teams are cross-functional, with all the skills as a team necessary to create a product Increment. Scrum recognizes no titles for the Developers in a Scrum Team, regardless of the work being performed by the person. Scrum recognizes no sub-teams, regardless of domains that need to be addressed like testing, architecture, operations, or business analysis. Individual Scrum Team members may have specialized skills and areas of focus, but accountability of creating a valuable increment belongs to the Scrum Team as a whole. It's always best to let the Scrum team decide how they want to assign members to each team based. The Scrum team might

	take factors such as team size, type of work, skills etc into consideration while splitting or assigning members to a team.

Question 19
 	
An organization has hired a Scrum master to help them "evolve" their product development using the Scrum Framework. The teams are currently working at a component level in this organization. This means that each team address one single application layer only (for example, UI, Database, core logic, security, testing and interfaces). The Scrum master introduces the concept of feature teams, where teams would need to have the skills to work on multiple layers throughout a Sprint and deliver a valuable software every Sprint. What are two things the Scrum Master should take into consideration when moving away from component teams toward feature teams? Select the two best answers
  A. Using the feature teams approach allows easier calculation of the productivity per team or even per member. Incentives on productivity are likely to speed up the transition to feature teams, and therefore the adoption of Scrum.
  B. Productivity will probably decrease during the initial transition. The decrease in productivity will be due to the change in mindset. The delivery of business value is still likely to increase.
  C. It's easier to track accountability and hold the appropriate people responsible for the work in component-based team.
  D. Members are likely to develop specialized skills quicker in a component-based team.
  E. One cannot do Scrum without feature teams. We should not continue adopting Scrum until teams are reorganized in feature teams.
  F. Gradually feature teams will become more productive as people from the different layers and components become accustomed to working and delivering unified functionality together, as one Scrum Team.
	Correct answer: B, F
	
	Feature team is a long-lived, cross-functional, cross-component team that completes many end-to-end customer features. A component team is a team whose primary area of concern is restricted to a specific component.
	
	With the move to Feature Teams, productivity may dip initially while the teams are getting used to working in this new way. Gradually feature teams will become more productive as people from the different layers and components become accustomed to working and delivering unified functionality together, as one Scrum Team. The Business Value is also likely to increase.
	
	A component team is a team whose primary area of concern is restricted to a specific component. Here is a quick comparison of Component and Feature Teams.

Component team	Feature team
Can be implemented in a Scrum Framework	Can be implemented in a Scrum Framework
More Communication Overhead	Less Communication Overhead
Optimized for delivering the maximum number of lines of code	Optimized for delivering the maximum customer value
Focus on increased individual productivity by implementing 'easy' lower-value features	Focus on high-value features and system productivity (value throughput)
Dependencies between teams leads to additional planning	Minimizes dependencies between teams to increase flexibility
Focus on single specialization	Focus on multiple specializations
individual/team code ownership	Shared product code ownership
Clear individual responsibilities	Shared team responsibilities

Question 20	**Correct answer: C**
Jane recently joined an organization as the Scrum Master, and she is asked to work in Scrum Team that will develop a new application. The new application will help employees manage their "timesheets" and "expense". Jane has started collaborating with the leadership teams and Product Owner on finalizing the budget, requirements, team members etc. During a meeting with the Product Owner, Jane learns that only the requirements related to "timesheets" (and not "expense") are collected so far. The Product Owner is unsure if it is enough to start the Development. What should Jane's response be? A. A separate Product Backlog needs to be created capturing the requirements just for expenses before the first Sprint. B. All the requirements need to be collected and understood in detail before the first Sprint. C. As long as the collected requirements will result into a valuable increment they can start. They can collect the "expense" requirements as they learn more. D. The Scrum Team is already finalized. Not starting the Sprint would result in waste of resources.	Scrum and Lean encourages to start with what one has and on the other not creating waste by going overboard and documenting too many requirements. Scrum only requires a Product Owner with enough ideas, a Scrum Team to execute on those ideas, and a Scrum Master to guide the process. Every Sprint should produce a valuable Increment. Scrum is founded on empirical process control theory, or empiricism. Empiricism asserts that knowledge comes from experience and making decisions based on what is known. As the Sprints progress the team will learn more from the work they have done.

Question 21	Correct answer: A,B,E
A Scrum Team of 9 members is working on building a new application to support the hiring processes in their organization. Charles is a new Developer and he has added an additional feature in the Increment which is not part of the Product Backlog. He did it because he was approached directly by one of the business stakeholders and it only took him 30 minutes to implement the requirements. This was discovered just before the Sprint Review by the Scrum team. What should the Scrum Team do? Select three best answers A. The team should reassess whether the feature should be kept or removed. B. Charles should ask Product Owner to add this feature to the Product Backlog because it is was asked by a Stakeholder. C. The Scrum Team should inform the Scrum Master about the request and remove Charles from the Team. D. The Scrum Team should retain the feature in the Increment but do not present it to the stakeholders. E. The Scrum Team should discuss the issue in the Sprint Retrospective.	The Product Backlog is an ordered list of everything that is known to be needed in the product. It is the single source of requirements for any changes to be made to the product. The Product Backlog lists all features, functions, requirements, enhancements, and fixes that constitute the changes to be made to the product in future releases. Implementing a feature which has not been groomed in the presence of the entire team during refinement or gone through the appropriate sprint planning sessions can have negative impacts on the increment. The team should also discuss this matter in the Sprint Retrospective so that everyone is aware and do not make the same mistake. Adding the item to the Product backlog just because it is developed does not make sense. Removing the item without assessing the impacts would not help either. Scrum Teams must follow the Scrum Values. Everything the team does should be transparent. Hiding the information from the Product Owner or stakeholders is not a good approach. Scrum Master does not remove individuals from the team for these kinds of mistakes. Scrum Master understands the mistake and helps the Team learn from it.

Question 22	Correct answer: G

A Kanban "Workflow" definition must include:
 	
  A. A shared understanding within the Scrum Team of how work is defined (work items).
  B. The start state of the process.
  C. The active states for the work items.
  D. The finished state of the process.
  E. A definition of how Work in Progress (WIP) will be limited.
  F. A set Service Level Expectation (SLE) that communicates a forecast of how long it should take to complete work items
  G. All of the Above.
	Kanban is a strategy which optimizes the flow of stakeholder value through a process that uses a visual, work-in-progress limited, pull system.
	
	Kanban is a visual system for managing work as it moves through a process. Kanban visualizes both the process (the workflow) and the actual work passing through that process.
	
	Kanban is a method that uses a work-in-process limited pull system as the core mechanism to expose operation (or process) problems and to stimulate collaborative improvement efforts.
	
	Each Scrum Team must create its definition of "Workflow" containing the following elements:
	
	  1. A shared understanding within the Scrum Team of how work is defined (work items).
	  2. The start state of the process.
	  3. The active states for the work items.
	  4. The finished state of the process.
	  5. A definition of how Work in Progress (WIP) will be limited.
	  6. A set Service Level Expectation (SLE) that communicates a forecast of how long it should take to complete work items.

Question 23	Correct answer: B,E
Smith is a Scrum Master. During the Daily Scrum meeting, one team member, who is also an important team member, consumes a lot of time every Daily Scrum. What should Smith do? Select the two best answers. A. Contact the team member's Manager and raise this as an impediment to the Manager and ask that they resolve this matter as quickly as possible. B. Smith should consider taking the person in private and coaching him about the event timebox and its advantages. C. Smith must suggest using a round robin timer mechanism, to limit the time each person can speak at the Daily Scrum so that everyone has opportunity to speak. D. Smith should allow the team member who take most time to talk last. E. Smith must coach the Scrum Team to help them find a way to solve the problem and own the solution as the team needs to be self-managing.	Smith should consider taking the person aside and asking them how they see their impact to the Daily Scrum, effectively coaching them into better working as an equal team member. Smith can also suggest coaching the Scrum Team to help them find a way own and solve the problem. The Scrum Master serves the Scrum Team in several ways, including: 1.Coaching the team members in self-management and cross-functionality; 2.Helping the Scrum Team focus on creating high-value Increments that meet the Definition of Done; 3.Causing the removal of impediments to the Scrum Team's progress; and, 4.Ensuring that all Scrum events take place and are positive, productive, and kept within the timebox.

Question 24

Sam is the Scrum Master for a Scrum Team. One of the Developers approaches Sam's and tells her that they are not completing the integration testing for all of the selected Product Backlog Items in the Sprint. Integration testing is part of the agreed definition of "Done". Developers have discussed with the Product Owner and decided to change the definition of "Done". Which two actions should Scrum take?

- A. Ask the Developers and Product Owner, "Will removing integration testing from the definition of "Done" allow the team to produce potentially valuable increments at the end of every Sprint. If not then, it should not be allowed.
- B. Make sure that the quality of the increment does not decrease by changing the definition of "Done". If it does, it should not be allowed.
- C. Disagree with the Developer and tell them that having a stringent definition of "Done" is important for the quality of the product, and they should follow it.
- D. Agree with altering the definition of "Done" as both the Developers and Product Owner agree.
- E. Ask the team to wait as the definition of "Done" can only be changed during Sprint Retrospective.

Correct answer: A,B

This question may sound like a repeat however it highlights the importance of quality in the Sprint. To being with, the Scrum Master serves the Scrum Team by leading them in the right path. The Scrum Master:
1) Coaching the team members self-management and cross-functionality.
2) Helping the Scrum Team focus on creating high-value Increments that meet the Definition of Done.
3) Removing impediments to the Scrum Team's progress.
4) Ensuring that all Scrum events take place and are positive, productive, and kept within the timebox

During the Sprint:
• No changes are made that would endanger the Sprint Goal.
• Quality does not decrease.
• The Product Backlog is refined as needed.
• Scope may be clarified and renegotiated with the Product Owner as more is learned.

Question 25

Charles has been hired as a Scrum Master for a company that has been doing business for over a hundred years. In order to stay competitive, they have started an initiative to digitize their legacy systems. The company has several Scrum Teams working on different components that will be integrated to a single platform. Charles and his team are responsible for building the back-office platform and integrating all other components. The Scrum Teams work in two-week Sprints and are expected to deliver all functionality in 2 months (4 Sprints). During development the requirement for one of the components changes. This is slowing down the progress Charles and his team have been making.

Because of these changes, Charles and his team estimate that they will not be able to deliver all expected work within the committed timeframe. The program manager in charge of the digitization initiative is upset with the Product Owner. As a Scrum Master, what could Charles do to help the Product Owner?

A. Ask the Product Owner to work with the program manager and the other teams on the ordering of the Product Backlog items. Be transparent and work on reducing the dependencies if needed.

B. Ask the Product Owner to work with the team and redefine the possible delivery date.

C. Ask the Product owner to remove all items from the Product Backlog for which development is forecasted to be beyond the expected date. These are likely to be low value anyways.

D. Ask the Product owner to extend the Sprint length. This way they would not miss the date.

E. Ask the Product owner to remove a few items from the Sprint Backlog which will compensate for the delay and help the team deliver on time.

F. Ask the Product owner to add additional developers to the team in order to increase velocity and meet the original date.

Correct answer: A,B

Long question isn't it? Similar questions might appear on the test. Be sure to focus on the important aspects of the question.

Remember adding additional resources to the team, extending the Sprint, remove Product backlog items to accommodate other Product backlog items, are not good ideas.

The Scrum Master should ask the Product owner reduce dependencies as much as possible. The Nexus Sprint backlog can highlight the dependencies across all the Scrum Team so appropriate actions can be taken.

Question 26	Correct answer: D,F,G
A scrum team has been creating a Product for the past 7 sprints. Overtime the relationship between the Product Owner and the Developers has suffered. The Developers are upset with the Product Owner for the constantly changing the requirements. The Product Owner is upset with the Developers for changing the work that needs to be done during the Sprint. What should the Scrum Master, do? (Select 3)	Conflicts are a natural occurrence and the Scrum Master coaches the Scrum Team on the value of resolving conflicts. Leaving conflicts unresolved can impact the Scrum values of openness and respect diminishing trust. Lower trust levels will impact the Scrum Team's effectiveness and can cause impediments in the future. It is the responsibility of the Scrum Master to remove impediments that hinder the team through conflict resolution and facilitation. End of the Day, the Scrum Master is responsible for the Scrum Teams effectiveness.

A. Take a break between Sprints (for a few days if needed) to organize a team building session to rebuild the relationship.

B. Explain the Developers that the Product Owner is accountable for the increment every sprint and thus the teams needs to be follow his guidance.

C. The Scrum Master's responsibility is to ensure the Scrum Team has a stable velocity. Any changes that negatively impact the team's velocity will be rejected by the Scrum Master.

D. During the Sprint Retrospective, ask the Product Owner and the Developers to address the issues. Have the Team discuss why the changes occur and what impact they have on the value of the product.

E. Developers and Scrum Masters should be able to resolve the conflict themselves as they are self-managing and self-organizing.

F. Coach the Product Owner about the importance of Sprint Goal. As long as the Sprint Goal is met by the Developers, Product Backlog items in the Sprint Backlog can change.

G. Coach the Developers that changes in requirements are expected in a sprint. Show them different techniques to manage change.

Also remember the entire team is accountable for an increment and not just the developers.

Here is what happens when a typical change is requested:

Here is what we came up with:

* Change is presented to the Product Owner who may add them to the Product Backlog at his discretion.
* The developers and Product Owner meet regularly to engage in Product Backlog Refinement, during which an estimate is added/updated to the PBI.
* The Scrum Team decides when to pull the change into a sprint at Sprint Planning.
* if an existing item requirement changes it can be moved back to the Product backlog (from the Sprint backlog) as long as it does not impact the Sprint goal.

Question 27

A new Product Owner who has joined an existing Scrum Team that has been working together for eight Sprints. The Scrum Team has grown to have a good understanding of the functionality of the product they have been building. The Product Owner, being new to the company, is unsure about her responsibilities. As a Scrum Master explain two acceptable ways of helping the Product Owner. (Choose the best two answers.)

A. You should advise the Product Owner to rely on Market Analysis, Developers and the Stakeholders to formulate the Product Goal and the Product Backlog. By asking questions and working with the developers and stakeholders, Product Owner will quickly be up to speed.

B. You should advise the Product Owner that, in today's highly competitive markets, it is important that the Developers are directly updated about the changing business priorities on a daily basis. The Daily Scrum allows the Developers to adapt to the changes in scope without delay.

C. You should advise the Product Owner to start building a good relationship with the Stakeholders of the product. Ongoing interaction with them is important to regularly align with changing organizational or market expectations. The Product Owner is also expected to invite the right Stakeholders to the Sprint Review meeting.

D. You should tell the Product Owner to make sure that there should be no ambiguities or possible misunderstandings on the Product Backlog items when they are handed over to the Developers. This is best done by capturing all the functional requirements during an analysis phase and documenting them thoroughly upfront.

Correct answer: A,C

The Product Owner is accountable for maximizing the value of the product resulting from the work of the Scrum Team. How this is done may vary widely across organizations, Scrum Teams, and individuals. Product Owner should focus on:

1. Key Stakeholder Involvement: In order to maximize Product value, the Product Owner should identify the key stakeholders for the product and involve them as necessary throughout the development effort.

2. Product Marketplace: The Product Owner should be expertly aware of the marketplace for the product. They should constantly be gathering and re-gathering information regarding the marketplace, so that the product value is maximized.

3. Product Release Decisions: The Product Owner is the one and only person who can decide whether to release the latest Increment of the Product. For Product value to be captured, a release of the product must occur.

The Product Owner:
1. The Product Owner is one person, not a committee.
2. Communicates regularly with the Stakeholders.
3. Creates new items in the Product Backlog.
4. Revises the priority of Product Backlog items
5. Work with the Developers on Product Backlog refinement.
6. Answers questions about the Product Backlog items and makes sure that everyone has the right understanding of Product Backlog items.
7. Checks the completed items with the Developers to ensure they are Done based on the "Definition of Done".
8. Collaborate with stakeholders, user communities, and subject matter experts.
Remember there will be always be ambiguities in the Product Backlog items (if not in all then in some). Updating the Scrum team every day about the market is not needed either. The Product owner should be able to drive the product backlog based on the market analysis, not update the team about it every day.

Question 28	Correct answer: C,D
Charles and James are talking about velocity and technical debts. In what two ways is velocity and technical debt related? (Choose the best two answers.) A. Adding higher estimates to technical debt product backlog items will allow the Scrum Team to maintain constant velocity therefore ensuring predictability. B. They are not related because technical debt is non-functional, and velocity is calculated based on end user functionality. C. A Scrum Team can artificially increase velocity by allowing technical debt to be incurred. D. As the Developers are working on new Product Backlog items, they may unexpectedly run into technical debt that will result the team's velocity dropping.	Technical debt is a natural occurrence when developing complex products. Technical debt covers functional and non functional aspects of Product backlog item. It is a concept in software development that reflects the implied cost of additional rework caused by choosing an easy solution now instead of using a better approach that would take longer. And how it is managed depends on the team AND context of the situation Velocity and technical debt aren't directly correlated, and velocity can't measure technical debt directly. However, velocity (when properly implemented) can act as a detective control to uncover hidden debt. Technical debt isn't necessarily bad. Just like financial leverage, there is good debt and bad debt. Taking on debt the project can afford may be a necessary choice to meet short-term goals. It's just important to only take on debt that the project can afford, and that the team can pay back! On the other hand the team should not simply consider remaining work as technical debt to show higher velocity (or show they are completing more work). The main problem with technical debt is when it's invisible. Gnome's Law of Transparency℠ says, "No invisible work, ever!" Visible debt won't reduce your velocity, but may reduce the speed at which new features can be delivered. Invisible work will act as a drag on velocity, which is an early warning that there may be unknown or unexpected technical debt that should be surfaced and addressed by the entire Scrum Team..

Question 29	**Correct answer: D**
Sid is a Scrum Master for a Scrum Team that is new to Scrum. At the halfway point of the Sprint, the Product Owner comes to Sid because he is concerned developers will not be able to complete the entire Sprint Backlog by the end of the Sprint. What should Sid do in this situation? A. Advise the Product Owner that the Developers owns the Sprint Backlog and it is up to them to meet their commitments. No one tells the Developers how to turn Product Backlog into Increments of potentially releasable functionality. B. Add more developers to the Scrum Team to meet the Product Owner's expectations. C. Motivate the Developers to meet their commitment to the Product Owner. D. Coach the Product Owner that the Sprint backlog is not a commitment, just a forecast. Developers cannot promise the entire scope that was forecasted during Sprint Planning. As more is learned during the Sprint, work may emerge that affects the Sprint Backlog.	Scrum is founded on empirical process control theory, or empiricism. Empiricism asserts that knowledge comes from experience and making decisions based on what is known. The Sprint Backlog is a forecast by the Developers about what functionality will be in the next Increment and the work needed to deliver that functionality into a 'Done' Increment. Developers modifies the Sprint Backlog throughout the Sprint, and the Sprint Backlog emerges during the Sprint. This emergence occurs as Developers work through the plan and learns more about the work needed to achieve the Sprint Goal.
Question 30 A member of the HR department is trying to understand Scrum and the accountabilities within this framework. A Product Owner is asked to put two everyday scenarios which would best describe self – managing scrum teams. Which two scenarios would best represent a self-managing Scrum Team? (Choose the best two answers.) A. Management works with the efficient Scrum Master to optimize the Scrum Team's progress during the Sprint. Developers take the Product Owner and Scrum Master's lead. B. Developers within the Scrum Team creates their own Sprint Backlog, reflecting all work that is part of the Definition of Done.	**Correct answer: B,D** A self-organized team is a team that is able to self-manage and decide how best to accomplish their work.

C. Scrum Team invites external people to the Sprint Planning to help them create a complete and detailed Sprint Backlog. D. Scrum Team members collaboratively select and re-plan their work throughout the Sprint. E. The Scrum Team members are strictly focused on the work within their functional role and always handing off the work to other roles in a timely matter. F. Good Scrum Teams are always able to meet their achievements.	
Question 31 Monica is a Scrum Master on a new Scrum Team. What would be the best way for her to determine if the Product Owner is interacting enough with the Developers during a Sprint? A. Check whether the Product Owner is actively engaged at the Daily Scrums. B. See whether the Product Owner has provided enough information at the Sprint Planning to make his/ her presence optional during the Sprint. The level of autonomy within developers can be the result of having the right presence from the Product Owner. C. Check whether the Increment presented at the Sprint Review meets the Product Owner's expectations. D. The Product Owner must always be present with the Developers. Unavailability of the Product Owner is prohibited in Scrum. E. Check whether the Increment presented at the Sprint Review meets the Sprint Goal.	**Correct answer: E** Outcomes of the Scrum Team are affected by the Product Owner's participation and availability. During a Sprint the Product Owner is responsible for answering questions from the Developers about items in the current Sprint and optimizing the value of the work the Team does. However, the Product Owner and Scrum Master are not expected to attend the daily scrum everyday (unless the developers need them). It is critical that the Product Owner is present during the Sprint Planning session. He / she would help the team select the high value product backlog items which would help them meet their Sprint Goal. The Product Owners absence in the Sprint Planning meeting is not a good idea because: 1.The Sprint goal is decided during the Sprint Planning meeting. The Sprint goal should be assigned to the Product Goal which is driven by the Product Owner. 2.High value items are picked from the Product Backlog and moved to the Sprint Backlog. Presence of the Product Owner would guide the developers to do so. Remember there might be times when a few items are missed during a sprint and thus the increment might not meet a Product Owners expectation. However at the end of the Sprint, the increment should always meet the Sprint Goal.

Question 32	Correct answer: A,D
During the Sprint Review, the Product Owner decides to release the current Increment to production. The Stakeholders suggest temporarily delaying the next Sprint in order to respond more quickly to user feedback after the release. The Product Owner prefers to continue to the next Sprint and make progress towards the next release. The Scrum Master begins facilitating the discussion. What would be two acceptable outcomes of the discussion? (Choose the best two answers.) A. Continue with the Sprints but shorten the Sprint timebox to allow for shorter feedback loops. B. Delay the next Sprint to allow the Scrum Team to work on new customer feedback. C. Continue with the Sprints but allow the Sprint Goal within the Sprint to change according to the customer feedback. D. Continue with the Sprints and include the customer feedback in the Sprint Backlog and Product Backlog as they come in. (as long as the Sprint Goal is not impacted)	A new Sprint starts immediately after the conclusion of the previous Sprint. Delaying the start of the next Sprint interrupts progress and can reduce the Time-to-Market. Shortening the Sprint length allows the team to respond quicker to changes outside of the Sprint plan and while still allowing delivery of business value. Adding user feedback to the Product Backlog helps the Product Owner with ordering the backlog to maximize the flow of value. During the Sprint no changes are made that would endanger the Sprint Goal, however the Goal can be drafted in a way which could accommodate client feedback as they come in.

Question 33	Correct answer: A
After several Sprints, a key Stakeholder starts using the product. The Stakeholder is surprised by the slow performance and complains to the Product Owner. The Product Owner comes to the Scrum Master asking for advice. What is the best action for a Scrum Master to take? A. Encourage the Product Owner to bring the performance concerns to the Developers within the team and work with them on how to improve performance, and ultimately have stronger Definition of Done. B. Ask the Product Owner to wait until the next Sprint Retrospective as it is the most opportune time to modify the Definition of Done. C. Bring the concern to the Developers in the Scrum Team. Ask the team to stop working on everything and correct the product, improve the performance testing right away. D. Explain to the Product Owner that it's up to the Developers to decide on acceptable performance standards as they own the Definition of Done.	The highest priority of agility is to satisfy the customer through early and continuous delivery of valuable software. The team can get together as soon as possible to expand their Definition of Done to include more stringent criteria for higher quality. Functionality which is already been developed can be revised to abide to the new Definition of Done. This upgrade work can be taken as separate Product Backlog items as needed.

Question 34

At the tenth Sprint Retrospective, the Product Owner mentions that he is surprised about the amount of technical debt that has built up in the system. He is not happy because as a result of the technical debt, the product is not able to support an adequate number of users. The Product Owner is also upset about the fact that the product will need several more Sprints to address the scalability issues in order to meet his expectations. What factors may have led to this?

- A. The Scrum Team might not have been transparent.
- B. Developers might not have been paying enough attention to technical quality of the code.
- C. The Scrum Team might not have used the past Sprint events effectively to inspect and adapt.
- D. Developers and the Product Owner were not having conversations around technical debt.
- E. All of the above.

Correct answer: E

Each component within the Scrum framework serves a specific purpose and is essential to Scrum's success and usage. Scrum's roles, events, artifacts, and rules are immutable and although implementing only parts of Scrum is possible, the result is not Scrum.

The emergent process and work must be visible to those performing the work as well as those receiving the work. With Scrum, important decisions are based on the perceived state of its three formal artifacts. Artifacts **that have low transparency** can lead to decisions that diminish value and increase risk.

Often the issue is that teams do not meet the definition of Done. Remember the Definition of Done creates transparency by providing everyone a shared understanding of what work was completed as part of the Increment.

When it comes to events, remember the Sprint is a container for all other events. Each event in Scrum is a formal opportunity to inspect and adapt Scrum artifacts. These events are specifically designed to enable the transparency required.

Question 35

Which two statements are the most accurate in regard to scaling Scrum for large projects requiring multiple Scrum Teams? (Choose the best two answers.)

- A. Customizing the core Scrum framework is necessary to be successful with Scrum at large scale. Customizing may also include application of only the events and accountabilities needed.
- B. A well-structured (and ordered) Product Backlog can minimize and often eliminate the need for Developers working on multiple Scrum Teams during a Sprint.
- C. Team members must work full time on a single Scrum Team.
- D. A person focusing on the Sprint Backlog of a single Scrum Team is often more productive

Correct answer: B.D

Content switching is a Scrum Anti Pattern and is not productive. A person or team working on a single problem at a time is typically more effective than one that is working on multiple problems simultaneously. They can fully focus and dedicate their energy to resolving the problem before moving to the next. Having a well-structured Product Backlog can help minimize dependencies and increase focus for each team.

than that same person working on multiple Scrum Teams at the same time.	
Question 36 A Scrum Team discovers that it doesn't have the tools and infrastructure to make each selected Product Backlog item done. What is the most appropriate action for the Scrum Master to take? A. Stop the Sprint and have the Developers work on the infrastructure before continuing. B. Hire additional members or experts to focus on tools and infrastructure only. Rest of the team can continue with their work. C. Coach the Scrum Team to improve its skills, tools and infrastructure over time. For now they can establish a Definition of "Done" that is actually possible to achieve given the current circumstances. D. Encourage the Product Owner to accept partially done Increments and complete the work in the Hardening Sprint.	**Correct answer: C** The Scrum Master serves the Team by coaching it in self-organization and cross-functionality. Infrastructure will always be evolving or will never be complete. The team should keep working on the architecture and infrastructure in a Sprint. For every Sprint, the team should look at creating something of value. The team should also focus developing functionalities and features in parallel with the architecture. While the architecture is build, the Definition of Done should be in synch with the current state of the architecture and not the future state. Hiring external members outside the team to help or accepting partially done increments are never good ideas.
Question 37 Charles is a Scrum Master on one of the Scrum Teams and needs your advice. Charles's Daily Scrum requires more than 15 minutes and the team has suggested dividing themselves into two separate teams in order to stay within the time box. As another Scrum Master, what would be the best response? A. Disagree – as the root cause may not be that the team is too big. B. Agree – You agree that dividing the team into two is a good strategy to allow the teams to learn how to run Daily Scrums quickly and effectively. Once they've learned to limit the Daily Scrum to 15 minutes, Charles can merge the teams again.	**Correct answer: A** The entire purpose of the daily scrum if for the team to come together and talk about the impediments. Breaking the team downs would not allow all the team members to be in the same room / meeting to discuss or give inputs to the needed topics. Dependency between the teams would increase and communication would decrease. Breaking the team down into multiple teams just to meet the timebox is not the solution. In a typical situation, different meetings outside the daily scrum can be conducted for extended discussions. Not offering to be involved is not the correct answer either.

C. Unsure – dividing a team into two cannot be decided based on this information. You offer to not be involved. D. Agree – this is an appropriate solution to the problem.	
Question 38 Your organization has formed a new Scrum Team and has assigned you as the Scrum Master. In what ways would you help the team start? A. Ensure the Scrum Team members have compatible personalities, have the tech leads clarify the expectations and responsibilities of each role, work hours and explain the performance rewards system. B. Have the Scrum Team members introduce their background experience with each other, ask the Product Owner to discuss the Product Goal and answer questions, and ensure the team understands the need for a Definition of "Done."	**Correct answer:** B Scrum Teams should have all of the competencies and skills to do the work in the Product Backlog which includes understanding the goals and history of the product and ensuring that they all know what "done" means. Each Scrum team decides how the group will work. Within this team, each member is equally important (no-hierarchy), but responsibilities are clearly defined. This means that each team member should get equal opportunity to voice his or her opinion. Together, they can then form a solution. Ultimately, the Product Owner gets the final say about prioritization, but all other discussions are guided by the Scrum Master to a solution everybody agrees with. Lead the teams to be more self-organizing teams which motivated individuals who work together toward a shared goal and have the ability and authority to take decisions and readily adapt to changing demands. Enable this by letting them know what the Product Goal is and answering their questions.

Question 39

Jonna is a Scrum Master who has been hired by an organization that is new to Scrum. She has been invited to meet the IT and product management team to kick-off the project. During the meeting the Product Owner asks how many Sprints will be needed to address the entire architecture and infrastructure. What are the two best responses for Jonna to explain how such work is handled in Scrum? (Choose the best two answers.)

   A. Jonna should explain that product management should not worry about technical solutions. Jonna should inform them that the Scrum Team will work with the IT department when needed and keep the Product Owner updated on additional time required each Sprint. The additional effort will be added to the velocity to manage the Sprint Planning.

   B. Jonna should coach the Product Owner and Developers to add the known work (w.r.t architecture) to Product Backlog to ensure transparency, have the Developers estimate the work and do this in early Sprints while also creating some business functionality in the early Sprints.

   C. Jonna should explain that it is more effective when architecture and infrastructure emerge alongside the development of business functionality. The additional advantage is that business value is created more quickly and earlier.

   D. Jonna should confirm that architecture and infrastructure is needed before starting on business functionality, but the estimated budget will be difficult to estimate. She should suggest that the first Sprint will be dedicated towards building the technical foundation in order to get an accurate estimation for any additional budget and time required.

Correct answer: B,C

Developers in the Scrum Teams should design and build a platform / a foundation (of Non-Functional requirements and High Value Functions) which would be used by as a Shared Architecture.

Each set of Scrum Team would work on this (to begin with) and work with each other to enhance it with time. Developers in the Scrum Team are responsible for creating the architecture.

The architectural and technical design discussions start as early as sprint planning and continue throughout the sprint as the design is being implemented (i.e. coding/construction).

Defects, non-functional testing (such as performance, reliability, usability testing) also uncover design issues or problems which result in design discussions and may result in changes to the underlying application architecture or specific components or designs.

The Applications overall architecture is not designed upfront, as the actual implementation of it emerges. The emergence of the Architecture is based on guidelines and agreed principles.The System's architecture is decided throughout the project, as understanding emerges, and the Developers learns more about the project.

Developers should have a set of Guiding Architecture Principles that they understand and follows when writing code.
There is no assigned Role (e.g. a software architect) whose job it is to makes sure a consistent architecture is developed. Developers makes sure that the architecture evolves based on the needs.
Developers plans some time each Sprint to discuss the architecture needed for the features planned in that Sprint.

Question 40	Correct answer: A, E
You have a Scrum Team that has been working together for over a year. The Scrum Team consists of eleven members who rarely collaborate and work within their functional boundaries. There are no Sprint Goals and most of the items in the Sprint Backlog are unrelated. The Scrum Team has concluded that it is not possible to create Sprint Goals based on the items in the Product Backlog. What might explain why the Scrum Team is finding it difficult to craft Sprint Goals? (Choose all that apply.) A. The Product Owner has not set the Product Goal and thus it's difficult to create / align the Sprint Goals. B. The Scrum Team is too big. C. Scrum might not be the best framework for this team. D. The Sprints are too long. E. The Product Owner is not ordering the Product Backlog items in the Product Backlog item.	The Product Owner typically comes to the Sprint Planning with a business objective / Product goal in mind and Product Backlog items related to the business objective. After deciding what can be done for the upcoming Sprint, the Scrum Team will craft a Sprint Goal that would be met through the implementation of the items. Prioritized items helps the team craft the Goal. The Sprint goal is not dependent on the size of the team nor length of the Sprint. Scrum is also a framework that's fit all projects, when implemented right.
Question 41 The director of engineering in your organization always stresses the importance of meeting deadlines in order for the engineering department to be seen as a reliable source for the product management department. The director has calculated that the team's velocity needs to increase an additional 15% to meet the commitment he made to management for the release date of the product. He asks Steven, the team's Scrum Master, to increase his team's velocity. Which would be the best two responses for Steven to take? (Choose the best two answers.) A. He helps the director understand that it typically takes a few Sprints for a team to gradually increase the velocity up to the level expected. Meanwhile he presents this to the team as a challenge and a company goal, leaving it up to them to figure out exactly how to achieve this.	**Correct answer: B, D** The Scrum Master serves the organization by helping employees and stakeholders understand and enact Scrum and empirical product development and causing change that increases the productivity of the Scrum Team. The Sprint Backlog is created during the beginning of the Sprint. The Sprint Backlog captures all the work which the developers identify as necessary, to meet the Sprint Goal. The Sprint Backlog is a plan by and for the Developers. The Sprint Backlog is made up of: 1) The Sprint Goal. 2) The Product Backlog items selected for the Sprint. 3) The actionable plan for delivering them are together as an increment and realizing the Sprint Goal. The Sprint Backlog is created during the Sprint Planning. The Sprint Backlog includes: 1) Items selected from the Product Backlog.

B. He informs the director of organizational impediments he is aware of that prevent the team from being more productive. He suggests collaborating with him on how to remove these impediments.

C. He educates his director on how it is part of a team's self-management techniques to improve velocity as needed. He invites the director to the next Sprint Retrospective to brainstorm on how they can improve.

D. He explains how a team uses the velocity of a Sprint primarily to forecast work for the next Sprint, not to perfectly predict future productivity. He refers the director to the Product Owner for all information concerning the progress of development.

E. He tells the director that this is not his responsibility in Scrum. He tells the director to work with the Product Owner to check whether the estimates on the Product Backlog are being respected during implementation.

2) Tasks created by decomposing the selected Product Backlog items (during refinement).

The Sprint Backlog is highly visible, real-time picture of the work that the Developers plan to accomplish during the Sprint in order to achieve the Sprint Goal. The Sprint Backlog is updated throughout the Sprint as more is learned. Developers keep adding tasks during the Sprint, so, the Sprint Backlog keeps getting updated. The Sprint Backlog is the Developers plan for the current Sprint. This plan is not detailed upfront.

Question 42

Steven is a Scrum Master for three Scrum Teams who are building a product using the same Product Backlog. Management wants to standardize how velocity is calculated across all three teams. This will help the management identify which teams are high performing and which teams need more support. What would be the best three responses Steven could provide to management? (Choose the best three answers.)

A. Velocity is the amount of work a Scrum Team does in a Sprint. This measure is unique to that team and used as an input to Sprint Planning.

B. Two teams doing the exact same work, putting in the exact same effort, could reflect different velocities as story points are relative to each team.

Correct answer: A,B,E

Working software is the primary measure of progress. Scrum is based on empirical process control theory where delivering working software frequently and measuring the impact helps the Product Owner maximize opportunity for the business to deliver value.

Agile Velocity measures the amount of work a single team completes during a software development iteration or sprint. It represents the **amount of story points completed over time and** can be visualized as the slope in a classic burndown chart.

Story Points are a unit of measure for expressing an estimate of the overall effort that will be required to fully implement a product backlog item or any other piece of work. Story Points are a **subjective measure** decided and agreed upon by an individual scrum team or organization.

C. Standardizing velocity across teams is a good way to understand which teams are producing the most value. D. Providing incentives based on velocity can increase the Scrum Team's motivation to produce more value. E. There is no direct relationship between velocity and value.	Also remember velocity and story points do not reflect the value of the work done. Velocity should not be used as a performance metric at the executive table and or as a team comparison metric.
Question 43 A team is conducting a Sprint Review where they have invited all the sponsors and stakeholders. One of the stakeholders indicates that due to recent market changes, there is risk and funding might be reduced for the project. This triggers tensions to rise and arguments break out at length between members. As a Scrum Master, what would be the best two actions to take? (Choose the best two answers.) A. Defend the original budget and request the stakeholders to adhere to the originally agreed funding for the product. B. Be objective. Schedule a meeting with the Scrum Team and be transparent on what is known and unknown. Ask the team to continue work until further notified. C. Encourage the stakeholders and Product Owner to focus on delivering the highest value items for the next Sprint D. Avoid getting involved as it is the Product Owner's responsibility to manage Stakeholder expectations. E. Inform everyone to start taking the appropriate actions based on the information they have. They can look for jobs outside the firm as needed.	**Correct answer: B,C** The Scrum Master is responsible for promoting and supporting Scrum by helping everyone embody the values of commitment, courage, focus, openness and respect. Leaders at the company can reduce the supply of invalid information by decreasing its demand. They can do by being transparent. The all-hands meeting is just one example. The Scrum master should always help the team focus on the Sprint Goal and Increment acknowledging the external challenges encountered on the way.

Question 44

During a Sprint Retrospective, a Scrum Team discussed several quality issues which prevented them from delivering a valuable Increment at the end of the Sprint. The Team did mention that they were able to achieve the needed high velocity. What are the best two responses for Steven, their Scrum Master? (Choose the best two answers.)

   A. Acknowledge the hard work but remind the Team that they need to further improve in order to do more in the next Sprint.

   B. Agree and acknowledge the with Team's hard work, so they will be motivated to do even more in the next Sprint.

   C. Facilitate a discussion on how to improve the quality to a level high enough for the Increment to be valuable, even if the measured velocity drops in the next Sprint.

   D. Stress the value of working software over measured velocity.

Correct answer: C,D

Scrum employs an iterative, incremental approach to optimize predictability and control risk. The primary objective of a Sprint (iteration) is to produce a valuable product Increment. Having an Increment will allow the Scrum Team to know the right thing to do in the upcoming Sprint. Having a velocity is important but working software is the primary measure of progress.

Acknowledge the hard work is fine however the team does not need to do "more". It needs to do the right thing by improving quality and delivery the required increment.

Question 45	Correct answer: B,D

Question 45

Your company has notified the stakeholders that they will be having the first release of a new product within ten Sprints. During the seventh Sprint, the Scrum Team discovers that they will not be able to include all of the expected features within the first release. The Product Owner believes if they remove some items from the Definition of Done they will be able to accelerate the development process. Developers objects to this idea as it will lead to technical debt. As a Scrum Master, what would be the best two ways to explain the impact of technical debt? (Choose the best two answers.)

A. As long as there is still technical debt in the current release, feature development for the next release cannot be started. The Product Owner must first agree to fixing this before allowing changes to the Definition of Done.

B. Releasing the version upon a reduced Definition of Done creates false assumptions about the actual state of the system. This will create many interruptions during the development of the next release as fixes will need to be done to the previous release caused from a reduction of quality.

C. The amount of technical debt will need to be analyzed in order to understand the impact on subsequent releases in order to allocate additional Sprints at the end of the project.

D. Reducing the Definition of Done will introduce unknown errors as development progresses and functionality is added. The system can become more difficult to stabilize as work progresses. Development for the actual release as well as future releases will be slowed down in unpredictable ways.

Correct answer: B,D

The Definition of Done helps the Scrum Team have a shared understanding of what it means for work to be complete, to ensure transparency. The Definition of Done is used to assess when work is complete on the product Increment. It also ensures that the work that is done is in usable condition and meets the quality standards for future sustainability.

Question 46	Correct answer: A
If there are multiple Scrum Teams working on the same product, all of the Scrum Teams must mutually define the Definition of Ready (DoR). The DoR is a checklist that the Product Owner must fulfill before a Product Backlog item is presented at Sprint Planning. The DoR protects the Developers from interruptions and increase in scope during the Sprint. It helps the team focus and meet the delivery date on time. Once the DoR is finalized, the specifications defined in the Product backlog items cannot change.	During Product Backlog refinement, detail, order, and estimates will be added or improved until the work on the backlog meets the DOR. By analogy with the "Definition of Done", the team makes explicit and visible the criteria (generally based on the INVEST matrix) that a user story must meet prior to being accepted into the upcoming iteration. By actively participating in Product Backlog refinement, a good Scrum Team will collaborate with the Product Owner in making sure that a standard such as this is observed.

A. False
B. True

- I (Independent). The PBI should be self-contained and it should be possible to bring it into progress without a dependency upon another PBI or an external resource.

- N (Negotiable). A good PBI should leave room for discussion regarding its optimal implementation.

- V (Valuable). The value a PBI delivers to stakeholders should be clear.

- E (Estimable). A PBI must have a size relative to other PBIs.

- S (Small). PBIs should be small enough to estimate with reasonable accuracy and to plan into a time-box such as a Sprint.

- T (Testable). Each PBI should have clear acceptance criteria which allow its satisfaction to be tested.

Just as completed items which fit the definition of "done" are said to be "DONE-done", items that fit the definition of ready are called "READY-ready".

Experienced developers are usually aware that a user story is meant to **represent an ongoing and evolving conversation with stakeholders, and not a fixed specification.**

Product Backlog items should be clear enough and have enough information for the Product Owner and Developers to understand the work that needs to be done and to create a forecast of Product Backlog items to implement the Sprint Goal. Nothing stops the flow of Sprints, for example, we do not delay the Sprint because the items are not ready. In such cases, the "unready" items would be selected for the Sprint anyway and refined during the Sprint. In the case that the Product Backlog items are not clear enough, Developers forecasts the most likely Product Backlog items to meet the goal and create a Sprint Backlog based on a likely initial design and plan. Once the time-box for the Sprint Planning meeting is over, the scrum team should start the Sprint and continue to analyze, decompose, and create additional functionality during the Sprint. At the end of the Sprint, the Scrum Team can discuss in the upcoming Sprint Retrospective why this happened and what changes will make it less likely to recur.

Thus, a DoR should never be considered a gateway to get the Sprint / Development started.

Question 47
An organization is planning to form five new Scrum Teams to work on building a single product. A few of the future team members ask the Scrum Master who will coordinate the work between the different Scrum Teams. What should the Scrum Master reply?

A. The Scrum Master will visit the five Scrum Teams daily to ensure alignment and that all Sprint Backlogs remain synchronized.

B. The Scrum Master will teach the Product Owner to work with the technical leads on ordering Product Backlog in a way to avoid too much technical and development overlap during a Sprint. This will help reduce coordination.

C. Teach them that it is their responsibility to form the teams such that each team will have the necessary skills, knowledge, and competencies to create an integrated Increment by the end of every Sprint. They themselves will be

Correct answer: C
Scrum Teams are structured and empowered by the organization to organize and manage their own work. This includes deciding how to form teams when multiple teams are needed. The resulting synergy optimizes the Scrum Team's overall efficiency and effectiveness. They are self-organizing.

responsible for coordinating all the work as needed. D. At the end of Sprint Planning, the Scrum Master will collect all Sprint tasks and create a consolidated plan for the entire Sprint. E. Advise the teams to minimize dependencies by working on separate development branches and integrate at the end of four Sprint cycles.	
Question 48 During a Product Backlog refinement meeting, the Product Owner introduces a new Product Goal that will be worked on for the next several Sprints. The Product Owner envisions several key features necessary to be delivered in order to meet Product Goal. One of the features in the Product Goal is enhanced audits and security. This non-functional security requirement is not applied to the increment delivered in the previous Sprints. What are the different ways the Scrum Team can handle these high-security requirements? (Choose the best three answers.) A. They should be implemented by a separate security team so that security can be resolved through application enhancements without impacting the functional development. B. During the Sprint Retrospective, the Scrum Team should assess how to add these expectations to their Definition of Done so every future Increment will meet these security requirements. C. The security requirements are added to the Product Backlog and addressed throughout the Sprints, combined with creating the business functionality in those Sprints. D. Work which needs to be done to change the existing increment can be added as separate Product backlog items.	**Correct answer: B, C, D** In order to ensure transparency, work that must be done to the product must be visible in either the Product Backlog or the Definition of Done. Non-functional requirements describe qualities of the system being developed. E.g. the system should be secure, extensible and have acceptable performance. The way to meet such requirements is: 1) Have them as a part of the Definition of Done and check the applicable Increment against these criteria. 2) Add them as the Acceptance Criteria to the applicable Product Backlog item. 3) Include them as Product Backlog item itself.

E. A complete list of security-related Product Backlog items needs to be created before starting a new Sprint. F. They should be planned in parallel Sprints so not to disrupt the feature development. After security concerns have been finalized, they will be applied to the work that is already completed before new feature development can continue.	

Question 49
 	
John has been working in a company as Project Director for 10 years. 15 different healthcare products fall under Johns control. In the past John has always had Products status reports send to him. These status reports have helped John understand about the work that has already been done on the Products and the work remaining. The company has recently moved to a Scrum Framework. John has approached all the Product Owners to produce such reports. Which is the best way to respond to John's request?
 	
  A. Politely tell John that Scrum does not support Project Managers as there is no such role defined in Scrum.
  B. Produce the Product status reports which John needs as the Product status reports produce transparency and Scrum is all about transparency.
  C. Share the Product Backlog with John and make sure he knows how to look for the information needed.
  D. Share the Stakeholder reports with John.
  E. The Product Owners should produce the report. They can delegate the work to the Developers or Scrum Master if needed.
	Correct answers: C
	
	One of the key pillars that support the empirical process control is Transparency. Transparency will help manage stakeholder expectations and allow the teams to effectively adapt if and when needed.
	
	A duty of the Scrum Team is to be transparent. Those who need information are responsible for getting it. So, people concerned about the progress can investigate the artifacts of the Scrum Team (Product Backlog, Sprint Backlog, increment itself) and visit Sprint Review, if needed.

Question 50	Correct answers: A

Kabir has been doing his best and helping other Scrum Team members. This action demonstrates which of the following?
 	
   A.   Value of Commitment.
   B.   High Performance.
   C.   Honesty.
   D.   Value of Transparency.
	People personally commit to achieving the goals of the Scrum Team by doing their best and helping others.Scrum Values give direction to the work done in Scrum, along with the work ethics the Scrum team should have. Commitment: The Scrum Team members should personally commit to achieving the Scrum Goals. Commitment is about dedication and applies to the actions, the effort, not the final result. The Scrum Teams should:
	
	· Commit to quality, commit to collaborate.
	· Commit to learn, commit to do the best they can, every day again.
	· Commit to the Sprint Goal, commit to be professional.
	· Commit to self-organize, commit to excellence.
	· Commit to the agile principles, commit to create working software.
	· Commit to look for improvements, commit to the Definition of Done.
	· Commit to the Scrum framework, commit to focus on Value.
	· Commit to finish work, commit to inspect & adapt.
	. Commit to transparency.
	
	Remember there is no value called Transparency. Scrum Values are :
	
	1. Commitment
	2. Courage
	3. Focus
	4. Openness
	5. Respect

Question 51	**Correct answers: B**

It's the third day of a 2-week sprint. A Developer approaches a Product Owner as he has questions about a functionality. The Product Owner does not know the answer and would need to reach out to the stakeholders in order to get the answer. The Product Owner does ask the Developer to wait till the Sprint Reviews when all the stakeholders meet. Should the Product Owner and Developer have to wait for this long?
 	
  A. True
  B. False
	Getting feedback from Stakeholders is a crucial activity in Scrum. Working with stakeholders frequently ensures the team to focus on the right things to build. Although it is required to have Stakeholders at Sprint Review, they can also engage with the Scrum Team during Product Backlog Refinement, Sprint Planning or anytime during the Sprint if the Scrum Team requires it.

Question 52
 	
What is management's role in Scrum? (Choose two best answers)
 	
  A. Managing the Product Owners and Scrum Masters.
  B. Managing the Finances and Budgets of the Teams.
  C. To provide the necessary environment for Scrum Teams to thrive and flourish.
  D. Provide support to the Scrum Teams as needed (by providing insight and resources that help Scrum Team improve).
	Correct answers: C, D
	
	The Management supports the Product Owner with insights and information which helps with developing a high value product. The Management also supports the Scrum Master to cause organizational changes that foster empiricism, self-organization, bottom-up intelligence, and intelligent release of software. The Management has no active role in the actual product development through Scrum. However, Management external to the Scrum team is incredibly important in setting the vision and strategy to guide the overall direction of the organization.
	
	.

Question 53	**Correct answers: E**
A Scrum Master has been complaining that the level of openness between team members of Scrum Team is not to the level expected. Management is aware that the success of a Scrum depends upon how people adapt to the Scrum Values. They are aware that Open communication is an Important Scrum Value. What could be the impacts of reduced openness? A. It becomes difficult to collaborate between team Members. B. Quality level of the Product could reduce. C. Stakeholder trust could decrease. D. Time to market could increase. E. All of the above.	The Scrum Team and its stakeholders agree to be open about all the work and the challenges with performing the work. The level of openness will directly impact the level of transparency. Decreased transparency in turn will lead to less collaboration, decreased trust and delayed market releases.
Question 54 A management team member does not understand the value of spending so much time on defining the "Definition of Done". As a Scrum Master, you can explain that the benefits of "Definition of Done" are: (Choose all that Apply) A. The definition of done helps determine the amount of work completed and amount of work remaining to create a valuable increment by the end of the Sprint. B. The definition of done is a checklist to monitor the Scrum Team members progress towards a task. C. The definition of done creates transparency and provides a common understanding of "done" state of the increment presented at the Sprint Review. D. It helps compare the Scrum Teams efficiency.	**Correct answers: A, C** When a Product Backlog item or an Increment is described as "Done", everyone must understand what "Done" means. Scrum Team members must have a shared understanding of what it means for work to be complete, to ensure transparency and is used to assess when work is complete on the product Increment. This definition of "Done" provides the team guidance on what it takes to make the increment valuable.

Question 55	Correct answers: B, E

A Scrum Team has requested additional time towards the end of the release to integrate with the work produced in the previous sprints increment. They also need time to do additional testing before releasing. (Multiple browser Testing, Multiple DB Testing etc.). What scenarios most likely occurred? (choose the best answers)
 	
  A. The testing team members must not be working at the velocity expected.
  B. The team's definition of done might not be comprehensive enough or incomplete. (integration work and testing might not be included)
  C. This is normal as end to end integration testing can only happen towards the end of the release and will need additional time.
  D. Scum must have been customized to the teams need.
  E. The Definition of done is being ignored by the Team.
	At the end of a Sprint, the new Increment must be "Done," which means it must be in valuable and meet the Scrum Team's definition of "Done".
	
	The Definition of Done is a formal description of the state of the Increment when it meets the quality measures required for the product. The moment a Product Backlog item meets the Definition of Done, an Increment is born.
	The Definition of Done creates transparency by providing everyone a shared understanding of what work was completed as part of the Increment.
	If a Product Backlog item does not meet the Definition of Done:
	1) It cannot be released.
	2) It cannot be even presented at the Sprint Review.
	If a Product Backlog item does not meet the Definition of Done, it returns to the Product Backlog for future consideration.
	All members of a Scrum Team must have a shared understanding of what it means for work to be complete, to ensure transparency.
	
	Definition of done should include:
	1) Conventions, standards and guidelines of the Organization which need to be followed at the minimum should be a part of the definition of one.
	2) Any compliance or regulatory requirements

Question 56	**Correct answers: B, D**
Scrum has a few rules defined within the framework. Which rules can be helpful in helping the team self-organize effectively? Choose two best answers. A. Creating the "Definition of Done" and "Definition of Ready" for every EPIC and Story. B. Timeboxing the events in Scrum to allow regular inspection and adaption opportunities. C. Defining the requirements clearly. D. Creating a valuable product by the end of each sprint. E. Creating a potentially shippable product by the end of each sprint. F. Having a mixture of skilled team members so external resource dependency can be completely eliminated.	Time-boxing promotes regularity and focus for self-organized teams. With the 2020 Scrum guide, the emphasis is more on producing one single valuable increment, regardless of it being in shippable state or not. Having a valuable Increment allows teams to collaboratively make decisions on what needs to be done next.
Question 57	**Correct answers: C, D**
An Organization has been following the traditional waterfall process for years. The management decides to start implementing Scrum and has hired a New Scrum Master. What should the Scrum Master do? Choose all that apply: A. Start with looking at the existing teams and divide them into multiple Scrum Teams. B. Start attending the Daily calls of every team and start enforcing Scrum. C. Schedule formal training sessions to coach Scrum. Arrange personal coaching sessions if needed. D. Make sure that the Scrum Events are scheduled for all the Scrum Teams.	The Scrum Master serves the organization in several ways, including: • Leading and coaching the organization in its Scrum adoption. • Planning Scrum implementations within the organization. • Helping employees and stakeholders understand and enact Scrum and empirical product development.

Question 58	Correct answers: A, D

A Toy company has recently hired James as a Product Owner. James has complete ownership over all the Toys manufactured in the company. His responsibilities will also include all financial aspects of the product which includes investments, budgeting, pricing strategies, and financial forecasting. Can Scrum be used to help James with these responsibilities and if so, how? (choose the best two answers)
 	
   A. Yes. The Scrum framework allows frequent inspection of the outcomes of the delivered Sprint Increments. James can understand what value is being produced each Sprint.
 	
   B. No. Budgeting and forecasting is outside the Scrum Framework.
 	
   C. Yes and No. Scrum can be used for operation development activities. The finance teams outside can help with the product owner with respect to investments, budgeting, pricing strategies, and financial forecasting.
 	
   D. Yes. James can manage the allocated budgets and investment using Scrum. Each release would be a assigned a set budget. The release can be further broken down into Sprints.
	The cost of developing, delivering, and sustaining products can impact how the flow of value is managed throughout the life of a product. Each Sprint is an opportunity to inspect the investment (financial, time, effort, etc.) against the returned value (customer satisfaction, revenue, etc.) of the work that has been delivered. The team can then decide on what it should do next to maximize the value of the investment.
	
	Release planning (not an official Scrum Event) in Scrum happens every sprint, either as part of the sprint review or in the normal course of preparing for the subsequent sprint.
	
	Release planning in Scrum consists of several activities:
	1. Review and update the release constraints of scope, date, and budget.
	2. Product backlog grooming.
	3. Review and update the minimum releasable features (MRFs)
	4. Product a sprint map (optional).
	
	A release is a combination of multiple Sprints. Each Sprint is an opportunity to inspect the investment (money invested, time, effort, etc.) against the returned value (customer satisfaction, revenue, product value).The cost of developing, delivering, and sustaining products can impact product value is managed throughout the life of a product. Calculating costs on a fixed-date release can be done as follows :
	
	1. Determine who is on the team.
	2. Determine the sprint length, in hours or days.
	3. Multiply personnel cost (per hour or per day) by sprint length to get a cost per sprint. For a fixed-date release, multiply the number of sprints in the release by the cost per sprint.

Question 59	Correct answers: D
A Scrum Master is tasked with helping an organization create Scrum Teams. The organization is new to Scrum. When forming teams, which of the following approaches would best conform with the values defined in Scrum? (choose the best answer)	It's important that Scrum Team members have trust between them. This trust is cultivated from the Scrum values of commitment, courage, focus, openness and respect. By embodying these values, the Scrum Team is able to maximize the benefits of empiricism.

A. A skills matrix would need to be created and Scrum Team members would need to be distributed to create a "Whole" Team.

B. The Scrum Master should create the teams according to what is needed for their project and work with the technical leads to assign members according to the needs of upcoming Sprints.

C. The Scrum Master should work with the leadership team to allocate members based on roles, titles, seniority and experience to ensure that all Scrum Teams have equivalent capacities.

D. Provide the future team members with boundaries and give them the support needed to self-organize into Scrum Teams.

Because the Scrum Team will be the one doing the work, it's most effective to have the future team members decide how to organize the teams as they will be the ones working together.

Question 60

Sid has been working in an organization for 10 years as Scrum Master. Due to his experience, Sid has been assigned to a product which will be worked on by three Scrum Teams. Sid recommends that the teams should get going and produce an integrated increment in the first Sprint itself. The Scrum team members don't even know each other's name yet. During the initial conversation, various members reject this idea. However various members propose different ideas on how an increment can be achieved. Of the proposed choices, which ones should Sid support? (choose two best answer)

A. Each Scrum Team delivers Increments in its own code branch. Once the Sprint Review is done, the code should be merged, and the testing should be completed.

B. Sid should let the Scrum Team decide. If majority of them say that it's not possible to create an increment in the first sprint, then Sid should accept the decision.

C. Each Scrum Team should deliver an increment at the end of each Sprint. At the end of the Sprint, new Product Backlog items will then be added to the next Sprint Backlog to check if integration is not complete.

D. Scrum encourages at least one functionality to be added to an increment every Sprint specially (when it's the first Sprint). This is not mandatory however will get the team going. All Scrum Teams must agree on a mutual understanding of 'done' that defines all work necessary to deliver a potentially shippable Increment that includes all previous Increments delivered for the product.

E. The Definition of Done for each team can vary as long as each Definition of Done, at the bare minimum, includes the criteria which make the increment compatible across all the teams.

F. Wait until enough of the infrastructure and architecture is in place before starting the first Sprints. This will increase the success of delivering integrated Increments in Sprint 1.

Correct answers: D, E

When a Product Backlog item or an Increment is described as "Done", everyone must understand what "Done" means. If there are multiple Scrum Teams working on the system or product release, the Scrum Teams must mutually define the definition of "Done" to have a shared understanding of what it means for work to be complete, to ensure transparency. Each Increment is additive to all prior Increments and thoroughly tested, ensuring that all Increments work together.

When multiple teams are working on the same product, there can be more than one Definition of "Done" for all of them. Each team might be working on a different part of the product (e.g. desktop application, mobile application, web application), or simply have different styles of work. If there are multiple Scrum Teams working together on a product, they must mutually define and comply with a shared Definition of Done. They can add their own specific criteria on top of this Definition of "Done" Criteria.
When different teams are working on the same product, they must observe a common Definition of Done which qualifies for the integrated increment.

The Definition of Done observed by an individual team should reinforce and not contradict any shared Definition for a product increment. For example, a team may incorporate a shared DoD as a subset of their own. Scrum Teams Definition of "Done" = Nexus Definition of "Done" + Optional Scrum Team Specific Definition of "Done" Criteria.

Version 32.0 "© 2019 Sid Bathia. All rights reserved."

Question 61	Correct Answer: D.E
Charles (Product Owner) is new to Scrum. 3 Scum teams work together on a Product and Charles has been assigned to this Product. Every Sprint Planning, the 3 Scrum Teams choose the work they are going to do (from the Product Backlog) for the Sprint. Charles feels the teams select very little work. How should work from the Product Backlog be distributed for multiple teams? (Choose 2 answers) A. Charles should be distributing the work from the Product Backlog to the teams, because he is responsible for the Product Backlog. B. Charles should work with the Scrum Master to assess the team's velocity. He should be distributing the work to the team based on each team's velocity. C. Each Teams individual team members / Developers should pull in the work (which they are going to work on) from the Product Backlog based on what they are comfortable with. D. Developers within the Scrum Team (or appropriate representatives of each team) should coordinate and pull work in from the Product Backlog. This should be in agreement within all team members (within and across the teams) and the Product Owner. E. Charles should talk about his concerns during the Sprint retrospective and discuss the reasons for the little work being picked.	During Sprint Planning the number of items selected from the Product Backlog for the Sprint is solely up to the Developers in the Scrum Teams regardless of the number of Teams working from the same Product Backlog. Only the Developers in the Scrum Team can best assess what can be accomplished over the upcoming Sprint.

Question 62	Correct Answer: A, B, C, D, E
The advantages of a Sprint Goal are: (Choose all that Apply): A. The Sprint Goal gives sense to the tasks and motivates the Team. People tend to be more enthusiastic and enjoy their work when they understand what it's for and how they contribute to the common cause. B. The Sprint Goal unites the Scrum Team. C. The Sprint Goal helps in managing risks. D. The Sprint Goal helps with focus and making decisions. E. The Sprint Goal helps manage stakeholders' expectations.	The Sprint Goal is an objective set for the Sprint that can be met through the implementation of Product Backlog. It provides guidance to the Scrum Team on why it is building the Increment. What needs to be done is a collaboration between all Scrum Team members and how to best deliver it is decided by the Scrum Team. The most effective way of meeting goals and objectives on a self-organized team is through the embodiment of the Scrum Values: courage, commitment, openness, focus, and respect. Advantages of a Sprint Goal: 1. The Sprint Goal gives sense to the tasks and motivates the Team. People tend to be more enthusiastic and enjoy their work when they understand what it's for and how they contribute to the common cause. 2. The Sprint Goal unites the Scrum Team. 3. The Sprint Goal helps in managing risks. Each Sprint can be considered a project with a fixed budget and date. The Sprint Goal indicates the risk that the Scrum Team mitigates during the current Sprint. The risk can be associated with functionality, technologies, human factors, the external environment, etc. 4. The Sprint Goal helps with focus and making decisions. 5. The Sprint Goal helps manage stakeholders' expectations.

Question 63

A Product Owner works with three Scrum Teams. During a Product Backlog Refinement meeting, the Product Owner introduces the teams to the new items created in the Product Backlog. The upcoming Sprint Goal is to create a front end / user interface / UX which allow corrections to existing system data. The new items introduced require the front end to be secured so only privileged users can make the corrections. This new UX standard will be more stringent than what was created in the previous Increments. Which of the following approach would be most appropriate going forward?

A. The Scrum Team should document all the requirements before starting so it does not to disrupt the development work during the Sprint. After UX requirements have been finalized, the team should apply the work to the completed items in the previous Sprint before continuing on new items.

B. The Scrum team should handle all the UX requirements in a separate Product or Sprint Backlog. Needed experts can work on this Backlog separately and get the work completed.

C. Assign the work to specialist an continue work as usual.

D. The Scrum Team should expand the Definition of Done (in the current or upcoming Sprint Retrospective) to add a more stringent criteria for meeting UX / security requirements and apply them going forward. For the items which are already completed in the previous Sprints (which do not meet the new UX standard), new product backlog items can be created to make them UX compliant.

Correct Answer: D

When multiple teams are working on the same project, there can be more than one Definition of "Done" for all of them. Each team might be working on a different part of the product (e.g. desktop application, mobile application, web application), or simply have different styles of work, and therefore require different Definitions of "Done". This is all right, if their definitions are compatible and have the capacity to create one Integrated Increment each Sprint.

All Scrum Teams must have a Definition of "Done" that makes their combined work potentially releasable. A Few Good Criteria to include in the Definition of Done are:

o Unit tests passed.
o Code reviewed Completed.
o Acceptance criteria met / Acceptance test passed.
o Functional tests passed
o Non-Functional requirements met.
o Integrated into a clean build
o Automated regression tests pass
o Feature level functional tests passed
o Meets compliance requirements

During each Sprint Retrospective, the Scrum Team plans ways to increase product quality by adapting and improving the Definition of "Done" as appropriate. So, Definition of Done changes with time.

Question 64	Correct Answer: B
A Scrum Team suggests applying a Definition of Ready (DoR) to the Product Backlog items. According to the team all the items within the DoR should be completed before starting the Sprint. They want it to be mandatory and this will also make the Sprint Planning easier. This should be allowed. A. True B. False	Product Backlog items should be clear enough and have enough information for the Product Owner and Development to understand the work that needs to be done and to create a forecast of Product Backlog items to implement the Sprint Goal. Nothing stops the flow of Sprints, for example, we do not delay the Sprint because the items are not ready. In such cases, the "unready" items would be selected for the Sprint and refined during the Sprint. In the case that the Product Backlog items are not clear enough, Developers would forecast "the most likely" estimates if needed. The team would create a Sprint Backlog based on a likely initial design and plan. Once the time-box for the Sprint Planning meeting is over, the team would start the Sprint and continue to analyze, decompose, and create additional functionality during the Sprint. At the end of the Sprint, the Scrum Team can discuss in the upcoming Sprint Retrospective why this happened and what changes will make it less likely to recur. The Definition of Ready can be useful but it should NOT be used as a gateway for Sprint Planning. As a guideline, it can be useful but as a process it can block the flow of value.
Question 65	**Correct Answer: B**
A Scrum Master works with 3 Scrum Teams. All three Scrum Teams work on the same Product. The Scrum Master is of the opinion that the teams spend too much time refining the Product Backlog items. How much time should be spent refining the Product Backlog? A. Not more than 10% of the capacity of the Scrum Team. B. As much as the Product Owner and Developers agree is necessary to create "Ready" Product Backlog items.	The Scrum Team decides how and when refinement is done. Refinement within a single team usually consumes no more than 10% of the capacity of the Scrum Team. For multiple teams as well, the suggested Timebox of Product Refinement (not mandated) is up to 10% of the capacity of a Scrum Team during a Sprint. However, Inspection and adaption may lead to this being adjusted over time as required.

Question 66	Correct Answer: C
A company has been doing really well selling its Product. The client base (number of clients) which the product caters to, has increased over a period of time. The demands of the clients have increased as well. The Scrum Team has also been gradually growing in size. The team decides it would be a good time to split into 2 smaller teams. What should be the primary concern for the 2 Scrum Teams working on the same Product Backlog? (Choose only one answer) A. Drop in initial velocity. B. Even distribution of work. C. Dependencies between the two teams. D. All of the above.	One of the responsibilities of a Scrum Team is to deliver a valuable increment by the end of their Sprint. Without a valuable increment, the Sprint is considered a failed Sprint, as the opportunity to inspect and adapt is lost. So, when multiple teams are working from the same Product Backlog, their primary concern should be to manage the risks that emerge from dependencies with the goal of creating an integrated, valuable Increment by the end of their Sprint. Drop in velocity is not incorrect either however it is only temporary. As teams get more acquainted with the setup, the velocity will increase.
Question 67 John is a new Product Owner. What action should John take if the Developers decide that Retrospectives are no longer necessary? A. John should talk to the Scrum Master and ask him to start facilitating more productive retrospectives. B. No action is needed by the Product Owner as the Scrum team is self-governing. C. Have a one to one with the team lead only and try to understand the issue. D. All of the above.	**Correct Answer: A** The Scrum Master facilitates Inspection and Adaption opportunities as requested or as needed. The Scrum Master ensures that the Scrum Team is meeting as necessary (all scrum events are conducted and are effective) and teaches the Scrum Team to keep the meetings within the time-box. The Scrum Master is responsible for the scrum team's effectiveness. A scrum team will be effective when all the events they conduct are effective.

Question 68

Kabir is a Scrum Master and has just joined the organization. He sees that the Daily Scrum is taking an hour instead of 15 mins which is the typical time-box. He observes that the majority of the time is being used by Charles who is a developer. Charles talks about important stats and graphs however this information is not always relevant to the event. Which actions should Kabir take? (Choose 2)

A. Work with the team so that they can discuss the problem and make suggestions. Allow them to take ownership of the solution.
B. Ask Charles to speak last so that everyone has a chance to talk at the Daily Scrum.
C. Suggest that each team member only take a maximum of 2 minutes to speak at the Daily Scrum.
D. Start facilitating the Daily Scrums.
E. Speak with Charles privately and coach him on the purpose of the Daily Scrum.

Correct Answer: A, E

The Scrum Master supports the Scrum Team by:
1) Facilitating Scrum Team's decisions.
2) Removing impediments that hinder the Scrum Team's progress.

A Scrum master also acts as a great Facilitator that sets the stage and provides clear boundaries in which the team can collaborate. This includes facilitation of the Scrum events to ensure they'll achieve the desired outcome and - most importantly - that the empirical process is optimized.

A Scrum master is a great coach that helps individuals and groups to continuously improve in how they deliver valuable outcomes as a team or as an organization.

Question 69	Correct Answer: C
During a daily call, Charles and John have been arguing over a Product Backlog item. Charles thinks that the Product Backlog item is done while John thinks it's not completely done. What should the Scrum Master do? A. The Scrum Master should bring the Developers together, go through the Definition of Done, and make the final decision himself. B. The Scrum Master should not interfere. The Team should be resolving their own conflicts. C. The Scrum Master should facilitate a session with all Scrum Team members to help them resolve the conflict, refine the Definition of Done if needed and allow them to become effective again. D. The Scrum Master should bring the Product Owner to the discussion and have him/her decide the work needed to make the item 'Done'.	A great Scrum Master recognizes team conflict in an early stage and can apply different activities to resolve it. A great Scrum Master understands conflict isn't necessarily wrong. Healthy conflict and constructive disagreement can be used to build an even stronger team. A good Scrum Master is an Impediment Remover that helps resolve issues that are blocking the team's progress, considering the self-organizing capabilities of the Team. Having the Product Owner in such discussions is a great idea. However, it would be great if the entire Scrum team including the Product Owner are present to discuss the definition of done and refine it needed.

Question 70	**Correct Answer: B, C, E**
Sid is a Scrum Master at Samsung. Samsung (Mobile Unit) has one single product with multiple Scrum Teams working on it. Some Scrum teams have been working at Samsung for 10+ years and some of them are relatively new. During a Product Backlog refinement session, the Product Owner informs the teams they need to manage the Guardrails warnings. Guardrail warnings are technical alerts each team gets if the code does not follow the standards. The developers lets the Product Owner know that each of their teams will need full-time help from Jake, the guardrail expert in their upcoming Sprints. Which of the following would be appropriate for Sid to consider? **(choose the best three answers)**	The Scrum Master is responsible for removing impediments within the current context of the situation AND helping the team stay within the boundaries defined by the Scrum framework.

A. Combine the teams into one them so they no longer need to share Jake's services.

B. Investigate whether applying additional techniques or frameworks for scaling Scrum would be helpful since you have multiple teams working on the same product with dependencies.

C. Developers can volunteer to take on Jakes work, if they have the expertise.

D. Sid should ask Jake to work with the organization to hire additional people so that he can train them.

E. Have the Product Owner and Developers re-order the Product Backlog items so that Jake can serve full-time on a single team (one team at a time) for a Sprint.

F. Propose a separate Sprint at the end of the project to work on items dependent on Jake's domain.

Question 71	Correct Answer: C, E, F
Which options show that a Scrum Team is self-Managed? (choose the best three answers) A. Developers are staying focused in working within their own functional role and are able to handoff the work to other roles at scheduled points of time. B. The Scrum Team has a high velocity and is able to reduce the frequency of the Daily Scrum. C. Scrum Team members are collectively deciding and re-planning their work throughout the Sprint to meet the Sprint and Product Goal. D. Individual Developers are cross-functional and are working in more than one Scrum teams. E. Developers in the Scrum Team creates their own Sprint Backlog during the sprint planning. Not only do they create it but they manage its evolution during the sprint as they learn more. F. Developers are able to meet the Sprint Goal.	Self-organized teams choose how best to accomplish their work, rather than being directed by others outside the team. Self-organized teams are also responsible for applying the most appropriate practices to provide transparency in order to optimize value, control risk, and manage expectations.
Question 72	Correct Answer: A
Allowing technical debt to be incurred can allow the Scrum Team to deliver more items in a given period of time. This gives the perception that the Scrum Team has a higher velocity than what it actually has. A. True B. False	Technical debt is a natural occurrence when developing complex products. It is a concept in software development that reflects the implied cost of additional rework caused by choosing an easy solution now instead of using a better approach that would take longer. And how it is managed will depend on the team AND context of the situation. Allowing technical debt to be incurred can allow the Scrum Team to deliver more items in the same period of time. This gives the perception that the Scrum Team has a higher velocity than what it actually has. More items delivered does not necessarily mean they are moving faster if they are taking shortcuts.

Question 73	Correct Answer: A, C
An organization has 5 Products, each with separate Product Backlog. Each Product Backlog has 2 dedicated Scrum Teams. How many Product Owners could the organization have? (Choose two) A. Five Product Owners. One for each product. B. 10 or less Product Owners assuming each Scrum team needs a Product Owner. C. One Product Owner for all five products.	For every Product, there is a Product Backlog. For every Product Backlog there is a Product Owner. The Product Owner can be fully committed to a single product or can be part time, as long as the product has a Product Owner. The Product Owner is the sole person responsible for maximizing the value of the product. This reduces complexity in knowing who is making what decisions and why. He/she may delegate his/her responsibilities to the Developers but will still remain accountable for the outcome of those responsibilities.
Question 74	**Correct Answer: A**
Kevin is a Scrum Master of a Scrum Team (9 members in total). The Scrum Team recently worked on building a website. The Scrum Team had successfully released the MVP (Minimum Viable Product) after 16 Sprints. The Scrum Team, over time has become very matured and self-managing. The MVP was received well in the market and the sponsors released additional funding to implement new functionalities in the upcoming Sprints. In one of the meeting Kevin notices that the same set of Developers are working directly with the Product Owner during every Product Backlog refinement. These Developers then communicate the requirements to the rest of the developers. What is the best action Kevin can take? A. Coach the team about the benefits of having all the needed developers during refinement session. It's fine if they continue to do what they are doing. B. Kevin should attend the Product Backlog Refinement meetings to make sure that different developers are present each time. This will give a chance for each developer to grow. C. Discuss the matter with Product Owner and ask him to invite all Developers to participate in the Product Backlog refinement.	The scenario in the question clearly indicates that the Scrum Team is very matured and self-managing. Such teams tend to organize work by themselves and are very clear about who will do what. If the same set of people are attending the Product Backlog refinement, it is very likely to be an agreement within the Scrum Team. They are accountable and in control of how they do things.

D. Bring up the matter in Sprint Retrospective and ask the other team members if they are feeling left out. E. Do nothing. It's not the Scrum Master place to comment.	
Question 75 Jane is a Scrum Master employed by the engineering department. The Director of Engineering considers using Scrum for a new project but wonders about the value of having all the Developer attend the Daily Scrum. She is concerned that the employees already attend allot of mandatory company meetings. Given the workload, the Daily Scrum would take away even more time. What are two outcomes of the Daily Scrum that Jane should explain on why the Daily Scrum is important? Select the two best answers A. The Daily Scrum serves as a reporting tool for Jane. As a Scrum Master she uses this meeting to learn about the task performed and remaining. She then uses the team's updates to plan their work for the next day, making sure that every team member is assigned the right tasks. B. Through the short, daily alignment of the Daily Scrum, Developers grow and improve a shared understanding of the most important work to be undertaken in the next 24 hours to achieve the best possible progress toward the Sprint Goal. This daily opportunity to inspect and adapt will enable the Developers to best tackle any unforeseen circumstances that might otherwise disrupt the team's progress. C. During the Daily Scrum, Developers update the Scrum board with the current status of their work and the progress made with as much details as possible. This increases transparency. D. Developers in the Scrum Team will produce a daily status report indicating how much time was spent working on individual tasks since the last Daily Scrum. The reports will help in discussing how the Sprint went at the Sprint	**Correct Answer: B, E** Developers in the Scrum Team use the Daily Scrum to inspect progress made toward the Sprint Goal and to inspect how progress is trending toward completing the work in the Sprint Backlog. Every day, Developers should understand how it intends to work together as a self-organizing team to accomplish the Sprint Goal and create the anticipated Increment by the end of the Sprint.

Retrospective meeting. The report will provide detailed insights into the accuracy of estimates versus actual time spent, which can be used to create better estimates at the next Sprint Planning. D E. During the Daily Scrum, Developers will inform the Scrum masters (and other developers) of impediments that are hindering their progress, and for which they have no means to resolve. They will enable Jane to help the team remove the impediments and be more productive.	
Question 76 At the tenth Sprint Review, the stakeholders seem disappointed, frustrated as well as angry. They say the product does not meet their needs. They say It will cost more than they anticipated. What factors could have led to this situation? Select two best answers A. The Product Owner has not been interacting frequently with the stakeholders. He should have kept them aware of the progress of the project. B. The stakeholders haven't been using the Sprint Reviews to actively engage, inspect and review the progress. C. Changes to the project plan were not adequately documented, planned and shared. The change request procedure was not diligently followed. D. The stakeholders were not allowed to enter the development area or be present at the Daily Scrum. Had they given the opportunity, the current situation could have been avoided. E. The Project Management Office (PMO) and its project managers have not been engaged adequately causing the project plan to become inaccurate.	**Correct Answer: A,B** A Sprint Review is held at the end of the Sprint to inspect the Increment and adapt the Product Backlog if needed. During the Sprint Review, the Scrum Team and stakeholders collaborate about what was done in the Sprint. Based on that and any changes to the Product Backlog during the Sprint, attendees collaborate on the next things that could be done to optimize value. This is an informal meeting, not a status meeting, and the presentation of the Increment is intended to elicit feedback and foster collaboration. The Product Owner is responsible for maximizing the value of the product resulting from work of the Scrum Team. How this is done may vary widely across organizations, Scrum Teams, and individuals. The Product Owner is the sole person responsible for managing the Product Backlog. Product Backlog management includes: • Clearly expressing Product Backlog items • Ordering the items in the Product Backlog to best achieve goals and missions • Optimizing the value of the work the Scrum performs • Ensuring that the Product Backlog is visible, transparent, and clear to all, and shows what the Scrum Team will work on next & • Ensuring the ScrumTeam understands items in the Product Backlog to the level needed.

Question 77	**Correct Answer: C**

A new Scrum Team that has been formed to build a Product. Most of the members are new to Scrum or have very little Scrum experience. During the first Sprint Review, the Increment didn't meet the Product Owner's expectation. Developers within the Scrum Team said that they built the Increment based on their understanding and interpretation of the Product Backlog items. What could have caused such a situation? (Choose the best answer)
  A. The requirements were too complex.
  B. The Scrum Master did not take over the administrative tasks as expected.
  C. The Product Owner and Developers did not spend enough time working together. Each day (and every event including the Daily Sprint) within a Sprint was an opportunity to inspect the Increment for the Product Owner.
  D. No specific reason as these types of situations are very common in new Scrum Teams.
	The situation most likely occurred since the Product Owner and Developers didn't collaborate and inspect the increment as needed. For any Increment to be delivered successfully, Developers must have a very good understanding of the requirements and the Definition of Done. They can achieve that by working closely with the Product Owner who can provide clarification on what is exactly expected from the Increment. Adaption and Inspection is important. The more the Product owner (or needed stakeholders) can adapt, the more the Scrum team can adapt to meet the expectations.

Question 78	**Correct Answer: B**

A organization requires all Increments to pass user acceptance testing (UAT) before it can be released to production. Is it typically a good idea to postpone UAT until the end of the project to prevent the developers being disrupted from their development work during the Sprints?
  A. Yes, because UAT is done in a hardening Sprint before the release Sprint.
  B. No, because the state of the Product Increment won't be transparent until the end of the Project. The increment could have less quality and the feedback loop would be too long if UAT is pushed to the end of the Project.
  C. It depends on the team's definition of "Done".
  D. Yes, because the Scrum Team is a self-organizing team and should not be disrupted during development.
	The purpose of each Sprint is to deliver Increments of value that adhere to the Scrum Team's current definition of "Done". UAT should be done as soon as possible as any delay in this activity will reduce transparency, quality and increase risk.

Question 79	**Correct Answer: C,D**
A Scrum Team is midway through the Sprint. They have completed working on Backlog items #8 and #9 during the current Sprint and item #6 and #7 in the previous Sprint. During the Sprint Review, the Scrum Team is presenting the Increment to the stakeholders. One of the stakeholder's requests information on how item number #8, #9 works together with #6 & #7. The Developer who is presenting at that point opens a different environment to show how #6 & #7 works but the stakeholder struggles to understand it because both the functionalities were not shown together in one environment. Select the two true statements about this situation? A. Stakeholder who didn't understand the functionality should be the coached by the Product Owner. B. It is normal to have multiple versions of the Increment until all the changes are integrated in the final Sprint in the release. C. The Team is not adhering to the definition of "Done" D. Items #8 and #9 were not integrated with the previous Increment. E. Team didn't perform the testing of #8 and #9.	The Increment is the sum of all the Product Backlog items completed during the current Sprint and the value of the Increments of all previous Sprints. The Increment must be in useable condition regardless of whether the Product Owner decides to release it or not. Even though Backlog items #8 and #9 are implemented by the Scrum Team, they are not integrated with the previous Increment. That's why the functionalities are present independently in two different environments. There is nothing wrong with the stakeholder wanting to see how the current Increment(8# and #9) work together with the previous increments(#6 & #7). Hence it is not DONE. Remember, an increment meet "done" only when one single valuable increment is produced by the Scrum team each Sprint.
Question 80 By the end of the Sprint, a Product Backlog item in the Sprint Backlog does not meet the team's definition of "Done". What two things should happen with the item? A. Extend the Sprint, to give you enough time to complete the item. B. Include it in the Increment to be inspected at the Sprint Review. Partly completed items can be reviewed at the Sprint Review. C. Do not include the unfinished item in the Increment. Do not show the item in the Sprint Review. D. Estimate the amount of work remaining to make it 'Done' and add it to the Product Backlog for the Product Owner to decide what to do with it.	**Correct Answer: C,D** Explanation At the end of a Sprint, the new Increment must be "Done", which means it must be in useable condition and meet he Scrum Team's definition of 'Done'. Scrum Team members must have a shared understanding of what it means for work to be complete, to ensure transparency. This is the definition of "Done" for the Scrum Team and it is used to assess when work is complete on the product Increment. Unfinished Items cannot be included in the Increment for Sprint Review.

Question 81

An organization very recently has transitioned from a traditional approach to a Scrum method. Things have been going as planned however the relationship between the Product Owner and the Developers team has gotten worse. Developers are not very happy with the Product Owner as he is constantly changing the requirements. The Product Owner is disappointed with the Developers for changing the estimations and how the work would be implemented. What should the Scrum Master, do?

A. Leave it to the Scrum team and not do anything. The Scrum team is self – organizing and should know how to resolve conflicts.
B. Facilitate a discussion between the Product Owner and the Developers focusing on the topic of change. Have the team discuss why the changes occur and the impacts it has on the product. Raise this issue during the Sprint Retrospective, if needed.
C. Increase the capacity of the team, so added scope will be managed.
D. Become the gatekeeper of changes. Any changes that impact the team's velocity should go through the Scrum Master first.
E. Explain to the Developers that the Product Owner is accountable for flow of value and his/her decisions should be respected in order to maximize the product value.

Correct Answer: B

Conflicts are a natural occurrence and the Scrum Master coaches them on the value of resolving conflicts. Leaving conflicts unresolved can impact the Scrum values of openness and respect diminishing trust. Lower trust levels will impact the Scrum Team's effectiveness and can cause impediments in the future. It is the responsibility of the Scrum Master to remove impediments that hinder the team through conflict resolution and facilitation.

The Scrum Master leads the team through healthy conflict and debate and supports the team in problem solving and conflict resolution.

Question 82	Correct Answer: B
Sid is a Product Owner who is new to Scrum. During the Sprint, he comes to Paul, the Scrum Master, stating that he is concerned that the Developers will not be able to finish the Sprint Backlog before the end of the Sprint. What would be the most appropriate response from Paul? A. Facilitate a meeting with the Developers and the Product Owner. Remind the Developers about their commitment of finishing the Sprint Backlog as agreed to in the Sprint Planning. B. Help Sid understand that the Sprint Backlog is a forecast of what the Developers believes it can accomplish in the Sprint. Forecast does not mean a commitment and its normal if the Sprint backlog is not completed. C. Tell Sid not to worry as the Developers are committed to complete the Sprint Backlog and no one should tell them how to do their work. D. Defer some of the work to another Scrum Team that has extra capacity.	Scrum is founded on empirical process control theory, or empiricism. Empiricism asserts that knowledge comes from experience and making decisions based on what is known. The Sprint Backlog is a forecast by the Developers about what functionality will be in the next Increment and the work needed to deliver that functionality into a "Done" Increment. The Developers modifies the Sprint Backlog throughout the Sprint, and the Sprint Backlog emerges during the Sprint. This emergence occurs as the Developers works through the plan and learns more about the work needed to achieve the Sprint Goal.
Question 83 Your Scrum Team is invited to a meeting where management announce that there will be budget cuts due to market changes and that funding for your team's product might be reduced. Tensions begin to rise within the team. As a Scrum Master, what would be the best course of action? (Choose two best answers) A. Work with the management to keep the original budget as the team has been doing well. B. Facilitate another meeting between the management and the Scrum team. The Scrum team should clear out their doubts. C. Ask the Scrum team to continue focusing on delivering the most valuable items for the next Sprint. D. Avoid getting involved as it is the Product Owner's responsibility to manage stakeholder expectations. E. Simply inform the team to stay busy until the information is officially announced.	**Correct Answer: B, C** The Scrum Master not only a servant-leader to the Scrum Team but also the organization. The Scrum Master helps everyone improve their interactions to maximize the value created by the Scrum Team. Value for the business and value for customers. The Scrum Master leads by example, by respect, and by the ability to influence the organization for the Scrum Team and its effectiveness. The Scrum Master should also lead by values, by helping everyone embody the values of commitment, courage, focus, openness and respect.

Question 84

A new Scum team has just started implementing Scrum. At their first Sprint Planning, Developers are not able to confidently make a forecast of Product Backlog items because of unclear requirements. However, the Scrum team as a whole has a clear vision of the business objective, they are hoping to achieve with the Sprint increment. Which of the following are the most appropriate responses? (Choose 2):

A. Developers should make a best guess on which items could be done that would most likely meet the business objective. They should create enough of a Sprint Backlog to begin implementation for the first few of days. They should adapt the Sprint Backlog as they learn more about the requirements.

B. Extend the Sprint Planning until the Sprint Backlog can be fully formulated, and commitment has been agreed upon.

C. Temporarily postpone the Sprint Planning to give the Product Owner time to make refinements to the Product Backlog items.

D. Use the upcoming Retrospective to discuss why this happened and what can be done to reduce the risk of this occurring again.

Correct Answer: A, D

All events are time-boxed events, such that every event has a maximum duration. This helps the team not only to stay focused but also improve the events in the future. Allowing events to be postponed or extending beyond time-boxes will make it more difficult to improve how the events are run as you would be enabling anti-patterns to solve process problems.

Developers modifies the Sprint Backlog throughout the Sprint, and the Sprint Backlog emerges during the Sprint. This emergence occurs as Developers works through the plan and learns more about the work needed to achieve the Sprint Goal.

References

Order of Scrum exams
https://www.scrum.org/resources/blog/best-order-get-all-scrumorg-certifications

Agile Manifesto.
Reference link: http://agilemanifesto.org/

The Three Pillars of Empiricism (Scrum) – Hiren Doshi.
T@https://www.scrum.org/resources/blog/three-pillars-empiricism-scrum

Empiricism, the act of making decisions based on what is – Ken Schwaber
https://kenschwaber.wordpress.com/2011/05/03/empiricism-the-act-of-making-decisions-based-on-what-is/

Agile is constant change
https://www.scrum.org/resources/blog/agile-constant-change

Updates to the Scrum Guide: The 5 Scrum values take center stage - Dave West
https://www.scrum.org/resources/blog/5-scrum-values-take-center-stage

So, What is Agile Really About? - Barry Overeem
https://www.scrum.org/resources/blog/so-what-agile-really-about

If your backlog is not refined then you are doing it wrong - Martin Hinshelwood
https://www.scrum.org/resources/blog/if-your-backlog-not-refined-then-you-are-doing-it-wrong

Culture Change An important ingredient for organizational Agility - Hiren Doshi
https://www.scrum.org/resources/blog/culture-change-important-ingredient-organizational-agility

Sprint. Sprint Goal and Scrum Values

5 Metaphors to Explore the Value of Scrum Values – Nagesh Sharma
https://www.scrum.org/resources/blog/5-metaphors-explore-value-scrum-values

There's value in the Scrum Values – Gunter Verheyen
https://gunterverheyen.com/2013/05/03/theres-value-in-the-scrum-values/

4 Ways to Coach with the Scrum Values - Stephanie Ockerman

Six Reasons Why You Need to Pay More Attention to the Sprint Goal - ILLIA Pavlichenko
https://www.scrum.org/resources/blog/six-reasons-why-you-need-pay-more-attention-sprint-goal

Getting to Done: Creating Good Sprint Goals - Stephanie Ockerman
https://www.scrum.org/resources/blog/getting-done-creating-good-sprint-goals

Getting started with a Definition of Done (DoD) - Martin Hinshelwood
https://www.scrum.org/resources/blog/getting-started-definition-done-dod

Calling All Industries: Your Process is Failing You - Donis Marshall
https://www.scrum.org/resources/blog/calling-all-industries-your-process-failing-you

Scrum Roles and Events

Reference: Characteristics of a Great Scrum Team - Barry Overeem
http://www.barryovereem.com/wp-content/uploads/Characteristics-of-a-Great-Scrum-Team.pdf

Reference: The 8 Stances of a Scrum Master - Barry Overeem's
https://www.scrum.org/resources/8-stances-scrum-master

Why you Need Only ONE Product Owner - Roland flemm
https://www.scrum.org/resources/blog/why-you-need-only-one-product-owner

Stances of the Product Owner - Robbin Schuurman
https://www.scrum.org/resources/blog/stances-product-owner

The Story Writer (A Misunderstood Product Owner Stance) - Chris Lukassen
https://www.scrum.org/resources/blog/story-writer-misunderstood-product-owner-stance

Leadership Skills and Planning

4 Secrets to Great Agile Leadership - Dan Sloan
https://www.scrum.org/resources/blog/4-secrets-great-agile-leadership

Scrum Mastery: 4 Steps to Optimize Product Value - Stephanie Ockerman
https://www.scrum.org/resources/blog/scrum-mastery-4-steps-optimize-product-value

Agile Coaching and Self-Organizing Teams

https://www.scrum.org/resources/blog/4-ways-coach-scrum-values

Reference: 5 Powerful Things About the Sprint - Stephanie Ockerman
https://www.scrum.org/resources/blog/5-powerful-things-about-sprint

Myth: Having A Sprint Goal Is Optional In Scrum - Christiaan Verwijs
https://www.scrum.org/resources/blog/myth-having-sprint-goal-optional-scrum

References: 5 Agile Leadership Tips for Creating Mature Scrum Teams - Ron Eringa
https://www.scrum.org/resources/blog/5-agile-leadership-tips-creating-mature-scrum-teams

Scrum Myths: There is No Planning in Scrum
https://www.scrum.org/resources/blog/scrum-myths-there-no-planning-scrum

Reference: Leading High Performing Teams - Edwin Dando
https://www.scrum.org/resources/blog/leading-high-performing-teams

Release planning and predictable delivery
https://www.scrum.org/resources/blog/release-planning-and-predictable-delivery

Organization Events and Culture

What Do Agile Leaders Do? - Kurt Bittner
https://www.scrum.org/resources/blog/what-do-agile-leaders-do

Freeze The Pond Versus Take The Hill Two Metaphors For Enterprise Agile Change - Kurt Bittner
https://www.scrum.org/resources/blog/freeze-pond-versus-take-hill-two-metaphors-enterprise-agile-change

Product Vision

10 Tips for Product Owners on the Product Vision - Robbin Schuurman
https://www.scrum.org/resources/blog/10-tips-product-owners-product-vision

Why – How – What: From Product Vision to Task - Peter Götz
https://www.scrum.org/resources/blog/why-how-what-product-vision-task

Mike Griffin – PMI-ACP® Exam Prep, A Course in a Book® for Passing the PMI Agile Certified Practitioner (PMI-ACP) ® Exam

https://www.visual-paradigm.com/scrum/definition-of-done-vs-acceptance-criteria/

Reference : Three Levels of Agile Coaching
https://www.odd-e.com/resources/papers/agile_coaching.pdf

Myth 9: Story Points are Required in Scrum - Barry Overeem
https://www.scrum.org/resources/blog/myth-9-story-points-are-required-scrum

Agile Coach Toolkit #5: Active Listening – Punit Doshi
https://www.scrum.org/resources/blog/agile-coach-toolkit-5-active-listening

https://www.guru99.com/code-coverage.html

https://www.agilealliance.org/glossary

https://www.toolsqa.com/blogs/test-approach-and-comparisons-between-atdd-tdd-and-bdd/

https://www.scrumalliance.org/community/articles/2013/march/spikes-and-the-effort-to-grief-ratio

https://dzone.com/articles/the-5-solid-principles-explained

https://blog.servicerocket.com/adoption/blog/2014/11/how-to-create-a-good-bug-report

https://visualstudiomagazine.com/articles/2008/10/21/code-metrics.aspx

https://www.inflectra.com/spirateam/highlights/understanding-alm-tools.aspx

https://www.atlassian.com/agile/software-development/branching

https://dzone.com/articles/three-rs-clean-code

https://www.infoworld.com/article/2949579/design-for-change-coupling-and-cohesion-in-object-oriented-systems.html

https://dzone.com/articles/scrum-and-devops

https://aws.amazon.com/devops/what-is-devops/

https://en.wikipedia.org/wiki/Software_testing#cite_note-Kaner_1-1

https://www.softwaretestinghelp.com/testers-in-tdd-bdd-atdd-techniques/

The Professional Product Owner and the Three Vs - Don McGreal
https://www.scrum.org/resources/blog/professional-product-owner-and-three-vs

https://www.business2community.com/strategy/professional-scrum-with-kanban-psk-dont-just-limit-wip-optimize-it-02084017

https://kanbanize.com/blog/aging-work-in-progress/

https://getnave.com/blog/aging-work-in-kanban/

https://kanbanize.com/kanban-resources/kanban-analytics/cycle-time-scatter-plot/

https://kanbanize.com/kanban-resources/kanban-analytics/cumulative-flow-diagram/

https://www.scrum.org/index.php/forum/scrum-forum/16795/my-journey-psk-i-and-how-i-passed

https://www.agilealliance.org/glossary/rules-of-simplicity/

https://hygger.io/blog/roles-in-extreme-programming-methodology/

https://www.guru99.com/performance-testing.html

https://searchwindevelopment.techtarget.com/definition/static-analysis

https://dzone.com/articles/layered-architecture-is-good

https://www.agilebusiness.org/page/whatisdsdm

https://www.productplan.com/glossary/moscow-prioritization/

https://resources.collab.net/agile-101/agile-methodologies

https://www.digite.com/kanban/what-is-kanban/

https://kanbanize.com/kanban-resources/getting-started/what-is-wip/

https://leankit.com/learn/agile/what-is-scrumban/

https://www.smartsheet.com/scrumban-choosing-middle-ground-between-scrum-and-kanban

https://www.scrum.org/resources/blog/4-key-flow-metrics-and-how-use-them-scrums-events

https://www.scrum.org/resources/blog/limiting-work-progress-wip-scrum-kanban-what-when-who-how

https://www.scrum.org/resources/blog/kanban-service-level-expectations-and-how-use-them-scrum

https://www.scrum.org/resources/blog/scrum-primer-kanban-teams

https://www.excella.com/insights/burndown-chart-vs-cumulative-flow-diagram-cfd